Chris Williamson describes t
Jeremy Corbyn and some of hi
amson himself. He reveals the
party machine by Labour's rig
its most unprincipled. William............................
tious and his trenchant views make uncomfortable reading.
But for those who want to see a socialist future, or anyone
who has ever voted Labour and wants to see it do better, this
is essential reading.

                                           Ken Loach, Filmmaker

Chris Williamson is a compelling and committed socialist and was Jeremy Corbyn's most loyal supporter in Parliament: that is why he had to be sabotaged at all costs. The left-wing came so close to Parliamentary victory under Corbyn but ultimately failed: Williamson gives an insiders' informed analysis of why this happened and what needs to happen if the Left are ever to gain ascendancy. This book is a fascinating account of his struggle and the way forward.

                  Alexei Sayle, actor, author, stand-up comedian

A monumental injustice was done to Chris Williamson and so many others during the period of hope and pain discussed in this book. Now, hear Chris Williamson speak, his is a story of brushing up against the parameters of a well-managed political system which can only assimilate so much. We have a carefully curated hierarchy of political subjectivity which is determined by the subjects adherence to certain pious hypocrisies imposed from above. Behind Chris there are millions like him who were cancelled out of the right to participate in this political system due to their dedication to a more just society.

                                Lowkey, musician and activist

Chris Williamson's '10 Years Hard Labour' is an eye-opening, and at times, infuriating, insider's account of the coordinated political assault on the British Left that took place inside a party that was once its home. It is also the inspiring story of a veteran of workers' struggles who stood on principle and weathered the establishment's attacks while so many around him caved.

Max Blumenthal, author, editor and founder of The Grayzone

Chris Williamson is as always concise, honest and optimistic - and his book is a must read. Detailing the campaign by Zionists and Labour Party conservatives to deny the British public of a once in a lifetime opportunity to be governed by principled people like himself and Jeremy Corbyn.

Miko Peled, author and human rights activist

Activists need to read this book to fully understand the extent to which powerful forces within the Labour Party were prepared to go to destroy any chance of a Corbyn election win. Chris Williamson has drawn on his experience to produce an analysis of the party following its defeat in the 2010 general election. His insight will hopefully enable us to be better armed next time.

Sheila Coleman, Hillsborough Justice Campaign

This book will bring joy to the hearts of those who have longed to see the reptiles of the Parliamentary Labour Party and Party hierarchy called out for treacherously undermining Corbyn. It also gives overdue vent to criticism of Corbyn himself for trying to appease the hyenas who were using the fabricated anti-Semitism issue to bring him down – a tragic mistake as futile as it was disloyal to people like Chris Williamson who stood their ground. This account demonstrates what happens when a party loses touch with its popular base and every sense of decency, which should prompt thousands to tear up their Labour Party cards in disgust.

Peter Ford, former British ambassador to Bahrain and Syria.

A Fascinating insight into the dirty underhanded shenanigans that happened inside the Labour Party covering the Miliband and Corbyn years. From a man who was loyal to its leadership but paid a heavy price for standing up for its members and activists.

This book exposes the collusion that happened inside the party to ensure the power remained in the hands of the few and the offer of radical change and hope would never get the opportunity to flourish.

**Ian Hodson, National President Bakers',
Food & Allied Workers Union**

Chris Williamson's emotional honesty and fierce political polemic make this 'ringside view' of an MP who was in the inner circle and shadow minister under both Miliband and Corbyn a shocking eye opener and powerful read.

The Left needs an honest account and reckoning of the rise and fall of 'Corbynism' - and I hope this book is the start of that much needed self-criticism and honest debate.

Salma Yaqoob, peace activist

An unflinching examination of the collapse of the left wing of the British Labour Party. Williamson courageously offers an inside account of corporate infiltration and how the party became reactionary and betrayed its origins. And he offers a searing indictment of the cannibalistic witch-hunt that libelled Corbyn and others with false accusations of anti Semitism to cleanse the party of the left. This is a necessary corrective history for British audiences and a warning for the left in all Western democracies.

Rania Khalek, journalist, Breakthrough News

IN MEMORY

To: Lonny, my late wife, who was my soulmate, and Marilyn Murray, who was one of the kindest people I have ever known.

Chris Williamson

TEN YEARS HARD LABOUR

Copyright © Lola Books 2022
www.lolabooks.eu

This work, including all its parts, is protected by copyright and may not be reproduced in any form or processed, duplicated, or distributed using electronic systems without the written permission of the publisher.

Printed in Spain by Cimapress, Madrid
ISBN 978-3-944203-48-5

Original edition 2022

Chris Williamson was born in Derby into a working class family in 1956. He left school at 15 to work in a factory, before training as a bricklayer. He has also been a market trader, a social worker, and a welfare rights officer.

He joined the Labour Party in 1976 and is a lifelong socialist, trade unionist, and animal rights campaigner. He has been a Labour councillor, council leader, and an MP.

He was a Shadow Minister under Ed Miliband and Jeremy Corbyn, and, from 2017 onwards, he was Corbyn's most vocal supporter inside the Parliamentary Labour Party.

He was suspended from the party in February 2019 and, after being briefly reinstated, was re-suspended in June 2019. Later, the High Court declared the second suspension to be unlawful, but a third suspension was imposed. He resigned from the party after Labour's National Executive Committee prevented him from standing as a Labour candidate in the 2019 general election.

Some of the information contained in this book is a matter of public record, the rest is an account of Chris Williamson's own unique insights based on documentary records he kept at the time.

CONTENTS

Acknowledgments	viii
Preface	ix
List of main acronyms	xi

CHAPTER ONE
   The starting gun   1
CHAPTER TWO
   New Labour's ghost   11
CHAPTER THREE
   "Red Ed"?   26
CHAPTER FOUR
   A disaster waiting to happen   35
CHAPTER FIVE
   Attack of the gammons   42
CHAPTER SIX
   A very amateurish coup   57
CHAPTER SEVEN
   Reality check   66
CHAPTER EIGHT
   Manufacturing a "crisis"   77
CHAPTER NINE
   Back into the lion's den   92
CHAPTER TEN
   "Though cowards flinch and traitors sneer"   107
CHAPTER ELEVEN
   Free agent   118
CHAPTER TWELVE
   Beginning of the end   127
CHAPTER THIRTEEN
   Betrayal   150
CHAPTER FOURTEEN
   "The silence of our friends"   163
CHAPTER FIFTEEN
   A Kafkaesque nightmare   178
CHAPTER SIXTEEN
   Rank cowardice   189

CHAPTER SEVENTEEN
   Fighting back   210
CHAPTER EIGHTEEN
   Total war   215
CHAPTER NINETEEN
   The fix   230
CHAPTER TWENTY
   Judgment day   241
CHAPTER TWENTY-ONE
   Turkeys voting for Christmas   248
CHAPTER TWENTY-TWO
   Independence   256
CHAPTER TWENTY-THREE
   Road to perdition   263
CHAPTER TWENTY-FOUR
   The "antisemitism" agenda   271
CHAPTER TWENTY-FIVE
   "If you don't fight, you will always lose"   286
CHAPTER TWENTY-SIX
   Making the revolution   299

Appendix   309
Notes   355
Name index   387

ACKNOWLEDGMENTS

Before I began writing this book, I viewed it as a daunting task, and I never imagined that I would be able to flesh out 10 years of history, memories, and experiences. It was a long slog, but I was hugely assisted by so many people.

This book would probably never have been written were it not for my comrade and confidante Paul Mallet. As the dirty tricks mounted up against me in my later years in Parliament, Paul continually badgered me to *"write it down for the book"*. I would like to express my gratitude to Lee Garratt, who encouraged me to take the plunge and put pen to paper.

I also want to thank Dave Middleton, who did an excellent job on my first draft, proofreading and highlighting where more clarity was required. I am particularly grateful to Ammar Kazmi for his meticulous attention to detail in editing the final draft. I owe them both a huge debt of gratitude for their assistance in helping me to bring this project to fruition and for sparing my blushes.

I must also thank James Shires and Sarah Russell, who reminded me about a number of happenings during the decade after 2010.

So many comrades had my back when I was under attack. They inspired me to record what was a unique and turbulent time for the labour movement. I will be eternally grateful to those thousands of grassroots activists for their incredible solidarity, and I hope they feel that I have done justice to this period of our history in which they played such an important part.

However, my biggest thanks must go to my partner, Maggie Amsbury. Throughout the many tribulations I faced in my parliamentary life, and especially during the time of the witch-hunt, she supported me unequivocally with true love and encouragement. She also motivated me to finally set the record straight for posterity.

All errors and inadequacies in this work are, of course, my own.

Derby, 2022

PREFACE

With some notable exceptions, left-wing British politicians have, in general, failed to engage in one of the greatest, timeless mediums of human expression: books. As a result, we continually fail to set the record straight and to promote our understanding of history, ceding ground to right-wing revisionists and propagandists to tell future generations the tales of our time. *"If there's a book that you want to read, but it hasn't been written yet, then you must write it"*, goes the clichéd – but nevertheless true – maxim of US American Nobel laureate Toni Morrison. That sums up the genesis of this treatise on my experiences of the Ed Miliband and Jeremy Corbyn eras.

Despite numerous works having been written about the period covered in this book, all of them are plagued by a failure to truly lift the veil and uncover its sordid underbellies. That is what I have tried to do now, for the first time.

Whilst I have done a lot of writing over the years, this is the first time that I've written a book. I've tried to make it as readable as possible, with short chapters filled with subheadings. I've also attempted to keep it as chronological as I can, but there are inevitably some relevant thematic overlaps that I've preferred to keep together.

Most political memoirs are written by people who are beguiled by Westminster, but I was never so enamoured. So, mine is a unique and critical perspective. I had a ringside seat to the action. I saw first-hand the machinations of the Miliband years, the explosion of hope generated by Corbyn, and the unscrupulous ways in which powerful vested interests plotted to take him down.

In this book, I recount my experiences of the post-New Labour era. I shed new light on the major policy battles between 2010 and 2015, and I examine why, despite what many had hoped, Ed Miliband failed to escape New Labour's clutches.

I also evaluate the Jeremy Corbyn epoch. Why did Labour's bureaucracy act as a hostile fifth column? How did Corbyn's trusted advisers let him down? Why were Labour MPs completely out-of-step with Labour's supporters? How did trade union leaders deliver a fatal blow to the Corbyn project? And how did the Socialist Campaign Group of Labour MPs facilitate the witch-hunt against longstanding anti-racist socialists? These are issues that many other commentators have simply refused to address.

After being relentlessly smeared, I now seek to set the record straight and offer some thoughts on the future of the movement that was awoken by Corbyn's transformative vision. Britain continues to face insecurity, tyranny, and war. It is thanks to powerful forces, who benefit from these tragedies, that neoliberalism continues to dominate Britain's domestic agenda and international policy, despite its destructive impact on the lives of ordinary people. The failure of the Corbyn project should serve as a cautionary tale as we rebuild from the rubble.

We don't have to accept the inequality and injustice that 40 years of neoliberalism have visited on the people of this country and those around the world. We must build on the solidarity that we saw at the height of the Corbyn years. In words inspired by Percy Shelley: we are many, they are few. If we want it, the world is ours to win.

LIST OF MAIN ACRONYMS

BICOM – Britain Israel Communications and Research Centre
BoD – Board of Deputies of British Jews
CAA – Campaign Against Antisemitism
CLP – Constituency Labour Party
CPS – Crown Prosecution Service
CST – Community Security Trust
DPP – Director of Public Prosecutions
DWP – Department for Work and Pensions
EHRC – Equality and Human Rights Commission
FBU – Fire Brigades Union
FCR – Fiscal Credibility Rule
IHRA – International Holocaust Remembrance Alliance
JLC – Jewish Leadership Council
JLM – Jewish Labour Movement
JVL – Jewish Voice for Labour
LAW – Labour Against the Witch-Hunt
LFI – Labour Friends of Israel
LOTO – Leader of the Opposition's Office
LRC – Labour Representation Committee
MMT – Modern Monetary Theory
MP – Member of Parliament
NCC – National Constitutional Committee
NEC – National Executive Committee
OULC – Oxford University Labour Club
PCC – Police and Crime Commissioner
PCH – Portcullis House
PLP – Parliamentary Labour Party
PMQs – Prime Minister's Questions
PRS – Private Rented Sector
SCG – Socialist Campaign Group of Labour MPs
TUSC – Trade Unionist and Socialist Coalition
UJS – Union of Jewish Students
UNSC – United Nations Security Council

CHAPTER ONE

THE STARTING GUN

In the early hours of 7 May 2010, at the election count in Derby North, I could feel a burning excitement in the pit of my stomach. The vote was looking dangerously close, and the stoicism I had previously been displaying was starting to wither. I'd already taken myself away from the frenzy and tried to compose myself outside and, when I returned, I was keeping a distance from the delirium of the count. Minutes felt like hours. *"Just give us the damn result!"*, I kept thinking. It was at that point of total exasperation when I finally saw a familiar face approaching. It was one of my closest comrades and confidantes, Fareed Hussain.

"You've won! You've won!", Fareed exclaimed, embracing me with a bear-like hug.
"No, no, I don't want to look. Don't tempt fate!", I said.
"Look at the votes piling up! You've done it!", he insisted.

To be elected to serve my hometown was one of the proudest moments of my entire political life. There we were, in the small hours of a spring day, marching to the local Labour club, where I belted out the words to 'The Red Flag' hymn. We had defied the predictions of local hacks and had bucked the national trend, and I was soon to be heading down to the House of Commons. The euphoria was indescribable.

In the following days, I spoke to many grassroots activists and trade unionists who were hoping that the Labour Party could be reimagined under a new leader. Britain had already endured over three decades of neoliberalism. New Labour, which in 2002 Margaret Thatcher reportedly described as her greatest achievement,[1] was finally out of office after 13 years in government. It was replaced by a Tory-Lib Dem Coalition Government that inflicted a new era of austerity on the country, underpinned by a deepened commitment to the same failed economic ideology of the previous decades. Those three decades had seen an exponential rise in inequality and a public policy regime that had essentially implemented socialism for the rich and crumbs from the table for the rest. The government found at least £500 billion to bail out the banks in 2008. But the British people, who'd been immiserated, never received a bailout.

When I arrived in the Palace of Westminster on 10 May 2010, it felt intimidating. I was in an unfamiliar environment, with its antiquated conventions and its archaic parlance, which sets it apart from the people whom it is supposed to represent. But I was determined not to be overawed by the place, and so I applied to make my maiden speech – the first speech given by a newly elected MP – on the first sitting of the new Parliament. I recall being in the Commons chamber feeling incredibly nervous. I was mindful of the great orators that had graced the green benches before me, and I had an enormous sense of self-doubt. It was a classic case of imposter syndrome. I felt like a fish out of water. I was also self-conscious about the convention of having to stand up at the end of every speech to catch the Speaker's eye, indicating that I wanted to participate in the debate. I knew that all my friends and family would be watching on TV, so the pressure was on.

When I was eventually called, a relief came over me. The debate under consideration was the Coalition Government's first Queen's Speech setting out their policy programme, so I had plenty to speak about. I talked about poverty, inequality, climate change, local government, and the previous Labour government's record. I was complimentary about some of New Labour's achievements (an indication of my naïvety at the time in not fully recognising how much of an Establishment tool it had been). I also expressed my concern that the Coalition's plans would *"take us back into a period in which people are forced into poverty pay"*, and make local authorities cut services *"to deflect attention away from the Coalition Government's proposals"*.[2] Given what happened in the decade that followed, my worries proved prescient.

I was full of hope and anticipation about what I could achieve as the MP for my home city. I wasn't going to just disappear into the Westminster village. I wanted to be a visible presence in the constituency: a resource for local people. So, when the outgoing Derby North MP Bob Laxton asked if I wanted to take over the lease on his constituency office, which was located on the third floor of an anonymous office block, I politely declined. I told him that I wanted a city centre shopfront so that I could be easily accessible to constituents. Laxton's reaction was priceless. He said, *"That's a big mistake. You want to make it as difficult as possible for people to get in touch with you"*. I thought that was a curious attitude for an elected politician, particularly as Laxton was a people person. It shows that 13 years in the Westminster bubble can addle the brain.

As I was to discover, parliamentary pomposity is endemic. A perfect example of this was when Jim Dowd, one of the few Labour MPs with a working class background, loudly lambasted me for having the temerity to show some students around the Members' Cloakroom. Dowd came in afterwards and started yelling at the top of his voice that *"strangers"* were not allowed to enter what he seemed to consider an inner sanctum. Dowd wanted access restricted to parliamentary plonkers like him. Just to reinforce the point, he complained to the House authorities who then installed a bigger sign at eye-level, reminding everyone that the cloakroom was for MPs only. The pompous prat stood down in 2017, and he later became one of 15 former Labour MPs who urged voters not to back Jeremy Corbyn in the 2019 general election.[3] They signed a full-page advert that appeared in a number of local newspapers across Labour's heartlands in the north of England, targeting marginal constituencies. Like so many other Labour MPs, Dowd should never have been allowed within a million miles of an elected role for the party.

However, those parliamentary peculiarities, as absurd as I found them, were not my main issue of concern. At the time, I had been the Labour Group leader in Derby for the previous eight years, and so I knew that local government was going to be in for a rough ride. I was therefore pleased to get a seat on the Communities and Local Government Select Committee. This gave me the opportunity to directly scrutinise and challenge the disastrous proposals being pushed by Eric Pickles, the Local Government Secretary throughout my first stint in Parliament.

Just as I was beginning to get to grips with the Select Committee, Ed Miliband appointed me as the Shadow Fire Minister in October 2010, only five months after I was first elected to Parliament. I guess it was a reward for the support I'd given him in his leadership bid. I'd backed Ed because I believed that he was the only contender capable of beating his brother David, the continuity New Labour candidate. There was growing dissatisfaction in the country with Blairite politics, and I was concerned that David Miliband would further alienate the party from working class communities. In fact, I think it would be fair to say that, without my support, Ed wouldn't have been elected; his margin of victory was miniscule, just 1.4 per cent over his brother. I not only voted for him myself (with a higher weighted vote as an MP), but I also led a mobilisation campaign in Derby North and Derby South where members gave Ed their first preference. Only 69 other constituencies did the same.[4]

Some mischievous, self-professed 'left-wing' critics have since slated me for not supporting Diane Abbott. The allusion is that my later support for Corbyn wasn't genuine, and that I was really a Blairite wolf in sheep's clothing who had somehow reinvented himself upon returning to Parliament in 2017. It's a curious criticism, because Dennis Skinner attracted no censure for backing David, nor did the seven other socialist MPs who also voted for Ed. In fact, only six left-wingers gave Abbott their first preference. If I had backed Abbott, David would have won and that would have meant, ultimately, that Corbyn would never have been given the chance to stand as leader in 2015.

Ditching New Labour?

Ed Miliband had promised to turn the page on New Labour. Many of us wondered whether he meant it and, if he did, whether he was even capable of doing so. He certainly didn't get off to a great start with the people he appointed to his Shadow Cabinet. To be charitable to him, the PLP wasn't exactly brimming with talent. During his reign, Blair had stuffed Labour's benches with empty suits: lackeys who would fill out space and blindly follow the whip. People like Jeremy Corbyn and John McDonnell were considered beyond the pale. Whilst Miliband did appoint Diane Abbott to the junior role of Shadow Public Health Minister, she was never in his Shadow Cabinet, and he sacked her three years later for *"fail[ing] to show sufficient loyalty"*.[5] Sadly, Miliband's first Shadow Cabinet was a *Who's Who* of New Labour drones.

There wasn't even a place for an experienced left-wing thinker like the late Michael Meacher, who had served with distinction as a government minister from 1997 to 2003 (later to be sacked by Blair). Meacher had even backed Miliband in the leadership election, but he received nothing in acknowledgment. I believe Meacher would have made an excellent Shadow Chancellor. He regularly spoke about the economy and tax issues, inside and outside the Commons. In 2012, he published a Private Members' Bill to address tax avoidance.[6] Compare Meacher to Alan Johnson, the man who Miliband appointed as his first Shadow Chancellor. Johnson admitted that he would need to *"pick up a primer in economics for beginners"*, and he then coined the absurd mantra about the Coalition *"cutting too far and too fast"*.[7] This particular Johnson refrain betrayed his deeply conservative economic perspective. Just like Denis Healey a quarter of a century earlier, Johnson had failed to grasp, or perhaps didn't understand, the fiscal and monetary policy levers available to a currency-issuing government like ours. To argue that the government was cutting too far and too fast was to concede that some level of austerity was necessary, when in reality austerity was making it harder to recover from the 2008 financial crash. In its 2012 World Economic Outlook, even the International Monetary Fund's chief economist, Olivier Blanchard, acknowledged that austerity was causing more economic damage than experts had anticipated.[8]

Johnson's tenure as Shadow Chancellor was over in less than three-and-a-half months when he resigned after his marriage broke down.[9] However, in the short period that he held the position, he wasn't totally useless. He at least had the courage to attack Chancellor George Osborne. The problem was that Johnson's rhetoric displayed and replayed the Tory line about running up debt, encapsulated in his catchy but unhelpful *"deficit deniers"* attack. He said, *"If countries ... had not run up debts ... to sustain their economies, people would have not lost their credit cards, but lost their jobs, lost their houses, and lost their savings"*.[10] It was a great soundbite, no doubt, but it was more economic mythology. The government had simply created the money through 'quantitative easing', via the Bank of England. The notion of paying back money that one owes to oneself is plainly farcical but, instead of making that very point, Johnson chose to perpetuate the debt fallacy, unnecessarily ceding political ground to the Tories. Consequently, Labour was consistently on the backfoot in the Commons chamber and in interviews with the corporate media.[11]

Ed Balls, Johnson's replacement, was even worse. The Balls blueprint was to tell the electorate that he wouldn't cut back quite as severely as George Osborne. In other words, he was offering austerity-lite. Both Johnson and Balls, uncritically and credulously, sought to appease, rather than to resist, the Coalition Government's austerity agenda. They validated the simplistic, neoliberal 'household budget' analogy about how the economy functions. This was a product of Thatcherism and has remained in the public consciousness ever since. They should have outlined an alternative economic model, explaining how an interventionist government, with its own sovereign currency, could eliminate poverty, maintain full employment, and provide world class public services in a thriving economy. Instead, they argued for 'Compassionate Conservativism'.

The Miliband leadership team was obsessed with trying to shake off the accusation that New Labour had spent too much whilst in office. There was even an absurd discussion at a PLP meeting about publicly apologising for government 'overspending' prior to the 2008 financial crash. This was policy by focus groups, and it was unconvincing nonsense that did little to win over wavering Tories. It just deterred people who would have otherwise voted Labour. What they ought to have apologised for was the extension of bank deregulation by Gordon Brown[12] and for not spending enough. The New Labour government could have embarked on a bigger fiscal stimulus for new infrastructure and housing projects, provided much needed investment in public services, and reintroduced meaningful regulation of banks. But New Labour was in thrall to neoliberal dogma, and so was Miliband. People were increasingly saying on the doorstep that there was very little from which to choose between Labour and the Tories. And they were right.

Meanwhile, in the land of make believe, a leading economist and former member of the Bank of England's Monetary Policy Committee, Danny Blanchflower, was drooling about Balls in his September 2010 column for the *New Statesman*. He concluded his flattery by talking up the potential parliamentary performance of Balls, saying that *"he certainly has the credentials to be the next shadow chancellor. If I were Osborne, I would shudder at the prospect of debating with such a sharp economist at the despatch box"*.[13] The reality was considerably different. Contrary to Blanchflower's acclamation, Balls was a disaster as Shadow Chancellor. As well as being an unusually poor performer at the despatch box, his oratorical impotence was in no way counterbalanced by his policy propositions. In fact, the opposition from Miliband's entire Shadow Cabinet to the Coalition's austerity agenda was feeble. The best that they could muster was that the cuts were too severe.[14] The party's leadership supported the public sector pay cap.[15] And when Rachel Reeves was the Shadow Work and Pensions Secretary, she said that Labour didn't want to represent people who were out of work.[16] It became increasingly clear that there was precious little hope of Miliband turning over a new leaf for the party. The New Labour page had been glued down.

Corporate infiltration

The influence of Labour's traditional allies in trade unions and civil society groups like the peace movement were treated with disdain. By contrast, lobbyists and corporate capitalists seemed to have the ear of senior party figures. Even securing a commitment from Labour's Shadow Cabinet for policies that reflected what many people thought were the party's most basic values, let alone 'socialist' principles, was like pulling teeth. When Miliband eventually committed Labour to scrapping the hated bedroom tax, over 18 months after the idea surfaced in the Welfare Reform Bill, it was presented like he was making a ground-breaking announcement.[17] To penalise low-income households for having a spare bedroom (by limiting housing benefit for council and housing association tenants) should have been wholeheartedly repudiated by Labour at the outset.

However, we shouldn't be too surprised about Labour's positioning back then. A similar restriction for private sector tenants had been introduced by the Tories in 1989, and it had been reinforced by the New Labour government in 2008.[18] Many of Miliband's frontbench, including Miliband himself, were ministers in that government. But Labour wasn't always such a brazen Establishment tool, and it didn't have to remain that way. Indeed, Labour in 1989 was forthcoming in the Commons about its opposition to those restrictions on private tenants[19] (although overturning them was omitted from the subsequent election manifesto in 1992). It wasn't until the 2017 manifesto that Labour offered any hope for private renters with its commitment to *"end insecurity for private renters by introducing controls on rent rises, more secure tenancies, landlord licensing and new consumer rights for renters"*.[20]

The deficiency in Labour's policy offer under Miliband was, I suggest, a direct result of welcoming corporate lobbyists. Labour even seconded staff from multinational accountancy companies to advise on policy, like KPMG and PricewaterhouseCoopers (PwC). After Miliband made me the Shadow Fire Minister in the Shadow Local Government team led by Caroline Flint, I discovered that a PwC employee had been seconded into the team. This has been recorded in an entry by Flint in the parliamentary Register of Members' Financial Interests in 2012.[21]

Even though I had only been an MP for a short time, I thought it was odd that the Labour Party should be accepting input on its policy positions from private corporations. I wondered what was in it for them. Looking back, I wish I had challenged this practice, which turned out to be widespread. It was revealed in 2014, for example, that Labour's frontbench had accepted over £600,000 for assistance with research from PwC alone, to help form policy on tax, business, and social security.[22] Furthermore, the following year, Miliband was forced to reveal the identity of a mystery £600,000 donor. It turned out that the individual was Martin Taylor, a Mayfair hedge fund manager.[23] Miliband also elevated Charles Allen to the House of Lords in 2013, who was a director of the cleaning and catering corporation ISS at the time. ISS had been criticised for its involvement in the privatisation of public services, including the NHS, and for profiteering at the expense of its low-paid workers.[24] Yet, that didn't deter Miliband, who invited Allen in 2011 to review and rebuild Labour's organisation.[25] Allen even chaired the Labour Party's executive board from 2012 to 2015.[26] This insidious influence on the party's internal structures and policy development by the corporate sector helped to stifle any ideas that would unduly fetter free-market capitalism.

This was highlighted in painful clarity at the 2011 Labour Party conference, at which I spoke at various fringe meetings to argue for rent controls. The Shadow Housing Minister, Alison Seabeck, disagreed with my stance. She and her partner, Nick Raynsford, who had been a Housing Minister under Blair, had attended one of the meetings at which I'd spoken. Seabeck collared me later that day to say my proposal would create a homelessness crisis because landlords would abandon the private rented sector (PRS) resulting in fewer homes being available to rent. Seabeck's approach was clearly blinkered by New Labour's neoliberal influence. She offered nothing new and only wanted to tinker with the existing broken system rather than replace it, as I was recommending. Seabeck's successor, Jack Dromey, was better, but his housing policy horizons were also limited.

I'd been advocating for a much more radical, and common sense, approach. Even if Seabeck's apocalyptic prediction about the PRS shrinking had been right, that wouldn't have mattered if it corresponded with an increase in public housing. That could be quickly achieved through a municipalisation programme where councils could acquire properties on the open market and then make them available for rent. This could also have been supplemented by a council house building programme and a mutual home ownership initiative. In addition to rent controls and providing new council housing, which is self-explanatory, I also produced an explicit policy idea for a future Labour government to embrace cooperative/mutual home ownership. It wasn't only me pushing these ideas; they were supported by groups like the Co-operative Party[27] and Defend Council Housing,[28] as well as the London Labour mayoral candidate Ken Livingstone.[29] Neither Seabeck nor Dromey took any of those ideas forward. Such was the innate conservatism of Miliband's Shadow Cabinet that Hilary Benn explicitly ruled out rent controls.[30]

Before moving on in Ed Miliband's Shadow Cabinet reshuffle later in 2011, Caroline Flint contributed some policy ideas on housing for Progress, a right-wing pressure group. In 2011, Progress published Flint's proposals in *The Purple Book*.[31] But she offered nothing to actually address the housing crisis. All she did was to suggest some punitive measures, such as housing ASBOs (anti-social behaviour orders) banning evicted tenants from living within five miles of their former homes.[32] The book mapped out a range of right-wing policy ideas for the Labour Party. In addition to Flint, the contributors included senior figures from the New Labour era, such as Andrew Adonis, Douglas Alexander, Frank Field, Tessa Jowell, Peter Mandelson, and Jacqui Smith. The late Michael Meacher said that the book was merely a collection of repackaged Conservative Party policies.[33] What's even worse is that Ed Miliband, who supposedly wanted to take Labour in a new direction, wrote the book's foreword.

The Progress pressure group was established in 1996 to support Tony Blair's ambition of turning Labour into a safe prospect for the corporate class. It was bankrolled for many years by billionaire Lord Sainsbury, who, although a former Labour minister under Blair, donated more than £2 million to the Liberal Democrats in 2016.[34] He also helped to finance the breakaway Social Democratic Party in the early 1980s.[35] It was obvious that Progress was a cuckoo in the Labour nest. It was so right-wing that, in 2012, GMB general secretary Paul Kenny called for it to be proscribed. He accused Progress of being a *"party within a party"*, evoking echoes of the attacks on the left-wing Militant group in the 1980s, which led to it being excluded from the party. However, Labour's response to the GMB's plan to table a motion against Progress was rather different to how Militant were treated. A party spokesperson was quoted as saying:

> *"We are a party that is reaching out to people, gaining new supporters and offering real change for the country in these tough times. The Labour Party is a broad church and we are not in the business of excluding people."*[36]

Yet a few short years later under Corbyn, Labour became obsessed with doing just that. At this point in time, however, the truly appalling nature of many senior figures in the PLP was beginning to become clear to me.

CHAPTER TWO

NEW LABOUR'S GHOST

When I was elected to Parliament in 2010 and saw what goes on behind the scenes in the corridors of power, the scales fell from my eyes. Were we, as Labour MPs, really the parliamentary representatives of the workers? The great socialist revolutionary Vladimir Lenin had once observed that *"the Labour Party ... is led by reactionaries, and the worst kind of reactionaries at that, who act quite in the spirit of the bourgeoisie ... [It] exists to systematically dupe the workers"*.[1] Lenin's description certainly resonates with my experience.

Miliband appointed Liam Byrne as his Shadow Department for Work and Pensions (DWP) Secretary. Byrne was the former Chief Secretary to the Treasury in Gordon Brown's administration, who left the idiotic note saying, *"I'm afraid there is no money"*, which became propaganda fodder for David Cameron. One of Byrne's early tasks was to lead Labour's response to the 2011 Welfare Reform Bill, a spiteful piece of legislation, in which he effectively outlined that Labour agreed with much of the Coalition Government's proposals. The bill introduced the hated Universal Credit system and bedroom tax, scrapped Council Tax Benefit for low-income households, abolished the Social Fund, and imposed more cuts in the support available for lone parents.[2] It also put a ceiling on the level of social security paid to claimants, including assistance with housing costs, which had ballooned thanks to the deregulation of privately rented housing 20 years earlier. Shortly after the Coalition published its proposals, Byrne tried to persuade the PLP, at its regular meeting, to accept the benefit cap. I spoke vehemently in opposition after he told the meeting that it was politically unsustainable to oppose it because of the spiralling cost of housing benefit. I made the point that the Labour Party shouldn't be accepting a position where the victims of a Tory policy failure were being punished. After all, it was our policy failure, too. Nothing had been done to address rising rents in the private sector in the 13 years that New Labour were in power. I argued that if there was concern about the cost to the public purse of the ballooning housing benefit bill, Labour should demand rent controls and a massive council house building programme, instead.

That speech generated my first run-in with Ian Austin. Most of the PLP agreed with me that we shouldn't be supporting measures that would create even more hardship, and many of them congratulated me on my speech at the end of the meeting. Two weeks previously, Austin had also been praising me for providing him with some background notes for a speech he wanted to make about cuts to the fire service in the West Midlands. So, when I saw him approaching me, I was anticipating another slap on the back, rather than a slap in the face. He confronted me in an aggressive, hectoring manner, accusing me of grandstanding. He continued his tirade in the corridor. As we walked down the stairs to the Commons Tea Room, Angela Eagle joined him in haranguing me for criticising Byrne's proposal.

Liam Byrne has form for pandering to the worst kind of far-right sentiment. Back in 2008, when he was the Immigration Minister, he announced that British citizens could be jailed for 14 years and fined £5,000 if their invited family members visiting from overseas broke immigration rules.[3] Pandering to racist sentiment like this only helped, rather than hindered, the rising UKIP tide. In spite of that, the party continued its racist assaults, culminating in the infamous anti-immigration mugs with which Ed Balls proudly posed during the 2015 general election campaign.

In March 2013, Byrne was at it again, this time over the workfare scheme of Tory DWP Secretary, Sir Iain Duncan Smith. Byrne had persuaded the Shadow Cabinet to instruct Labour MPs to abstain on a bill reversing a Court of Appeal ruling that the government had acted unlawfully by requiring benefit claimants to do unpaid work. The case had been brought against the government's so-called *"back to work"* scheme by a graduate who was required to work for free at Poundland, and it was colloquially known as the 'Poundland case'.[4] The Court of Appeal decision meant that 250,000 unemployed workers should have received a total of £130 million in backdated benefit payments, but the government's retrospective legislation prevented this.

Hilary Benn broke the news about the plan to abstain on the Jobseekers (Back to Work Schemes) Bill, at a meeting of his shadow ministerial team. He told us that the Shadow Cabinet had made the decision earlier that day. I was stunned. I'd attended a consultation meeting the previous evening, called by Byrne himself, to get a steer from Labour MPs, and they were unanimous in saying that we should vote against the Coalition's plan. But Byrne and the Shadow Cabinet disregarded the outcome of that consultation exercise and gave Duncan Smith a free pass. When Benn asked for comments, I made my views crystal clear that the Shadow Cabinet was out of line. Benn said he didn't want to debate it and closed the meeting. Paul Blomfield, Jack Dromey, Helen Jones, and Roberta Blackman-Woods were the other MPs in the team, but they didn't raise any objections.

I then penned a memo to the Chief Whip, saying that the Shadow Cabinet's plan was politically inept, intolerable, and insupportable. When I delivered it to the Chief Whip's office, Byrne was already there talking to the whips to find out who was going to rebel. When I said I was thinking of resigning from the frontbench over the Shadow Cabinet's imposition of a whip to abstain, he asked to speak to me privately. I told him bluntly that his plan to abstain was utterly untenable. I said that the government's emergency legislation to penalise people in poverty was *"fucking outrageous"* to which he responded by simply saying *"I know"*. He tried to justify his position by saying that he'd wrung some concessions from Duncan Smith on the bill and had persuaded him to establish an independent review of the benefit sanctions regime. He also wrote a piece for *LabourList*, in which he said:

> "People are very angry about the jobseekers bill ... Labour MPs are furious. Labour councillors and activists are angry. And they are right to be. This bill is an emergency fix to almighty incompetence at Iain Duncan Smith's DWP. Our decision not to support the bill in the Commons but to abstain was very, very difficult."[5]

His excuse was pitiful, incredibly irritating, and singularly unconvincing, because the people making the *"very, very difficult"* decisions are never the ones affected by them!

After my exchange with Byrne, I took soundings from other members of the Socialist Campaign Group on what to do, including John McDonnell. They all said it was better to have my voice on the frontbench supporting the Fire Brigades Union's (FBU) campaign against government plans to cut firefighter pensions. I'd been working closely with the FBU since Miliband had appointed me as Shadow Fire Minister two-and-a-half years previously. During that time, I'd been urging them to reaffiliate to the Labour Party and was making some progress on that front. The FBU general secretary Matt Wrack – who was sceptical of Labour at the time – was always resistant to my overtures, but most of the other senior FBU officials were amenable to the idea. I was also committed to assisting the firefighters in their pensions dispute and resisting Coalition plans to privatise the fire and rescue service.[6] So, taking account of the bigger picture, I swallowed hard and abstained on the bill after all. I found the requirements of collective responsibility imposed on frontbenchers incredibly restrictive at times like this, particularly because, as a junior Shadow Minister, I had no direct input into Shadow Cabinet decisions. It isn't easy to navigate the competing pressures between conscience and losing the opportunity to develop other policy areas by breaking collective responsibility on an unrelated matter. But, in any event, my days on the frontbench were numbered.

Parliamentary parlour games

The following month, in April 2013, Margaret Thatcher died. David Cameron recalled Parliament during the Easter recess to pay tribute to her. It was an unprecedented move, previously reserved for matters of national emergency. Even the most swivel-eyed Thatcherite Tory would concede that her death didn't constitute a national crisis. The last time a former Prime Minister had passed away during a recess was James Callaghan. He also died during an Easter recess, but tributes were paid when the House returned. That was the convention that Cameron broke, with barely a whimper from the Labour leadership, even though Parliament was set to return only a few days later. In spite of the colossal waste of time and money involved, Miliband ordered his MPs back to London for the eulogies. What the hell was he thinking? Thatcher was the bloody architect of the neoliberal era that had inflicted so much pain and misery on working class communities all over Britain! She'd made greed a virtue. It was another example of how detached the Labour leadership had become from the people it claimed to represent. Whilst Miliband was insisting on participating in a parliamentary pantomime to glorify a tyrant, street parties were being organised in working class neighbourhoods to celebrate her death.[7] I didn't expect Miliband to join those celebrations, but I was appalled at his glowing homage. He even legitimised her assault on the post-war consensus when he said that *"she was right to recognise that our economy needed to change"*.[8] To make matters worse, Miliband represents a former coalfield community that was devastated by Thatcher's economic butchery. Miliband did at least preserve some of his dignity by making some modest criticisms towards the end of his speech:

> *"it would be dishonest and not in keeping with the principles that Margaret Thatcher stood for not to be open with the House, even on this day, about the strong opinions and deep divisions there were, and are, over what she did. In mining areas such as the one I represent, communities felt angry and abandoned. Gay and lesbian people felt stigmatised by measures such as Section 28, which today's Conservative Party has rightly repudiated."*[9]

Miliband's critique of the devastation Thatcher had wrought, however, was shamefully deficient.

Prior to the recalled session, my refusal to participate was noted by the whips, who began to apply pressure on me to attend. Jonathan Ashworth, who previously worked for Miliband before being gifted the safe seat of Leicester South, was the East Midlands whip and was tasked with demanding my attendance. I never had much time for him. He was only selected for the 2011 by-election after Labour's candidate selection process was stitched up by the party's National Executive Committee (NEC), who kept local favourite, Ross Willmott, off the shortlist. I lobbied Harriet Harman, who was an NEC member at the time, about Willmott being barred from the shortlist and to request that local members be allowed to decide who they wanted. What I didn't know then was that Ashworth had previously worked for her, too. He was her political secretary when she was the acting leader upon Gordon Brown's resignation following the 2010 general election. So, I wasn't impressed that the little squirt was attempting to hector me into submission. Like most of the PLP, Ashworth has never done a proper day's work in his life. He's just another archetypal careerist who progressed from student politics, to working for the Labour Party, to being a special adviser, to then becoming an MP. In his last phone call to me on the issue, he made an implicit threat to my position as a Shadow Minister. I had to make it crystal clear to him that, no matter what he said or did, I was not going to participate in such a grotesque parliamentary spectacle designed to whitewash Thatcher's diabolical legacy. As it happened, I was already busy presiding at the official reopening of a post office in my constituency that had been arranged for some time.

Later in 2013, the FBU were stepping up their industrial action against the government. Ministers wanted to force firefighters to work longer, pay more into their pensions, and receive less in retirement. The government also wanted to renege on a previous commitment regarding the normal retirement age for firefighters. In 2006, New Labour had increased the normal pension age from 55 to 60 for new recruits to the fire and rescue service, but they gave assurances that existing staff would retain their current pension rights. I was vetoed by Hilary Benn when I wanted to publicly endorse the FBU's industrial action, but I still joined their picket lines. I used my position on the frontbench to excoriate Tory Fire Minister Brandon Lewis for causing the dispute, and I laid the blame for any strike days at his door.

Much to the displeasure of the Miliband leadership, the FBU called a day of action during the 2013 Labour Party conference in Brighton. So, I don't think I enamoured myself with the leadership when I attended and spoke at a picket line outside a Brighton fire station, and then gave an interview to BBC News. Shadow ministers were expected to distance themselves from all industrial disputes, not join picket lines and speak out on the side of the workers. They were supposed to be 'statesmanlike' neutral observers or, better still, to actively criticise the unions. I always believed that was an incongruous imposition, given the party's links to the trade union movement. Two weeks after being appointed as the Shadow Fire Minister in October 2010, I made the mistake of allowing a statement to be prepared for me by Caroline Flint's office. She was the Shadow Local Government Secretary before Miliband appointed Hilary Benn to the role. It was about a planned strike by the London firefighters on bonfire night over the proposed imposition of changes to their shift patterns.[10] There was little, if any, nuance in the statement: no criticism of the heavy-handed management tactics, just criticism of the industrial action. I felt the words sticking in my throat as I was saying them at the despatch box. I never made that mistake again. It is toe-curlingly embarrassing to read it back years later.

Miliband never supported any industrial action whilst he was the leader, and he seemed to relish criticising the unions whenever there was a dispute that attracted media attention.[11] He sounded like a robot on occasions when commenting on strikes, repeating the same line over and over again about the public being *"let down"* by trade unions and employers alike.[12] When Miliband announced a reshuffle of his frontbench in 2013 after Parliament returned following the conference season, I wondered what he had in store for me. I eventually received a phone call from one of his staff asking me to meet Miliband in his office. When I arrived, he looked ill at ease, so I guessed that he was planning to sack me. He broke the news by saying, *"I'm sorry, I haven't got space on the frontbench for you"*. I didn't have the presence of mind to say, *"Can't you ask people to squeeze up a bit?"*. Instead, I found myself reassuring him. I was trying to ease his awkwardness.

Later that day, I bumped into Lisa Nandy, who at that time was friendly and supportive towards me. She said Miliband had wanted to sack her as well but, rather than putting him at ease about it, she had apparently launched a verbal assault against him for his disloyalty to her. The upshot of that exchange was that Miliband ultimately changed his mind and kept her on the frontbench, but with a different portfolio. According to Nandy, when he called to offer her a different position, she had said that was also unacceptable, resulting in Miliband hanging up on her. She then wrote to him apologising for her outburst and said she would agree to the alternative shadow ministerial role after all, which he accepted. She suggested that I should write to him asking for a meeting to determine why he had replaced me.

I took Nandy's advice, and a meeting was arranged the following week on 16 October 2013, after Prime Minister's Questions. Miliband was cagey when I met him. I told him that many people were saying that he'd sacked me because I was too close to the FBU, but he insisted that wasn't true. When I said, *"Well, did you think I was shit as the Shadow Fire Minister then?"*, he was even more adamant that he didn't believe that, either. However, he went on to refer to how difficult it must've been for me to have had to deal with the fallout from the industrial action by the firefighters. I told him it wasn't difficult at all. I said I completely supported them and that I wanted to be more forthright in my backing of the FBU, but that Hilary Benn had overruled me. Miliband replied, *"Oh yes, he mentioned that to me"*. But I didn't get a coherent explanation from him as to why he'd removed me. He implied that I'd been dropped by accident, because of the impact of other moves. He said that I'd just been *"caught in the crossfire"*, whatever that was supposed to mean. He asked how long I'd been on the frontbench, which was a slightly strange question, given that it was Miliband himself who'd originally called to offer me the position. What it indicated, however, was that he took little to no interest in junior shadow ministerial positions. When I told him that I'd been on the frontbench for three years, he said, *"Oh well, you've had a good go then"*, as if I should've been thankful! There was an out-of-touch, Oxbridge arrogance about his attitude. He had removed me from a role I was passionate about for no good reason, and he was treating it like I'd had *"a good go"* on a theme park roller coaster. His disposition was positively clammy.

Shortly after seeing Miliband, I bumped into Tom Watson, whose office was next door to mine. It might be surprising to learn that, back then, Watson was also very friendly and supportive towards me, like Nandy. I guess they didn't see my politics as any kind of threat in those days. Watson had resigned his role as Labour's general election coordinator a few months previously, because of the controversy over the selection procedures in the Falkirk constituency involving Karie Murphy, who worked for him at that time,[13] and who'd later go on to work for Corbyn. When I told Watson about my meeting with Miliband, he said that it was almost certainly Hilary Benn who had wanted me out because of my proximity to the FBU. He explained that, in his experience, you need someone in your corner, like the Chief Whip or your Shadow Cabinet member, when a reshuffle takes place. It seems I'd had neither.

A few months earlier, before being sacked, I'd also had a run-in with Chief Whip Dame Rosie Winterton, after I'd missed an inconsequential vote in the Commons. I was absent because I'd been making a keynote speech at a Local Government Association conference in Brighton in my capacity as the Shadow Fire Minister. I had used the occasion to highlight the government's plans to privatise the fire and rescue service.[14] I also gave a guarantee that if I were in government, there would be no privatisation on my watch, and any externalised services would be brought back in-house. The previous day, the Pairing Whip, Mark Tami, had confronted me about my absence. When I explained where I'd been and told him that the vote on an amendment to the Health and Social Care Bill had come sooner than anticipated, he calmed down a bit. However, he was clearly still indignant about me prioritising the opportunity to set out my opposition to privatising a key public service over being in Parliament to participate in a vote that wasn't even close.

Winterton had summoned me to her office to give me a dressing down. The interaction illustrated the absurdity, dysfunctionality, and preoccupation with trivialities of the PLP's whipping system. Once I arrived, Winterton kept me waiting for half an hour. When I was eventually beckoned into her room by her assistant, she didn't even lift her head from her desk or utter a word for around a minute. She just continued writing something in a notepad, leaving me standing in the doorway like a naughty schoolboy called to the headteacher's office after being caught smoking behind the bike sheds. When she did finally deign to speak to me, she was incredibly supercilious and insisted that I must write a letter of apology to Alan Campbell, the Deputy Chief Whip. I had to bite my tongue when I responded, because I felt like telling her a few home truths. I stuck to reiterating how the vote had been called earlier than expected, how my vote would have made no difference, and why my absence did not imply that I wasn't concerned about the implications of the Health and Social Care Bill. I pointed out that I'd been working hard on the campaign against the bill, to which her riposte was, *"We're all working hard on it, Chris"*. That was manifestly not true.

For example, the previous week, I'd joined a handful of other Labour MPs who'd been collecting signatures for a petition against the bill. The idea was to walk over to the Department for Health together so that Andy Burnham, the Shadow Health Secretary, could present them all at the same time. I'd been petitioning in Derby City Centre every weekend for the previous six weeks and had collected over 12,000 signatures, whereas the other MPs had only mustered a few hundred at most. Their combined efforts amounted to less than 2,000, so the signatures collected in Derby represented over 90 per cent of the combined total. One of the MPs in attendance was Luciana Berger – who later went on to treat me as one of her top bogeymen – and she was effusive about my petitioning acumen as we walked back to Parliament together. She was curious about how I'd managed to dwarf the efforts of the other MPs. *"Oh, that's so inspirational"*, she gushed, when I explained the on-street campaigning I was leading in Derby at the time. But in Winterton's myopic mind, participating in pointless parliamentary parlour games trumped campaigning on the streets.

As I was out of favour with Winterton and Benn, it's hardly surprising that Miliband gave me the boot. I was replaced as Shadow Fire Minister by Lyn Brown, who told me she didn't want the job. She said she was more interested in other policy areas and said that she'd wanted to continue as a whip. FBU members didn't take kindly to the move, and many of them were calling for me to be reinstated. Brown said she was getting a hard time in meetings with firefighters and repeatedly asked me if I would help her by intervening to ease the tension, which I did each time she asked. I continued to support the firefighters from the backbenches and maintained a close and fraternal relationship with the FBU.

War! What is it good for?

There were two issues about which I felt profoundly uncomfortable during my first term as an MP. They have been the source of much sniping and distortion by right-wingers and 'soft left' commentators, so I think it is important to set the record straight. The first related to a House of Commons motion supporting the United Nations Security Council (UNSC) motion 1973 regarding the situation in Libya in the aftermath of the Arab Spring. I supported the motion in the hope that, by doing so, a peaceful settlement could be reached in the Libyan civil war. The motion read as follows:

> "That this House welcomes United Nations Security Council (UNSC) Resolution 1973; deplores the ongoing use of violence by the Libyan regime; acknowledges the demonstrable need, regional support and clear legal basis for urgent action to protect the people of Libya; accordingly supports Her Majesty's Government, working with others, in the taking of all necessary measures to protect civilians and civilian populated areas under threat of attack in Libya and to enforce the No Fly Zone, including the use of UK armed forces and military assets in accordance with UNSC Resolution 1973; and offers its wholehearted support to the men and women of Her Majesty's armed forces."

The tragic events that unfolded in Libya proved that my reasoning was hopelessly optimistic. The misinformation about Mu'ammar al-Gaddafi was overwhelming and I feel ashamed that I was taken in by the disinformation. I have since spoken to people who have lived and worked in Libya who have painted a very different picture to the mainstream one. The experiences of Dave Roberts, who was my agent in the 2019 election, have been particularly illuminating for me. He'd been to Libya and seen for himself the social programmes that al-Gaddafi's administration had implemented. I am still remorseful to this day for going along with the parliamentary groupthink on this issue. I've since made a public statement saying:

> "I bitterly regret ... voting for a Parliamentary motion backing UN Security Council Resolution 1973, enforcing a No Fly Zone in Libya. The consequences of this imperialist intervention were catastrophic."[15]

I should have listened to Yasmin Qureshi who'd told me that she was deeply concerned about the motion. She thought it would be used as a pretext for regime change to enable oil companies to get their hands on Libya's huge resources. Qureshi was one of only 10 Labour MPs who opposed the motion. The other Labour MPs who opposed the motion were Katy Clark, Graham Allen, Ronnie Campbell, Jeremy Corbyn, Barry Gardiner, Roger Godsiff, John McDonnell, Linda Riordan, Dennis Skinner, and Mike Wood. Five other MPs also voted against: two SDLP MPs, Mark Durkan and Margaret Ritchie; one Green MP, Caroline Lucas; and one Tory, John Baron.

With the benefit of hindsight, it's now obvious that the parliamentary motion supporting UNSC 1973 was merely a fig leaf to justify military intervention by British forces. A 'no-fly zone' sounds like a common-sense, passive proposal. But the reality is anything but. It requires complete air dominance, meaning the shooting down of aircraft and the destruction of all air defences such as anti-aircraft batteries. So, the no-fly zone was a Trojan horse for full-scale NATO military intervention. My gullibility about NATO's intentions seemed to be shared by the Libyan government itself, which had accepted the UNSC resolution. In responding to the UNSC decision, Libyan Foreign Minister Moussa Koussa announced an immediate ceasefire and a stoppage of all military operations. He said:

> "Libya has now got knowledge of the resolution, and in accordance with article 25 of the UN charter and given that Libya is a member of the UN Security Council, Libya is committed to accept the UN Security Council resolution."[16]

There was no justification for the use of military force and the decision to do so was an act of egregious imperialist aggression. Far from protecting the Libyan people, as was stated in the parliamentary motion for which I voted, Britain and NATO caused unthinkable suffering. Libya was once ranked at the top of all African countries in the UN's Human Development Index (HDI), *"which ranks standard of living, social security, health care and other factors for development"*.[17] In 2010, Libya's global HDI ranking was 53,[18] but it had slipped to 105 by 2019.[19] So, Libyan people have faced a sharp downturn in their living standards as a result of NATO aggression. That's in addition to all the death and destruction.

The other issue that made me feel decidedly uneasy was the parliamentary motion to support air strikes in Iraq against ISIL, or Da'esh, in September 2014. Earlier in the year, Da'esh had *blitzkrieged* through northern Iraq and were on their way to reaching Baghdad. The group had emerged as a direct result of Western imperialism and, in addition to their occupation of huge swathes of Iraq, they had also taken over large parts of neighbouring Syria. Unlike the 2003 invasion and the 2011 Libyan intervention, the Iraqi government in 2014 had explicitly invited a British military presence. I was nevertheless wary about another incursion by British armed forces. I spoke extensively to Labour Party members, and I consulted constituents in Derby. My local paper even ran a poll to ascertain what voters thought. The whips put me under heavy pressure to support the leadership. Two days before the debate, Ed Miliband asked to see me after PMQs in his office behind the Speaker's chair. I told him that I was incredibly hesitant about backing air strikes and was concerned about how the situation could escalate. He said, *"Trust my judgement on this Chris. We're going to be in government in less than a year and we need to be united on this"*. Miliband's electoral navel-gazing didn't seem like a good reason to bomb another country. I didn't commit to anything, only telling him that I'd think about it.

When the debate took place two days later, I was still unsure about what to do. Corbyn spoke in opposition to the motion. He referred to the plight of migrants fleeing previous military interventions in Afghanistan, Iraq, Libya, and Mali, for which British MPs had voted. He acknowledged the horrors being inflicted by the Da'esh death cult, but he also referenced the consequences of previous military adventures, which had led to the growth of the Taliban, al-Qa'eda, and Da'esh itself. I intervened on Corbyn's speech to ask:

> *"Will my Honourable Friend comment on the argument that the air strikes have so far prevented the expansion of ISIL forces? Would more air strikes go further in preventing ISIL from taking more ground?".*[20]

Corbyn replied by referring to the imprecise nature of air strikes and he gave the example of a school that had been bombed by mistake a few weeks earlier. When the division was called, I was still in a quandary, and I was considering various issues. For example, the country's most senior religious scholar, Grand Ayatullah Sayyid Ali al-Sistani, had issued a major edict. It called on Iraqis to be united against Da'esh, and to take collective responsibility for vanquishing them. Swiftly thereafter, tens of thousands of Iraqis, many of them teenagers, had volunteered to fight. They formed the Hashd al-Sha'bi, or the Popular Mobilisation Forces (PMF). It seemed to me that this was quite unlike 2003. But Corbyn opposed British air strikes and voted No. I had a tough decision to make. In the end, I walked through the Aye lobby.[21] I had been swayed to support the action, in large part because, at the time, I thought it would support the Iraqi resistance. The 2014 air strikes against Da'esh, on Britain's part at least, thankfully proved to be a limited venture.

In this instance, my regret is that the air strikes, although limited, helped to open the door for NATO powers to take action against the Iraqi resistance that it had purported to support. Two of the heroes who'd been instrumental in crushing the Da'esh menace – Abu Mahdi al-Muhandis (Deputy Chairman of the PMF) and Hajj Qassem Soleimani (Commander of Iran's Quds Force) – were viciously murdered in a drone strike in January 2020 ordered by the then US President, Donald Trump. The very leaders who had been on the frontlines protecting the world from Da'esh were bumped off in a cowardly, remote control attack, devoid of honour and humanity, let alone legality. The world owed a debt of gratitude to Abu Mahdi and Hajj Qassem. Instead of being lauded, they were depicted as 'terrorists' by the rogue, gangster states that make up the NATO conglomerate. The soil of Iraq is drenched in the blood of so many heroic martyrs, who sacrificed their lives to defeat Da'esh. The air strikes did nothing in comparison. Instead, they were weaponised against Iraq's heroes. It wasn't only Abu Mahdi and Hajj Qassem who were targeted, countless other members of the resistance have been exterminated in NATO air strikes since then. US military presence in Iraq also continues to this day, despite repeated calls by Iraq's Council of Representatives, and the Iraqi people themselves, for the withdrawal of US troops.[22]

My experiences have shown me that decisions on military action have real, long-term consequences. They shouldn't be made in haste, and there are too few people in Parliament who are knowledgeable and courageous enough to take a stand against British imperial bloodlust. Decisions claimed to be in the 'national interest' are really in the interests of corporate capitalism. War is phenomenally profitable for a few, whilst being devastating for those who have to live under it. The gaining of access to natural resources generates enormous profits for private companies, huge dividends for shareholders, and bumper bonuses for top executives. It also helps to spread the influence of British and US empire, whilst crushing resistance movements and those who are at the forefront of the fight against barbarism.

The shadow of New Labourism continued to linger on in the Miliband years. It manifested itself through cruelty towards people reliant on social security, anti-trade unionist positions, and militarism. None of these Blairite tendencies was cured under Miliband. The failure to move on from New Labour would prove to be a fatal mistake.

CHAPTER THREE

"RED ED"?

As the 2015 general election drew closer, discussions around policy intensified, but the paltry policy propositions promoted by Miliband and his Shadow Cabinet were decidedly dour and uninspiring. This shambolic shower were setting the party on a collision course with democratic devastation at the polls. The public were crying out for an alternative to austerity and were in no mood for a return to the New Labour prospectus. The fact that the party had lost almost five million voters between 1997 and 2010 didn't seem to register with the party's leadership and their advisers.[1]

The writing was on the wall when Vince Cable, who was the Coalition's Business Secretary at the time, was steamrollering legislation through Parliament to privatise Royal Mail in 2011. Chuka Umunna was the Shadow Cabinet member charged with leading Labour's opposition to the bill, but he was half-hearted at best. Umunna was an admirer of the New Labour ghoul Peter Mandelson who had been the Business Secretary under Gordon Brown. Mandelson had wanted to press ahead with part-privatisation of Royal Mail in 2009, but he was forced to abandon the idea the same year. He said an insufficient number of "credible bidders" had come forward to take the proposed 30 per cent stake because *"market conditions ha[d] made it impossible to conclude the process"*.[2] It wasn't that he had changed his mind about the principle of part-privatisation though. There had been no Damascene conversion about selling off vital public services. The privatisation plan was merely stalled rather than abandoned. So, privatisation wasn't anathema to Umunna. I can recollect being on a conference call with him in 2013 to discuss tactics with other MPs. I urged Umunna to give an unambiguous commitment to renationalising Royal Mail when Labour gets back into office. His retort was illuminating, *"We can't do that; the city wouldn't wear it"*.

This deference to free market capitalism defined the Miliband years. It was particularly apparent in 2014, during the series of so-called 'fireside chats' that the Shadow Cabinet were holding in their Westminster offices to discuss potential manifesto policies. These were intimate conversations involving only six or seven backbench MPs on each occasion. I remember vividly one such meeting with the Shadow Transport Secretary, Mary Creagh. I'd already attended a few of these discussions with other Shadow Cabinet members and I was usually the first out of the traps, so I decided to let others go first at this meeting. Half an hour went by with the other MPs asking about anything and everything to do with transport, apart from the obvious issue of renationalising the railways. I eventually asked Creagh directly if we were going to commit to bringing the railways back into public ownership to create some clear blue water between us and the Tories. Her response was underwhelming. She said we were going to have a mixed economy on the railways. I stressed that such a policy would not go down well with members or with the public at large. I pointed out that all the franchises would be coming up for renewal in the next Parliament, so all we would have to do is wait until they expire before bringing them into public ownership. The other MPs in the meeting included Jenny Chapman and Diana Johnson, who looked at me like I was some sort of political dinosaur. Jonathan Reynolds, who was also present, then started eulogising about the apparent quality of a privatised service operating in his constituency. Sitting in the corner of the room was John Cryer, who at that time was masquerading as a left-wing MP. I waited for him to come in to support me but, instead, he just sat there like a stuffed dummy. What I subsequently discovered was that Cryer was hoping to be elected as Chair of the PLP and was currying favour with right-wingers, so he didn't want to blot his copybook with them. Later that evening, I bumped into Chapman and Johnson who were giggling about my stance on the railways. They were astonished that I still thought outright nationalisation was a good idea. Yet, opinion polls consistently showed that a huge majority of the British public supported renationalisation.[3] These Blairite cut-outs were living in their own world.

The 'mixed economy on the railways', to which Creagh referred, made no sense. Labour's policy was to establish a public sector agency to bid against the private train operating companies for the franchises.[4] It was an overly bureaucratic crackpot concession to the private corporations who had been ripping off passengers since John Major's Tory government finalised the privatisation of the network in 1997.

The other fireside chats were no better. The Shadow Education Secretary Tristram Hunt wasn't offering anything materially different to the Coalition. Free schools and academies were to remain in place with no coherent oversight by local authorities. His proposals for schools were based on recommendations by former New Labour minister David Blunkett.[5] This wasn't surprising; it was New Labour that started the disastrous academisation agenda in the first place. Its architect was New Labour aficionado Lord Andrew Adonis, a former member of the Social Democratic Party, a right-wing group that broke away from Labour in 1981. Indeed, the Tory Education Secretary, Nicky Morgan, said explicitly that, *"One of the first acts of the Coalition Government was to turbo-charge Lord Adonis's academy programme"*.[6]

I attended another pointless consultation meeting with Blunkett and Hunt, which had been arranged to listen to the reaction of Labour MPs. Even the right-wing dominated PLP were unhappy with the Blunkett plan, and every Labour MP who came to that meeting opposed it. But Blunkett was having none of it. He dismissed out of hand the option preferred by MPs to bring academies and free schools under the umbrella of local authorities. He proclaimed that this would lose the party the election. The only role local authorities would have would be to appoint directors of school standards from a list approved by the Education Secretary, with powers to intervene in underperforming state, academy, and free schools. But that was a poor substitute for proper democratic supervision, and so Labour's grand plan for schools was to leave the fragmented system in place. The picture wasn't much better for higher education, with students still being subjected to tuition fees, although the payments were to be capped at £6,000 instead of £9,000.[7]

At the fireside chat with Ed Balls, where I brought up the question of public ownership of the railways again, his rejoinder was to ask what the limits of my nationalisation ambitions were. *"Would you nationalise BT?"*, he asked sarcastically. *"Yes"*, was my reply, but I pointed out that I was only asking for a more modest commitment to take over the rail franchises as they came up for renewal. Balls wasn't interested. He had no appetite for anything vaguely socialist, even though the 2008 financial crisis had demonstrated the case for bringing the commanding heights of the economy into democratic public ownership. Balls was only interested in tinkering with the lopsided system that was increasing poverty and inequality. The public were neither impressed nor fooled by his maladroit manoeuvres, such as his plan to means-test the universal Winter Fuel Payment. But Balls was belligerent when challenged about the futility of his gimmicks.

Whilst I had some sympathy for Balls when, in 2013, David Cameron called him *"the most annoying person in modern politics"*, I can't say I was shocked by the remark.[8] Balls was a belligerent politician, and that cost him his seat at the 2015 general election. He wasn't made to suffer, though. As a privately educated PPE graduate, Balls had a feather-bedded landing after losing favour with the voters in Morley and Outwood. The Establishment always look after their own. Balls's charmed existence outside of Parliament has included being appointed Chair of Norwich City Football Club, becoming a senior fellow at Harvard University, and regularly appearing on light entertainment TV shows. He was also wheeled out on occasions to attack Corbyn in the pages and broadcast channels of the corporate media. And he even took to Twitter after the 2019 election to insult me. I had criticised all three Labour leadership candidates for kowtowing to the McCarthyite demands being made by the Board of Deputies of British Jews,[9] a group that supports the racist, settler-colonial ideology of Zionism. For that, Balls defamed me as a *"ridiculous and bigoted anti-Semite"*.[10]

Widening Labour's appeal

Midway through Miliband's leadership, I recall speaking to Tom Harris about broadening Labour's voter base. Harris represented Glasgow South before losing his seat in the 2015 SNP landslide. Whilst we were in Parliament together, Harris and I got on well, despite his Blairite inclinations. In one conversation with him, I said our task was to appeal to non-voters who feel disenfranchised. We needed to inspire people by giving them a reason to vote Labour. I told him that, in my view, the political process had failed them, and non-voters were the biggest cohort in every election. Harris's reaction was extraordinarily cynical, and it summed up everything that is wrong with Westminster politics. He metaphorically patted me on the head whilst patronisingly saying that I didn't understand. *"The thing about non-voters is they don't vote, so don't bother wasting your time on them"*, he said. As well as writing a regular column in the ultra-Conservative *Daily Telegraph*, Harris subsequently went on to set-up a political consultancy firm that commends the corporate sector and promotes privatisation.[11]

Harris's contempt and arrogant dismissal of the electorate was commonplace on Labour's benches. The same attitude was also apparent when Labour MPs in the most marginal seats started meeting together with party officials to begin campaign planning, a couple of years before the 2015 general election. I had a slender majority of just 613, whilst Balls only had a lead over his Tory rival of 1,101, so we attended a lot of meetings together. Arnie Graf, the US-based community organiser who Miliband had brought in to advise the party, spoke at one of these meetings about the importance of community organising. After the 2015 defeat, Graf exposed how out-of-touch the party had been when he revealed that officials *"didn't know a single worker on the minimum wage"* for Miliband to talk to during a press event.[12] Had Balls listened to Graf and taken the UKIP threat more seriously, the party's strategy could have neutralised UKIP.

Balls had dismissed the findings of some detailed work that had been commissioned to assess the threat posed by UKIP in Labour's marginal seats. In Balls's constituency of Morley and Outwood, UKIP took 7,951 votes and, in my seat, they secured 6,532 votes. I can vividly remember Balls in one of these meetings belligerently asserting that for every vote UKIP takes from Labour they will take three or four from the Tories. His intransigence impacted on the party's response to the UKIP threat, which was never taken seriously enough. Corbyn later summed up the feelings of many when he said a lot of people had voted for UKIP in 2015 out of despair.[13] Balls thought that Labour could see off UKIP by talking tough on immigration. He was so certain of his position that he told Sky News that he hoped to use one of Labour's anti-immigration mugs to do a toast to a Labour government upon victory.[14] The mugs were a reprehensible diversion that played to the lowest common denominator of prejudice. They were not only morally wrong, but they were also politically inept. It did nothing to encourage would-be UKIP voters to switch their support, and it deterred others from voting Labour. Given the closeness of the result in Derby North, it probably did enough damage to cost me my seat in 2015. I certainly had a number of former Labour voters tell me on the doorstep that they wouldn't be voting Labour precisely because of the anti-immigration mugs. In the end Balls's hubris was his nemesis.

He was one of many senior Labour figures who were not convinced about the need to build local parties along the lines advocated by Graf. These are the same individuals who opposed Corbyn, and despised the fact that, when he was elected leader, Labour *did* become the mass party that Graf had advocated. After the 2017 general election, there was a huge opportunity to develop Graf's community organising model but, sadly, it never materialised, partly because of the counter-revolution in the Labour Party, to which Balls contributed. It made effective community organising impossible. New members were treated with disdain, and Balls told *BBC Newsnight* in a 2016 interview that he was *"afraid Jeremy Corbyn has brought in new members"*.[15] Isn't bringing in new members something to be celebrated rather than something of which to be afraid? Many of those new members were previously non-voters, the very people whom Tom Harris had dismissed as being a waste of time.

Separately, I'd been advocating a radical green agenda, but the party failed on that front as well. Miliband had steered the Climate Change Act through Parliament in 2008, so I had high hopes that, under his leadership, Labour would embrace a progressive environmental programme. But the party's green manifesto was woefully inadequate, even though it said that *"tackling climate change is an economic necessity and the most important thing we must do for our children, our grandchildren and future generations"*.[16] For example, it left fracking in place, said nothing about reforesting the uplands, allowed the utilities to be run for profit by global corporations, and it was silent about making energy efficiency a national infrastructure priority. The best it could muster was a commitment to *"a major drive for energy efficiency*",[17] whatever that was supposed to mean. The plans for an *"independent National Infrastructure Commission"*[18] only highlighted investment in flood prevention, without giving any specifics. Warm words were no substitute for specific plans. Had the party taken a stronger line on the environment and made it a programme priority with clear policy lines, Balls might have survived, as the Green Party polled 1,264 in Morley and Outwood. A creative campaign focussing on things like creating well-paid green jobs, democratising the utilities to slash household utility bills, and going after the polluters could have made the difference, but Miliband was too timid.

With less than 12 months to go before the 2015 general election, most Labour MPs were behaving like lemmings running hell for leather towards an electoral cliff. This air of unreality in the PLP was intensified after the 2014 local council elections. The atmosphere at the next PLP meeting was buoyant after Labour had done well in middle class areas. Many Labour MPs were standing up in turn to announce that Labour was no longer a party of the working class in their respective constituencies. Their tone was celebratory when they explained how many working class voters were deserting the party. They displayed an arrogant, self-satisfied, couldn't-care-less attitude about the loss of working class supporters because they thought they were being replaced by more affluent middle class voters. Andy Slaughter, the Labour MP for Hammersmith and Shepherd's Bush, gleefully spoke about how middle class voters had thrown out the Tories in Hammersmith and Fulham Council. There was an unattractive swagger about his account of the result. As the meeting was breaking up, he asked me if Labour still had many working class supporters up in Derby North. When I said I hoped so, he was dismissive of their significance as a cohort in the electorate. But the suburbanite tendency in the PLP, that was typified by Andy Slaughter's haughty psephology, were living on borrowed time. They would have their smug smirks wiped off their faces by working class voters in the subsequent general election.

In desperation, as the general election drew closer, the late Michael Meacher and I convened a discreet meeting of like-minded MPs just before Christmas 2014. We met in a small committee room in Portcullis House, adjacent to the Palace of Westminster.

We were joined at the meeting by just three other MPs: Michael Connarty (then MP for Linlithgow and Falkirk East), Ian Lavery (MP for Wansbeck), and Steve Rotheram (then MP for Liverpool Walton). All of us were extremely concerned about the deficiencies in Labour's offer. After a lengthy discussion, we agreed to draw up and publish a progressive policy proposal to put pressure on the leadership. We wanted to see the election manifesto committing Labour to opposing austerity, and to supporting the full renationalisation of the railways and the repeal of anti-trade union laws. Connarty was particularly worried about the situation in Scotland, where the SNP were riding on the crest of a nationalist wave, because the Scottish people had lost patience with Westminster politics. He felt that, unless Labour changed tack, the party could be wiped out in the ensuing general election.

Under Miliband and Balls, Labour was out of step both with its members and working-class voters, whose support was needed to secure a Labour government. Labour's leadership team had allowed themselves to be manipulated by the Tories into supporting austerity, which was economically illiterate, electorally disastrous, and gave political cover to the Coalition Government's leaders. This was an inevitable consequence of putting neoliberals in charge of developing Labour's economic policy.

But it wasn't just the emaciated economic offer at the 2015 election that was informed by Team Miliband's injudicious entanglement with neoliberalism. It also influenced the entirety of Labour's 2015 manifesto. What resulted was the election of a majority Tory government for the first time in 23 years. The Tories gained 26 seats, including mine, giving them an overall majority, whilst Labour lost 24 despite slightly increasing its vote share. I believe that the progressive policies that Meacher and I had proposed, calling on Labour to reject austerity, could have made a material difference to the election outcome. Our statement was eventually signed by just 15 Labour MPs and published by *LabourList* on 26 January 2015.[19]

It is clear to me that Miliband won the 2010 leadership election under false pretences. He had portrayed himself as an alternative to New Labour. He promised to put members centre stage, claiming that if the party had listened to them when it was in government, it wouldn't have made as many mistakes. He described himself as *"the most credible candidate of change"*.[20] *Conservative Home* labelled him 'Red Ed', an undeserved sobriquet that was picked up by the corporate media.[21] His record as leader was more like a New Labour tribute act, starkly illustrated in Labour's 2015 manifesto. I remember, in 2010, congratulating him after he had addressed the PLP in a leadership hustings. Thinking back to that encounter, he was talking to Luciana Berger and Chuka Umunna when I joined the conversation. I urged him to, *"Keep that passion and be yourself"*, but he seemed far more interested in the counsel of two right-wingers than anything I had to say. These were two right-wingers, let's remember, who were later at the centre of the efforts to sabotage Jeremy Corbyn's leadership, and who ultimately left the party as part of the right-wing breakaway Change UK group in 2019.

Had Miliband taken my advice, things might have played out differently. I don't believe he was naturally inclined to be so right-wing. Some have argued that he didn't know what he believed and wanted others to make decisions. But I think he was afraid to be himself, and he eventually took comfort in speaking through the mediums of focus groups, corporate lobbyists, and policy wonks. He was never a conviction politician, but he clearly had some beliefs of his own when he stood for the leadership in 2010. His loss of spirit was to be his undoing.

CHAPTER FOUR

A DISASTER WAITING TO HAPPEN

The loss of the 2015 general election had been a foregone conclusion, and it was the direct result of Ed Miliband's failure to make good on what he had promised during the 2010 leadership contest. If Miliband's intentions were initially genuine when he announced his ambition for Labour's top job, he soon changed his tune. Not only were his Shadow Cabinet dour and uninspiring, but his advisers in the leader's office were no better. His ridiculous mantra about what he referred to as the *"squeezed middle"*[1] failed to convince voters. I'm not sure if he even believed it himself. It seems they were all merely attempting to continue with Tony Blair's idea of a 'big tent' policy.[2] Of all people, it was John Prescott – Labour's deputy leader under Tony Blair who had been a ship's steward and trade union activist before entering Parliament – who in 1997 stupidly said, *"We are all middle class now"*.[3]

To concentrate Labour's appeal on middle class voters and to try to outmanoeuvre UKIP was a damfool scheme. An indication of just how ill-judged the *"squeezed middle"* tagline was in winning over the electorate was revealed by a study undertaken by Oxford University's Department of Sociology in 2016. Researchers found that six out of 10 people in Britain considered themselves working class. They felt that it was their family background, rather than their occupation or whether they went to university, that determined class. The study also found that just under half of those in 'middle class' jobs (classified as managerial or professional) said that they were working class.[4]

So, Ed Miliband's pitch was aimed at just 40 per cent of the electorate. Worse still, polling evidence showed that the cohort he was trying to woo was much more inclined to vote Conservative than Labour.[5] Copying Blair's 'big tent' policy meant disregarding working class concerns. Peter Mandelson had once arrogantly asserted that working class voters *"have nowhere else to go"*.[6] This was not only morally wrong but, by 2015, it was well and truly out of date. Many working class voters had either stopped voting altogether or were supporting other parties. Labour lost almost three million votes in 2001 compared to four years earlier, and it won that election with the lowest number polled by a winning party since 1929.[7] In the 2010 election, Labour's vote had fallen by just under five million compared to 1997.[8] In spite of these startling statistics, Miliband decided to follow the Mandelson maxim. The blinkered policy wonks in the leader's office, who thought it was a good idea to pursue that strategy, were too clever for their own good. These were the same blinkered policy wonks who thought it was a sensible idea for Labour to pinch the 'One Nation' phrase coined by Benjamin Disraeli, a nineteenth century Tory Prime Minister.[9] These 'strategists' (I use the term loosely) were convinced that a strategy focussed on 35 per cent of the electorate would be sufficient to win the election.[10] Miliband had lit the fuse on an electoral time bomb that was set to explode in his face on 7 May 2015.

It is unsurprising that the Labour Party lost the 2015 election miserably. Many cited the party's lacklustre manifesto, whose six key pledges were carved into the notorious 'Ed Stone' (a hulking 2.6 metre limestone slab),[11] as the reason for defeat. Jon Cruddas was scathing about the manifesto, and he had helped to write it![12] He said:

> *"We gamed out the electorate but we got it wrong, and then the music stopped on election day and we didn't realise the scale of it until one minute past 10 on election night ... We ended up with a cost-of-living, transactional politics which drew on polling figures that were based on sand. That is the reality of it".* [13]

Meanwhile, the Green Party, which had campaigned on an anti-austerity platform, gained over a million votes for the first time in its history. I lost my Derby North seat by the narrow margin of 41 votes, whilst the Greens had secured 1,618 in all. It was a similar story in many other marginals.

Labour's election strategists had decided that the party would focus any additional resources on gaining target seats that were needed to give Miliband enough MPs to form a government.

Labour's campaign team was chaired by Douglas Alexander and included MPs Jonathan Ashworth, Gloria De Piero, Michael Dugher, Toby Perkins, and Lucy Powell, all of whom subsequently opposed Jeremy Corbyn's leadership.[14] Furthermore, most of the people advising them were New Labour re-treads such as Torsten Bell (a former adviser to Alistair Darling) and Spencer Livermore (a former aide to Gordon Brown).[15]

The strategists left constituencies like mine to fend for themselves, even though I only had a majority of 613 at the time. The party's campaign managers took the complacent view that all the seats Labour had won in England and Wales in 2010 would not change hands. In the previous general election, my campaign had benefitted from communications about the party's plans being directly mailed to voters in Derby North, and we enjoyed additional organisational support as well. However, in 2015, none of that was available. So incompetent were the team at the party's head office who were running Labour's hapless 2015 election campaign that they omitted to declare £123,748 in election expenses, including £7,614 for the 'Ed Stone'. This resulted in a maximum fine of £20,000, which was the biggest electoral fine in more than two decades.[16] The Electoral Commission said, *"It is vital that the larger parties comply with these rules and report their finances accurately if voters are to have confidence in the system"*.

Meanwhile, Julie Hilling, Labour's candidate for Bolton West, who was defending a majority of just 92, told me she had asked for additional assistance. The feedback she was hearing on the doorstep ran counter to the national opinion polls. But she told me that, rather than getting the extra support she needed, she received an angry phone call from Labour's Chief Whip, Rosie Winterton, upbraiding her for undermining the 'key seat strategy'. Hilling went on to lose her seat by 801 votes. Winterton's vote share also slumped in her Doncaster Central constituency.

Unlike Hilling, the response we were receiving on the doorstep in Derby North suggested that I would win comfortably. We did in fact beat the Tories in six out of the seven wards that comprise the constituency. The bookies had me as the odds-on favourite to retain the seat, and an Ashcroft poll had me winning Derby North with a majority of more than 9,000. We ran a strong local campaign and had done extensive work throughout the constituency in the previous five years. I'd rejected the template election address produced by Labour's head office, because it included the Balls stamp of anti-immigration rhetoric. I was neither prepared to put my name to the racist pledge to deny social security to immigrants for two years, nor to the economically illiterate reference to cutting the deficit every year. I had written a detailed report on community cohesion the previous year as a policy background paper, which was then quietly binned by Yvette Cooper, who also happens to be married to Ed Balls. I was not about to do a volte-face less than 12 months later. Our election literature in Derby North reflected the constituency work that I'd done, which included leading the campaign to save the rail manufacturing industry in the city, which we hoped would resonate with voters.

Election day

Prior to the election, I met with representatives from the Trade Unionist and Socialist Coalition (TUSC) to discuss my position on opposing austerity, and my support for a higher minimum wage, trade unions, public ownership, and scrapping tuition fees. After our meeting, TUSC agreed not to field a candidate against me, as they understood that we shared the same socialist positions. Sadly, there was no such agreement forthcoming from the Green Party. Their local members told me that, *"It's safe to vote Green because you're going to win by a landslide"*, and they selected a very effective local candidate, Alice Mason-Power. She gave a powerful performance at the various hustings events. When I spoke to her after one of those public meetings, she said that I should join the Green Party. My response was that we would have a better chance of delivering the policies we both supported if Green Party members joined Labour. However, in hindsight, that was a misplaced assurance on my part. Even if they had joined (and many Green Party members did join under Corbyn),[17] Labour's bureaucrats and the PLP would have simply disregarded their wishes.

The final national opinion polls showed that Labour and the Tories were neck and neck, suggesting certain victory for Labour in Derby North. After a long day getting out the vote, I sat down with my partner Maggie, just before 10:00pm to listen to the bombshell exit poll before getting ready to attend the count.

To my horror, they were predicting that I was on course to lose. When we got to the count at Derby Arena, I felt ill. As soon as I arrived, journalists descended on me for my reaction to the exit poll. I confidently told them that I didn't believe it, but deep down I knew that exit polls were rarely wrong. I don't know if it was a bug or a reaction to the possibility of defeat but, as the night wore on, I felt increasingly unwell. My daughter Simone bought me a bottle of water, and I went to sit in a bathroom cubicle away from prying camera lenses to see if I could compose myself. But nothing seemed to work. I told my agent, James Shires, that I was going back to the constituency office with Maggie. He said that he would keep me up to date with developments.

When I got back to the office, I was throwing up in the bathroom and the updates from the count weren't making me feel any better. The news was that it was too close to call, but it looked like the Tories were just ahead. Then we were informed that it looked like we had just shaded it. Every time the phone rang, I felt a frisson of fear. Eventually, Maggie took a call saying that the declaration was imminent and that I needed to come back to the count. I said to Maggie that I wasn't sure whether I was well enough. I splashed some cold water on my face, but it was no good, I just couldn't face going back. We decided to go home, and I went to bed.

My two children, Fionnbharr and Simone, took a break from the count to come home to check how I was, and to tell me that the outcome had gone to a recount. I was worried about how I was going to pay the mortgage if we did lose, and I was concerned about the impact on my staff team who relied on me for their livelihoods. I was not independently wealthy, and, unlike many MPs, I had no secondary source of income. As a committed socialist, I certainly wasn't going to be offered any lucrative political consultancies. Fionnbharr and Simone were trying to comfort me and said they would rally round as a family to get through this potentially adverse situation. After the third recount, the result was eventually declared at around 9:30am, almost 12 hours after the polls had closed. The Tories had won by just 41 votes.

The shock of defeat: what went wrong?

The result was a bitter pill to swallow, not least because we discovered on the day that a number of Irish voters in Derby North had been incorrectly registered as European citizens. That meant that they were ineligible to vote in UK general elections. We received several phone calls from aggrieved supporters who had said they had only been able to vote in the local council election that was being held simultaneously. A few days after the election, we found out that the true scale of the problem was substantial. At least 60 other Irish citizens had been incorrectly registered, and I was contacted by several households who had been unable to vote for me because they had been removed from the register after moving house. One family of Labour voters had been in touch to say they went to vote at the polling station serving their new address but were told they were not on the electoral register there. So, they went to the polling station covering their former address where they had previously voted, only to find that they were not registered there, either. Others told me they had been unable to cast proxy votes for people who were unable to vote in person, even though they had the appropriate documentation to do so. There had been some breakdown in the system which meant that the names of these proxy voters had not been included on the list given to presiding officers at the polling stations.

I decided to take legal advice to determine whether I had a chance of succeeding with an election petition, which is a legal device to declare an election void and force a re-run. But time is of the essence and the deadline for submitting such a petition is just 21 days after the date of the election, so I needed to move fast. I took soundings from John Cooper QC, who said I had a strong case, but the cost implications of losing were prohibitive. I was already worried about what I was going to do for an income without taking on the liability of a costly legal case that could run into six figures. I needed to attempt to get the costs underwritten.

I approached the Labour Party head office for assistance, but they wouldn't help. I later discovered that there was a political intervention at a senior level vetoing any support. John McDonnell said he would approach trade unions to see if any financial backing could be obtained that way. I even approached

Queen guitarist, Brian May, who was aware that I'd led efforts in Parliament to stop the badger cull, which was an issue about which he felt strongly. We had got on well together when I met with him in Parliament to discuss the campaign against the cull. He was supportive of my case, but he didn't feel he could underwrite the costs as he said that would appear political, and he had established a non-political organisation before the election called Common Decency.[18] He did say, however, that he was prepared to offer public words of support and encouragement. In the end, I ran out of time and just had to accept defeat.

CHAPTER FIVE

ATTACK OF THE GAMMONS

After the 2015 general election, I had sunk into a Slough of Despond for several weeks, until Jeremy Corbyn secured the requisite number of nominations to stand in the Labour leadership campaign. I didn't expect him to win but I thought he would do better than many were suggesting, and certainly a lot better than the 200-to-1 odds the bookies were offering. Corbyn's entry into the contest gave me a new lease of life, and I threw myself wholeheartedly into supporting his campaign. I spoke at numerous CLP nomination meetings in support of Corbyn. The first one was at Broxtowe CLP. I remember looking at the attendees and thinking that I was unlikely to secure a majority for Corbyn. I guess I'd been influenced by the propaganda that his support was confined to the margins. In other words, young idealists, bohemians, and hippies. Nobody in the room fitted those descriptions but, when the votes were counted, Corbyn won overwhelmingly. That meeting suggested to me that, contrary to expectations, Corbyn had appeal across the board, not just amongst young people and old radicals.

The Broxtowe experience was to be repeated at every CLP nomination meeting I attended, and so it was obvious that something significant was happening. Tony Blair didn't help his own side when he suggested that people whose hearts were with Corbyn should *"get a transplant"*.[1] When it looked like Corbyn actually had a chance of winning, the Establishment went into meltdown. The registered supporters system, which had been brought in under Ed Miliband in the hope of marginalising the left, had badly backfired. Tens of thousands of people flocked to join the party to vote for Corbyn. He was a breath of fresh air, unlike the other candidates. He unashamedly advocated for socialism and an end to austerity.

In early 2015, the prospect of the Labour Party becoming a vehicle for socialism and, later that year, Corbyn being overwhelmingly elected as leader, seemed about as likely as finding life on Mars. Yet, that miracle became a reality on 12 September.

Something with which nobody had reckoned, however, was the ferocity of the opposition to Corbyn's leadership from Labour MPs and bureaucrats.

An early warning of PLP scheming

At the 2015 Labour Party conference, I was approached by Dave Wilcox, who was a Labour councillor on Derbyshire County Council at the time. He said that the Labour Group wanted me to help with local election preparations, as the election was coming up in just over 18 months. The council leader, Anne Western, was a big Corbyn supporter, so I was pleased to assist. They were offering a paid position and, initially, I took on the role with Sarah Russell, who was my caseworker and a Labour councillor in Derby. She was an outstanding organiser, and we set about structuring the campaign together through to the Christmas break, when Sarah continued in the role on her own through to the county elections in 2017. One of the first things I did was to contact the Labour MPs in the county to explore how we could work together towards securing a Labour victory, which would ultimately help consolidate their own votes. I was surprised that Toby Perkins, who had previously been so supportive, simply ignored my emails and wouldn't take my calls.

I later discovered why Perkins had been cold shouldering me when I was attempting to become the Labour candidate for the Derbyshire Police and Crime Commissioner (PCC). The PCC election was due to take place in 2016, and I'd sent out an email to members throughout the county seeking their support to be the Labour nominee. To my surprise, I received a surly reply from Perkins. He wrote:

> "If I had been asked six months ago about this, I would have thought it was inconceivable that I might not have supported you for this post, but some of the things that I have read from you in recent months ... give me tremendous cause for concern".

Clearly, Perkins had objected to my forthright support for Corbyn, and to my criticism of the PLP malcontents who I'd called out for their unwillingness to accept Corbyn's landslide victory. He also seemed to take exception to my opposition to Labour MPs voting for yet more air strikes. In late 2015, I had joined the calls encouraging rank and file members in Labour-held constituencies to press their MPs to oppose David Cameron's call for an air offensive in Syria. Perkins was one of those Labour MPs who were eventually persuaded to go through the No lobby. He told me in an email that he *"was very torn"* about which way to vote, and he made excuses for the Labour MPs who had voted with the government, insisting that they were *"not bad people"*. According to Perkins, I was *"part of a simplification of what was a multi layered and very difficult decision"*. To my delight, on the same day, Perkins's office manager got in touch to say she would be happy to support my PCC campaign.

In a later exchange, where I'd privately taken Perkins to task for an atrocious statement he had made about Ken Livingstone, he confirmed that he didn't vote for me to become Labour's PCC candidate. He said the reason was that he considered me to be *"a combatant in a civil war"* of which he apparently wanted no part. That was a transparently false statement, as Perkins was an enthusiastic cheerleader for, and a participant in, the PLP coup against Corbyn in 2016. Perkins is an archetype of the PLP's mindset. His behaviour illustrated how shallow these Westminster village inhabitants really were. In May 2015, he had told me that he was *"a big fan"* of mine, and that I was *"a considerable loss to the PLP"*. Yet, a few short years later, in 2019, Perkins joined in the efforts to drum me out of the Labour Party for which I'd been campaigning before he started infant school.

However, I guess I shouldn't have been so surprised by Perkins's behaviour. Earlier in 2015, when I was speaking in support of Corbyn at the Nottingham South CLP leadership nomination meeting, Perkins spoke in support of the Blairite candidate, Liz Kendall. The meeting was being held at the Nottingham Mechanics' Institute, which has its own bar. Whilst we awaited the result, I went to buy a drink for the speakers. Perkins had declined my offer to buy him one, but he later congratulated me on my speech. I thanked him and responded with a jocular enquiry about whether that meant he was jumping ship. But his melancholy demeanour suggested he wasn't in the mood for light-hearted banter. He replied gloomily, *"The only jumping I'll be doing is off a bridge or out of the party if Corbyn is elected"*. He didn't stay for the result, which was an overwhelming victory for Corbyn. Had he done so, his mood would have no doubt worsened; not one solitary member at the packed meeting had voted for Kendall.

Another indication of the change in attitude inside the PLP towards Corbyn's supporters became apparent when I attended Dame Margaret Beckett's annual CLP fundraising dinner after I had lost my seat. It illustrated the petty animosity of Labour's old guard who resented the extraordinary uprising by ordinary party members that Corbyn's candidacy had precipitated. Beckett's dinners always begin with a ridiculous reverential routine, where guest speakers and senior labour movement figures from past and present are introduced with musical fanfare. I'd endured the ritual for the previous five years when I was a fellow Derby MP, although the dubious privilege was never extended to me during the eight years when I led Derby's Labour Group, including the four years when I was leader of Derby City Council.

After I came out in support of Corbyn, it seems I was returned to the ranks of the *personae non gratae* at Beckett's Derby South events. At the two Derby South CLP dinners I attended during my parliamentary hiatus following the 2015 election, there was the usual rollcall for Beckett's top table guests and assorted labour movement Z-listers. On both occasions, they included my Derby North predecessor, Bob Laxton, but excluded me. Whilst I was pleased to be spared the pretentious pageant, it seemed like a deliberate snub. On the first occasion, I thought it was just an oversight, but then it happened again. It was blindingly obvious that it was intentional when the same thing happened for the third time, after I'd been re-elected as MP for Derby North in the 2017 general election. On that occasion, Sir Keir Starmer was the guest speaker and even he was embarrassed, prompting him to namecheck me at the beginning of his after-dinner speech. This is, of course, an incredibly trivial matter in the overall scheme of things. However, it does indicate the depth of resentment that was felt by Labour's right-wing grandees, who had lost control over what they considered to be their fiefdom.

Mr Popularity

It is hard to believe now but, in the 2010–2015 Parliament, I had been popular among my peers in the PLP. Even the ultra-right-wing Labour MP John Mann was friendly back then. Mind you, that might have been because he was a Leeds United fan and I used to get him tickets for the football when they were playing Derby County at Pride Park. I was acknowledged by the Parliamentary Internet Communications and Technology Forum as the most loyal Labour MP in the House of Commons in 2014. I managed to contain my disdain for the direction in which Miliband's Shadow Cabinet were taking the party without resorting to the out-and-out sabotage that Corbyn was to face.

When I lost my Derby North seat, I was inundated with messages from Labour MPs commiserating with me. A fellow Derbyshire MP, Toby Perkins, who represents Chesterfield, was the first to call. He was really upset that I'd lost my seat. I was touched by his kind remarks but thought his analysis of what should come next to be way off beam. Perkins said, *"Well, we've tried a left-wing manifesto now and we can see it doesn't work"*. I thought to myself, *"If that's your idea of a left-wing manifesto, why did you join the Labour Party in Tony Benn's former constituency?"*. Chris Leslie, who represented Nottingham East at the time, also called me and said he would help me find alternative employment. He said that he was keen to keep in touch and that he was concerned about my situation. Michael Meacher best summed up my own feelings when he called me to offer his commiserations. *"Our leaders have got a lot to answer for"*, he said.

The leader and deputy leader, Ed Miliband and Harriet Harman, also went out of their way to send me personal handwritten letters expressing their sympathy. Miliband wrote:

> "I am so sorry that you lost your seat. It was a dreadful shock and the narrowness of the result makes it even harder. I hope you are bearing up under the very difficult circumstances. I know you will bounce back and if I can help in any way, please let me know. You were a great supporter of mine, and I am very grateful for that. With all best wishes."

To see the above document please scan this QR code.

Harman wrote an even more effusive letter. She said:

> "I am so deeply sorry that you have not been re-elected. You were such an asset to the PLP with all your life experience and your work as council leader. Even though you were in the PLP for too short a time, you gained a huge amount of respect and admiration. I hope you will help us find our way forward. With thanks and best wishes for the future. In solidarity."

To see the above document please scan this QR code.

But Miliband's *"best wishes"* and Harman's *"solidarity"* were short-lived, as was the support from other erstwhile parliamentary colleagues, who I'd previously considered friends. In my naïvety, I had fully expected that my one-time colleagues would respect the democratic will of the overwhelming majority of grassroots party members when they elected Jeremy Corbyn as leader. How wrong I was!

Take, for example, Lisa Nandy. She went from being a putative torchbearer for the left in the 2010–2015 Parliament, to backing the coup against Corbyn in 2016. She later became a fully-fledged witchfinder general, discovering 'antisemites' around every corner. On 29 June 2019, the *Financial Times* published an opinion column she had scribbled that represented a gratuitous hatchet job against me, which included the defamatory assertion that I had been engaged in *"Jew-baiting"*.[2] Before that, however, our relations had already soured. I knew something was amiss when I saw her at the 2016 Labour Party conference in Liverpool. It was initially a friendly chat as we hadn't seen each other in-person for over a year. But her mood darkened when I mentioned the party's change of direction under Corbyn and McDonnell. She went off on a rant about McDonnell and displayed what can only be described as a persecution complex. She told me about all the 'abuse' she was supposedly receiving online, for which she held McDonnell responsible. She said she was even getting abuse at her advice surgery from one particular individual. I tried to reassure her that we all get online abuse, but she was adamant that hers was different. When I said, *"You can't hold John responsible for trolls and stalkers"*, she became even more antagonistic, telling me she was *"very disappointed with this conversation"*. She was clearly frustrated that I refused to indulge her fantasy about being a victim of some elaborate conspiracy masterminded by McDonnell. That vivid imagination for non-existent conspiracies was clearly at work again, when years later she, figuratively speaking, donned the witchfinder's high-crowned hat, cape, and bucket-top boots.

2015 Oldham by-election

Shortly after Corbyn was elected leader, my old comrade Michael Meacher passed away after a short illness. My office in Portcullis House had stood opposite Meacher's and, as I had a Nespresso machine, he used to regularly pop in for a coffee. He was delighted when Corbyn was elected party leader and said it was a *"seminal day in British politics, marking the coming together of the two great conditions needed for transformational change"*.[3] He would have been distraught to see the Corbyn project destroyed. During the 2010–2015 Parliament, ours were often the only voices in the PLP arguing for more progressive policies. Meacher was one of the first Labour MPs to make me feel welcome upon my election to Parliament in 2010, when I was still feeling somewhat discombobulated by the rarefied Westminster atmosphere.

Jim Kennedy, who was a Labour NEC member back then, broke the sad news to me over the phone. Kennedy was also upset, but he knew that a candidate would have to be selected to replace Meacher, and he was urging me to throw my hat in the ring. I was reluctant to do so, because I didn't know much about the Oldham constituency, and I was hoping to fight Derby North again in the next general election if local members still wanted me. But Kennedy said there would be no better way to pay tribute to Meacher than by continuing his legacy and ensuring that Corbyn had another supportive MP. I said I would think about it. Kennedy's point about carrying the torch for Meacher eventually persuaded me to go for it, provided that a credible local candidate did not emerge. Then the leader of the local council, Jim McMahon, expressed an interest and Mo Azam, a local Jeremy Corbyn supporter, said he was going to stand. I was going to withdraw at that point, but Alex Halligan, a local Momentum organiser who was close to Jon Lansman, asked me to stay in the contest as that would help Azam.

I went through the motions and gave a strong speech at the selection meeting, but the outcome was cut and dried. McMahon won with 232 votes to Azam's 141. I think I gained 18 first preference votes, but it was gratifying to learn that nearly all of Azam's supporters had given me their second preference votes, and that the vast majority of McMahon's had done so as well. The corporate media had speculated about Labour losing the by-election, which they said would prompt a leadership challenge to oust Corbyn. Bear in mind that this was only a few months after Corbyn had overwhelmingly won the leadership contest! But, despite their best endeavours, McMahon went on to comfortably win the seat with an increased share of the vote (albeit on a smaller turnout). This vote should have fortified Corbyn's standing in the PLP, but it did nothing of the sort. If anything, it encouraged the fifth columnists to step up their efforts to destabilise his leadership.

Corbyn's local government timidity

I had been described as a local *éminence grise* by one Derby-based commentator during the two years I was out of Parliament. I guess that was why Unison approached me in 2016 to intervene in a long-running regrading dispute with the Labour-controlled council. Following a job evaluation exercise, the council were planning to cut the salaries of teaching assistants in the city by up to 25 per cent. The negotiations had reached an impasse and I was asked to help break the stalemate. The council leader, Ranjit Banwait, was a good friend of mine and he was coming under intense criticism for the council's stance. Jeremy Corbyn had even become involved and had phoned Banwait to urge him to reach a settlement. The local Unison branch secretary, Nicole Berrisford, had also spoken about the dispute from the rostrum at the 2016 Labour Party conference. The pressure was then further intensified when Unison's general secretary, Dave Prentis, joined local Unison activists on the streets in Banwait's own ward to highlight what the council was doing.

I persuaded Banwait to allow me to lead informal negotiations to reach a settlement. A number of meetings then took place with three Unison representatives to find a solution. I was joined in those meetings by Lisa Eldret, who was the council cabinet member dealing with the issue, and James Shires, the local Labour Party agent. We made good progress and, separately, I went through the council's statement of accounts to identify where the funding could be found to meet Unison's reasonable demands. There was plenty to go at, too. The council had over £88 million in unallocated reserves, an explicit budget risk reserve of just under £12 million, and had only used £280,000 of £13 million it had previously set aside for equal pay claims. When any preceding job evaluation exercises had resulted in staff grades being reduced, workers were eligible for salary protection, but that system had been abandoned because of government funding cuts. Nevertheless, full salary protection for the teaching assistants was easily achievable, it just required political will to make it happen.

The council's chief finance officer took exception to my intervention. In a private email to Banwait, he compared me to Eric Pickles because I had identified where the council had reserves it could use to settle the dispute. Pickles was the Local Government Secretary at the time and was obsessed about reserves held by local authorities.[4] Ultimately, an agreement was reached through the meetings that I'd brokered, and Nicole Berrisford, along with a large number of the teaching assistants, later campaigned for me in the 2017 general election. However, a few months after the election, the council reneged on the agreement.[5] The following year, Labour lost control of the council and Banwait lost his seat to UKIP. To add insult to injury, the new council administration reached an agreement with Unison in a matter of weeks.[6]

The teaching assistants dispute was a salutary lesson in how the government had devolved blame to local councils for cuts made in Westminster. Banwait had led a valiant campaign demanding a 'Fair deal for Derby'. I presented a petition in the House of Commons calling on the government to provide more resources, which was inevitably ignored.[7] The campaign did garner a lot of local support and it was replicated by other Labour councils but sustaining public support for five or six years is difficult. The cuts kept on coming and were being implemented by Labour authorities. Attempts to pin the blame on Tory ministers lost traction and the focus of frustration returned to the council. It was a neat trick that was assisted by the local newspaper and radio station. They were constantly criticising the council, but they said very little to hold Tory MPs in the area accountable for cuts that they were supporting.

I began to wonder what the point was of having Labour in local government if all it did was the Tories' dirty work. There had to be a better way. Ironically, an alternative was possible thanks to the Coalition Government. I hadn't been aware of its potential until I was returned to Parliament in 2017 but, when I discovered it, it generated a hostile reaction from Labour's right-wing, who are more comfortable making cuts than reversing them. Labour's inability, or reluctance, in local government to mobilise communities against the cuts, and to provide a positive example of what Labour could do when in power, was damaging the party's prospects for the following general election. Corbyn had failed to urge Labour councils to use the powers at their disposal to eliminate the housing crisis and to reverse the cuts imposed by central government. Instead, they were left wringing their hands in despair. Where were the likes of Ken Livingstone, Linda Bellos, Ted Knight, and David Bookbinder? A return to the days of municipal socialism was desperately needed, to force local authorities to serve the interest of local communities and to build a credible foundation for parliamentary elections.

The Trident dichotomy

The new direction in which Corbyn, and the vast majority of regular party members, wanted to take the party was tested at the 2015 Labour Party conference, a fortnight after he won the leadership. Scrapping Trident, the so-called nuclear deterrent, which is a military vanity project that can never be used, was a cornerstone of Corbyn's leadership campaign. Understandably, he wanted to change the party's policy, which was to support the Trident renewal programme. But party managers and some trade union leaders conspired to ensure that a vote on the issue was blocked. John Woodcock, the right-wing MP, who represented Barrow and Furness where the replacement Trident submarines would be built, was cock-a-hoop. He was quoted in the *Guardian* claiming that it was good that Labour members had *"rejected the CND left's plan to prioritise returning the party to the days of 1980s unilateral nuclear disarmament"*. With no hint of irony, given his role as a prominent PLP saboteur, he welcomed such bureaucratic subterfuge, because he claimed that he didn't want a re-run of *"old battles that risk splitting Labour apart"*. The likes of Woodcock and certain trade union leaders erroneously claimed that the Trident renewal programme was essential to protect jobs. But Corbyn had already made clear, in his leadership policy paper published in August 2015, that he was committed to securing those high-tech, well-paid jobs through defence diversification. He had said:

> *"I am committed to ensure that in transitioning away from nuclear weapons, we do so in a way that protects the jobs and skills of those who currently work on Trident, and in the defence sector more widely. This will help grow the British economy".*[8]

Corbyn explained that the investment being poured into Trident could sustain 31,000 high-tech, well-paid jobs, compared to the 11,000 equivalent occupations being maintained by the Trident project.

Corbyn's defence diversification proposal was, and still is, desperately required, and not just for the jobs linked to Trident. Employment in the British arms industry has been in decline for decades, but no government has ever adopted a formal strategy for arms producers to diversify away from military work. In 2016, it was estimated by the ADS Group (an arms industry lobby that represents the aerospace, defence, security, and space industries) that there were 142,000 jobs in the sector compared to 405,000 in 1981. Of those 142,000 jobs, a CND study found that around 11,000 are currently linked to Trident.[9] The Lucas Aerospace Combine Shop Stewards' Committee produced the pioneering *Lucas Plan* in 1976, demonstrating how they could utilise their skillsets and the company's technologies for alternative, socially useful applications.[10] These included wind turbines, solar energy, and hybrid vehicles. They were ahead of their time in proving that high-tech skills in the arms industry were readily transferable. It just takes political will, and a change in the political mindset, to make it happen. Corbyn was someone who seemed to have both of those requisite qualities.

Despite Corbyn's clear commitment to a defence diversification strategy, Unite the Union's and GMB's Rolls Royce branches in Derby were unhappy with my support for his Trident stance. They had firmly endorsed me when I was the local MP in the 2010–2015 Parliament, and I had worked closely with Unite in the campaign to save the rail manufacturing industry in the city a few years prior. We had also collaborated in highlighting the impact of offshoring skilled manufacturing jobs. Additionally, I had discovered that Rolls Royce were using agencies to bring in highly skilled workers from India but were paying them a fraction of the going rate. I had alerted Unite to this exploitation, which was going on under its nose. So, I felt that I had a good relationship with the Rolls Royce unions, and, during the 2015 leadership election, I had made several attempts to broker a meeting with their senior shop stewards. I wanted to reassure them that a Corbyn-led Labour government would not sacrifice any jobs, and that Corbyn's defence diversification and industrial policy would instead increase the number of high-tech jobs. After Corbyn became leader, the shop stewards finally consented to a meeting, but they were not convinced. They said defence diversification was *"pie in the sky"*. I realised that we had a lot of work to do to reassure them. I contacted Corbyn to say that he needed to reemphasise his commitment to retaining existing high-tech jobs and creating more whenever the opportunity might arise. I made the same point to John McDonnell when he later visited Derby. But, in the end, my loyalty to Corbyn had cost me the support of these influential union branches.

Despite being out of Parliament at the time, I wanted to continue doing advocacy work. I planned to establish an advice centre in my former constituency office, and I spoke with various local trade union branches. I hoped that they could help me with some seed corn funding to get the project off the ground. But when I approached Unite, the local full-time official, Tony Tinley, refused point-blank. Tinley is a brusque trade union bureaucrat with a touch of the Napoleon complex about him. He said, *"Don't bother approaching the industrial branches"*. He was deeply hostile about Corbyn and told me that I was *"spitting in [Unite's] face"* because I had been photographed in front of a banner with a ☮ peace symbol on it.

In spite of a lack of support from local unions, I maintained my stance. I addressed a CND fringe meeting before the 2015 Labour Party conference had concluded. I urged delegates to use the months ahead to make the case for defence diversification, to maximise the chances of next year's conference agreeing to support scrapping Trident. Within a couple of weeks, I was on the road, putting forward arguments to CLPs up and down the country. I found myself pushing at an open door and every constituency, bar one, was overwhelmingly supportive of what I was saying, and many were unanimous in their opposition to Trident. Most of the meetings had a speaker arguing in favour of the party's existing policy, but they cut no ice with grassroots members. The only exception was when I spoke at Wolverhampton South East CLP, which was represented in Parliament by the Blairite military hawk Pat McFadden. They had invited John Woodcock to make the case for the present policy position but, unlike every other meeting that had an open show of hands, McFadden called for a secret ballot. Whilst the votes were being counted, I spoke informally to some of the members in attendance. One of them told me that none of the new members had been invited to the meeting; he had only found out about it by accident. When the vote was eventually announced in favour of renewing Trident, no figures were given, which left me feeling rather suspicious.

I continued to push the case for scrapping Trident right up to the 2016 Labour Party conference. A couple of weeks beforehand, Sir Paul Kenny – the outgoing GMB general secretary who'd been appointed a Knight Bachelor the previous year – incorrectly claimed that the Trident programme was essential to protecting jobs. On BBC Radio 4's *World at One* programme, he said:

"If anybody thinks that unions like the GMB are going to go quietly into the night while tens of thousands of our members' jobs are literally swannied away by rhetoric then they've got another shock coming".

I contacted GMB's general secretary-elect, Tim Roache, to say that Kenny's remarks were unhelpful. I thought Roache was an ally. He had spoken in glowing terms about Corbyn. His reply to my message about Kenny was startling. He compared Corbyn's proposal to scrap Trident to Margaret Thatcher's assault on the coalmining industry and the decimation of the coalfield communities when all the pits were closed. When I said Corbyn's not going to throw anyone on the dole, and urged him to examine his record, Roache said Corbyn had no record and claimed that he had never done anything. The way right-wing MPs like Woodcock, and reactionary trade union leaders such as Kenny and Roache, indulged in sophistry to make unjustifiable accusations, was essential to the witch-hunt that enveloped, and then destroyed, the Corbyn project.

Roache ended up as one of the leading witch-hunters, demanding my suspension in February 2019. He was one of many who shocked me with the ferocity of their attacks. Just over three years previously, in the autumn of 2015, he had approached me when he was the chair of the Centre for Labour and Social Studies (CLASS) think-tank. He wanted to appoint me as the director and urged me to apply. He was said to have been very disappointed when I decided to pull out before the interview, as the job would have been mine if I had wanted it. Yet, just over three years later, Roache was among those leading the efforts to crush me politically. Then, the following year he was forced to resign *"amid allegations of sexual assault, cover up and a 'casting couch' culture at GMB"*.[11] Coincidentally, John Woodcock had resigned in 2018 from the Labour Party before facing allegations about sexual harassment that were made by a woman aide.[12] Woodcock was subsequently elevated to the House of Lords by Boris Johnson, who then asked him to lead an investigation *"into 'far-left hijacking' of Black Lives Matter and Extinction Rebellion"*.[13] He now styles himself as 'Lord Walney'. Such are the characters of those who sought to destroy my parliamentary platform.

The Labour Party is brimming with individuals like those whom I've recently mentioned. They are exemplars of what are commonly described in social media parlance as 'gammons': red-faced reactionaries, full of hatred and contempt for anything that might mildly improve all our lives. With every fibre of their beings, these malcontents attacked Corbyn, me, and everyone who ever supported us. I don't know from where, deep inside them, this inexplicable loathing for humanity comes. But millions have had to pay the price for their bitter neuroses.

CHAPTER SIX

A VERY AMATEURISH COUP

In the run-up to the 2016 referendum on European Union membership, I spent the evenings and weekends knocking on doors, running street stalls, and speaking at public meetings across the Midlands in support of a Remain vote. I argued on a 'Remain and Reform' platform. On the day of the referendum, I'd been on the go from 5:00am until the polls closed at 10:00pm. I was due to attend the count in Derby, but I was so exhausted from campaigning that I fell asleep after returning home. When I eventually arrived at the count, the outcome was clear, and journalists descended on me to ask for my reaction. Whilst others appeared to be losing their heads, I remember feeling sanguine about the Leave victory. It wasn't the outcome that I had preferred, but I was prepared to accept it and to make the most of it.

However, the plotters in the PLP were on manoeuvres. They used the outcome as a pretext to oust Corbyn, something which they'd been attempting to do ever since he'd been elected nine months prior. Indeed, there was speculation that the PLP had been hoping to use the local election results, a month before the referendum, as their pretext, but Labour had performed much better than most had expected.[1]

Corbyn had been a Eurosceptic for decades, and he was a trenchant critic of the various treaties that the British government had ratified during his time in Parliament. However, he swallowed his distrust of the EU and enthusiastically fought on a 'Remain and Reform' platform in the referendum, sensibly refusing to campaign on the same platform as the Conservatives. The repercussions of Ed Miliband's disastrous decision to campaign alongside the Tories in the Scottish independence referendum in 2014 saw Labour all but wiped out in the general election 12 months later.

Labour's pro-EU campaign was being overseen by a torpid Alan Johnson, who took a technocratic and boring approach. Corbyn, by contrast, put in an energetic and exhilarating effort. Angela Eagle, who would later mount an ill-fated leadership challenge, said he was *"pursuing an itinerary that would make a 25-year-old tired"*.[2] Corbyn won over many sceptical Labour voters. Polls showed that 63 per cent of Labour supporters voted remain.[3] Despite this success, the knives were out for Corbyn. Whilst Nicola Sturgeon was being hailed because 64 per cent of SNP voters had backed Remain, Corbyn was being demonised. As far as most of the PLP were concerned, it was all his fault that the country had voted to Leave the EU. Ann Coffey and Margaret Hodge wasted no time in tabling a PLP motion of no confidence in Corbyn, which was carried by 172 votes to 40. The PLP hoped this would force Corbyn to resign, but he was made of sterner stuff than they'd imagined. A leadership contest was now inevitable.

The coup attempt by the PLP was met with an immediate and massive show of support for Corbyn from grassroots members. The night before Labour MPs voted on the no confidence motion, a huge rally was organised opposite the Palace of Westminster in support of him. I was in the 10,000-strong crowd that crammed into Parliament Square that balmy June evening.[4] Several MPs addressed the enormous gathering from the top of the FBU's converted fire engine, including Dennis Skinner, Richard Burgon, John McDonnell, and Angela Rayner. Tosh McDonald, who was at that time the President of the train drivers' union ASLEF, gave a typically passionate speech. To loud approval, he told the crowd that the support for Corbyn was so immense that, unlike in 2015, we'd have to organise outdoor rallies to accommodate the crowds supporting him this time. And he wasn't wrong: most of Corbyn's rallies in 2016 were held outdoors with huge numbers in attendance. But the biggest roar of the evening came when Corbyn himself addressed the throng. *"Don't let the media divide us; don't let those people who wish us ill divide us"*, Corbyn warned.[5] Those words were continually ringing in my ears three years later when that was precisely what his opponents had succeeded in doing.

But, at that point, all was looking well. Like most ex-MPs, I retained a parliamentary pass, and so I agreed to show some of the people who had attended the rally around the parliamentary estate. Whilst I was waiting for them to clear security in Portcullis House, Corbyn came walking by on the way to his office. He looked incredibly calm, as if he didn't have a care in the world, despite the enormous pressure he was under from the revolting

PLP. He stopped to have a chat with me, and he agreed to wait for the people I was with so I could introduce them to him. He was typically gracious with all of them and spent time talking to them all before we moved off. I took the group onto the Commons Terrace, where I saw Andy McDonald and Karl Turner having an argument about Corbyn. Turner scurried off without speaking to me. McDonald then told me about what had happened at the PLP meeting earlier that evening, which was subsequently described as *"brutal"* by *LabourList*.[6] McDonald informed me that the behaviour of the PLP was savage. He was really upset about what he had witnessed, and he had tears in his eyes as he told me, *"No man should be put through what Jeremy went through tonight"*. He described how the atmosphere was intensely menacing, *"They were like a lynch mob. If they'd had a rope, I swear they would have strung him up. It was utterly disgusting behaviour"*. I was appalled. Worriedly, I said, *"But he can't step down. There's too much riding on him. We need him to stay no matter what"*. McDonald's description of the monstrous behaviour he had witnessed convinced me that we had to assert the right of grassroots members to hold these scumbags to account for their intolerable behaviour.

The coup takes shape

Owen Smith eventually emerged as the challenger, and I spent the summer of 2016 touring the country speaking in support of Corbyn's bid to retain the party leadership. When the PLP coup began, I gave an interview to *BBC Newsnight*, in which I said that Labour MPs had declared a civil war on the membership and it's a civil war that the membership was determined to win. Following the PLP coup, I spoke at Corbyn's first campaign rally at Conway Hall. I told the jam-packed audience that Labour's coup-plotting MPs might as well have been in league with Lynton Crosby, who was the Conservative Party's chief spin doctor at the time. Crosby, I said, could not have done a more effective job had he planted sleepers inside the PLP to wreak havoc following the EU referendum result, which had plunged the Tories into chaos.[7] This led to an avalanche of protestations from Labour MPs after someone in the audience posted about my comments on Twitter. *"How could you say that about your friends, Chris?"* was the common theme running through all their messages. The late Jack Dromey was one of the complainants. I forwarded my op-ed in the *Morning Star* to him, in which I referred to a number of right-wing PLP renegades who had set their faces against Corbyn's programme and connived together to plot his downfall. He then replied, enquiring plaintively, *"Am I a right-wing renegade, Chris?"*. I had got on well with Dromey in the 2010–2015 Parliament and I wasn't looking for an argument. So, I replied saying that I didn't think he was a renegade, but that I was incredibly disappointed that he'd gone along with those who were. We never re-kindled our friendship.

Another MP who supported Owen Smith, and convinced himself that Smith was going to win, was Karl Turner, Labour MP for Kingston upon Hull. Turner and I were both originally elected in 2010 and we always got on well together. We stayed in touch after I lost my seat in 2015. In May 2015, Karl posted a tweet saying, *"Bring back our vegan brickie"* with a link to Kevin Maguire's 'Commons Confidential' diary piece in the *New Statesman* with the same headline.[8] Maguire's snippet said:

> *"Asked which defeated MP the staff would most miss, a copper on one of Parliament's gates answered Chris Williamson. He was possibly Britain's only vegan bricklayer-turned-MP. The red environmentalist was a Tory scalp by 41 votes in Derby North, in part due to the Greens taking 1,618 votes back in fifth place. Staff loved Williamson because he was polite and displayed no airs and graces. Unlike some."*

Given that Turner and I had a good relationship at the time, I pleaded with him to remain loyal to Corbyn and to not resign from the frontbench. In fact, I had messaged a large section of the other frontbenchers, too, including Lisa Nandy and Owen Smith himself, urging them to get behind Corbyn and respect the decision of grassroots members to elect him. All of them ignored me apart from Turner, who did me the courtesy of responding, if only to say that he was going to resign. He said he had his reasons without telling me what they were. He then had a pop at me on Twitter over the orchestrated Shadow Cabinet resignations that were staggered to cause maximum embarrassment to Corbyn, which I'd publicly criticised. He said, *"The trouble is Chris you and*

I both know what you spout is utter and complete BS? Now stop!".[9] He followed that up with another broadside, *"Me and Chris were good mates in Parliament. We agreed politically on most things then but I won't let him talk crap!"*.[10] Turner, whilst quite a personable character, seems to have gained a reputation for being a rude loudmouth, especially on social media. It didn't bother me because I knew what he was like. I recall messaging him to ask him not to engage in a public spat, to which he responded by saying:

> *"Chris I'm happy to have a public spat with you when you speak shite at the rate you do of late ... You piss me off when you spout shite. Stop it because I can't stop myself calling you out ... Now I say this to you and anybody else I will NOT tolerate letting the Tories win big without challenge and if JC is the leader they will. It's called the bigger picture Chris. For FUCK sake tune in!".*

He then rang me just after midnight to sound off in a similar vein. But, after an hour-and-a-half discussion, he had calmed down and we ended the call cordially. He didn't change his mind about backing Smith, however.

Nevertheless, the resolve of grassroots members to spike the guns of the saboteurs was clear when we organised a rally in Derby for Corbyn's leadership campaign. Thousands turned up to the open-air meeting on Cathedral Green to hear his message of hope. I had the privilege of introducing Corbyn on that lovely, cloudless summer's day. To look out at the multitude of expectant faces was awe-inspiring. When the rally concluded, Corbyn was mobbed, and I had to virtually drag him away to get him to the station to catch the train up to Matlock for the second rally of that day. When we arrived in Matlock, there was another huge crowd awaiting him, whom he addressed from the bandstand in Hall Leys Park. At the end, Corbyn was mobbed once again. The trains only came once an hour and, because he spent so much time speaking with enthusiastic supporters and having selfies with them, he missed his train. It was a consummate performance by a people's champion who was genuinely interested in what people had to say. That wasn't a Derbyshire one-off either, it was repeated at every campaign meeting he attended. It contrasted sharply with his predecessor. I remember seeing Ed Miliband looking decidedly uncomfortable when he was interacting with the public and glancing round for one of his aides to 'rescue' him. Blair, Brown, and Kinnock were even worse. The only other leader I've seen who looked comfortable and genuinely interested in people was John Smith.

Whilst Corbyn's campaign went from strength to strength, Owen Smith's was tanking. Smith and I were both first elected in 2010, and Miliband brought him into his Shadow Cabinet in 2012. Smith used to present himself as a 'lefty' and treated me as a sounding board to obtain a left perspective following discussions at Shadow Cabinet meetings. He had no real roots in the labour movement. He was born into a middle class family and his employment history had all the characteristics of a privileged middle class kid. He was a BBC Radio 4 producer, before becoming a special adviser to a cabinet minister, and then he moved to Pfizer where he became Head of Government Affairs and Policy. He tried to construct some working class credibility by launching his leadership campaign at Orgreave, the scene of the infamous police riot that saw rampaging coppers attacking miners for trying to save their jobs and communities. Smith hadn't reckoned with my friend and comrade John Dunn, who was a veteran of the miners' strike. Dunn was also one of the Clay Cross councillors who took on Ted Heath's government in the early 1970s over higher rents for council tenants. He is also one of the leading members of the Orgreave Truth and Justice Campaign. Dunn interrupted Smith's publicity exercise to tell him he was shamelessly exploiting what had happened at Orgreave for his own political ends. In an article for *Labour Briefing*, Dunn said he told Smith:

> *"While you were busy making pharmaceutical companies rich, we were struggling on and it is disgusting that you are exploiting and hijacking our struggle ... What you are doing in this so-called leadership battle is no different to what the [Union of Democratic Mineworkers] scabs did to my union in undermining our strike!"*[11]

Smith didn't reply and dived into a getaway car, wound up the window, and sped off. A few days later, Dunn was suspended from the Labour Party. But he had the last laugh after he received a random email from Smith's campaign asking if he had voted.

He responded by saying he was still waiting for his ballot form to arrive, without saying he wanted to vote for Corbyn. Lo and behold, two days later his voting papers turned up in the post. It was just another example of the corrupt system being overseen by right-wing apparatchiks who were doing everything in their power to skew the vote in favour of Smith.

Staff subterfuge

During the 2016 coup, I also received a message out of the blue from the left-wing MP for Easington, Grahame Morris, who offered me a job in his office as a political assistant. Morris had been promoted to the Shadow Local Government brief, after nearly all the Shadow Cabinet and frontbench had walked out. I was happy to help out. However, although I was working for Morris, my contract of employment was technically with the Labour Party, even though my salary was to be paid out of parliamentary 'Short Money'. This is funding that is provided to support opposition parties, which was introduced in 1975 and was pioneered by Ted Short, who was a Labour MP and served as deputy leader of the party. The funding is made available to all opposition parties in the House of Commons that have secured either two seats, or one seat and more than 150,000 votes. Short Money is used to assist opposition parties in carrying out their parliamentary business, which includes funding the running costs of the Leader of the Opposition's office.

The fact that my contract was with the party caused an insurmountable problem almost immediately. Three days into my new role, I was contacted by Emilie Oldknow at Labour's head office to say I would have to change my social media profiles. My Facebook home page had a photo of Corbyn and me together, and I had added a 'Keep Corbyn' Twibbon on my Twitter display picture. She said that, as party employees, we had to be neutral in the leadership campaign. There was no way I was going to be neutral, so I handed in my notice with immediate effect five days after I started, even though this meant a substantial financial sacrifice. The leadership campaign was too important, and I was not prepared to sit on the side-lines during this crucial battle for the soul of the Labour Party. Oldknow's remarks about the restrictions that applied to anyone working for the Labour Party turned out to be breathtakingly two-faced. In April 2020, she was named in a leaked dossier detailing the bureaucratic subterfuge and sabotage at the heart of the Labour machine.[12] It seems that, when she was telling me that party staffers had to be neutral, she was actively working against Corbyn's leadership.

The subterfuge went right to the very top. The party's general secretary at the time, Iain McNicol, was a hard-line Corbyn opponent. I am told that, in 2015, McNicol had offered his resignation to Corbyn. He had no desire to work under him. As the course of history demonstrated, it was a huge strategic miscalculation on Corbyn's part not to have accepted it. Indeed, it was probably Corbyn's first big failure of judgement. As the 2016 leadership challenge got underway, it was reported that McNicol was *"willing to put his job on the line"* to ensure Corbyn was kept off the ballot paper.[13] McNicol had obtained legal advice based on an erroneous reading of the party's rules, which suggested that Corbyn couldn't automatically re-stand. The NEC, on that occasion, narrowly overruled him.[14] McNicol also oversaw a huge purge of Corbyn's supporters. Labour Party staffers were instructed to trawl through members' social media accounts to find pretexts for suspension, and the NEC imposed a six-month cut-off date. This meant that thousands upon thousands of members who had joined in the six months prior to the leadership election were barred from voting.

The NEC's sharp practice was successfully challenged in the High Court by Christine Evangelou, the Rev Edward Leir, Hannah Fordham, Chris Granger, and 'FM' (a teenager). Mr Justice Hickinbottom said, *"For the party to refuse to allow the claimants to vote in the current leadership election, because they have not been members since 12 January 2016, would be unlawful as in breach of contract"*.[15] John McDonnell welcomed the High Court judgment and said that *"the decision taken to freeze out new members since January was an affront to democracy and went against everything the party stands for"*.[16] But McNicol and the right-wingers on the NEC were not finished. They used party funds to take the issue to the Court of Appeal, where they succeeded in having the High Court judgment reversed. One particular submission made by David Goldstone QC, the barrister acting for the new members, has proven to be prophetic. Goldstone said that to give the NEC sweeping powers to impose retrospective exclusion and disenfranchisement was to provide *"scope for abuse"*. Given the various machinations that happened afterwards, there is no doubt that the Court of Appeal provided such a precedent. Regrettably, the five new members were ordered to pay £30,000 towards the party's costs within 28 days, and permission to appeal to the Supreme Court was denied.

The scale of the gerrymandering was truly staggering. As a result of the arbitrary six-month cut-off date, around 130,000 otherwise-eligible voters were prevented from participating.[17] Furthermore, I am aware of estimates that hundreds, if not thousands, of members were suspended. Projections from the *Skwawkbox* suggest that the total number of excluded voters may have been far higher, with potentially 250,000 members, affiliates, and registered supporters being deprived of their votes.[18]

I've heard first-hand accounts from eyewitnesses in Labour Party regional offices where everything had been put on hold to find excuses to exclude would-be Corbyn supporters. I was told that, whenever one of the functionaries found an excuse to exclude someone, they would shout at the top of their voice, *"I've got one"* or *"Gotcha!"*. Everyone in the room would then applaud and cheer. The overzealous vetting procedures saw people being barred on the flimsiest of grounds. One of the most bizarre reasons for excluding a Corbyn supporter was because she had allegedly posted *"inappropriate content on Facebook"*. That *"inappropriate content"* was her sharing of a Facebook post linked to a video by the Foo Fighters band, which included the caption, *"I fucking love the Foo Fighters"*.[19]

However, in spite of all the odds, the underhanded scheming, the manoeuvring, and the manipulations by the PLP and the party bureaucracy, Corbyn won the second leadership election by an even bigger margin than he did in 2015. Corbyn was changing the face of British politics.

CHAPTER SEVEN

REALITY CHECK

Labour governments have never gone as far as they could, or indeed should, have gone in transforming society. That was certainly true of the New Labour governments led by Tony Blair and then Gordon Brown. In fact, their regimes actively built on the Thatcherite legacy they inherited. Tony Blair even admitted that he *"always thought [his] job was to build on some of the things [Thatcher] had done rather than reverse them"*.[1] New Labour was an extreme example of the perverse policy priorities pursued by Labour administrations, but the sad truth is that all Labour governments have helped to maintain the status quo in Britain. The reason for this is that Labour ministers have always listened more attentively to the corporate capitalist lobby than they have to their own grassroots supporters.

There was hope that this would change when Harold Wilson led the party back to power in February 1974 and secured an overall majority in the October election of that year. The party's radical manifesto committed the government to *"bring about a fundamental and irreversible shift in the balance of wealth and power in favour of working people and their families"*.[2] Tragically, any hope of a fundamental shift was abandoned under James Callaghan, Wilson's successor. Callaghan's government was startled by apocalyptic briefings from civil servants in the Treasury. As a result, Callaghan's Chancellor, Denis Healey, went to the International Monetary Fund (IMF) for a $3.9 billion USD loan in 1976. Healey's decision was based on a false premise that Britain was hostage to currency speculators.[3] Whilst Thatcher is credited with inflicting monetarism on the country, the genesis can be traced back to Callaghan and Healey. They could've defeated the speculators by locking their funds behind capital controls and blocking imports. Instead, and in the teeth of opposition from grassroots Labour Party members, trade unionists, and left-wing MPs, they chose to punish the British people by deliberately pushing up unemployment through public spending cuts. Inevitably, working class communities, which overwhelmingly voted Labour, were hit hardest by the Labour government's refusal to use the economic instruments already at their disposal. When Thatcher came to power in 1979, she enthusiastically embraced and turbocharged the approach initiated by the outgoing Labour administration. We've been living with the consequences of neoliberalism ever since.

Just before Healey went cap in hand to the IMF, delegates to the Labour Party conference overwhelmingly voted to nationalise the UK's four major banks and most of the insurance industry. Healey described that decision as an *"albatross"*, and Callaghan said his government would not carry it out.[4] However, Healey subsequently conceded that the IMF loan was unnecessary.[5] His admission once again demonstrated that if the Labour membership had more control over party policy, the parliamentary elites would make fewer mistakes. This was something Ed Miliband pointed out in his leadership bid 34 years later, although he failed to follow through on it.[6]

Healey's legacy has continued to influence the party's economic thinking right up to the present day. During the 2015 Labour leadership election campaign, one of the candidates, Andy Burnham, decided to publicly apologise for New Labour's spending. In response to a question from a member of the public, he said, *"Sorry. It was a mistake, we should not have allowed the deficit to get that high"*.[7] This sort of thinking continued in the four years that John McDonnell was Shadow Chancellor. I argued, from around 2018 onwards, that we should use Modern Monetary Theory (MMT) as a lens to provide a better understanding of Britain's fiat monetary system. The British government issues our currency, so it can never run out of money, which creates enormous opportunities to intervene in the economy to eliminate the problems that blight so many lives. MMT would provide a coherent economic framework for assessing the consequences of government policy choices and explode the myths about government borrowing and the deficit. I made the point that MMT could enable Labour to demonstrate that its desire to lift people out of poverty, reduce inequality, modernise the country's infrastructure, and improve public services, was not reliant on a tax and spend programme. This wouldn't make taxation irrelevant: it is needed to generate a value for the currency, tackle inequality, bear down on inflation, and drive behaviour change. Taxation can also be used to create space in the economy when it is at full capacity, to allow spending on government programmes without causing inflation. In other words, we could've argued for 'fiat socialism'[8] instead of being restricted to typical Keynesian thinking. I spoke alongside Bill Mitchell about the prospects that MMT would offer a Labour government at a fringe meeting during the 2019 Labour Party conference.[9] The audience was made up of conference delegates and supporters. They eagerly took-up the ideas that Bill and I spoke about. But McDonnell could never break out of this 40-year-old economic straitjacket.

The 2017 Labour manifesto was hailed as a radical alternative to the previous four decades, and I described it as the best since 1945. But, the truth is, it needlessly restricted Labour's ambitions. It failed to repudiate the parameters set by neoliberal doctrine. McDonnell continually reinforced the tax and spend myth, like when he joked about the only numbers in the Tory manifesto being the page numbers.[10] It was a great one-liner, but it was ultimately unhelpful in trying to expand our horizons.

Labour, moreover, produced a compendium to its manifesto, *Funding Britain's Future*, detailing which taxes would be imposed to fund an incoming Labour government's programme. The approach wasn't too dissimilar to John Smith's 'Shadow Budget' in 1992, which led to the infamous Saatchi and Saatchi 'Double Whammy' Tory campaign attack ad. The McDonnell approach inadvertently bestowed a status on the billionaire class that they did not deserve, because it implied that we needed them to fund a good society. It also played into the Thatcherite contention that the economy works like a household budget and allowed right-wing opponents to regurgitate her remark that socialist governments *"always run out of other people's money"*.[11]

So, when Alan Sugar told Piers Morgan in December 2018 that he would leave the country if Jeremy Corbyn became Prime Minister,[12] I said I'd happily chauffeur him to his private jet. We don't need bumptious billionaires; they are a big part of the modern malaise that afflicts our country today.

Whatever happened to Corbynomics?

The tragedy is that an MMT understanding *had* been advocated by Corbyn in his 2015 leadership bid, when he was being advised by Richard Murphy, co-founder of the Tax Justice Network. Murphy's ideas about 'People's Quantitative Easing' gained traction at the time.[13] It was this ingenious break with the 40-year-old neoliberal orthodoxy that led right-wing former Shadow Chancellor Chris Leslie to label it 'Corbynomics'. It was meant to be an insult to undermine the new economic direction being taken, but it was a rather snappy strapline that captured the zeitgeist of the Corbyn project. I had fully expected that Murphy would be brought in as a key adviser when Corbyn won the leadership contest. I remember speaking to him on 12 September 2015, outside the Queen Elizabeth II Centre where the leadership results were being announced, and we walked down to the pub where some of Corbyn's supporters were congregating. I got the feeling that he was expecting a call, but the call never came. That was a huge tactical error. If Labour had formally embraced fiat socialism, fallacies about the fiscal deficit, public spending, and so-called government borrowing could have been destroyed from the get-go. Murphy's insight would have been invaluable in communicating a progressive economic alternative. Looking back, I suspect it was McDonnell who didn't want Murphy on the inside, because he was sceptical about MMT.

In January 2019, Stephanie Kelton, a leading MMT expert who had advised Bernie Sanders during his 2016 Democratic presidential nomination campaign, was in London for a lecture tour at the invitation of Mariana Mazzucato. Her 2020 book *The Deficit Myth*[14] is a must-read treatise on monetary and fiscal policy. I took the opportunity to ask her if she would be willing to talk to McDonnell about MMT but, when she agreed, McDonnell made a feeble excuse to avoid meeting her. He also said that he'd already met Bill Mitchell, who is probably the world's pre-eminent MMT economist. When I pressed McDonnell about MMT, he displayed a fundamental misunderstanding, claiming that MMT couldn't be utilised in Britain because pound sterling wasn't a reserve currency. Mitchell subsequently told me that when he met McDonnell, he advised him that his Fiscal Credibility Rule (FCR) would potentially limit an incoming Labour government's ability to intervene in the economy.[15] Instead of adopting a FCR, Mitchell had suggested that Labour's fiscal ambitions could be defined by full employment and price stability, but his advice was spurned.

Unsurprisingly, opposition to MMT didn't just come from McDonnell. In early 2019, Jonathan Reynolds, who was the Shadow Economic Secretary to the Treasury at the time, had attacked my stance in an article published by *LabourList*.[16] In response, I wrote an opinion piece defending MMT and criticising the FCR. However, when I approached Sienna Rodgers, who was the *LabourList* editor at the time, she refused to publish it, saying that she only accepted articles from MPs who hold the Labour whip, and I'd been suspended. My response was instead published in the *Morning Star*.[17] The main thrust of my argument was that MMT would free an incoming Labour administration from the unnecessary economic shackles that had bedevilled previous Labour governments, and it would help to facilitate Labour's progressive programme.

Despite the early promise of 'Corbynomics', I was the only MP pushing for a paradigm shift in economic policy. McDonnell argued that he had built flexibility into the FCR, meaning that, in the event of an economic downturn that required a fiscal stimulus to avoid a recession, the FCR could be suspended. This point was echoed by Reynolds. What neither McDonnell nor Reynolds admitted, however, was that it would be technocrats in the Bank of England who would determine when the targets could be suspended. As Bill Mitchell says, that is a basic Monetarist tenet: monetary policy has primacy over fiscal policy, which is neoliberal-centric. The FCR would have imposed a senseless restraint on a future Labour government. It even included crass neoliberal framing such as:

> "everybody knows that if you're putting the rent on the credit card month after month, things needs to change. And that is why we would commit to always eliminating the deficit on current spending in five years".[18]

Writing about MMT in the *Financial Times*, Martin Wolf, the paper's chief economics commentator, summed up why people like

McDonnell are pushed down the blind alley of tax and spend. Wolf said:

> "In my view, [MMT] is right and wrong. It is right, because there is no simple budget constraint. It is wrong, because it will prove impossible to manage an economy sensibly once politicians believe there is no budget constraint".[19]

That, in a nutshell, sums up the problem. If politicians and the public realised that money was no object for governments in currency-issuing nations like Britain, our wealthy elites would lose control of the economic narrative. That would make the justification for austerity untenable and the failure to eliminate poverty unsustainable. Even under Corbyn and McDonnell, Labour never cut through the economic eyewash. It was another wasted opportunity.

Intended and unintended consequences

It could've all been so different had Tony Benn, who led the charge to democratise the party from 1979 onwards, not lost his seat in the 1983 general election. He was stitched up by the Labour Establishment following a review of constituency boundaries. Unhappily, stitch-ups are a routine story with which we've become all too familiar since 2015. Had Benn held his seat in that election, I believe that he would have later been elected leader, and the party would have taken an entirely different direction. Instead, Neil Kinnock became leader, and his era served as the midwife to New Labour. He diminished the already limited influence of Labour's grassroots and restructured Labour's bureaucracy, paving the way for Tony Blair to transform the party in his own image. He also went on a charm offensive with the deregulated financial sector, which was dubbed the 'Prawn Cocktail Offensive', having private luncheons in the City of London. After Labour lost the 1992 election, it prompted Tory grandee Michael Heseltine to mockingly quip, *"Never before have so many crustaceans died in vain"*.[20] That purposeless crustacean-cull cast a long shadow and was still influencing McDonnell's economic prospectus a quarter of a century later.

The lack of internal democracy under Blair was dismal, but it improved slightly in one respect: electoral college percentages. The electoral college system for leadership elections had originally been brought in as part of the democratic reforms led by Tony Benn, before which the election of Labour leaders was the sole purview of the PLP. In its first iteration, 40 per cent of the votes were given to affiliated trade unions and socialist societies, whilst 30 per cent went to the PLP, and another 30 per cent went to Constituency Labour Parties (CLPs). Under Blair, the electoral college percentages changed. The three constituent parts each had an equal 33 per cent of the vote. Had those proportions been in place at the outset, Benn would have defeated Denis Healey in the deputy leadership election in 1981 by a comfortable margin. Such an eventuality would have enabled Labour to avoid the subsequent New Labour debacle.

Just imagine how much better today's world would be had that New Labour era not occurred! We would have a PLP that is fit for purpose and accountable to the membership for decisions taken in Parliament. Grassroots party activists would be venerated not denigrated, and they would be in the vanguard of a social movement, making democracy work for the many, not the few. Think of the international policy dividends that would have been made possible as well! The war in Iraq and Afghanistan would have been averted or, at least, there would have been no British involvement. And the Labour Party would have been unambiguously on the side of oppressed peoples around the world. Ponder the benefits in terms of domestic policy, too! The creeping privatisation of our NHS, fragmentation of our education system, imposition of tuition fees, expansion of private finance initiatives, reduction in manufacturing jobs, and much more besides, could've all been avoided. To the disadvantage of us all, it wasn't to be.

However, 30 years later, an unexpected opportunity arose to refashion the role of the Labour Party in Tony Benn's image. Ray Collins, who was Labour's general secretary during the first year of the Miliband era, was tasked with drawing up an alternative system to the electoral college. No one understood at the time what a seismic decision that would turn out to be. Ironically, many of the Labour Left opposed the idea. I was present at a meeting of the PLP where Collins spoke about his proposals.

There was scepticism from MPs on both the left and right of the political divide. Many Labour MPs were unhappy about losing influence, particularly the entitled Blairites. After lengthy negotiations, trade union leaders went along with the plans. At the beginning of 2014, the GMB's general secretary, Paul Kenny, who was knighted the following year, said the unions would support a new one-member-one-vote system to elect the Labour leader.[21] But he added that they would not accept any *"watering down"* of their collective voice.[22]

Miliband originally asked Collins to undertake the review following the Falkirk constituency selection affair in 2013. Eric Joyce was the Labour MP who had won the seat with a majority of 7,843 in the 2010 general election. However, a vacancy had arisen when Joyce had to resign from the party, but not as an MP, after head-butting two Tory MPs in the House of Commons Strangers' Bar in February 2012.[23] He also attacked several other Conservatives during the fracas and was unrepentant when he was arrested, telling the police that he head-butted Tory MP Stuart Andrew because *"he deserved it"*.[24]

The ensuing Falkirk selection contest descended into a bitter slanging match between Unite the Union and the Blairite Progress faction. Unite's preferred candidate was Karie Murphy, who worked in Tom Watson's office at the time. Progress accused Unite of trying to fix the selection in favour of Murphy by recruiting new party members from within Unite's significant local membership. Grangemouth Refinery employed a large number of the local Falkirk workforce and many of them were members of Unite. Progress claimed this was unfair, despite the fact that they were recruiting members themselves and their favoured candidate, Gregor Poynton, even admitted to paying the membership fees for new recruits.[25] As far as I was concerned at the time, it seemed much ado about nothing. I couldn't understand why recruiting party members was being portrayed as crooked.

What happened next was truly remarkable. In responding to the commotion that had been whipped up by the corporate media, fuelled by entitled right-wingers who were disgruntled about working class supporters gaining the upper hand in Falkirk, Miliband called in the police.[26] The allegation was that Unite were engaged in a ballot-rigging exercise and were signing-up union members without their consent and in breach of data protection regulations. However, the police concluded that there were insufficient grounds for any criminal inquiry.[27] In the end, it was all for nothing. Labour lost the seat to the SNP in the 2015 general election by the huge margin of 19,701 votes and were routed throughout the whole of Scotland, returning just one MP compared to 41 in 2010.

Following his dumbfounding police complaint, Ed Miliband focussed his energies on trying to limit the influence of trade unions within the party. He told Collins that he wanted to recast the party to make it *"a genuinely mass membership party reaching out to all parts of the nation"*.[28] Little did he know what he was about to unleash. I vividly recall Miliband, in his shirtsleeves, passionately trying to sell the idea to a sceptical PLP, telling us to imagine a party with up to 400,000 or more members, affiliates, and registered supporters. He told the PLP that he didn't want anyone contributing to the Labour Party through affiliation fees unless they'd deliberately chosen to do so. He said he wanted people to make an *"active, individual choice on whether they become part of our party"*,[29] rather than being automatically affiliated. To achieve Miliband's objectives, Collins made several recommendations. He proposed a more transparent link and a closer relationship with trade unionists. He wanted fair and transparent selections and a central register of all constituency development plan agreements with trade unions.[30] These were the agreements in some constituencies where trade unions provided funding directly to CLPs.

But the recommendation that was to shake the political world to its core 18 months later was the proposal to replace the electoral college for leadership elections to a one-member-one-vote system. The rib-tickling irony is that the intention of those behind the plan was to marginalise the left. As we know, it did the very opposite. The inappropriately named 'centrist' commentariat and assorted right-wingers who were pushing this idea arrogantly assumed that support for mass-socialism was dead and buried. How wrong they were! Ed Miliband's 400,000 prediction was quickly surpassed when Corbyn won the Labour leadership. At the height of the Corbyn surge, there were almost 600,000 full members of the party alone, without taking into account the proliferation in affiliates and registered supporters.

Misplaced hopes

When Corbyn took up his position as Labour leader on 12 September 2015, there were hopes that, this time, things would be different. I'd witnessed a microcosm of the revolution that people had been expecting when I was outside London's Queen Elizabeth II Centre, where the results of the leadership contest were being announced. I'd travelled down with my partner Maggie to do an interview with *Telesur* who were covering the outcome of the election because of Corbyn's interest in Latin American politics. Whilst we awaited the declaration of the result, we began chatting with Helen Martins and Paul Steele, a couple from Kent who had been inspired by Corbyn's ideas. They were impressed to discover that as an ex-MP I was not only supporting Corbyn, but that I was a vegan, too. There was a large crowd outside awaiting the outcome and when the news emerged of Corbyn's landslide victory people were literally dancing in the street. It was a moment I'll never forget. So many hopes and expectations were encapsulated in that instant. Maggie and I went on to become good friends with Paul and Helen, who threw themselves into campaigning for the party in their constituency. Paul later paid a heavy price for his Labour activism as he had one of his fingers bitten off by a ferocious dog when he was delivering leaflets. He is a folk guitarist and had to learn to play his guitar in a different way because of his injury. Paul and Helen are just two of the millions of people who were betrayed by the cowards and traitors who make up the PLP.

In Corbyn, we had elected a genuine socialist to lead the party, whose programme was overwhelmingly popular with the public (notwithstanding the timidity on economic policy). And we had a mass-membership to take that message out to the country. What we had not reckoned with, however, was the lengths to which the Labour Right and the party bureaucracy would go to frustrate and sabotage the democratic will of the rank-and-file membership. Nor had we realised how much those internal groupings inside the party were in bed with the corporate capitalist Establishment. And we definitely didn't anticipate how they would combine with the Israel lobby to smash the prospect of an anti-imperialist, pro-peace international policy. The vested interests who backed Miliband's plan made up for their miscalculation by engaging in the dirtiest political war of attrition since the Labour Party was founded. The scale of the betrayal was even worse than Ramsay MacDonald's perfidious decision to throw his lot in with the Conservatives to form the National Government in 1931.

The brazen way in which the Labour Establishment conducted themselves was without precedent, and their contempt for democracy was just jaw-dropping. Lord Peter Mandelson was one of the chief ringleaders. He was recorded in February 2017 saying:

> *"Why do you want to walk away and just pass the title deeds of this great party over to somebody like Jeremy Corbyn? I don't want to, I resent it, and I work every single day in some small way to bring forward the end of his tenure in office. I work every day. Something, however small. It may be an email, a phone call, or a meeting I convene, or people I see, or Labour MPs I encourage, or young people I take out and try and galvanise them. Every day, I try to do something"*[31]

The arrogance and sense of entitlement he displayed in that audio recording exposed the mentality of the Westminster fraternity with which we had to contend. Yet, in spite of the forces ranged against us, I believe that we still could've made concrete achievements had we done things differently. We should've taken some lessons from Ed Miliband's Marxist father, Ralph Miliband, who had already written, 60 years earlier, about many of the issues we came to face. Ralph's book *Parliamentary Socialism* remains a must-read for understanding much of the problems that plagued the Corbyn project. He aptly observed that Labour's history *"has been punctuated by verbal victories of the Labour Left which ... have had little influence on the [party's] conduct"*.[32] That remains true to this day. That is why I firmly believe that to move forward, and to give people hope that politics can make a positive difference, it is crucial to examine what went wrong. That is how we will avoid making the same mistakes in future.

CHAPTER EIGHT

MANUFACTURING A "CRISIS"

Bogus 'antisemitism' accusations against Jeremy Corbyn can be traced back as early as the 2015 leadership election. Corporate media outlets had pounced on Corbyn on various occasions. For example, the *Telegraph* ran a story falsely claiming that a Labour MP had called Corbyn an 'antisemite'. Corbyn was repeatedly questioned about his associations with various pro-Palestine activists, who themselves were smeared.[1] There was a particularly grotesque display on the part of Channel 4's Krishnan Guru-Murthy, who interrogated Corbyn about his invitations to Parliament of representatives of Hamas and Hizballah. The pro-Israel Community Security Trust even claimed that Corbyn *"seem[ed] to gravitate towards"* 'Holocaust deniers' and 'antisemites'.[2] However, these smears were just part of the background noise at that time. On the day Corbyn was elected leader, the BBC published a page of quotes from those who both supported and opposed him, but no-one mentioned anything about 'antisemitism'.[3]

It wasn't until early 2016 that the manufactured 'antisemitism crisis' began to gain traction. The Oxford University Labour Club (OULC) served as the epicentre. The saga was triggered by the OULC's decision to endorse Israeli Apartheid Week,[4] prompting one of their co-chairs, Alex Chalmers, to resign and use the moment to make groundless allegations.[5] Chalmers was a former intern with the Britain Israel Communications and Research Centre (BICOM), a pro-Israel lobby group, so it is reasonable to assume that he had ulterior motives in seeking to damage the pro-Corbyn OULC's reputation.[6] Of course, the corporate media had a field day with the confected controversy, and they indulged in an outpouring of contrived outrage. The Union of Jewish Students (UJS), which is a member of the World Union of Jewish Students (WUJS) – itself an affiliate of the World Zionist Organization – was behind the slurs.[7] The WUJS campaigns to strengthen the ties of Jewish students with Israel. It has even produced a *hasbara* (pro-Israel propaganda) handbook for Zionist student activists to equip them with talking points that dehumanise Palestinians and defend illegal settlements in Palestine. The handbook explicitly states that it is designed to provide, *"Jewish students with the tools to defend Israel ... to lobby for support for Israel, and pressure for an end to Palestinian violence"*.[8] The campaign of vilification by the UJS against the OULC had nothing to do with Judeophobia. It was part of a concerted effort to take down an anti-imperialist, pro-Palestine leader of the Labour Party who was known to be a critic of Zionism. Corbyn's response was manna from heaven for these unscrupulous complainants and their accomplices in the Fourth Estate. Rather than challenging the veracity of their claims, Corbyn supported the decision of Labour's NEC to commission Baroness Janet Royall to conduct an inquiry into the OULC. Despite Royall's links to Labour Friends of Israel,[9] it seems that even she couldn't find a way to legitimise the smear. In fact, she concluded that she had *"received no evidence that the [OULC] is itself institutionally antisemitic"*.[10]

It was when the Royall Inquiry was announced that I first found myself in the crosshairs of the Zionist lobby. I was subjected to a pile-on for having the temerity to tweet that I hoped she wouldn't find any evidence of Judeophobia in the OULC. The faux furore was initiated by Ian Austin, which led to Zionist extremists calling for me to be expelled from the Labour Party and accusing me of racism. The party didn't respond to their contemptible claims, but it was a portent of things to come. Paradoxically, two-and-a-half years after I'd defended them, the OULC had been appropriated by Zionists and was used to accuse me of, and condemn me for, 'antisemitism' in an open letter.[11]

Later in 2016, Corbyn gave succour to the Zionist lobby still further by asking Shami Chakrabarti to conduct an *"Inquiry into antisemitism and other forms of racism"* in the Labour Party.[12] She had stepped down as director of Liberty a few months beforehand. She introduced her report by finding that, *"The Labour Party is not overrun by antisemitism, Islamophobia or other forms of racism"*.[13] But the credibility of her conclusions was compromised when she was given a seat in the House of Lords shortly after her report was published. The decision to launch the inquiry was cynically used by Israel apologists to reinforce their spurious statements that Labour was being invaded by 'antisemites' because of Corbyn.

Once the report was available, it attracted various negative epithets such as *"whitewash"*[14] and *"weak"*.[15] Corbyn's approach was diminishing his position as leader, not strengthening it, and far from protecting his own and the Labour Party's reputation, it was doing the opposite. There was no evidence at that time, or indeed since, that the online 'antisemitism' constantly being cited was emanating from Labour Party members. On the contrary, the available evidence showed it was the far-right who were responsible for the minority of genuine claims of Judeophobia.[16] In any case, it is a mistake to get bogged down in a fight over statistics, which were evidently on Corbyn's side. The smear campaign was not about Judeophobia. It was a political attack, for political reasons, designed to achieve political ends.

Rather than elevate the status of bogus 'antisemitism' accusations, Corbyn could've put himself in a much stronger position by calling them out for what they were. His own record on challenging bigotry, including Judeophobia, was exemplary. He had the perfect justification for contesting these slurs. His reputation spoke for itself, and many of the people being targeted were left-wing anti-Zionist Jews. Moreover, the non-Jewish members being singled out like Marc Wadsworth and Ken Livingstone had long records of fighting bigotry, stretching back to the 1970s. Wadsworth had founded the Anti-Racist Alliance in 1991. Livingstone had earned the sobriquet of 'loony lefty' in large part because of his stance against bigotry when he was the leader of the Greater London Council (GLC) in the early 1980s. Corbyn should have used those facts to push back against the con artists who were flagrantly weaponising Judeophobia for political ends. By not doing so, the situation deteriorated further.

Another friend bites the dust

I was genuinely bemused by the 'antisemitism' accusations when they first hit the headlines. The outrageous suspension of Ken Livingstone in April 2016, following a ferocious ambush by the uncouth and loudmouthed John Mann, was a watershed moment. Corbyn's response to the rumpus was truly dreadful. It was one of many catastrophic errors of judgement he made in response to the manufactured crisis, not to mention a disheartening betrayal of a fellow socialist whom he had known for 50 years! Corbyn even told the BBC that Ken had *"continued to make offensive remarks which could open him to further disciplinary action"*.[17] However, contrary to Corbyn's assertion, there was nothing remotely offensive about what Livingstone had said. Instead of showing solidarity with a longstanding and loyal comrade, Corbyn sought to placate the mob.

The following month, Michael Dugher, who was the Labour MP for Barnsley East at the time, used his Twitter profile to launch an attack on Livingstone. Dugher masqueraded as a lefty in the same way that Owen Smith had done during the 2010–2015 Parliament. I used to get on with him quite well in those days. We regularly engaged in banter about football, as he supported Nottingham Forest, who are the local rivals of Derby County, which is my team. Dugher's left-wing credentials were always suspect, however. He was a special adviser to the arch-right-winger, John Spellar from 2001 to 2002. He then worked as a special adviser to Geoff Hoon when he was the Defence Secretary during the illegal war against Iraq.[18] He was also employed as a corporate lobbyist for Electronic Data Systems[19] a US multinational whose clients included the UK Ministry of Defence,[20] the US Navy[21] and Shell.[22] In the two years before he was elected to Parliament, he was Gordon Brown's chief political spokesperson from 2008 to 2010. However, he gave the impression that he supported issues like renationalising the railways and scrapping the bedroom tax. He even shared a platform with Jeremy Corbyn, Ian Lavery, and me during the 2012 Labour Party conference at a fringe event on rebuilding Britain.

I decided to message him when I saw his tweet, to urge him to stop the public bickering as it only assisted our political opponents. I referred him to an interview with the Jewish American political scientist, Norman Finkelstein, which addressed Livingstone's suspension.[23] However, Dugher was unmoved and responded saying, *"Livingstone remains in denial. I'm not going to shut up about antisemitism, Chris, and I hope Jeremy's inquiry produces some practical changes"*. I naïvely believed that he was acting in good faith, so I pointed out that Livingstone had done more than most people inside and outside the party to stand up against racism. I explained that many people in the Jewish community were appalled at the way in which Judeophobia was being weaponised to attack Corbyn's allies. I said, *"Let's tackle genuine anti-Semitism but let's not indulge in a witch-hunt. I must say, in my 40 years as an active member of the party, I've never witnessed any anti-Semitism in the party. Have you?"*. He claimed he had seen lots and that Livingstone was a Judeophobe. I still gave Dugher the benefit of the doubt but told him I was *"gobsmacked"* by his reply. I reminded him that Livingstone's criticisms of Israel and his reference to the Ha'avara Transfer Agreement during a radio interview did not make him Judeophobic. Our exchange continued, but it made no difference to his deliberately obtuse attitude towards Livingstone. In his last response, he said that Livingstone *"was just being a twat"*. But he was at pains to stress that I was *"not antisemitic at all"*.

Later that month, Dugher turned his attention to Jackie Walker,[24] the former vice chair of Momentum whose initial suspension had been overturned.[25] I once again took him to task, telling him to *"give it a rest"*, pointing out that Walker was Jewish and should never have been suspended in the first place. However, again, it made no difference. He simply said, *"Sorry mate. I asked for a full explanation. What's wrong with that. And, by the way, I'm not giving up the fight against antisemitism 'a rest'. Sorry you see it like that"*.

I realised Dugher was a lost cause as the insults kept on coming no matter what I said. Eventually, he started publicly attacking and misrepresenting me, too. My deteriorating relationship with Dugher was symptomatic of what was happening to my association with the vast bulk of the PLP. I was initially saddened by the way they were turning against me, but I eventually realised that they were no loss. They were never real friends or comrades in the first place. Dugher eventually announced his resignation from the Labour Party, the week before I was suspended in February 2019, claiming it was *"institutionally anti-Semitic"*.[26] But his real motivation, I believe, was revealed in an interview with the *Jewish Chronicle* just after Labour's 2015 general election defeat. He said it was *"a fundamental and rather catastrophic political management error"*[27] when Ed Miliband imposed a three-line whip on Labour MPs to support Grahame Morris's parliamentary motion to recognise the Palestinian state in 2014.[28] Corbyn's longstanding support for the Palestinian people, and his persistent criticisms of Israel's colonial abuses, put Ed Miliband's stance in the shade. Dugher was the polar opposite of Corbyn. He had been vice chair of Labour Friends of Israel and, in 2015 he told an LFI 'We Believe in Israel' conference that he was *"proud to call [him]self a Zionist"*. He even invoked the war criminal Henry Kissinger during his address.[29] Corbyn's relentless refusal to reject the obviously dishonest claims about an 'antisemitism crisis' enveloping the Labour Party provided the perfect cover for Zionists like Dugher.

The political lynching of Marc Wadsworth

The racist treatment of Marc Wadsworth should go down as one of the most deplorable episodes in Labour history. Wadsworth is a veteran anti-racist activist and journalist. At a press conference to launch the recommendations contained in the Chakrabarti Inquiry in 2016, Wadsworth had called out Ruth Smeeth MP for allegedly fraternising with a hack from the *Daily Telegraph*. Smeeth had served for several years as one of Israel's chief lobbyists in Britain, between late 2005 and mid-2007.[30] Before she stood for public office in May 2010, she joined the Community Security Trust, which has been reported to have links to Israel's Mossad spy agency.[31] During the Corbyn years, she regularly and shamelessly threw around 'antisemitism' allegations like confetti.

Wadsworth's 'crime' was to ask a question at a press conference! The incident was captured on video and was uploaded onto YouTube by the *Skwawkbox*. Wadsworth started off by making a factual observation, saying:

> *"I saw that the* Telegraph *handed a copy of a press release to Ruth Smeeth MP, so you can see who is working hand in hand."*[32]

At this point, he was noisily interrupted by several people sitting around Smeeth who drowned out what he was saying by repeatedly screaming, *"How dare you!"*. It seemed Smeeth's cackling cronies took exception to a black man publicly exposing her duplicity. A voice off camera can be heard saying, *"Do you have a question?"* Wadsworth then continued:

> *"The question is this, right. If you look around this room, how many African, Caribbean, and Asian people are there? We really need to get our house in order, don't we? And that was a recommendation of the report."*[33]

The former political correspondent of the *Sun*, Kevin Schofield, who was sitting directly behind Smeeth, can then be clearly heard saying to the BBC's John Pienaar, *"That's antisemitism at the launch of an antisemitism report"*. At this point, Smeeth dramatically rushed out of the room, crying crocodile tears. Meanwhile, Wadsworth was concluding his intervention:

> *"And the Labour Party has to change in terms of the representation of [Special Advisers], not just having white boys who run things."*[34]

Wadsworth is a campaigning journalist who led the Labour Party Black Sections movement in the early 1980s and advised the family of Stephen Lawrence, a black teenager who'd been murdered in London by racist thugs in April 1993.[35] Wadsworth elevated the family's case to international status when he introduced Nelson Mandela to them the following month, and he featured extensively in a three-part BBC documentary on the case that was screened in April 2018. Wadsworth was expelled a week after the documentary was aired. The charge sheet against him was pure poppycock. Smeeth blatantly lied about what had happened. In a widely reported statement, she said:

> *"It is beyond belief that someone could come to the launch of a report on antisemitism in the Labour Party and espouse such vile conspiracy theories about Jewish people, which were ironically highlighted as such in Ms Chakrabarti's report, while the leader of my own party stood by and did absolutely nothing"*.[36]

It was obvious from reading the rest of Smeeth's bilious statement that this was just a political stunt. She asserted that, *"People like [Wadsworth] have no place in our party or our movement and must be opposed"*.[37] She then went on to make it all about Jeremy Corbyn:

"Until today I had made no public comment about Jeremy's ability to lead our party, but the fact that he failed to intervene is final proof for me that he is unfit to lead, and that a Labour Party under his stewardship cannot be a safe space for British Jews. I have written to the General Secretary of the Labour Party and the Chair of the Parliamentary Labour Party to formally complain about this morning's events".

Corbyn should have intervened in Wadsworth's case to say it was clearly a mendacious complaint without any merit whatsoever. After all, Corbyn had witnessed the entire incident. I was outraged at Wadsworth's treatment and, shortly after I was re-elected in 2017, I met him at a public meeting at which I was speaking. He had already been suspended for over a year by that time, and I resolved to use my position as an MP to assist him. We kept in regular contact and met up at the House of Commons to discuss his case on several occasions.

When Wadsworth's case was eventually listed for consideration by the Labour Party's National Constitutional Committee (NCC) in April 2018, I agreed to speak on his behalf and accompany him to the hearing. The NCC is basically a kangaroo court, where the only meaningful question would be whether or not you want a blindfold before being despatched by a metaphorical firing squad. The chair of Wadsworth's NCC hearing was one of the party's worst witchfinder generals, the notorious right-winger Maggie Cosin. She had presided over the hearing that expelled Cyril Chilson the previous month. Chilson is of Jewish heritage and is vehemently pro-Palestine. His parents had survived Auschwitz and the death march in 1945, yet he too was accused of 'antisemitism' and expelled.[38] Cosin had even threatened to have Chilson thrown out of his own hearing for querying the status of the Chakrabarti Report. As an aside, I had stood against Cosin for a seat on the NCC in 2016, which was elected by delegates at that year's party conference. Luke Akehurst, secretary of the right-wing Labour First group, was so desperate to stop me being elected that he put a message out offering to buy a drink for every delegate who voted against me.

The evidence that Wadsworth had done nothing wrong was so overwhelming that I thought even Cosin wouldn't be able to find against him. Clive Lewis and Keith Vaz had also provided written statements in support of Wadsworth, and he was being represented by a solicitor. So, together with the video evidence, his case should have been watertight. The day before the disciplinary meeting, Wes Streeting was attempting to rally MPs to influence the outcome. Streeting, who went on to write for Rupert Murdoch's *Sun* rag after Sir Keir appointed him to the Shadow Cabinet in 2021, was one of the most outspoken PLP malcontents during Corbyn's leadership. He circulated the following hyperbolic note to Labour MPs and peers:

> "Apologies for the impersonal message, but I wonder if I can enlist you to provide some practical moral support for our friend and colleague Ruth Smeeth next Wednesday morning (25th April)
>
> "She is giving evidence against Mark [sic] Wadsworth – the guy who abused her at the antisemitism inquiry launch – and we expect there to be a protest outside against her.
>
> "To give Ruth some moral support and solidarity I am assembling a group of Labour MPs and peers in Westminster Hall at 9:40am. We will then walk with Ruth to Church House nearby. We won't be allowed in with her, but I can't tell you how much a strong turnout will mean to her – and how much better it would be if we outnumber the protesters.
>
> "So, if you can make it let me know by email or text."

Around 50 right-wing Labour MPs heeded his call the following morning, which resulted in a sickening spectacle as they marched in unison down Victoria Street to secure a figurative lynching of a black man. The gruesome procession included many of the most aggressively right-wing Labour MPs, including John Mann, Margaret Hodge, Jess Phillips, Chris Leslie, Louise Ellman, Gareth Snell, and Luciana Berger.[39] The only thing missing was the burning torches. It was like a scene out of *Mississippi Burning*. The whole charade was arranged for the benefit of the cameras. Smeeth had rejected an offer to use a different entrance to avoid any demonstration, but she insisted on arriving through the front door. Whilst Streeting's lynch mob were gathering in Westminster Hall, I was having a morning coffee with Wadsworth in the Red Lion pub next door to Parliament. He looked calm and determined. We were both confident that there was no case to answer. Corbyn's office had been pressing me to ask Wadsworth to ensure there was no show of solidarity for him outside his hearing. Their reasoning was *"it won't help Jeremy if there is a demonstration"*, but it was Wadsworth who was facing the prospect of expulsion, not Corbyn. To Corbyn's inner circle, Wadsworth's plight was pretty much incidental and irrelevant, so we ignored their request, and the vigil went ahead.

It was a bright sunny morning as we walked across Parliament Square to the venue. Before we got there, I received a call from Amy Jackson, a staffer from Corbyn's office, who had been seconded from Unite the Union. She wanted to alert me to the fact that there was a large press contingent awaiting our appearance. When Wadsworth and I arrived at Church House, the MPs had already surrounded his supporters. The camera crews and journalists all had their backs to us as we neared the entrance, and we could've slipped in virtually unnoticed, but Wadsworth stopped to give some interviews and was immediately surrounded by microphones and TV cameras. I went in to find the waiting room. As I walked along the corridor, I was confronted by Smeeth's sidekick, Gareth Snell, then MP for Stoke-on-Trent Central, who followed her around like a great big lolloping St Bernard puppy dog. He was incandescent with rage when he saw me. *"What the hell are you doing here?!"*, he bellowed. I wasn't prepared to engage in an argument with him, so I calmly replied, *"I'm here to give evidence, Gareth"* and just continued walking. At which point, he blew a gasket, repeatedly blurting out, *"Evidence?! Evidence?! Evidence?!"* at the top of his voice. It was an unedifying encounter, but it was typical of the hectoring, boorish behaviour of many right-wing Labour MPs.

When the hearing finally got underway, I had to stay in the waiting room until I was called to give my statement. When I was eventually summoned, I said my piece and answered questions from Wadsworth's solicitor and the Labour Party's advocate. Cosin looked distinctly uninterested in what I had to say. But I was still confident that Wadsworth would be exculpated. Naomi

Wimborne-Idrissi, who is a founding member of Jewish Voice for Labour and was vice-chair of Chingford and Woodford Green CLP, also gave evidence in support of Wadsworth later that day. Wimborne-Idrissi was subsequently suspended for eight months in December 2020 for saying she was *"uncomfortable"* about party members being suspended over accusations of Judeophobia. Wadsworth's other witness was David Rosenberg from the Jewish Socialists' Group, who threw the hearing into turmoil when he comprehensively demolished the definition of 'antisemitism' that the party had been applying. The party and their lawyers were so discombobulated by Rosenberg's expert evidence that they were forced to call an adjournment to find out what definition Labour's NEC had agreed. They were misusing the 'Macpherson principle', which had arisen out of Sir William MacPherson's 1999 report into the racist murder of Stephen Lawrence. The Macpherson principle recommends that complaints of incidents of racism (which are subjective) should be recorded and investigated as such. However, the ultimate determination of whether something really is racist is an objective process. Instead, the NCC had been applying an asinine interpretation that resulted in the loss of any objective component: if Smeeth *said* something was racist, then it apparently *was* racist. Many self-professed 'socialists' still do interpret the Macpherson principle in that way. The irony is lost on these chumps that, were it not for people like Wadsworth, who helped to establish the Justice for Stephen Lawrence campaign, there would have been no Macpherson Report in the first place!

I was speaking at a meeting in the West Country that evening, so I had to leave the hearing at around 4:00pm. As I was travelling back from that meeting late at night, I took a call from Wadsworth at around midnight who told me his case was going into a second day. I was bemused. *"What else have they got to talk about?"*, I asked. Wadsworth sounded dejected and told me, *"They're going to expel me"*. I reassured him that, if they did, I'd continue to fight on his behalf to get it overturned, but he was resigned to his fate. The next day, Wadsworth's expulsion was confirmed as he'd predicted, and I issued the following statement on 27 April 2018:

> *"I am astonished by the National Constitutional Committee's (NCC) perverse determination of Marc Wadsworth's case. It flies*

in the face of the evidence that was presented and offends against the principles of natural justice.

"The NCC's decision has all the hallmarks of predetermination and tramples on the Labour Party's record of standing up for fairness. I will therefore continue to stand four-square behind Marc and assist him in his efforts to clear his name, and his reputation as a veteran anti-racist campaigner, which have been besmirched by this absurd NCC ruling."

The whole process was a sham, but it proved beyond a shadow of a doubt that the Labour Party's disciplinary system was thoroughly discredited and being abused for partisan purposes. It was at that moment when I realised that it wasn't just the PLP that needed to be remade; the Corbyn project could not succeed unless the party's broken bureaucracy was transformed, too. As things stood, it was rotten from top to bottom. Jennie Formby had just been appointed as the new general secretary and I was hopeful that she would start to turn things around. But, as we were to discover, she made matters considerably worse.

Meanwhile, the campaign for Wadsworth was entering a new phase. He embarked on a speaking tour to build support for his reinstatement, and he launched a crowdfunder to mount a legal challenge against his expulsion. I joined him at some of those meetings. I repeatedly raised his situation, and I was told that Gordon Nardell QC, who had been brought in by Formby to help with the party's disciplinary procedures, was looking at his case. A few months after Wadsworth had been expelled, Formby and Karie Murphy, one of Corbyn's inner circle, told me that they welcomed Wadsworth's legal challenge. They felt it would help to stem the tide of vexatious Judeophobia accusations that were invariably politically motivated. However, as it turned out, those were weasel words. I asked for a written assurance that the party would not pursue Wadsworth for costs in the event of him losing the case, but no such assurance was forthcoming. Paradoxically, given Formby's superficial support for Wadsworth's reinstatement, she later cited my speech at his Manchester campaign meeting as one of the reasons for suspending me in 2019. Ironically, in that same speech, I had lauded Formby's appointment as general secretary and said that I had the *"utmost confidence"* in her. In any event, Wadsworth eventually withdrew his legal challenge, because the risk of financial ruin at the hands of the Labour Party machine if he were to lose in the High Court was a real possibility.

Wadsworth is not an isolated case. The truly despicable treatment to which he was subjected is commonplace. Hundreds, if not thousands, of grassroots members have suffered a similar fate. Unsung heroes of the movement, who in some cases have given 50 years or more to campaigning for the Labour Party, have been unceremoniously kicked out on trumped-up charges. The people behind these abhorrent tactics are cynical, callous, and ruthless, and their victims were let down by a failure of the Corbyn leadership to defend them. It speaks volumes about the party's values that someone like Ruth Smeeth, who was the architect of the smears against Wadsworth, ever held the Labour whip in the first place.

Wadsworth did achieve some vindication in 2021, however, after he won a libel action against the *Jewish Chronicle*, which had carried a hit piece against him. They'd falsely alleged that he was involved in an initiative to track down Jewish Labour activists at their private addresses in order to intimidate, threaten, or harass them into silence. Wadsworth secured a public apology and was awarded substantial damages.[40] But he has not received any apology from the Labour Party, which was responsible for the nightmare that he was forced to endure.

Wheeling out a has-been

In March 2019 (the month after I'd been suspended from the Labour Party), former Labour Prime Minister Gordon Brown recorded a video in which he shamelessly invoked the Holocaust to launch an attack on his own party. It was an astonishing intervention. In the first half of Brown's two-minute piece-to-camera, he said:

> *"The Labour Party has a long, proud and noble tradition of standing up against prejudice, bigotry, discrimination, anti-Semitism and racism – from apartheid to Islamophobia ... And we must never equivocate on what is unequivocally wrong".*

Brown's reference to *"standing up against ... apartheid"* was ironic, given his support for the State of Israel, which practices an even more brutal version of apartheid than South Africa did. Indeed, African National Congress (ANC) activists, and even the late Archbishop Desmond Tutu, have said, *"Israel is far worse than apartheid"*.[41] But Brown conveniently ignored this reality and pivoted in his video from talking about Labour's record on standing up to bigotry, to launch a full-frontal assault on Labour:

> *"the Labour Party let the Jewish community and itself down. They should never have allowed legitimate criticism, that I share, of the current Israeli government to act as a cover for the demonisation of the entire Jewish people. Solidarity means standing up with those who are under attack, and that's why I'm joining as an affiliated member, the Jewish Labour Movement and I urge all my colleagues to do the same ... We will never allow evil to triumph over good."*[42]

Like many apologists for the racist State of Israel, Brown claims to share *"legitimate criticism ... of the current Israeli government"*. But one would be hard pressed to find Brown making any criticisms of Israeli governments, past or present. In 2009, he made some timorous remarks about Israel's repeated bombardments of Gaza. However, there are plenty of examples of him lavishing praise on the Zionist state. He was the first British Prime Minister to address the Knesset. In his speech on 21 July 2008, he said:

> *"To be able to come here at the invitation of your Speaker and of your Prime Minister Olmert – and to applaud you and the citizens of Israel for the courage you have shown in the face of adversity, resolution in the face of conflict, resilience in the face of challenge – is, for me, a singular honour indeed ... And to those who mistakenly and outrageously call for the end of Israel let the message be: Britain will always stand firmly by Israel's side."*[43]

Brown also heaped praise on the Zionist terrorist Menachem Begin and the false 'peacemaker' Yitzak Rabin. Absurdly, Brown's dishonourable intervention in the 'antisemitism' controversy wasn't countered by Corbyn or his office, and it added yet more fuel to the fire.

Misunderstanding the Zionist strategy

Corbyn's response to the ceaseless attacks from the UK's Israel lobby, and its allies in the corporate media and in Parliament, added an endless supply of fuel to the fire. There was a failure on his part, which filtered down to his supporters on the Labour Left, to recognise the attacks for what they truly were. Instead of denouncing those Zionist bigots for the racists that they are, he indulged their attacks, and, in so doing, gave them credence. But Corbyn wasn't solely responsible. He was surrounded by an assortment of naïfs and even 'liberal' Zionists, from whom he took counsel.

Instead of waging a political counter-offensive, Corbyn and his allies argued the toss over statistics, focussing on how few people, as a percentage of the total membership, had been accused of 'antisemitism'. When that didn't work, they trotted out the even more desperate line that 'one antisemite is one too many', setting themselves up for failure against an impossible standard of discipline. Eventually, Corbyn began to concede on the question entirely. The strategy of appeasement became more and more demanding, and, consequently, more and more unsustainable.

Zionist racists are maximalists: if you give them an inch, they will take a mile. No concession will appease them. They are like sharks who, once they have smelt blood, only become more bloody-minded. Had Corbyn and his team recognised that from the outset, the mischief-makers would have no doubt moved on to other attack lines. When he did repudiate other nonsensical calumnies, such as the one about him being a Czech spy, the smears failed to gain traction.[44] The failure to tackle the manufactured 'antisemitism crisis' head-on would later play a large part in the undoing of the Corbyn project.

CHAPTER NINE

BACK INTO THE LION'S DEN

When the 2017 general election was announced, I was sitting in a café with an old school friend's son, who was thinking of resigning from the Labour Party over Brexit. He was a Remainer who was unhappy about Corbyn's stance on the EU. I was trying to persuade him to get behind Corbyn and to accept the outcome of the referendum. I made the point that the main issue wasn't whether we were in or out of the EU, it was about ensuring we had the right progressive social, economic, and foreign policies in place. After all, poverty, inequality, and precarity had all increased exponentially whilst we were inside the EU. The EU isn't a utopia. In the midst of our conversation, I received a phone call from local Labour Party agent James Shires, giving me the news that Prime Minister Theresa May had called a snap election. After I put down the phone, the focus of our conversation switched to how we would win back Derby North. We knew that, if Labour were to have any chance of securing a majority, we would have to win back the seat I'd represented until 2015.

It was by no means certain that I'd be the Labour candidate. Party members were not being consulted, and candidates were going to be selected by a three-person panel of Labour's National Executive Committee (NEC). Nevertheless, we started campaigning in earnest, and I put together an outstanding team to help coordinate our efforts in the weeks leading up to polling day. Ammar Kazmi, Jyoti Wilkinson, Lewis Bassett, Peter Davies, Sarah Russell, and countless others, put in a herculean effort for the duration of the election campaign. Fortuitously, Margaret Beckett, Derby South's MP since 1983, was on the panel to choose the Derby North candidate and, despite our many political differences, she recognised my commitment to the party. There were a number of other potential candidates who asked to be considered, so it was an anxious few days awaiting the panel's decision. When it was confirmed that I was the official Labour candidate, a number of prominent left-wing figures suggested that I should distance myself from Corbyn. Richard Burgon openly admitted that he was one of them, when I spoke at a meeting of his CLP in early 2018. They considered Corbyn an electoral liability and they said that the most important thing was to get me and other Corbyn-supporting candidates elected, after which we could regroup. I wasn't prepared to do that for two reasons. First, it would be a dishonourable thing to do, as Corbyn was a friend and a comrade. Second, I felt that Corbyn was an electoral asset. So, I issued a press release stating that I was the most Corbyn-friendly candidate standing anywhere in Britain, and in England's most marginal seat no less.[1] I said that the election in Derby North would be a test case for 'Corbynism'. Corporate media hacks, and right-wing members of my CLP, thought that I'd signed my own suicide note with that press release. In particular, the enmity towards Corbyn and me by some right-wing Unite members was still running deep, even though we'd failed to get the party to drop its commitment to renewing Trident. It was fed back to me that a senior Rolls Royce shop steward was urging his workmates not to vote for me, even if that meant letting the Tories take Derby North again.

The 2017 general election campaign in Derby North was the best campaign of which I have ever had the privilege of being a part. There was a carnival-like atmosphere and the number of activists who were flooding into the constituency was unparalleled. We even had some people over from Bernie Sanders's team, who gave the canvassers a morale-boosting pep talk before many of the campaign sessions. But the success of our campaign was in spite of the party's bureaucracy, not because of it. Labour's defensive strategy meant that seats like mine were not prioritised. But Momentum, which had designed its own mobile app, did an amazing job in mobilising activists to come to Derby North. On some occasions, we had so many volunteers that we ran out of leaflets and canvass sheets.

We also went out of our way to target non-voters and UKIP supporters. I made the point to Brexit voters, who had bought in to the 'Taking Back Control' rhetoric, that Labour was the only party truly committed to giving people power over their own lives again. Labour was the only party willing to take on the vested interests of multinational corporate capitalism, to bring back our utilities into public ownership, to end exploitation of workers, and to stop the abuse of tax havens. On polling day, we worked flat out from 6:00am. Once we could do no more, the core team came back to my house to await the outcome of the exit poll. We sat in my front room with bated breath, anxiously watching the clock. I remember Ammar Kazmi, a young student who went on to work in my office, telling us that the exit poll had been overseen by Professor John Curtice. It was Curtice who had predicted the 2015 general election results with stunning accuracy. So, we were preparing to accept the exit poll as gospel. When it finally came through at 10:00pm, there was unbridled joy. Everyone in the room jumped up, punching the air and hugging each other as though England had just scored the winning goal in a World Cup final. It looked like we had proved all the sceptics and saboteurs wrong, and so it proved to be. Our opponents had anticipated a wipe-out for Labour across the country but, instead, we gained 30 seats. We turned a voting deficit of 41 in Derby North to a majority of 2,015. The juxtaposition between our reaction and that of the anti-Corbyn candidates, filmed in the BBC documentary 'Labour: The Summer that Changed Everything',[2] illustrated the chasm between us. Whilst the likes of Aberavon MP Stephen Kinnock, son of Neil Kinnock, had his mouth open aghast, grassroots Labour activists across the country were overwhelmed with happiness.

Political pundits had been pontificating about Corbyn supposedly not being a real contender for Prime Minister, not least because of the daily character assassinations perpetrated by the media and his own MPs. Yet, much to the scorn of the British Establishment, Corbyn presided over Labour's biggest increase in vote share since 1945. The Establishment realised that they'd seriously underestimated him, and that sent a shiver down their spines. But, as they realised the scale of their failure, things were about to get a whole lot worse.

The shape of things to come

When I was returned to Parliament in 2017, the ambience in Westminster was worlds apart from my previous stint, as was the interest in my views by the corporate media. Shortly after being elected, I gave a lengthy interview to Rowena Mason, deputy political editor of the *Guardian*.[3] I told her that the smears that had been levelled against Jeremy Corbyn were *"proxy wars and bullshit"* and the allegations against him of 'antisemitism' were a *"really dirty, lowdown trick"*. This prompted the first big pile-on against me from bad faith actors, and it was fomented by the likes of Ruth Smeeth, who, within days, was publicly calling for action to be taken against me.[4] Interestingly, in 2009, it was exposed by WikiLeaks that Smeeth had been listed as a *"strictly protect"* source in a US intelligence cable.[5] Smeeth had also had a career as a spin doctor, working as the director of public affairs and campaigns for the Britain Israel Communications and Research Centre (BICOM) from late 2005,[6] before taking up a position with Nestlé in mid-2007.[7] The fact that she was still able to stand in the 2010 election, and be elected as a Labour MP in 2015, is a withering indictment of the Labour Party's corrupt bureaucratic processes.

I was then contacted by Jeremy Newmark, who was the chair of the Jewish Labour Movement (JLM) at the time, to ask for a meeting. After discussing the request with Richard Burgon, the MP for Leeds East, I agreed to meet. The meeting was cordial, but when I said that other Jewish members agreed with the position that I'd taken in my *Guardian* comments, he insisted that those Jews were a tiny fringe, and it was only the JLM that spoke for Jewish party members. The process of 'othering' anti-Zionist Jews in the party, which has only become worse since then, began very early on. There I was, as a Labour MP, being instructed on the 'correct' line to adopt regarding numerous Jewish party members by representatives of an explicitly pro-Israel, Zionist organisation. These characters considered themselves to be the only 'real' Jews in the party. Such a concept was as much an abhorrence to me then as it is today.

Newmark subsequently resigned as JLM chair following claims of financial impropriety during his time as chief executive of the Jewish Leadership Council (JLC). The *Jewish Chronicle* recounted how an internal audit into Newmark's conduct, whilst he was the JLC chief executive, reported that he deceived the organisation out of tens of thousands of pounds.[8] It also reported that he had misled charities about the cost of projects on which he had worked. The audit report found that, during Newmark's time at the JLC, £111,734 could not be accounted for and an additional £266,189 merited further examination. However, after reviewing the case, the Metropolitan Police's serious fraud team decided not to proceed with its investigation.[9]

Newmark's departure from the JLM made no difference to its antagonism towards the Labour Party, even though it claimed to be Labour's oldest affiliate. The truth about JLM's rhetoric regarding its historical affinity to the Labour Party is quite different. Whilst previously going by the name of Po'ale Zion (Workers of Zion), it was reconstituted in 2015 by Newmark, which was uncovered in Al Jazeera's 2017 documentary 'The Lobby'. He said he had done so because of what he called *"the rise of Jeremy Corbyn"* and *"Bernie Sanders in the states"*. The hostility against Corbyn's leadership culminated in the JLM refusing to fully support Labour at the 2019 general election.[10]

The fact that Newmark's outbursts were ever treated with any credibility by staff in the leader's office illustrates just how badly they served Corbyn and the socialist movement he had roused. Three years before Corbyn was even elected leader, Newmark was involved in making false allegations of Judeophobia in a case against the University and College Union (UCU). The formal judgment of the Employment Tribunal was scathing about him. It *"rejected as untrue the evidence of ... Mr Newmark"* and described his claims as being *"preposterous ... utterly unfounded ... extraordinarily arrogant"* and *"disturbing"*.[11] Yet, Corbyn's top advisers took a credulous approach towards him, never questioning his motivations.

Moreover, two Labour MPs were also excoriated by the same Employment Tribunal after giving evidence, namely John Mann (now Lord Mann), and the subsequently disgraced Denis MacShane, who was jailed for six months for fraud in 2013.[12] Yet, Mann, who is strongly pro-Zionist and pro-Israel, and who has accepted thousands of pounds in donations and junkets from Israel lobby groups over many decades, was also left unchallenged by Corbyn's staff. A good example of that failure was when Mann aggressively ambushed former GLC leader and London mayor Ken Livingstone, accusing him of being *"a Nazi apologist"* and *"a disgusting racist"*[13] after Livingstone had referenced the 1933 Ha'avara Agreement during an interview with Vanessa Feltz.[14] Instead of defending Livingstone, Corbyn and his staff supported his suspension. Mann, on the other hand, faced no commensurate reprimand or punishment for his thuggish and threatening behaviour. By supporting Livingstone's suspension, they were colluding with Mann's denial of a historical fact, that the Zionist movement in Germany collaborated with the Nazis. In fact, Mann had accused Livingstone, in his typical red-faced gammon manner, of calling Hitler *"a Zionist"*, something which Livingstone had never claimed. Corbyn's team either failed to research the veracity of Livingstone's remarks about the Ha'avara Agreement, or wilfully ignored the truth. Either way, it was an abject failure on their part. Livingstone's suspension was not only an act of collaboration in a vile smear campaign, but it was also an act of historical revisionism. It is admitted in a paper published by the State of Israel's official Holocaust memorial, Yad Vashem:

> *"In retrospect, and in view of what we know about the annihilation of European Jewry, these relations between the Zionist movement and Nazi Germany seem especially problematic".* [15]

So, Livingstone was sacrificed on the altar of political expediency, based on historical revisionism by pro-Israel zealots. To add insult to injury, the infamous 'Leaked Report' in April 2020 ('The work of the Labour Party's Governance and Legal Unit in relation to antisemitism, 2014–2019') revealed that Corbyn's staff had urged for Livingstone to be expelled in 2018, after he had initially been suspended for two years.

By the time I'd regained my seat in Parliament, therefore, the damage had already been done. The obsequious prostration of the leader's office before the anti-Corbyn reactionaries and the Israel lobby in 2015 and 2016 had set the tone for the rest of Corbyn's leadership. That crucial period would prove to be formative and would ultimately result in my suspension from the party in 2019, and it would later contribute to the downfall of the entire Corbyn project.

A government in waiting?

After Labour had performed far better than expected in the 2017 election, Corbyn enjoyed a brief honeymoon period with the PLP. The abusive pre-election verbiage, to which he had previously been subjected by Labour MPs, was temporarily put on hold. At the first PLP meeting following the election, I arrived early in Committee Room 14, a cavernous gothic meeting space in the Palace of Westminster where the PLP and Conservative 1922 Committee hold their weekly meetings. I found a suitable vantage point from which to observe the proceedings. I wondered what reaction Corbyn would receive. I had heard first-hand accounts about how bad some of the meetings were over the previous two years when Corbyn had been in attendance, so I was standing ready to jump into the fray. But, to my amazement, he received a prolonged standing ovation when he arrived. Even Dame Margaret Hodge, who had tabled the PLP motion of no confidence against Corbyn the previous year, was applauding, albeit through gritted teeth, as was her Zionist confederate Joan Ryan.

But Corbyn's positive reception was merely the calm before the storm. The PLP's resentment about the new direction the party was taking remained undimmed, and I became a proxy for their attacks against Corbyn. It was abundantly clear that these individuals, with whom I'd previously been friends, were my 'friends' no longer. Within a matter of weeks, I was being targeted by right-wingers inside the PLP. I didn't mind being the focus of their ire because it drew the flak away from Corbyn, for whom I was prepared to sacrifice political capital to protect. Unlike other Socialist Campaign Group MPs, I was willing to fight fervently for the anti-imperialist, socialist policies that had delivered Corbyn's two landslide leadership election victories. Consequently, I became a go-to talking head for broadcast media, which infuriated most of the PLP, party headquarters, and Corbyn's advisers.

Staff in the leader's office continually tried to prevent me appearing on the main news media outlets, frequently asking me to pull out of programmes or to reject requests for comment. They also tried to replace me whenever they could with an alternative spokesperson. I went along with this for a while, but it was frustrating when criticisms in the media either went unchallenged, or were inadequately rebutted, by spineless stand-ins. I remember having a blazing row over the phone with John Prescott's son, David Prescott, who was working as a media adviser to Corbyn. He called me to complain about my appearance on *BBC Newsnight* the previous evening to defend Corbyn's historical statements about

Venezuela. I had agreed to be a guest on the programme after the office of the Shadow Foreign Secretary, Emily Thornberry, had issued an ill-informed statement, completely misrepresenting the situation in Venezuela. The statement described Nicolás Maduro's presidency as *"increasingly authoritarian"*, implied the violence on the streets in 2017 was his government's fault, and erroneously suggested he was violating human rights.[16] Her comments had no context, no reference to US sanctions, no mention of the US funding of violent right-wing opposition groups in Venezuela, and no acknowledgment of the economic sabotage by that country's powerful oligarchs. Shadow Foreign Minister Liz McInnes had even arrogantly asserted that it was up to Maduro to prove that such groundless allegations were wrong.

When I explained to Prescott that, in all the programmes on which I'd appeared, I was only reinforcing the positions Corbyn had previously taken in his leadership campaigns, his response was instructive. He said, *"Those were the leadership elections, but we're a government in waiting now, so we have to be more circumspect"*. I told him that his strategy was utterly wrong-headed, and that the only way we were going to win sufficient support to get into government was by continuing to be an insurgent force in British politics. I reminded him that Ed Miliband's obsession with triangulation had destroyed Labour's prospects in 2015 and that we must not make that mistake again. I said Labour's route back to power was to inspire non-voters and to give them a reason to vote Labour. But Corbyn's advisers had acquired delusions of grandeur. Rather than focussing on what had made Corbyn appealing in the first place, they'd honestly convinced themselves that they were on an unstoppable path to 10 Downing Street, and that all they had to do was steer clear of anything 'controversial'. They believed that the next election would be a replay of 2017, not realising that the 2017 election had led to the British Establishment redoubling their efforts to kill Corbynism. David Prescott's recitation about a government in waiting was in keeping with the attitude of the Labour Party for the best part of a century.

As long ago as 1923, when the general election resulted in a hung parliament, the Labour Left pressed the leadership to take office and attempt to implement a socialist programme. But this idea was dismissed. Philip Snowden, one of the 'turncoats' who later supported the First National Government under Ramsay MacDonald, revealed a mindset that persists to this day. Referring to the left's demands, he said:

> *"We might use the opportunity for a demonstration and introduce some bold socialist measures, knowing, of course, that we should be defeated upon them. Then we could go to the country with this illustration of what we would do if we had a socialist majority. This was a course which had been urged by the extreme wing of the party, but it was not a policy which commended itself to reasonable opinion. I urged very strongly to this meeting that we should not adopt an extreme policy but should confine our legislative proposals to measures that we were likely to be able to carry. We must show the country that we were not under the domination of the wild men".* [17]

Snowden's preoccupation about being perceived as not being *"under the domination of the wild men"* would not have been out of place among Corbyn's team. This obsession with 'optics', against a hostile press that was never going to be won round to our cause, was extremely foolish.

The most hated man in Parliament

A recurring attack line by both Tory and Labour MPs was my support for the self-determination and sovereignty of the Venezuelan people, and for the social progress the Venezuelan government had made since the election of Hugo Chávez in 1998. On one occasion, when I challenged Foreign Office minister Sir Alan Duncan in the House of Commons about his government's stance on Venezuela, I was jeered by both sides of the House. It seems that they took exception to me quoting UN rapporteur Alfred de Zayas, who had said that the US was waging economic warfare against Venezuela. He had also said that US sanctions were not only illegal, but that they could also amount to crimes against humanity. Duncan's response was meant to knock me but, instead, I found his childish, but palpable, anger hilarious. To loud cheers from both sides of the Commons chamber, he said:

"My Rt. Honourable Friend, [Sir Nicholas Soames, Winston Churchill's grandson] referred to 'Poundland Lenins'. I have just seen in this House one who is not even worth a penny, let alone a pound. I recognise when I see it, as do Members on the Opposition Benches, unreconstructed ideological nonsense – he is a throwback and he brings shame; indeed, I am astonished he has even been prepared to show his face in this House today".

It was obvious that I'd got under Duncan's skin. In fact, I'd already been the subject of his ire beforehand. Only a month previously, on 10 December 2018, Duncan had written a diary entry describing me as *"the odious Chris Williamson, the hard-left Labour MP who is probably the most hated man in Parliament"*.[18] Then, after his attack against me in the Commons, he wrote in his diary on 28 January 2019:

"[I] was able to sock it to the obnoxious Chris Williamson, who is hated by us and even more so by his own side. An unreconstructed leftie, whose beliefs are those of Castro, Chávez and Maduro, not to say Marx, Lenin, Trotsky and Mao, he is a Momentum nasty who is working to have many moderate Labour MPs deselected. They hate him with a passion, so I laid into him and relished every moment of it. Nice plaudits afterwards from both sides, especially Labour."[19]

Such accolades! Not only did Duncan place me in the ranks of so many great revolutionary leaders, but he also made clear the contempt in which I was held by the coterie of imperialists and neocons who sit on both sides of the Commons. I cannot think of a better bunch of people to be hated by. The majority of those who sit on the green benches are self-serving, venal vultures. Not only have their policies plunged millions of Britons into poverty, but they have also inflicted misery, death, and destruction upon the peoples of other countries through sanctions, bullets, and bombs.

In the meantime, a large section of the PLP continued to look for any opportunity to misrepresent and spin anything I said, as a way of manufacturing outrage. Their mischief-making was often positively juvenile. One such example was when I commented on some statistics showing that sexual offences against women on trains had more than doubled in the previous five years. I initially just shared a *Skwawkbox* report on social media,[20] which reminded its readers that Corbyn had floated the idea of women-only carriages during the final stages of the 2015 Labour leadership contest.[21] When I was subsequently contacted by reporters, I said the statistics suggested there may be some merit in examining the idea if there were public support for it. Incredibly, this resulted in wall-to-wall headlines and an inevitable backlash from Labour MPs. Some of them even resorted to pasting a sarcastic poster on my Westminster office door, prompting yet more headlines.[22] Jess Phillips, the right-wing Labour MP for Yardley, couldn't wait to jump in with a ludicrous straw man argument suggesting that I was proposing to give up on prosecuting assaults.[23] She doubled down on her deliberately obtuse response with an op-ed in the *Guardian*, in which she patronisingly offered to *"cut [me] some slack"*.[24] This is the woman who described the arch-right-wing Tory MP Jacob Rees-Mogg as *"charming and funny, kind, mad and totally himself"*.[25] Of course, right-wing interlopers like Phillips are not interested in facts when they can misrepresent someone to show them in a bad light. It is tawdry politics, but it was a tactic that Phillips and her ilk repeatedly used to undermine Corbyn and his supporters. These characters specialise in superficiality. In November 2021, she criticised Tory MPs with second jobs, yet she has also enjoyed an income from her own extra-parliamentary activities.[26] She even had an £8,000-a-year sideline working for top Tory donor and former Conservative deputy chairman Lord Ashcroft's firm.[27] That's not to mention the £15,000 she was reportedly paid to host a single episode of the BBC's *Have I Got News for You* in December 2021.[28] With a record like that, Phillips needs all the *"slack"* she can get before offering it to anyone else.

Mind you, when it comes to displaying double standards, Phillips was only doing what seems to come naturally to those in the PLP, including Sir Keir Starmer. In 2017, Starmer was poised to take a lucrative consultancy role for the pro-Israel law firm Mishcon de Reya,[29] until Corbyn vetoed the move.[30] Yet, according to the Register of Members' Financial Interests, Sir Keir Starmer still received over £20,000 from external earnings in the six months before the 2019 general election whilst he was a Shadow Cabinet member.[31] Even after he became the Labour

Party leader, the register shows that he also received almost £41,000 from external earnings, including a payment of £17,598.60 on 24 August 2021.[32] Unsurprisingly, he was caught out after trying to make political capital out of Tory MPs taking second jobs. In an interview with Sky News in November 2021, when he was asked why he was in talks about taking a paid consultancy in 2017, he said, *"No I wasn't, and we... I was in discussions, nothing happened".*[33] Quite what the difference is between *"talks"* and *"discussions"* is not clear.

A parliamentary boot boy

In my view, one of the most obnoxious and most aggressive right-wing Labour MPs, who was always in the vanguard of the 'antisemitism' smears, was Ian Austin. He was so appalling that he was more like a parody of a Labour MP than a real one. Former Tory leader and Prime Minister, David Cameron, once referred to him as one of Gordon Brown's *"boot boys"* during an exchange at Prime Minister's Questions, as long ago as 2006.[34] *"Boot boy"* was an apt description then, and it could still be applied today.

I had a number of run-ins with Austin when I returned to Parliament in 2017. The first occurred at the beginning of September that year. I was on my way back to my office in Portcullis House (PCH) after a meeting in the leader's office, which is located in the Norman Shaw South building. As I came down the stairs and entered the foyer, I saw Austin coming from the opposite direction. There is a footbridge connecting the two buildings and Austin followed me along the footbridge, so, when I got to the door leading into PCH, I held it open for him as a courtesy. But in a display of pure pig-headed petulance, Austin refused to walk through the doorway. I insisted, but still he refused. It was a stupid stand-off, but I wasn't going to back down, so I said: *"Stop being so fucking ridiculous and walk through the door that's being held open for you by a comrade".* At this point, he relented and walked through but, with venom in his voice, he screwed up his face and spat out the words, *"You're no comrade of mine!".* As we walked together into PCH, I told him we were both members of the Labour Party so we were de facto comrades whether he liked it or not. When we reached the staircase, he launched into a diatribe about 'antisemitism' and accused me of making Judeophobic remarks. I told him that was categorically untrue, and I challenged him to show me the evidence for his slur. He had no answer to that, other than to say, *"You think you're so virtuous, don't you?"*, and then he started ranting about Ken Livingstone.

The clash was reported in the *Skwawkbox* after they'd been tipped off by someone who had overheard Austin's loutish conduct as he berated me on the PCH staircase.[35] When Austin was contacted by *Skwawkbox* for a comment, he held me responsible. But I hadn't contacted them. Nevertheless, Austin flew into a rage and, in a state of high dudgeon, he rang my office to speak to me. *"I've just had an email from the* Skwawkbox ... *saying that I was involved in a public argument at Portcullis House last night ... Have you spoken to them?"*. Before I could answer, he said, *"Yes, you've spoken to them ... you've gone running to your mates at* Skwawkbox *to wind up the mob"* (by *"mob"* he meant grassroots members). *"You call me 'comrade', and then you ring* Skwawkbox*? You're a disgrace!"*, he ejaculated, before hanging up. I'd been on the receiving end of his aggression since the 2010–2015 Parliament. But this incident suggested that Austin had taken his bellicosity to a new level.

Austin was clearly indignant about Corbyn's leadership, and the high esteem that I was being afforded by many rank and file members. That was evident in 2016 when, in a packed House of Commons chamber, he yelled, *"Sit down and shut up"* whilst Corbyn was speaking at the despatch box in response to the Chilcot report.[36] Corbyn was making the point that the Iraq War was *"an act of military aggression launched on a false pretext"*, which the Chilcot Inquiry acknowledged.[37] But it was all too much for Austin. He continued to berate Corbyn. *"You're a disgrace!"*, he shouted, when Corbyn pointed out that *"dozens of my Labour colleagues ... voted against the war"*.[38] Austin's spiteful interruptions necessitated an intervention by the Speaker who said, *"If people want to witter away, they should leave the Chamber. It is boring and we do not need you"*.[39] The Speaker was dead right. The reaction of MPs to Austin's oafish performance was revealing because it drew more criticism from MPs representing other parties than it did from Labour MPs. That was another illustration of the gulf between the PLP and the vast majority of grassroots party members, who backed Corbyn to the hilt.

Such a public display of gross insubordination, particularly as it happened during the consideration of such a sombre topic, should have resulted in some form of disciplinary action. Austin's splenetic heckles most definitely brought the party into disrepute, yet he received no meaningful censure. In my opinion, Corbyn should have withdrawn the whip. Such a move would've been loudly applauded by grassroots members. The fact that he failed to do so was an indication that, despite his resilience in refusing to resign after the PLP's vote of no confidence the previous week, he was unwilling to assert his authority. It was a huge tactical error. It provided evidence of the gargantuan double standards that the party applied. Whilst grassroots members were being suspended for minor infractions, disgruntled MPs could do whatever they wanted without consequence. Less than a year before, Corbyn had secured the biggest political mandate in the party's 116-year history from its members, affiliates, and registered supporters, so he had every right to take action against Austin. Despite Corbyn winning the second leadership contest by an even larger margin than the first, he was still failing to command any respect from the PLP. Taking firm action against a recalcitrant right-winger like Austin would've shown, once and for all, that he meant business. Corbyn's weakness in this regard just created a rod for his own back in the following years. It just encouraged the PLP to take more and more liberties, and to treat him with increasing contempt.

In addition to the incident in PCH, Austin regularly hurled abuse at me in the division lobbies and corridors around Westminster. He is a serial bully whose aggressive behaviour should have been stamped out. At one point, it looked like he might finally get taken to task. I had seen him screaming at the party chair, Ian Lavery, in the division lobby. It was yet another appalling example of the man's unhinged behaviour. After an abusive conduct investigation was launched against him, it was soon dropped by the party's bureaucrats.[40] He was initially put under investigation around the time that Dame Margaret Hodge was to potentially face disciplinary action for calling Corbyn a *"fucking antisemite and a racist"*.[41] That incident took place in the Commons chamber behind the Speaker's chair, in front of Tory MPs. But the investigation against her was dropped shortly afterwards.[42] When the charges against Austin were dropped, he was hubristic and displayed no remorse about his actions. He claimed, *"Frankly, they should never have threatened this in the first place. The way this whole issue has been handled is unacceptable and the time it has taken is appalling"*.[43] Meanwhile, the bureaucrats were stepping up the exclusions of anti-racist socialists who supported Corbyn.

Despite Austin's yobbish persona, he is like a cockroach in a nuclear winter. He continues to scuttle from place to place. Not long after resigning from the Labour Party in February 2019, Tory Prime Minister Theresa May appointed Austin as her Trade Envoy to Israel in July 2019.[44] I was unsurprised to see him later being 'ennobled' by Boris Johnson in 2020, sitting as an 'independent' in the unelected House of Lords.

Ultimately, what is clear is that Westminster is rife with duplicity and cowardice. Against the backdrop of the 2017 general election, the detractors of the Corbyn project had become seriously desperate. Despite a brief period of reprieve, the PLP were soon back to their old tricks, and they wasted no time in attacking me as a proxy for attacking Corbyn. I was Corbyn's strongest parliamentary ally, and they knew it. Corbyn was being tamed by mugs like David Prescott, who were too clever for their own good, thinking that they were playing a big game of three-dimensional chess, and that they were masters of *realpolitik*. Meanwhile, I was the only person on the front line who was willing to be Corbyn's flak jacket. Whether it was fake 'antisemitism' allegations or hot air about Venezuela, I threw myself, repeatedly, on the grenades being flung in Corbyn's direction. And, frankly, I did so gladly. I wasn't upset about being attacked by other MPs in the Commons or in the media. But what I simply couldn't understand, and what did leave me continually frustrated, was the timidity of Corbyn and his team. Rather than maintaining their insurgency and radicalism, they started to believe their own hype. They became increasingly embarrassed of people like me, and the grassroots activists who'd put them in their lofty positions, as they tried to ingratiate themselves more and more into the political and media classes. That was always going to be a hopeless endeavour.

CHAPTER TEN

"THOUGH COWARDS FLINCH AND TRAITORS SNEER"

Unlike so many Labour Party conferences that I've attended over the years, the 2017 conference in Brighton had a positive, energetic vibe. I found myself in great demand to speak at numerous fringe meetings. So much so, in fact, that I missed most of the conference itself. All the fringe events were full to the gunwales. The Labour Representation Committee (LRC) was oversubscribed to such an extent that I had to address a huge overspill crowd outside the Friends Meeting House before speaking to a standing-room-only audience inside. All the speakers were doing likewise. John McDonnell recalled when LRC meetings were lucky to get a dozen people in attendance. The topic of conversation was all about how many historic defeats they'd sustained on the conference floor. How times had changed, we all thought.

The meeting that I enjoyed the most that year was the joint Cuba and Venezuela Solidarity fringe event. The Venezuelan ambassador was due to speak. This whetted the appetite of the corporate media hacks because of the ongoing street protests in Venezuela at that time. So, the meeting was swarming with reporters. They saw it as an opportunity to try to embarrass Corbyn because of his previous statements in support of the social progress Venezuela had made under Hugo Chávez. Channel 4's Michael Crick attempted to doorstep me as I entered the venue, but I told him to come inside and listen to my speech if he was interested in my views. Sensing the potential for negative headlines against Corbyn, the ambassador stayed away. But sitting amongst the huge audience were these poison-pen merchants from the mainstream print and broadcast media outlets, so I wasn't going to lose the opportunity to give those characters both barrels. Their reporting on the situation in Venezuela had been, and remains to this day, truly appalling. I singled out a few of them that I could see, including Crick and *Observer* columnist Nick Cohen. The meeting was chaired by the Corbyn-supporting Lincoln MP Karen

Lee. The assembled hacks took great umbrage when she wouldn't allow them to ask any questions. Writing for the *Spectator* after the event, Cohen referred to me as follows:

> *"On the platform was Chris Williamson, a Corbyn supporting MP. His menacing rhetoric, bald head and bulging eyes meant that to my mind there was a touch of Benito Mussolini about him".* [1]

It seems that the corporate hacks took exception to being told a few home truths about their partial reporting on Venezuela.

The Jackie Walker character assassination

Outside conference that year, I met Jackie Walker for the first time. Walker had been suspended for a second time on bogus 'antisemitism' allegations, following her comments about the definition of 'antisemitism' when she attended a Jewish Labour Movement 'training event' at the 2016 Labour Party conference. Her remarks were secretly recorded, and then deliberately misrepresented, prompting a torrent of faux outrage. Walker is herself Jewish, and she is married to a Jewish man, but that didn't stop the attack dogs trying to trash her reputation. The real reason she was picked on was precisely because she is a prominent and influential anti-Zionist Jewish woman. She was the vice chair of Momentum before her suspension, an outspoken socialist, and a key ally of Corbyn. It is obvious why she had to be taken down. But when she was in the eye of the storm, rather than defending her, the Momentum steering committee removed her as the organisation's vice chair. Momentum's chair, Jon Lansman, was quoted as saying, *"I spoke to Jeremy Newmark of the Jewish Labour Movement this morning, he's very upset and I can understand that – I work closely with Jeremy".* [2] The previous day, it was reported in the *Jewish Chronicle* that Lansman had *"reached the end of his tether and wanted her to be thrown out of the group".* [3]

Before Momentum moved against Walker, Manuel Cortes, a Corbyn supporter and general secretary of the TSSA union, called on her to resign, saying:

> *"I am asking Jackie that, in the interests of unity, she resigns at once from our party and also as vice-chair of Momentum. If she doesn't, both the Labour party and Momentum need to act to get rid of her at once. Furthermore, TSSA will seriously reconsider our union's support for Momentum if she is still in post by this time next week".* [4]

The concept of 'solidarity' is supposed to be a fundamental trade union principle. But Cortes was yet another 'optics left' merchant – a superficial 'socialist', more obsessed about how things looked rather than how they really were – who'd undergone a solidarity bypass. Like many other influential members of the 'movement', he would stand on platforms making tubthumping speeches but, when it came to the crunch, he couldn't walk the walk. A classic labour movement anthem, 'The Red Flag', contains the refrain, *"Though cowards flinch and traitors sneer / We'll keep the red flag flying here"*. Whilst many love to chant those words, it would be more appropriate for them to substitute the last line with, *"We'll run away crying in fear"*. They have no backbone. When speaking after her first suspension, Walker made a prophetic prediction:

> *"I have been spat at and beaten by racists. I have marched against the fascists, defended minorities, am of Jewish decent as is my partner. If they can do this to me, they can do it to anyone".* [5]

How right Walker was! The unwillingness by the leadership and other influential figures to offer support in her hour of need was an inexcusable example of disloyalty. Solidarity is a two-way street. It was another case of political self-harm. The consequences of their predisposition to leave comrades in the lurch were catastrophic.

In March 2016, Lord Michael Levy, a Zionist, threatened to quit the party unless the leadership sent a *"clear message"* that it will not tolerate 'antisemitism'. An early indication that the leadership would crumble in the face of this confected moral panic was given by John McDonnell. *"Out, out, out"* was his response to the *Independent*. Instead of standing up to the liars who were deliberately conflating anti-Zionism with Judeophobia, he said, *"If people express these views, full stop they're out"*.[6] That lily-livered reaction signalled to right-wingers like Levy, who piggybacked on the artificial 'antisemitism crisis', and the malicious bullies in the Israel lobby, that this could be successfully used as a wedge issue. It was their opportunity to split the Corbyn movement, and it was an opportunity that they seized with both hands thanks to the feeble acquiescence of Corbyn and McDonnell. Levy subsequently let the cat out of the bag when he claimed that *"using the word Zionists as another form of anti-Semitism frankly can no longer be tolerated"*.[7]

Walker was one of the early victims of this pernicious push against socialists and anti-imperialists in the party. I knew about Walker's story and had admired the principled stand she had taken. It was therefore a great privilege to finally meet her outside the Brighton conference centre, but she thought I wouldn't want to be seen with her, let alone have my photograph taken alongside her. I reassured her that nothing could be further from the truth, and we posed for a selfie. I praised her courage and I told her that the way she had been treated was dreadful. When she shared the photograph on social media, the predictable headlines ensued.

Walker and I became good friends after that meeting and I regularly spoke out in her defence. She later embarked on a tour with her one-woman show *The Lynching*, which she wrote and performed herself. It tells Walker's life story, from when her parents were civil rights activists in the US in the 1950s, to the fake 'antisemitism' accusations that enveloped her almost six decades later.[8] Walker's parents were victims of the 1950s Red Scare witch-hunt led by the right-wing Republican Senator Joseph McCarthy, which resulted in Walker's mother being deported to Jamaica in 1956. How ironic that, 60 years later, Walker found herself being targeted by a McCarthyite witch-hunt aimed at destroying the left inside the Labour Party!

In March 2018, when I was due to speak alongside the local Labour MP, Fiona Onasanya, at a meeting in Peterborough immediately after one of Walker's performances, I was put under enormous pressure to pull out. Onasanya buckled under the weight of opposition to her being on a platform with Walker, but there was no way I was going to be bullied into submission. Staff from the leader's office were on the phone, asking me not to attend. Even some of my own team were urging me to think again.

But, as I said to all the naysayers who were supposedly onside, solidarity is more important when it's difficult than when it's easy. My appearance at Walker's powerful and poignant performance prompted yet more national headlines. The chair of the self-appointed Jewish Leadership Council was given a platform on BBC Radio 4's flagship news and current affairs programme to demand that I spurn any further meetings in support of Walker. I then received the following message from Ben Folley from Corbyn's office:

> *"I understand the Chair of the JLC has said on Today Programme you should not be doing further meetings with Jackie Walker. I think you need to heed this given the sensitivity and pressure on Jeremy right now. Happy to discuss how we move forward".*

Corbyn and his staff were once again in full retreat mode. When it was rumoured that Walker and I would be speaking together at another event, Shadow Cabinet Minister, Barry Gardiner, told the *Today Programme* that his personal view was that it would be *"wrong to share a platform with somebody who has expressed the views that she has"*. What had Walker said to cause Gardiner to make such a statement? The truth is, she had said nothing remotely problematic. Yes, she had spoken out about the holocaust perpetrated against black Africans. Yes, she had spoken out in support of the Palestinian people and against the State of Israel's atrocities. Yes, she had spoken out against the so-called 'Law of Return' that gives all Jews around the world more rights to Palestinian land than those enjoyed by the Palestinian people themselves. In 1970, the State of Israel granted automatic citizenship not only to Jews, but also to their non-Jewish children, grandchildren, and spouses, and to the non-Jewish spouses of their children and grandchildren.[9] Should calling for greater recognition of the horrors of the slave trade, speaking out about the plight of Palestinians, and opposing the Law of Return transform someone into a pariah? Walker's ancestors were both Jewish and slaves. Gardiner had no right to imply that Walker had said anything inappropriate. The febrile atmosphere bludgeoned every MP but me into accepting the false narrative. I was, literally, the only MP prepared to challenge it publicly.

Of course, staff in the leader's office and Corbyn's allies in the PLP should have also been supporting Walker, not walking by on the other side or, worse still, pouring fuel on the fire to figuratively burn her at the stake. Their cowardice even put Walker's personal safety at risk. For example, when the film *WitchHunt*, directed by Jon Pullman, was due to be previewed at a fringe event in Liverpool during the 2018 Labour Party conference, the building had to be evacuated following a bomb threat by Zionist extremists. Walker was subjected to intolerable abuse and intimidation, but she bore it with great fortitude and maintained her dignity throughout. Walker was ultimately expelled in 2019 by the same kangaroo court that had expelled Marc Wadsworth 11 months previously. It seemed that prominent black rights campaigners were no longer welcome in the Labour Party.

I should have realised that we were on a hiding to nothing in Wadsworth's reinstatement bid when a senior Corbyn staff member told me in May 2018 that Shami Chakrabarti was pleased when Wadsworth was suspended. This individual said Shami was *"trying to appease people who accused her of a whitewash"*. The staff member was referring to her 2016 report on 'antisemitism and other forms of racism', which Corbyn had commissioned.

Grenfell victims betrayed

In her role as the Shadow Attorney General, a position to which Corbyn had appointed her in September 2016, Shami Chakrabarti's intervention in the aftermath of the Grenfell disaster in June 2017 was also unwelcome and unhelpful. Less than a week after the 2017 general election, one of Britain's worst modern-day disasters occurred when 72 people lost their lives in a fire that engulfed the Grenfell Tower block in North Kensington. The Royal Borough of Kensington and Chelsea (RBKC) Council had been criticised long before the fire by the tenants for not listening to their concerns. In November 2016, the local tenants group issued a stinging rebuke to the Kensington and Chelsea Tenant Management Organisation (KCTMO) that managed the tower block. In their newsletter, the tenants made the following ominous prediction:

> "It is a truly terrifying thought but the Grenfell Action Group firmly believe that only a catastrophic event will expose the ineptitude and incompetence of our landlord, the KCTMO, and bring an end to the dangerous living conditions and neglect of health and safety legislation that they inflict upon their tenants and leaseholders. We believe that the KCTMO are an evil, unprincipled, mini-mafia who have no business to be charged with the responsibility of looking after the everyday management of large scale social housing estates and that their sordid collusion with the RBKC Council is a recipe for a future major disaster.
>
> "It is our conviction that a serious fire in a tower block or similar high density residential property is the most likely reason that those who wield power at the KCTMO will be found out and brought to justice!"[10]

Just under three weeks after that fatal inferno, Corbyn appointed me as the Shadow Fire and Emergency Services Minister, a role I'd undertaken previously under Ed Miliband. My immediate priority was to obtain justice for the survivors, families, and the local community. I was determined to do everything in my power to fight for the people who had been affected by this horrific incident. I wasn't going to stand by and allow the issue to be kicked into the long grass, or for people to have to wait for more than two decades for justice, like the heroic Hillsborough campaigners had to do. I was clear that justice meant taking steps to prevent anything like this ever happening again, and that meant demanding reinvestment in our public services and retrofitting sprinkler systems, as a minimum. It also meant using my platform to speak up for the Grenfell survivors from the House of Commons despatch box and in the media. So, the day after my appointment to the frontbench, I called for the chair of the Grenfell Tower inquiry to either step down or be sacked. Ministers had selected a retired judge, Sir Martin Moore-Bick, for the role but residents were unhappy. I argued that tenants' views had been ignored for years, so it was essential that the government listened to what local people were saying and put someone in place in which the community had confidence. Emma Dent Coad, who was Kensington's newly elected Labour MP, added her voice to the chorus of objections to

Moore-Bick's appointment. She called for him to be replaced by someone with a *"human face"* to restore the inquiry's credibility with survivors.[11] She added that he was *"a technocrat"* who lacked credibility with victims.[12] BME Lawyers 4 Grenfell also weighed in to call on the Prime Minister to:

> *"withdraw [Moore-Bick's] appointment given [his] lack of credibility and appoint a Chair with a professional history and experience of appreciating the needs of social housing in this diverse community all too often ignored by the wealthiest Borough in the country".*[13]

Even Jenny Chapman, who was then a right-wing Labour MP, before Sir Keir Starmer installed her in the House of Lords after she lost her seat in the 2019 general election, was opposed to Moore-Bick's appointment. Commenting on Dent Coad's remarks, Chapman told BBC Radio 5 Live:

> *"There is little purpose in the inquiry proceeding if it doesn't have the confidence of the residents. I don't think you can just dismiss the comments of the local Member of Parliament."*[14]

But Chakrabarti had other ideas. On discovering what I'd said, she convened an urgent meeting with me, the Shadow Home Secretary Diane Abbott, and the Shadow Justice Secretary Richard Burgon. She opened the meeting by saying, *"We've got ourselves into a bit of a pickle"*. Chakrabarti argued that it wasn't for parliamentarians to interfere in an independent judicial process. But my point wasn't to interfere with the process itself. I just wanted to ensure that we spoke up for local people who were unhappy with Moore-Bick as the inquiry chair.

After all, Moore-Bick had an air of the Establishment about him. In one case, *Nzolameso v City of Westminster*,[15] his Court of Appeal judgment had to be overturned by the Supreme Court. The case related to a black single mother, Titina Nzolameso, who has Type II diabetes, hypertension, and diabetic retinopathy, and who is also HIV positive. She had been made homeless with her five children when her housing benefit had been cut. Westminster City Council decided to rehouse her 50 miles away in Bletchley, near Milton Keynes. Nzolameso appealed the decision until it reached Moore-Bick, who was one of three judges who ruled that the council had fulfilled its obligations, even though she had been moved to a location where she had no support networks for herself or her family. Moore-Bick didn't bother to challenge or scrutinise the council's decision, or their knowledge of their statutory obligations; he said that they could be assumed to know them. In essence, Moore-Bick let the council off the hook. The Supreme Court, on the other hand, *did* scrutinise the council's decision-making and found that they'd failed Nzolameso in various ways.[16] Was this a man who could be trusted to look deeply into the causes of the Grenfell disaster, and work to hold those responsible to account? It didn't seem that way to me.

However, Chakrabarti insisted that Moore-Bick was a *"lovely guy"* and *"a shy man"*, although what either of those descriptions had to do with his suitability was lost on me. I persevered with the view that, if our commitment to straight-talking, honest politics meant anything, we had to demonstrate that we understood the concerns of ordinary people. Chakrabarti immediately snapped back saying, *"But I'm an ordinary person, Chris, and I do understand the concerns of ordinary people"*. I nearly laughed. Chakrabarti is about as far removed from the lives and experiences of the working class community around Grenfell Tower as it is possible to be. She is a Baroness, before which she was a professional, middle class barrister, rubbing shoulders with the metropolitan liberal elite.

Diane Abbott and Richard Burgon said very little in the meeting, but both of them agreed with Chakrabarti that we had to accept Moore-Bick as the inquiry chair. I was less than pleased that, when it came to the crunch, some of Corbyn's closest and most senior allies were unwilling to speak up for a working class community that had been hideously wronged. It also left me with egg on my face. I was on the record saying that I supported the community's calls for Moore-Bick to go and I was due to appear on Nick Ferrari's LBC breakfast show the following morning. I was sure that he'd ask me about my position regarding Moore-Bick, and sure enough he did ask me point-blank about whether I still thought he should be sacked. The previous day, Lord Chancellor and Justice Secretary David Lidington gave Moore-Bick his unequivocal backing. He said, *"Sir Martin Moore-Bick will lead the inquiry into this tragedy with impartiality and with a determination to get to the truth and see justice done"*. I was therefore able to bludgeon my way through the interview with Ferrari. When he tried to drive a wedge between the party's pathetic official position and my support for Grenfell's residents, who wanted a different chair, Lidington's intervention enabled me to tell Ferrari that my position was now irrelevant. The minister had made it clear that Moore-Bick would not be replaced. I said the focus should turn to ensuring that Moore-Bick had the right people to advise him, who understand and represent the interests of the community.

I should never have been put in that position by Chakrabarti's insistence on a cosy, kid glove relationship with the judiciary. It was another example of the *"government in waiting"* mentality to which David Prescott had referred. It was also an early indication that Abbott and Burgon weren't quite the class warriors I'd thought they were. We should have been kicking over the traces, not conforming to bullshit parliamentary protocols like a bunch of mealy-mouthed lickspittles.

Sadly, that pretty much sums up the Socialist Campaign Group of Labour MPs (SCG), which is a self-selecting collection of supposedly likeminded individuals that was reconstituted in 2017 by Richard Burgon. It was intended to be an antidote to the 'Core Group', which comprised MPs who had not joined the 2016 PLP coup against Corbyn. The 'Core Group' also included supportive MPs like me, who had either come back or been elected for the first time in 2017. However, there was a feeling that it had become too staid and wasn't providing any policy innovation. But the SCG quickly went down the same route. I remember the Crewe and Nantwich MP, Laura Smith, bitterly complaining to me about the way in which the weekly SCG meetings functioned. She felt that it was only concerned with cheerleading the leadership and totally failed to provide a critical evaluation of the shadow cabinet's decisions, an assessment with which I completely concurred.

Where was the introspection and self-criticism? The SCG's stance was a massive error of judgement and stood in sharp contrast to the way it had functioned during the Ed Miliband years. It meant that all the parliamentary pressure on Corbyn was coming from the right-wing of the PLP. There was no countervailing, left-wing force being exerted by the SCG to create the space to consolidate and develop the policy programme that had won Corbyn two landslide leadership elections. The SCG's failure contributed to Corbyn's catastrophic decisions to repeatedly make concessions to the PLP's right-wingers, who had been politically incapacitated, albeit temporarily, after the 2017 election. By the end of that year, they were seizing back the initiative, and, by the end of 2018, they were once again dominating the agenda, aided and abetted by the corporate media.

In addition to the weakness being demonstrated by Corbyn and his team, there was no strength to be found from leaders in the trade union movement or among supposed left-wingers in the PLP, either. It felt as if I was carrying more and more weight on my shoulders. If not me, then who? It was becoming an increasingly difficult and lonely responsibility.

CHAPTER ELEVEN

FREE AGENT

Only six months into my stint on Corbyn's frontbench as Shadow Fire Minister, on 11 January 2018, I resigned. My discontent with the constraints of collective responsibility had been brewing for quite some time. The catalyst for my departure was the ridiculous outcry about an innovative, temporary measure I'd proposed to give Labour councils some budgetary breathing room. Councils up and down the country had been struggling, and continue to struggle, under the burden of swingeing budget cuts. My suggestion was that local authorities could help reverse Tory austerity by levying a redistributive council tax in every borough. Councils could use the *existing* statutory powers at their disposal to require wealthy households to shoulder a much higher proportion of the council tax burden. This would enable councillors to improve their local services, whilst freezing or even reducing the council tax liability for between 80 to 85 per cent of the households in their local communities.

Whilst the reaction to my proposal was hysterical and brutal, the funny thing is that I'd been promoting the idea for months before it appeared on the radar of right-wing hacks. I had floated the proposed measure in meetings with the 'Core Group' of (ostensibly) Corbyn-supporting Labour MPs, at which Corbyn's advisers were in attendance. I had also spoken about it alongside Shadow Cabinet members at public meetings, and I'd written several articles,[1] with no critical comments from anyone. It only turned ugly when the anti-Corbyn, liberal hack Paul Waugh covered the issue in a *HuffPost* article on 9 January 2018. After that, a plethora of unfriendly headlines followed.[2]

Ultra-Blairite MPs, like Wes Streeting, couldn't wait to denounce me. Predictably, he misrepresented what I was suggesting. He said that I was proposing to double council tax for everyone, which was the very opposite of what I'd been recommending.[3] The right-wing Shadow Local Government Secretary, Andrew Gwynne, was said to have been *"furious"* and he issued the following statement denouncing my suggestion:

"This proposal is not our policy and it won't be. Unlike this proposal, we recognise that each council area has a different ability to raise income locally and so we will look at that as part of a fair redistribution mechanism, linking social need, health inequality, urban deprivation and rural sparsity."[4]

But Gwynne's statement was meaningless without a Labour government. Offering tea and sympathy was no substitute for real action in the here and now, and that is what my proposition sought to provide. It was a creative use of legislation, which, curiously, had been passed by the Coalition Government and pushed through the House of Commons by none other than Sir Eric Pickles.

The response from Corbyn's staff was pathetic. Whenever they were confronted with hostile headlines, their first instinct was to retreat and to make ham-fisted attempts at 'damage control'. They asked me to renounce the idea and apologise, claiming that *"Jeremy was furious"*. When I refused, Amy Jackson – a secondee from Unite the Union into the leader's office, who was responsible for liaison between the leader and the PLP – told me over the phone that I would have to resign. I subsequently met in-person with Corbyn. He wasn't furious at all. In fact, he was curious about my proposal. He went through the various plans that Labour had for local government, including replacing council tax with a different system. I told him I supported those changes but that they were all 'jam tomorrow' schemes. We would need a general election before we could implement them, and we needed solutions *today*. The truth was that Labour had nothing to offer at a local level other than saying the party would manage the Tory cuts better than the Tories would. We were then joined in the meeting by Seumas Milne and Amy Jackson. The conversation continued for another 15 minutes or so, and we were not getting anywhere. To break the stalemate, I eventually said that I could probably serve the movement and support Corbyn more effectively from the backbenches. It was clear that Jackson just wanted me gone from the frontbench, so she enthusiastically agreed. Seumas said that my resignation would help, as there were virtually no friendly outriders in the PLP. Ever since the flurry of resignations during the attempted coup in 2016, nearly all the loyalists were on the frontbench, which restricted their ability to defend Corbyn at PLP meetings and in public. However, Corbyn said he didn't want to lose me from the frontbench. I said, *"Well, appoint me as the Shadow Local Government Secretary then"*. Corbyn responded by asking me if that was what I wanted. I told him that it was his decision, but that I could either make a difference heading up our policy agenda from inside the Shadow Cabinet, or I could work from the backbenches. I suggested that, if he didn't want to sack Gwynne, I could take over John Healey's brief as Shadow Housing Secretary as an alternative. We were offering nothing on local government and our housing policy prospectus was weak and timid. I said that we needed to be much bolder and to enthusiastically champion the rights of Generation Rent, who were being left behind. Whilst I was keen to continue working with the firefighters, the halfway house of being a junior Shadow Minister simply wasn't working. I wanted to speak out about the ideas I had, and, if I was going to be gagged as a Shadow Minister, I would sooner not be one. However, Corbyn asked me to think about it overnight before making a final decision, and so I agreed.

The following morning, I had a meeting with all of my office team. We went round the table, with everyone expressing a view about whether or not I should go. They ended up being pretty evenly split about it. Some of them made the point that resigning would be better for me, because it would liberate me from some of the ridiculous constraints of the frontbench. Others argued that my resignation might be damaging to Corbyn's leadership, and that I should make use of my frontbench profile to assist the movement. I could see that some of them were taking the whole situation to heart, so, after we'd finished our discussion, I decided to lighten the mood by playing (and singing along to) The Clash's song, 'Should I Stay or Should I Go?'. My team were often victims of my serenading.

I then received a call from John McDonnell, who urged me not to resign. I tentatively agreed, so long as we could discuss the potential of a progressive council tax again at the following Monday's meeting of the Core Group. But, by the afternoon, person/s unknown in Corbyn's office had told the media that I'd resigned, and my phone started ringing off the hook. Meanwhile, right-wing Labour MPs were briefing that I'd been sacked.[5] What is clear is that, when it looked like I might remain on the frontbench, someone in the leader's office decided to bounce me into resigning by tipping off the hostile corporate media. It was the insidious hand of 'machine politics' in action, which was a trademark tactic of the Unite the Union bureaucracy. But machine politics was the very antithesis of what Corbyn represented, and so it was particularly disappointing to see its insidious influence at work at the very heart of Corbyn's operations. I thought, so much for the 'straight talking, honest politics' that Corbyn had advocated in his leadership campaigns and when he was first elected as the party leader![6] The news also seemed to catch some of Corbyn's team off-guard. James Schneider was deployed to conduct damage control, and he sent me a statement to sign-off in order to quell the media onslaught, which said:

> *"I will be standing down from my role with immediate effect so that I can return to the backbenches, where I will be campaigning on a broader range of issues. I will continue to loyally support the leadership of Jeremy Corbyn from the backbenches and hope to be a voice for the party's members."*[7]

Schneider also penned the following response from Corbyn:

> *"I am grateful for Chris' work on the frontbench, particularly on fire safety following the appalling Grenfell Tower Fire. I know that on the backbenches, Chris will be a strong campaigner on a range of crucial issues as well as serving his constituents with dedication."*

In the end, I was content with resigning. I was almost there of my own volition! But the way that I was nudged into it left a bad taste in my mouth.

Becoming a target

My departure from the frontbench coincided with an announcement of what was meant to be a transformative 'Democracy Review'[8] of the Labour Party. The NEC had agreed it only a couple of months prior.[9] The Democracy Review was supposed to be a real opportunity for the Corbyn project to do away with the party's Kinnockite and Blairite structures, which disempowered grassroots members and reserved powers for largely unaccountable and opaque committees. I argued that the review should be strengthened by widening its terms of reference to require Labour MPs to be made accountable to the grassroots members in their constituencies through a process called 'open selection'. That would have required every Labour MP to undergo a 'primary' between every general election, during which local members could decide if they wanted the incumbent to continue or to be replaced with someone else. This process would not have been a new phenomenon in the Labour Party. Mandatory reselection was introduced in 1979, and then scrapped by Kinnock in 1990. It is also not unique to the Labour Party. Elected positions in every other organisation in the country, from trade union officials to boardroom directors, to community organisations to pressure groups, are subject to regular elections by the members/shareholders of their organisations. Even the secretary of Corbyn's allotment association is subject to an open selection once a year at their Annual General Meeting. The President of the United States of America, the most powerful nation on Earth, must also be re-endorsed by their party before running for a second term. Yet, Labour MPs seem to think that they should be exempt from any democratic oversight by their members. Unless and until the PLP is made accountable to grassroots party members, it will remain a law unto itself.

I was motivated to bring about open selection because to win an election with an unaccountable and hostile parliamentary party would have made it impossible to deliver an anti-imperialist socialist programme. A large proportion, probably a majority, of the PLP simply would not have voted for it. By voting with the Tories, as these right-wing malcontents undoubtedly would, Corbyn's manifesto would be dead in the water. We saw a significant group of Labour MPs vote against the settled will of the party's grassroots members on Europe in 1972. Were it not for these Labour Europhile MPs, led by Roy Jenkins (who later established the SDP, gifting Thatcher two landslide victories), Ted Heath would have lost his bid to join the European Economic Community (as it then was). The PLP with which Corbyn was lumbered would be even worse than their 1970s counterparts and they would not think twice about sabotaging key elements of the party's programme. Indeed, a Corbyn-majority government may have been hijacked, and Corbyn's premiership may simply have been robbed by a right-winger. Therefore, it was crucial to democratise the party's policy-making procedures. That meant: reconfiguring its bureaucratic machine at Head Office and in the Regional Offices; removing the PLP's effective veto over who can stand as a candidate for leader; and, crucially, making Labour MPs accountable to party members.

My calls for greater accountability enraged most of the PLP. Nearly all of them knew that their lucrative positions would be vulnerable if they were subject to a re-selection contest against Corbyn-supporting socialist candidates. Even before I'd started the Democracy Roadshow,[10] in which I travelled the country to meetings speaking in support of open selection and other democratic reforms during the summer of 2018, the level of resentment towards me boiled over on various occasions. Some MPs verbally abused me in the House of Commons division lobby and in the corridors around Westminster. Right-wing MP Lucy Powell even took to Twitter to publicly rebuke me for speaking at a meeting without informing her friend Anna Turley, then MP for Redcar.[11] As a courtesy, visiting MPs are expected to inform the local MP in advance if they are to hold a political event in their constituency. However, the pair were left red-faced after it emerged that I wasn't speaking in Turley's constituency, but rather the one adjacent to hers. Ascertaining the facts had evidently been less important than a rush to condemn and fan sectarian flames.

I launched the Democracy Roadshow with Tosh McDonald, president of the train drivers' union, ASLEF, at the start of the summer recess in 2018. We made a promo video, in which Tosh and I rode his Harley-Davidson motorbikes to the strains of Steppenwolf's 'Born to Be Wild' and a voiceover from me.[12] The video is still available on YouTube. I had never ridden a motorbike before, let alone a 1200cc Harley-Davidson. Luckily, we were able to shoot the video on a quiet, private road, but it was still nerve racking. My heart was racing throughout, and I never managed to get beyond second gear. I think I looked calm and professional in the video, though. Shortly after I embarked on the Democracy

Roadshow, John McDonnell announced at a Core Group meeting that he was going to do his own speaking tour. He said he was planning to use the summer recess to arrange meetings in the constituencies of some of the PLP saboteurs. *"I'm going into the bastards' own back yards"*, he told us. I don't know whether McDonnell ever went ahead with those meetings, but they certainly didn't cause any ripples if he did.

"Assassinate Chris Williamson"

When the Democracy Roadshow got into full swing, the animosity went into overdrive. Lyn Brown, Labour MP for West Ham, posted a malicious message in a WhatsApp chat group that was leaked to me. The subsequent exchange illustrated the level of bitterness inside the PLP. Brown wrote, *"Thinking of crowdfunding to assassinate Chris Williamson. Anyone in?"*. When the Labour MP for Bradford West, Naz Shah, responded by saying, *"😧 u ok Lyn (((((HUGZ))))))"*, Brown doubled-down. *"Because I'm planning a painful murder?"*, Brown said. That prompted Shah to respond saying, *"Well there is that but for u to be planning that surely... can't be good. I can literally hear you saying that"*.

After Brown discovered that I'd seen her messages, she was embarrassed and highly apologetic. Lloyd Russell-Moyle had threatened to report her to the police unless she made a fulsome apology. She insisted on buying me lunch to make amends. When we met, she told me that I was giving the PLP a collective nervous breakdown. I told her to tell them to calm down and join the debate. I was only speaking at meetings where their own local members had invited me, and the local Labour MPs were encouraged to attend. In fact, in a few constituencies, local Labour MPs did join the Democracy Roadshow! I told Brown that democracy was nothing to be fearful about, and, in any event, open selection was a relatively small part of what I was speaking about in my meetings. I agreed to give her a list every month of constituencies where I would be speaking. She said she would then broker a meeting with the relevant MPs before I attended. None of them took up the offer.

Roy Hattersley, a right-wing former Labour MP and deputy leader between 1983 and 1992, also decided to pile in. He even claimed to have attended one of my meetings, although we weren't introduced. The reason was because Hattersley had made it up. He said he had attended an event with me at Wortley Hall in the Penistone and Stocksbridge constituency, which was represented at the time by pro-privatisation Labour MP, Angela Smith. I was astounded that such a senior figure in the party would resort to a barefaced lie, particularly when there were so many witnesses to the fact that he was telling a tall tale. But these right-wing figures are shameless. Hattersley used the pretence of attending one of the Democracy Roadshow meetings to call on Corbyn to condemn it as *"wrong in principle and deeply damaging to Labour's prospects of election"*.[13] However, Hattersley's hallucination backfired on him. It prompted grassroots activists to start photoshopping his *Spitting Image* caricature into photos of meetings where I was speaking, which they then posted online.

Later, on 20 August 2018, Labour grandee Barry Sheerman, MP for Huddersfield, wrote to Corbyn to vent his feelings. He posted his missive on social media. He said, *"I am deeply concerned that the future of our party will be put in jeopardy if Chris Williamson's activities are not promptly condemned by you as leader of our party"*.[14] But it seemed that Sheerman was more worried about his own future, rather than that of the party's, and he had good reason to be. The Huddersfield town hall meeting was absolutely packed. Standing room only. On a show of hands at the end of the meeting, there was unanimous support for open selection and there was clearly no love lost between them and their MP. That response in Huddersfield was repeated all over the country.

Chuka Umunna, who was one of the most prominent right-wing malcontents, reacted angrily when grassroots members in his own constituency invited me to take the Democracy Roadshow to Streatham. *"Call off the dogs"*, was his blunt message to Corbyn.[15] By *"dogs"*, he meant Labour Party members who were demanding a greater say over their own party's policies and who should represent them in Parliament. Following Umunna's ultimatum, I began my speeches at the remaining Democracy Roadshow events up to the 2018 conference with 'Who Let the Dogs Out' – the title of the hit song by the Baha Men. This caused much mirth and hilarity, particularly when a large section of the attendees responded with, *"Who, who, who, who,*

who?". Umunna's kneejerk outburst was just one more example of the sense of entitlement with which the vast majority of the PLP were inculcated. The meeting in Streatham was jammed with attendees who were passionate about democratic reforms, and Umunna's members voted unanimously in favour of open selection. Umunna later went on to help found the ill-fated and short-lived Change UK party. His arrogance was even embedded in the name, which could be shortened to 'ChUK', similar to what the neoliberal President of France, Emmanuel Macron, had done with his party 'En Marche!'. Mr 'Chuk' later abandoned ship by joining the Liberal Democrats, even though six years earlier he had said that *"you can't trust a word the Lib Dems say"*.[16]

Neil Coyle, yet another aggressively right-wing Labour MP, penned an article for the *House Magazine*, in which he launched a broadside against the Democracy Roadshow. In his green-ink rant, he suggested that the tour was a ploy so that people would *"support [me] for leader when the time comes"*. Displaying a complete absence of any self-awareness, he said, *"Williamson seems to think people would rather see Labour fighting itself than for the issues affecting their daily lives"*.[17] This is the same guy who had sent a series of abusive texts to Corbyn over an extended period saying things like *"you're weaker than a mosquito on an elephant hide"*.[18] He also used the corporate media to criticise Corbyn's staff,[19] and he was even quoted in the *Sun* newspaper saying that the Shadow Cabinet was *"a complete washout"*.[20]

The reason they were all squealing was because there was a genuine grassroots uprising taking place. It scared the living daylights out of the cosy and complacent Westminster village. Right-wing Labour MPs could see their cushy lifestyles being snatched away by the pesky grassroots members who were, for the first time, asserting their rights to take control of their own party. That was anathema to those MPs. When Neil Kinnock had made a bombastic speech at a noisy PLP meeting in 2016 during the attempted coup against Corbyn, in which he implied that the party belonged to Labour parliamentarians, MPs cheered him to the rafters.[21] But, as a free agent, liberated from the clutches of the frontbench, I was determined to act as the champion of the membership, and to shatter these MPs' pretensions.

CHAPTER TWELVE

BEGINNING OF THE END

In spite of the overwhelming support from grassroots members for open selection, Jeremy Corbyn sought to placate Labour's parliamentary goons by supporting a fatuous 'compromise' at the 2018 Labour Party conference. Rather than ensuring all Labour MPs had to undergo a process of re-endorsement by their local parties before standing again for Parliament, he opted to mildly enhance the existing 'trigger ballot' system. This would make it slightly easier for local members to initiate a deselection campaign. It was pitiful on two counts. First, it failed to provide the real accountability for which members were desperately crying out. Second, it meant that members would have to mount a series of negative campaigns *against* their MPs, rather than it being a positive process. It seemed like Corbyn was suffering from a form of Stockholm syndrome. His failure to implement open selection was, without doubt, the weakest, most self-defeating strategic miscalculation of his entire leadership. If nothing else, it signalled to the PLP that their positions were under no threat whatsoever. Contrary to what many of them initially believed after the 2017 general election – that their careers would soon be on the chopping block – Corbyn had shown that he and the entire movement around him was a paper tiger.

But this gargantuan blunder doesn't just fall on Corbyn's shoulders. It was only made possible by all of the trade union delegations at the conference, apart from the Fire Brigades Union. They closed ranks to kill open selection. Len McCluskey is particularly culpable. He led his Unite the Union delegation to vote against their *own* democratically decided policy. Unite's votes would have seen the proposal carried by a majority of around 14 per cent. Opponents of the move were disingenuously presenting it as an attempt to weaken the role of the trade unions in the party. They portrayed it as a battle between grassroots party members on the one hand, and trade union members on the other. But when Ammar Kazmi, the delegate from Rushcliffe CLP, spoke from the conference podium, he exposed that false dichotomy.

He asked CLP delegates to raise their hands if, alongside their Labour membership, they were also members of a trade union. Unsurprisingly, a forest of hands went up. But it made no difference. The die had already been cast. Those trade union delegations did incalculable damage. McCluskey has since admitted that open selection was *"a missed opportunity"*. He has also tried to exculpate himself by saying, *"I was asked by Jeremy Corbyn to support the compromise and get the other unions to agree"* because the *"leadership [was] worried [that open selection] would provoke a split in the parliamentary party at a delicate time"*. He even said, *"I was furious that the unions and I were getting the blame for something the leadership wanted"*.[1] Where was the pugnacious 'Red Len' we'd all heard about? Couldn't he have argued the point with Corbyn if he felt so strongly about it? Isn't McCluskey responsible for his own actions? 'Corbyn asked me to do it' is a poor excuse. McCluskey was a leader in his own right, and his union had made its stance on open selection clear.

Having spent the summer months in 2018 campaigning on the issue, I was furious at Corbyn's and the unions' collective capitulation. I wrote an opinion piece in the *Morning Star*, saying that democracy would not be squashed by a *"bureaucratic machine"*. It was published on 26 September, the final day of conference, on the morning of Corbyn's speech.[2] McCluskey took exception to my article and, when he saw me in the conference exhibition area, which was crowded with people awaiting Corbyn's address, he interrupted a conversation I was having with three other people. He launched a finger-wagging, expletive-ridden tirade. I had my back against the wall, with McCluskey in my face attempting an impersonation of Alex Ferguson's hairdryer treatment. I repeated, *"Unite's policy was to support mandatory reselection"*. He retorted, *"It's also Unite's policy to support Jeremy Corbyn"*. I replied, *"Of course, and I support Jeremy"*. McCluskey's response was incredibly petulant, *"Well, with supporters like you, he doesn't need fucking enemies"*. I told him that he was being unfair. His parting shot was to howl, *"It isn't unfair, Chris. And don't accuse us of 'machine politics' again. You're playing a fucking right-wing argument"*. He then strutted off, probably to brief the media about the altercation.

Despite McCluskey's red-faced rant, I didn't want to pour fuel on the fire. I played the incident down when I was subsequently contacted by reporters, asking me for a comment about my "*clash with Len McCluskey*". I told them that their version of events was mistaken, and I said, "*I wouldn't describe it as a clash – we had a conversation, that was all*".[3] But McCluskey's spokesperson escalated the situation by saying, "*Len decided to give Chris a piece of his mind. There is anger at him attacking Unite for a rule change that was supported by Jeremy Corbyn's office*".[4] Then, in an article for *LabourList*, McCluskey accused me of using "*ultra-leftist terminology ... and ... undermining the wishes of Jeremy Corbyn*".[5] I have a video recording of the altercation, and I was urged by my staff to release it in retaliation, but I preferred to allow cooler heads to prevail. In the end, it seems that McCluskey now understands the error of his ways. He said, "*I took [Chris's] head off. I actually lost my own head a bit which I shouldn't have done*".[6] In a further concession, he added:

> "*the trigger ballot system that was adopted proved to be a failure. ... no MPs were successfully triggered, squandering a golden opportunity to change the PLP. Campaigners for open selection ... were right. If I could turn back the clock to the 2018 conference, I would push for open selection.*"[7]

I welcome McCluskey's change of heart, although it can never change what happened at that fateful and historic conference. I just wish more senior pro-Corbyn figures like him would admit what went wrong.

IHRA debacle

Earlier in September 2018, the Labour Party's NEC had adopted the 11 'illustrative' examples that accompany the International Holocaust Remembrance Alliance (IHRA) 'Working Definition of Antisemitism'.[8] The party's eventual adoption of the IHRA Working Definition was the culmination of a concerted spring and summer offensive by an unholy alliance of Zionist zealots and right-wing neoliberals.

On 26 March 2018, the Board of Deputies of British Jews (BoD) organised a protest in Parliament Square against Jeremy Corbyn and alleged 'antisemitism' in the Labour Party. The whole event made a mockery of the struggle against genuine racism. Underlining the dishonesty of the occasion was the attendance of right-wing politicians, including Norman Tebbit, whose so-called 'cricket test' in 1990 infamously questioned the loyalty of people with South Asian and Caribbean heritage in Britain.[9] But even though the protest was clearly engineered by extremists, the recreants in Corbyn's office were desperate to avoid any criticism of the demonstration. Amy Jackson breathlessly pleaded with me not to speak out against the brazen mud-slinging circus, and she even asked me to urge Jewish Voice for Labour (JVL) not to mount a counter-protest. Whilst I didn't call out the shameful charade, I refused to do anything to deter those who wanted to voice their support for Corbyn. Inevitably, the corporate media coverage focussed on the anti-Corbyn demonstrators. It failed to report on how many of them abused and harassed those who'd turned out to peacefully voice their opposition to the IHRA Working Definition. Elderly Jewish women who expressed their support for Corbyn were referred to as *"kapos"* and one young Jewish man was told to *"go back to the ghetto"*.[10] *"Kapo"* was a term for a prisoner in a Nazi camp who was assigned by SS guards to supervise forced labour or to carry out administrative tasks. This abuse was being meted out by far-right hoodlums wearing symbols associated with anti-Palestinian terrorism and the violent, racist Kahanist movement. Some of these characters were wearing T-shirts emblazoned with Menachem Begin's image. Begin masterminded the terrorist bombing of Jerusalem's King David Hotel in 1946, killing 91 people, and he was later elected as Israel's Prime Minister.

The BoD and the Jewish Leadership Council (JLC) had also sent a foul open letter to the Labour Party to coincide with the demonstration. The purpose of this twin-track assault was to monster Corbyn. The content of their letter was pure propaganda. They claimed:

> *"[Corbyn] issues empty statements about opposing antisemitism, but does nothing to understand or address it. We conclude that he cannot seriously contemplate antisemitism, because he is so ideologically fixed within a far left worldview that is instinctively hostile to mainstream Jewish communities ... Jeremy Corbyn is now the figurehead for an antisemitic political culture, based*

on obsessive hatred of Israel, conspiracy theories and fake news that is doing dreadful harm to British Jews and to the British Labour Party". [11]

They had absolutely no evidence whatsoever for their assertions. But, instead of speaking out against these assaults on his and the party's reputations, Corbyn issued a timorous apology and sought an urgent meeting with the letter's authors. He allowed himself to be bullied into saying:

"I recognise that anti-Semitism has surfaced within the Labour Party, and has too often been dismissed as simply a matter of a few bad apples. This has caused pain and hurt to Jewish members of our Party and to the wider Jewish community in Britain. I am sincerely sorry for the pain which has been caused, and pledge to redouble my efforts to bring this anxiety to an end". [12]

But there was no evidence to support Corbyn's assertions. He was effectively parroting lines from the Zionist spin machine. When Jennie Formby subsequently revealed the figures for alleged 'antisemitism' in the party, it gave the lie to Corbyn's statement. The statistics proved that allegations of 'antisemitism' were infinitesimal.

By September 2016, the Labour Party's membership had already swelled to around 550,000.[13] Between April 2018 and January 2019 the party received 673 allegations of 'antisemitism' against members of the Labour Party. The accusations represented just 0.122 per cent of the party's membership. Out of those 673 complaints, 96 were immediately suspended, 146 received a reminder of conduct, and 211 were issued with a Notice of Investigation. In 220 cases, there was insufficient evidence of any breach of the party's rules. So, that meant just over 0.08 per cent of the membership were subject to any vaguely credible charges. Of the remaining 453 cases, 96 were issued with a Notice of Investigation or suspension. In other words, less than 0.02 per cent of the membership. That figure was further broken down to reveal that only 42 members were referred to the National Constitutional Committee (NCC). Aside from those, 16 members were issued with a formal warning (representing less than 0.003 per cent of members), and 25 were issued with a Reminder of Conduct (or just over 0.0045 per cent of the party's membership). Seven cases were closed and six were referred for further investigation. The NCC had expelled 12 members, representing 0.002 per cent and six members received other unspecified sanctions.[14] Even if one accepts that the expulsions and other disciplinary actions were legitimate – and most if not all of them weren't – the number of 'antisemitism' cases inside the party didn't even constitute a pinprick. But the right-wingers in the PLP, the corporate media hacks, and the Zionist lobby were not going to allow the facts to get in the way of their smear campaign.

By seeking a meeting with the BoD and the JLC, Corbyn was yet again playing into the hands of his detractors in the Zionist lobby and the neoliberal Establishment. It didn't matter what he did, he was never going to pacify them. He was also, yet again, turning his back on his loyal left-wing, anti-Zionist Jewish supporters, many of whom had already been suspended. It was as if Corbyn was living out Albert Einstein's theory of insanity, doing the same thing over and over again and expecting different results.

By early September 2018, the IHRA issue had truly boiled over. The NEC was due to discuss the issue, and anti-Zionist Jewish members of the party in JVL decided to organise a rally outside the meeting to oppose the adoption of the 11 'illustrative' examples. They asked me to speak, and I ended up addressing a large crowd. Many of those who had come to voice their opposition were Jewish. There was a tiny counter-demonstration, comprising roughly a dozen Zionist chauvinists. But the corporate media's framing of the images outside Labour's headquarters did their best to equate the numbers protesting for and against.[15] In reality, the Zionist zealots, which included some known far-right extremists, were heavily outnumbered.

When I concluded my speech, I was surrounded by a media scrum. Whilst the reporters were firing a series of questions at me, one of the fanatics from the counter-demonstration, Damon Lenszner, was using a megaphone to scream abuse at me. He repeatedly yelled *"Labour fascist!"* and made some other incoherent remarks about me being *"at the top table, eating the scum off Corbyn's plate"*.[16] Lenszner, and former vice-chair of the Zionist Federation Jonathan Hoffman (who was also part of the counter-demonstration), subsequently pleaded guilty to charges of harassment and threatening behaviour after attacking Palestine solidarity protesters in Carnaby Street. They'd changed their initial 'not guilty' plea following a plea-bargaining agreement with the prosecution, who dropped the related assault charges.[17] Lenszner was originally charged with assault by beating, whilst Hoffman was charged with common assault and using threatening words and behaviour under Section 4 of the Public Order Act 1986.[18]

The point that I'd been making to reporters was that even Kenneth Stern, who helped to draft the almost-identical predecessor to the IHRA text, had highlighted the misuse of the IHRA. In 2011, he issued a statement saying that the definition *"was being abused [and] employed in an attempt to restrict academic freedom and punish political speech"*.[19] On 7 November 2017, he gave evidence to the US House of Representatives Committee on the Judiciary, during which he again expressed his criticism of the IHRA Working Definition. Yet, in 2018, Labour's NEC adopted it in its entirety. The naïvety of those who just saw its adoption as a smart tactic, rather than a morally bankrupt and damaging turn, was infuriating. Among the chief cheerleaders for its adoption was the leader of Momentum, Jon Lansman.[20] As we were soon to discover, the adoption of the IHRA Working Definition was a pretext to target lifelong anti-racist, pro-Palestine socialists like me.[21] It is, for all intents and purposes, a Zionist charter to suppress criticism of Israel. Indeed, five of the 11 examples refer to the State of Israel.[22] IHRA Example 7 suggests that referring to Israel as *"racist endeavour"* is 'antisemitic', even though its foundation was inherently racist. Three quarters of a million Palestinians had to flee their homeland at the point of a gun, whilst thousands of others were massacred.[23] Example 10 states that it is 'antisemitic' to draw comparisons between contemporary Israeli policy and that of the Nazis, yet a number of Jewish Holocaust survivors make that very comparison, as do many other Jewish people.[24] The late Gerald Kaufman made a powerful and emotional speech in the House of Commons in 2009 during which he drew a direct parallel between the actions of the Nazis and the deeds of Israeli soldiers. He said:

"My grandmother was ill in bed when the Nazis came to her hometown of Staszów. A German soldier shot her dead in her bed. My grandmother did not die to provide cover for Israeli soldiers murdering Palestinian grandmothers in Gaza.

"The current Israeli government ruthlessly and cynically exploit the continuing guilt among gentiles over the slaughter of Jews in the Holocaust as justification for their murder of Palestinians. The implication is that Jewish lives are precious, but the lives of Palestinians do not count.

"On Sky News a few days ago, the spokeswoman for the Israeli army, Major Leibovich, was asked about the Israeli killing of, at that time, 800 Palestinians – the total is now 1,000. She replied instantly that '500 of them were militants'. That was the reply of a Nazi. I suppose that the Jews fighting for their lives in the Warsaw ghetto could have been dismissed as militants". [25]

When Corbyn failed to push through the democratic reforms and to oppose the discredited IHRA Working Definition, he simply strengthened his enemies who saw it as a sign of weakness. It was maddening to witness the inability of Corbyn's advisers to never learn from the light of experience. They organised high-profile encounters for Corbyn to prostrate himself before antagonistic Zionist organisations like the BoD, the JLC, and the Jewish Labour Movement (JLM). They continually claimed that each new act of subservience would finally *"draw a line"* under the phoney 'antisemitism crisis' that was engulfing Corbyn's leadership. But it did no such thing. In fact, it did the very opposite. These organisations used those meetings as opportunities to further humiliate and undermine Corbyn.[26] They wanted him out because they found it unconscionable that someone like Corbyn could be the Leader of the Official Opposition, let alone a potential future Prime Minister. It was hopelessly naïve to expect that giving ground to such out-and-out zealots would stop their attacks.

No backbones to be found

I repeatedly pleaded for an end to the appeasement strategy and for a vigorous defence of Corbyn's reputation, in addition to a determined push back against the attacks on grassroots activists who were being targeted and smeared. Corbyn's most loyal supporters were being picked off one by one, and yet he remained silent about it, as did the SCG, despite my repeated exhortations that the concessions were proving disastrous. On 9 September 2018, I spoke with members at a Democracy Roadshow meeting in Portsmouth, at which I made the following exasperated observation:[27]

> *"We've tried to reason with people who are completely unreasonable. And every concession that we've made has just been taken, 'We'll have that, and then we want some more'. And then another concession's made, and they think, 'Right, thanks very much ... we'll have that, and then we want some more. Right, we've got Ken Livingstone ... we want the next person. Yep, we've got Marc Wadsworth out the way ... we want the next person. Jackie Walker, get rid of her. Get rid of Chris Williamson'. They're after me as well! Ultimately, what they want to do is topple Jeremy. They will not be satisfied until either Jeremy's stepped down, died, or has been removed."*

Prominent left-wing anti-Zionist Jews were being denounced. These included Jackie Walker, Tony Greenstein, who is the son of a Rabbi, and Cyril Chilson, whose parents survived Auschwitz. In fact, I was the only MP willing to speak out publicly against the witch-hunt. For that, I was depicted as a *"Jew baiter"*[28] and charged by the Labour Party's bureaucrats for a *"pattern of behaviour"*[29] that could bring the party into *"disrepute"* – for defending left-wing Jews! Despite Corbyn's oft-repeated line, *"We won't walk by on the other side"*, that was precisely what he did when his most loyal supporters, who were his praetorian guard, were being smeared, suspended, and expelled.

Despite the September setbacks, CLPs and trade union branches continued inviting me to their meetings. So, I carried on traversing the country to defend Corbyn's leadership, to advocate socialist policies, and to promote greater party democracy. There was still a huge appetite among rank-and-file members for the hopeful and empowering vision that I was setting out at these meetings, and the collective energy engendered by them was palpable. Members felt valued and part of a bigger project to genuinely transform the country. When I spoke at Democracy Roadshow events, I would stress that the democratic reforms we were discussing were not a navel-gazing exercise. They were fundamental to being able to deliver a socialist domestic programme and an anti-imperialist international policy. I reminded members that it was Tony Benn who in 1973 said, *"Our long campaign to democratise power in Britain has, first, to begin in our own movement"*.[30]

There was no doubt about the formidable forces that would be ranged against a Corbyn-led Labour government. By way of example, the week after Corbyn was elected as leader in September 2015, the *Sunday Times* carried a story about the military's response to him. They'd spoken to *"a senior serving general"* who was threatening treason should Corbyn be elected. This senior ranking soldier had warned that *"feelings [were] running very high within the armed forces"* about the possibility of a Corbyn government, adding, *"You can't put a maverick in charge of a country's security"*. The general even threatened a *"mutiny"* if attempts were made to scrap Trident, leave NATO, or shrink the size of the armed forces. He told the *Sunday Times* that there would be consequences. He was quoted as saying:

> *"The army just wouldn't stand for it. The general staff would not allow a Prime Minister to jeopardise the security of this country and I think people would use whatever means possible, fair or foul, to prevent that."*[31]

It was an ominous warning that we were in for one hell of a fight. And we needed to prepare for it. We needed to make sure that the parliamentary party had enough people in it to back Corbyn up should he face difficulties as Prime Minister, and we needed strong grassroots support throughout the country. Corbyn, and the people around him, failed to grasp this.

Despite the threats and the insults, members felt invigorated. The vested interests that we were up against were daunting, but it invoked a sense of collective solidarity at the same time. We knew that we were under siege, and that was bringing out the best in people. There was a real feeling that the Labour Party was embarking on the 'moral crusade' to which Harold Wilson had famously referred in 1962.[32] But, as well as bringing out the best in decent grassroots party members, it also brought out the worst in Corbyn's critics and the storm clouds were gathering. The unhappy reality was that the Corbyn project was now in full retreat. The saboteurs in the party's bureaucratic machine, the right-wing PLP malcontents, the reactionary old guard in the CLPs, and the Zionist lobby could all smell blood following the NEC and conference capitulations in September 2018.

Members of the Socialist Campaign Group of Labour MPs (SCG) were frightened of their own shadows. For example, when Naomi Wimborne-Idrissi, JVL's media officer, asked me if I could arrange a meeting between the SCG and senior JVL officials, SCG members were reluctant. They said that if we invited JVL, we would also have to invite the JLM. It wasn't clear to me how they'd reached that conclusion. I stressed that JVL were our allies, that it was our meeting, and that we could invite whomsoever we wanted. We were not accountable to the racist JLM. Eventually, a meeting was agreed, but it had to be an unofficial one and outside of the SCG's normal weekly meeting schedule. When it did eventually take place, only Grahame Morris and Lloyd Russell-Moyle joined me for the encounter.

No-platforming strategy flops

Once Parliament returned after the conference season, the demand for me to speak at meetings, to my surprise, increased. This prompted my opponents to invoke all sorts of deranged tactics against me, trying to get my speaking engagements cancelled. But when they realised that their efforts to intimidate organisers into revoking invitations to speak were failing miserably, they began to target proprietors of venues, instead. This, generally, was unsuccessful. On the odd occasion that they did succeed, an alternative location was always found. For example, when I was invited by Sheffield Labour Students (SLS) to speak at an event entitled 'Why We Need an Anti-War Government', there was a social media and on-campus campaign to get it stopped. The SLS committee was bombarded with complaints, and they were ultimately browbeaten into pulling the plug. The committee issued a statement saying that they were postponing the meeting indefinitely, until the then-ongoing Scotland Yard police investigation into allegations of Judeophobia within the Labour Party had been resolved. The Metropolitan Police had launched a criminal investigation following allegations of Judeophobic hate crimes within the party, that were allegedly contained in a leaked 'dossier'. The LBC radio station had obtained a copy of the 'dossier' and had passed it to Cressida Dick, the Met's Commissioner at the time, when she appeared on one of their programmes. A police spokesperson had subsequently stated that, *"A criminal investigation has commenced into some of the allegations within the documentation. Early investigative advice is being sought from the Crown Prosecution Service".*[33]

This had the desired effect by those who had produced the 'dossier', as it gave the hostile corporate media an excuse to run yet more negative headlines. But after the event on the university campus was cancelled, Sheffield Labour Left (SLL) stepped into the breach to host the meeting. They initially booked a conference room at the Jurys Inn Hotel, but the hotel cancelled the reservation after receiving several *"anonymous threats"*. However, SLL were *still* able to find an alternative venue, and they got Sheffield TUC to sponsor the meeting as well. It was eventually held at the Sheffield Trades Club on the date for which the event had originally been planned, and the adverse publicity increased the expected attendance.

On another occasion, I was due to speak at Cities of London and Westminster CLP, who lost access to a venue after the Zionist lobby put the frighteners on. But as the constituency covered the Palace of Westminster, I was able to host the meeting myself in a room in Portcullis House. There was clearly a concerted effort being waged in universities across the country to pile on the pressure against me. Cities of London and Westminster CLP itself was put under enormous pressure for inviting me to speak. Labour student bodies in London passed motions to boycott campaigning in the marginal seat, including Birkbeck, LSE, UCL, and KCL. The Birkbeck group posted a statement on Twitter, saying:

> *"Due to @WestminsterCLP's invitation of anti-Semite Chris Williamson to speak, Birkbeck Labour have immediately ceased all support for their campaign. We urge other Labour societies to join us until he is uninvited and an apology issued. Anti-Semitism has no place in our party."*[34]

The Labour group at the LSE also posted a statement saying:

> *"Following Westminster CLPs invite to Chris Williamson MP to speak, we follow @UCLlabour in no longer campaigning in the CLP until the invitation is rescinded and an apology issued. Antisemitism is not acceptable in any form within our party, and we condemn it completely."*[35]

These fraudulent 'antisemitism' claims had all the features of the slanderous statements that were made against the OULC by the Union of Jewish (UJS) students in 2016. I don't doubt that the UJS were involved in the campaign against me, too. The JLM were certainly implicated and *LabourList* reported that they'd even met with London Labour students to discuss my invitation from the CLP.

The Scotland Yard investigation that was used as a pretext to cancel the Sheffield meeting was an indication of the lengths to which the Zionist lobby were prepared to go in destroying the Corbyn project. The fact that the Metropolitan Police, an instrument of the British state, willingly participated in a partisan effort to undermine Britain's Official Opposition was reminiscent of the tactics deployed by tyrannical regimes around the world. And they were doing it at the behest of a hostile foreign regime. The Zionist BoD worked overtime to destabilise Corbyn's leadership and went out of their way to malign me at every turn. We know from the 2020 annual report of the BoD trustees that they have *"strengthened their links to the Israeli Ministry of Strategic Affairs and the [Israel Occupation Forces] Spokesperson Department"*.[36]

An Israeli human rights lawyer suggested that Israel's hand was behind the attacks on Jeremy Corbyn. The lawyer, Eitay Mack, was also concerned about ties between two British ministries and the BoD, the Community Security Trust, and Labour Friends of Israel.[37] Together with the then Israeli Prime Minister, Benjamin Netanyahu – who took to Twitter to attack Jeremy Corbyn[38] – the evidence of Israeli state involvement in trying to subvert democracy in Britain is overwhelming. Were they the ones behind the 'dossier'? In January 2020, Cressida Dick confirmed that five files had been passed to the CPS but, as far as I know, nothing came of them. This episode should send shivers down the spine of everyone who cares about our democracy.

Mudslingers go for broke

Whilst the 'antisemitism' hysteria continued to spread, I was doing my best to fight a rear-guard action. Towards the end of 2018, I was invited to speak at a fundraising dinner for Labour's outstanding Bournemouth East parliamentary candidate, Corrie Drew. The event took place at Bournemouth AFC's football stadium on the first day of the Christmas and New Year parliamentary recess. It was a huge success. The club's assistant manager also spoke, and there was a large and enthusiastic number of attendees. But that positivity was overshadowed the following day by more concocted objections from the usual suspects. They were complaining about a petition that I'd shared on Twitter. It opposed the Blockheads being barred from performing at a council venue in Islington because a celebrated saxophonist, Gilad Atzmon, was due to perform with them.

A few minutes after I posted the tweet, I was contacted by Asa Winstanley from the *Electronic Intifada*. He was concerned that my tweet would be weaponised against me because of Gilad Atzmon's public statements, of which I was unaware at the time. In fact, I'd never heard of Gilad Atzmon before being asked to share the petition. I was told that he was an ex-Israeli soldier who was pro-Palestinian and highly critical of Israel and was therefore being barred from performing because of the 'antisemitism' delirium. But, after my exchange with Winstanley, I deleted the tweet, about 12 minutes after I'd posted it. I also posted an apology. However, that didn't stop the troll farms and individual opponents from launching another assault against me, resulting in my tweet trending on Twitter. The feigned furore was because of Atzmon's political opinions, which had drawn criticisms from pro-Palestine activists and Zionists alike. But he wasn't making a speech at a political rally. He was merely playing his saxophone with his band. Nevertheless, the maximalist strategy employed by the Zionist lobby – which seeks to eradicate its opponents from public life – rendered Atzmon's musical performance a legitimate target.

The following month, in January 2019, the febrile atmosphere intensified still further with even more preposterous accusations. As Holocaust Memorial Day approached, I had a photograph taken of me signing the Holocaust Educational Trust's (HET) Book of Commitment in the House of Commons. Almost every single MP does this every year. I then posted the photograph with the following message on social media:

"It is Holocaust Memorial Day on Sunday. Hatred and bigotry led to the unimaginable horrors of the Holocaust. We must never forget and always strive to build a better, peaceful and compassionate world through love and solidarity."[39]

Bizarrely, this led to yet another hysterical pile on, which included an open letter being sent to me by the chair of the JLC, Jonathan Goldstein. He claimed that he was *"disgusted"* that I had signed the Book of Commitment.[40] The pro-Israel TV presenter, Rachel Riley, joined in the scrimmage, tweeting:

"To coin a phrase: Hands off our grief @DerbyChrisW Chris Williamson's record on antisemitism is of the lowest regard with the Jewish community, this'll be seen by many as a baiting spit in the face to those fighting hatred".[41]

Even by Riley's standards, the hyperbole contained in that tweet was off the scale. But it appears that she has form for making gratuitous and unfounded public accusations about 'antisemitism', and her celebrity status means that it reaches a wider audience. In my view, she has proven to be a valuable asset of the UK's Israel lobby in their attempts to delegitimise anti-imperialist activists. On the day I was initially suspended, in February 2019, she shared a tweet from the BoD making a ridiculous complaint about me *"hosting a film by Jackie Walker"*.[42] Riley added the caption, *"Full title Jew-baiter Chris Williamson"*.[43] The fallout from the Book of Commitment incident demonstrated that my Zionist opponents were prepared to weaponise everything and anything I did, in order to destroy my parliamentary platform.

Judas Jennie

As the weeks went on, the odium I was incurring from pro-Israel extremists and their right-wing allies in the PLP was reaching fever-pitch. I received a phone call from Karie Murphy to ask if I would be willing to meet with Jennie Formby to discuss the complaints being made about me. I told her I would be delighted to do so.

At that point, I still thought Formby was an ally. She had always been very friendly up until then. I remember – when I was standing to be selected as Labour's candidate for Derbyshire Police and Crime Commissioner in 2016 – that Formby overruled the local Unite political committee after a full-time official in Derby, Tony Tinley, had tried to fix the nomination against me. She was a senior officer at Unite's head office at that time. Moreover, just after I'd been confirmed as Labour's candidate for the 2017 general election, Formby sent me an unsolicited message of support. She wrote, *"Brilliant news you've been reselected … wish I lived closer so I could campaign for you but still plenty to do down here"*. The following year, she privately told me that she was putting herself forward to be Labour's general secretary. She also said that she was concerned about Momentum's founder, Jon Lansman, who was trying to derail her bid after announcing that he wanted to be general secretary himself.[44] She said he was *"behaving disgracefully … Corbyn cannot have someone with such a massive ego as GS, this is about the project not self-promotion (which I don't do very well!!)"*. She confided in me about her frustration with Lansman's efforts to take the position. She said, *"Shame Jon Lansman is briefing so unpleasantly against me, it's not exactly comradely and the right-wing of course love it"*. When I told her that I thought Lansman should stop his unacceptable shenanigans, and that her appointment would *"warm the hearts of hundreds of thousands of members"*, she responded effusively, saying, *"Cheers Chris, that means a lot"*. Then, exactly one year before she suspended me, Formby complained to me that Lansman was *"a hypocrite"*. She told me he *"sent me a text ... saying I must go for the job and I'd be brilliant!"*.

The last friendly private communication I received from her was in April 2018. It was about a PLP meeting I'd missed because I was in the Commons supporting Corbyn in a debate about Syria. She wrote, *"You would have enjoyed last week's PLP (not) but were quite rightly prioritising Syria"*.[45] She also referred to the 'antisemitism' issue, saying *"a lot of my time is changing structures so the whole party works together, as well as dealing with AS, so hopefully things will calm down a bit"*. However, far from damping things down, she poured petrol on the fire that had been set by Labour's political arsonists.

It was quite an eye-opener to witness her hostility towards me when we met in Parliament in early February 2019. Karie Murphy was also in attendance, but she didn't contribute much to the discussion. When I arrived, Formby was already sitting down. I sat at one end of a long table, and Murphy sat at the other, whilst Formby sat at the side halfway between us. She looked tired. The meeting did not go well. Formby told me that she received more complaints about me than every other member of the Labour Party put together. I said, if that's true, that's simply proof of a concerted smear campaign against me. She admitted that the complaints were nonsense but, when I suggested that she should *"tell them to fuck the fuck off"*, she was exasperated. She was at pains to point out that they'd not taken any action on the complaints. But I countered by saying, *"Why would you Jennie? You've just acknowledged that they're a pile of shite"*.

The conversation zig-zagged around different aspects of the witch-hunt. She then turned to the Democracy Roadshow, enquiring, *"Why do you have to attend so many meetings?"*, before patronisingly proclaiming, *"You're not Jeremy, you know"*. I then went into some detail about the content of my speeches at the rallies. I stressed how well my presentations were being received all over the country, with members leaving meetings fired up and more determined to fight for a Corbyn-led Labour government. But both she and Murphy looked conspicuously unimpressed, and Formby rudely retorted, *"But, if I was an MP, I'd be pissed off if you came into my constituency"*. It was obvious from this encounter that neither of them was interested in building a genuine mass social movement. They were both obsessed with the Westminster bubble, and they couldn't see beyond its ramparts. Two weeks later, Formby revealed her true colours when she suspended me from the party.

The dam starts to crack

With the benefit of hindsight, it's clear that the couple of weeks or so in February 2019, between my tumultuous meeting with Jennie Formby and my eventual suspension, were the most crucial in my downfall. The sheer pressure against me was becoming unsustainable.

On Sunday 10 February 2019, I attended the premiere of the documentary *WitchHunt* in London. The film revealed the distortions surrounding the attempts to expel Momentum's former vice-chair, Jackie Walker, from the Labour Party.[46] At the request of Jewish Voice for Labour (JVL), I booked a committee room in Parliament to screen the film for the benefit of MPs. JVL were also conscious of security concerns, and they wanted a safe place to hold the screening. They'd had to abandon a previous attempt to show it at a fringe event during the 2018 Labour Party conference because of bomb threats from Zionist extremists. On the morning of 25 February 2019, a young man from Corbyn's office asked me to attend and speak at the PLP that evening because Corbyn was also going to be present to talk about Brexit. I asked if he was sure about Corbyn wanting me to be there because most of the PLP hated me and Corbyn already had a hard time at these meetings. But he insisted that Corbyn needed some friendly faces in the room. I duly complied with the request. As soon as Corbyn had finished his presentation, I indicated that I would like to speak. But the chair, John Cryer, didn't call me until the proceedings were almost over. By that time, the meeting had degenerated into another hatefest.

Whilst the focus was supposed to be about Brexit, the issue of 'antisemitism' was raised almost immediately. Ruth Smeeth was called to speak before me, and she used the opportunity to unleash a stream of invective about the fact that *WitchHunt* was due to be shown in the Palace of Westminster. She said, *"It has been brought to my attention that one of our colleagues has booked a committee room to show the Jackie Walker film."* At that point, there was an exaggerated sharp intake of breath by around 250 of the 400 or so attendees. It felt like they were sucking out all of the oxygen in the room. It was akin to the audience reaction at a pantomime when the principal boy talks about some dastardly deed by the villainous character. She then went on to say, in a menacing tone, *"I don't know who it is yet, but I can assure you I will find out."* A sarcastic chorus of, *"Well done, Chris!"* then erupted from around the room. Their reaction was so over the top and farcical, it wouldn't have been out of character had they gone into full pantomime audience mode and called out to Smeeth, *"He's behind you!"*. I sat there, unmoved, as they indulged in their asinine antics.

When I was eventually called to speak, I was greeted by a cacophony of sounds by a group of bellowing bullies who tried to howl me down. But I ploughed on regardless. I had to shout at the top of my voice to make myself heard. I saw Corbyn nudging the chair to get him to call the rowdy rabble to order on several occasions. I started off my contribution by trying to be conciliatory. I suggested that we had all joined the Labour Party to fight for social justice at home and abroad (although, on reflection, most of them in that room were not interested in either). But when I quoted a passage from the late Jo Cox's maiden speech, in which she said that *"we have far more in common than that which divides us"*, most of the MPs and peers in attendance went apoplectic. It was an incredible spectacle, and it provided a field day for the corporate media hacks who were all gathered outside Committee Room 14 where the PLP meeting was being held. The volume of the hecklers meant that I had to raise my voice to such an extent that the assembled reporters could hear every word. One of them, Paul Waugh, the *HuffPost*'s executive editor of politics, posted a running commentary of my speech on Twitter. His first offering said, *"Chris Williamson making v strong defence of Corbyn at PLP. Heckled by MPs"*. This was followed by one saying, *"Oohs and jeers from some MPs as he says "As Jo Cox said 'there's more that unites us than divides us'." Williamson has backed a Labour Brexit"*. His final tweet in the thread stated, *"One Lab MP left mid-Williamson: 'I can't bear listening to any more of that c*nt.' PLP in action folks"*.[47]

Following the PLP shouting match, we held a Core Group meeting where Corbyn's staff were in attendance. The issue of the *WitchHunt* film was raised, and John McDonnell said he wasn't sure if it was his office who had booked the room. Amy Jackson was agitated about it, which wasn't surprising because the default position for the leader's office was always to crumble in response to smear merchants and bullies. She said to me, *"Please don't tell me it's you that booked a room to show the Jackie Walker film."* I refused to indulge her and laughed off her question without answering it.

The following day, however, when I was showing the committee room I had booked to Naomi Wimborne-Idrissi and Glyn Secker from JVL, Jennie Formby contacted me about the booking. She issued a veiled threat that, if I didn't cancel it, she would suspend me from the party. Whilst I complied with her request, it made no difference. She suspended me anyway the following day.

Formby was under pressure from the PLP and the party's deputy leader, Tom Watson, who the previous September had publicly said Formby should quit if the 'antisemitism' issue wasn't dealt with by Christmas 2018.[48] Meanwhile, Watson and his PLP cronies were doing everything in their power to exaggerate the invented crisis to make sure it continued on. Just three days before Formby suspended me, Watson appeared to issue more threats via the corporate media. He said that he was going to *"take personal charge of antisemitism and bullying complaints made by MPs"* and that he would *"hold the party's management of the complaints to account"*.[49] He had no constitutional standing to do so. But that didn't matter. His statement served its purpose in generating another set of negative media stories.

Parliamentary piffle

Exactly one week before I was suspended, a debate on 'Antisemitism in Modern Society' was arranged on the floor of the House of Commons. The purpose of the debate was a pretext to launch a volley of abuse against Jeremy Corbyn. All the MPs who spoke in that debate were united in their support for the apartheid State of Israel, and nearly all of them harboured a visceral hatred of Corbyn. Poor Jeremy had to sit on the frontbench, listening to a series of splenetic tirades from a bunch of bad faith actors who were playing to the gallery. MPs from both Labour Friends of Israel (LFI) and Conservative Friends of Israel (CFI) operated like a parliamentary tag team during the debate, in an attempt to land as many blows against Corbyn as possible. LFI is extremely influential in the PLP. Around half of all Labour MPs were members of the group at that time. The way LFI operates has led many to conclude that it is merely a front for the Israeli Embassy. Michael Rubin, who is a director of LFI,[50] told an undercover Al Jazeera reporter that the outfit worked *"really, really closely together"* with the Embassy, and that, *"It's just publicly we just try to keep the LFI as a separate identity to the Embassy"*.[51] CFI boasts an even bigger proportion of Tory MPs, with around 80 per cent of them signed up.[52]

In confronting those bigots, Corbyn should have adopted a different approach. Instead of turning the other cheek and allowing those pretenders to get away with making outrageously false statements, they should have been challenged there and then. The white flag approach meant that pro-Israel MPs were falling over themselves to kick Corbyn. Dame Margaret Hodge for example, claimed that:

> *"under the leadership of [Jeremy Corbyn], a platform has ... been given for antisemitism, which was always present on the hard-left fringes, but has now moved into the mainstream of my party. That is why we have experienced a surge in abuse against us – abuse particularly targeted against female Jewish MPs".* [53]

Luciana Berger, who had resigned from the Labour Party two days earlier, used the debate to claim that she had received *"thousands of messages of anti-Semitic abuse and hate"*.[54] But she didn't bother to clarify that none of them was from grassroots Labour Party members. Consequently, her experience of online abuse by far-right trolls caused her to reach the perverse *"conclusion that the Labour party [was] institutionally antisemitic"*.[55] Dame Louise Ellman said, *"the Labour party allowed the antisemitic bullying"* of Berger, and she claimed that *"today's Labour Party is perfectly at ease with anti-Jewish conspiracy theories*".[56] And ex-Labour MP Ivan Lewis, who resigned after being accused by a 19-year-old woman of sexual harassment,[57] had the gall to complain about what he described as Corbyn's *"longstanding support for the hard left's demonisation of Zionism"*.[58] He bemoaned the fact that grassroots members in the Blairite Berger's constituency had passed a vote of no confidence in her. But that only came after years of them putting up with her right-wing bile against Corbyn. Lewis tried to suggest this implied the beginning of a sinister plot against Jews in Britain.[59] These calumnies could, and should, have been rebutted.

The BBC ups the ante

The weekend before I was suspended, I was interviewed on Radio 4's *Today Programme* by Nick Robinson, who tried, and failed, every which way to make the fake 'antisemitism' indictment stand up. Later that day, he returned to the topic on Twitter,[60] making a statement that he subsequently had to withdraw after the BBC upheld a complaint about it. Many of those who'd heard the original interview were unimpressed by his interrogation techniques.[61] But he continued to bring up our encounter in the months that followed. In a speech that he gave eight months after he interviewed me, he said:[62]

> *"Chris Williamson told me on the* Today Programme *he's never seen antisemitism in the Labour Party ... Well, I've seen it Chris, the people in this room have seen it Chris, the people in the Labour Party fighting it have seen it Chris, and we will never stop pointing it out."*[63]

Despite his position as one of the BBC's most senior and experienced political journalists, Robinson's rhetorical rants simply don't stand up to scrutiny. Less than a fortnight before he spoke to me, the official figures relating to alleged Judeophobia had been published indicating that a negligible number of members had been implicated. Of those who had been accused, only 12 had been 'found guilty' of 'antisemitism'.[64] At least one of those 12 was himself Jewish, and the son of Holocaust survivors. Another was the son of a Rabbi. I don't want to accuse Robinson of being a partisan liar, but his thundering declarations that he and multifarious others had *"seen"* 'antisemitism' in the party stretch credulity beyond breaking point.

The Corbyn project, which had reached a high in 2017, and which had been fortified in 2018 after winning a majority on the NEC and then taking the general secretary position, had, by early 2019, begun to sharply decline. Corbyn's insurgent nature, which had won him two leadership elections, had been chipped away by a team of useless and incompetent advisers. At the 2018 Labour Party conference, which represented the conclusion of the months-long Democracy Review, Corbyn could have implemented whatever rule changes he wanted. He could have remoulded the Labour Party in his own image, shattering the bureaucracy created under Neil Kinnock and Tony Blair. He could have solidified the left's position at the top of Labour politics for a generation. Instead, alongside machine politicians like Len McCluskey and quislings like Jennie Formby, he initiated the beginning of the end for the very movement that he had helped to bring into existence in 2015.

CHAPTER THIRTEEN

BETRAYAL

On 27 February 2019, my 43 years as a devoted Labour activist would be brought to an ignominious end. It's a day that I will never forget.

The furore that led to my suspension from the Labour Party had started the day before. Yet another ridiculous uproar had erupted, this time about a speech I had given to a large Sheffield Momentum rally the previous weekend. I had addressed the never-ending 'antisemitism' aspersions being cast against the party:

> *"We are not a racist party, are we? We're not an 'antisemitic' party. We are the party that stood up to racism throughout our entire history. And now we – Jeremy, me and others – are being accused of being bigots, of being 'antisemites'. And it's almost as if we're living within the pages of George Orwell's* Nineteen Eighty-Four.

> *"The party that's done more to stand up to racism is now being demonised as a racist, bigoted party! And I've got to say I think our party's response has been partly responsible for that, you know? Because, in my opinion – I never have, I've got to say – we've backed off far too much, we've given too much ground, we've been too apologetic. What have we got to apologise for? For being an anti-racist party?*

> *"And we've done more to actually address the scourge of anti-Semitism than any other political party – any other political party. And, yet, we are being traduced, and grassroots members are being traduced. And I'm not going to stand for, or tolerate that, in any way shape or form and I will not allow these people to slag-off decent, hard-working, socialist members of our party. I'm just not going to do it because it's an absolute bloody travesty what they're saying about party members".* [1]

My speech had been well received by the crammed meeting. There had been a huge amount of warmth, positivity, and enthusiasm about taking our socialist and anti-imperialist agenda forward, and so the meeting itself was a triumph. In fact, it was considered so successful that the Momentum group posted a video of my entire speech on their Facebook page alongside an upbeat write-up about the day.

It wasn't until Liz Bates, who was the Westminster correspondent for the *Yorkshire Post* at the time, picked up on the speech that it became a news story. Interestingly, before arriving at the *Yorkshire Post*, Bates had worked as a communications officer for right-wing Labour MP John Healey. That Bates had, it seems, been probing through footage of me in the first place shows how obsessed both right-wing lobbyists and media hacks had become in trying to find a pretext to take me down. She clipped an out-of-context, 43-second extract of my speech and posted it on Twitter. In a sensationalist Tweet that would have been worthy of a hack working for Murdoch's *Sun*, she wrote:

> *"WATCH: Chris Williamson tells a Sheffield Momentum meeting that Labour has been "too apologetic" about anti-Semitism..."*

As is self-evident from my remarks, I had said nothing of the sort. I had said that Labour should stop apologising given that, in fact, the party had done an excellent job of tackling the *"scourge"* of Judeophobia. Bates, however, framed my remarks in a completely disingenuous and cynical way. She later posted a thread on Twitter,[2] which included a link to her highly partial and extremely prejudicial *Yorkshire Post* story.[3] It was a smear. But the veracity of Bates's reportage was of no interest to the PLP's right-wing vultures, nor to the Israel lobby who seized on her misrepresentations like a pack of hungry hyenas. Their clamouring had no effect on me. This wasn't the first time I'd been put through the wringer by these morons. I went to bed as they continued to rage on, thinking that they would have regained their senses by the morning.

I woke up to discover that the wolves were still at it. I had become the target of a media feeding frenzy with demands for Corbyn to throw me out of the party. I was still in bed when I received a curt call from Amy Jackson of the leader's office on that Wednesday morning. When I answered the phone, she said, *"You're leading every fucking news broadcast, you need to come and see us in LOTO"*. So, I had a shower, made some breakfast, and got ready to face the day. After clearing a few emails on my laptop, I set out for Westminster at around 10:30am, wondering what the day had in store for me. As I sat on the train that morning, I had no idea how big the shitstorm was going to get. When I made my way up the escalator to Portcullis House from the Tube, I saw the party chair, Ian Lavery, talking to the *Daily Mirror's* Kevin Maguire at the top of the stairs. Lavery greeted me with a big hug and urged me to keep going. Right on cue, there was more faux outrage from the usual herd of right-wing MPs. They considered such an open display of friendship towards me to be beyond the pale. The *Northern Echo* had reported the reaction of one of them. Newcastle North MP, Catherine McKinnell, said that Lavery's embrace was *"disturbing if true"*.[4] It was disturbing that Lavery had given me a hug?

When I eventually arrived at Corbyn's office, an ashen-faced Amy Jackson met me in the reception area. I asked if Seumas Milne was joining us. *"I'm dealing with it"*, she insisted. After I had agreed to issue a statement, we were joined by Milne and Karie Murphy. All three of them were in full retreat mode. Milne said that Corbyn needed to get on the front foot, as the issue was likely to come up at PMQs. He felt that Corbyn should pre-emptively announce that I was to be investigated; if a penalty were imposed after Theresa May had called for action against me, Corbyn would look weak. At that point Murphy exploded. *"Fuck off, Seumas"*, she said, adding, *"You know Jeremy said he wants a line drawn under this with a statement"*.

At no point did they consider defending me. Clearly, the pathetic poltroons in Corbyn's office were about as much use as the proverbial chocolate teapot. They simply folded in the face of the synchronised onslaught, as they always did. My comments at the Sheffield rally had been perfectly legitimate. If only they had reflected on their previous debacles, like with Ken Livingstone, perhaps they would have realised that they were simply playing into the hands of their internal and external enemies. But it seems they were so focussed on 'optics' and 'gaining power' that any deviation from their whitewashed plan had to be quashed.

What they failed to understand is the fact that, whatever they had done, the corporate media, the Establishment, and Labour right-wingers were determined to ensure that Corbyn would never become Prime Minister. To throw his praetorian guard under the bus was the worst possible response to that triumvirate of counter-revolutionaries.

Before coming to the meeting, I'd made the mistake of not watching the full recording of my speech. Without knowing exactly what I'd said, I lost confidence in my position. I wondered whether, perhaps, I had misspoken and unintentionally said something untoward. So, I agreed to make a qualified apology as a favour to Corbyn and his team. When I subsequently watched the video, I realised I had said nothing wrong after all. The mood was so oppressive that it initially made me doubt myself. I regret yielding to the pressure because my qualified apology was weaponised by Tom Watson's PLP posse, which was then accentuated by the corporate media and the Zionist lobby.

After issuing my apology, I thought it best not to go into the Commons chamber for PMQs that day. I stayed in the room where I had just met with Corbyn's team, and I watched it on the TV. Sure enough, Theresa May did indeed call for me to be suspended in response to a question from the then deputy chair of the Conservative Party, James Cleverly.[5] Amy Jackson stayed in the room with me whilst PMQs was taking place. Shortly after May's interaction with Cleverly, Formby decided to launch a formal investigation against me. Formby had succumbed to the coercive tactics of the PLP, corporate media, and the Israel lobby. Meanwhile, Corbyn sat on his hands and the so-called 'Socialist Campaign Group of Labour MPs' couldn't bring themselves to 'campaign' against this blatant injustice against one of their own. They did not possess a shred of personal loyalty. I wasn't even allowed to attend any further meetings of the SCG.

Many of my erstwhile 'friends' from the 2010–2015 Parliament were falling over themselves to castigate me, including Ed Miliband and Harriet Harman. In fact, an unimpeachable source told me that Miliband had called Corbyn to say that, unless I were suspended by the end of the day, *"30 MPs are going to walk"*. Corbyn should have welcomed their departure. If he had called Miliband's bluff, I very much doubt that all, or even any, of the 30

MPs in question would have left. Those characters are self-serving careerists, and they knew that, unless they stood as a Labour candidate, none of them would be returned to Parliament at the next election. I also have it on good authority that John McDonnell had been spooked by the recent departure of the Independent Group of MPs. The week before I'd been suspended, seven Blairites had resigned from the Labour Party at a highly-orchestrated press conference. Instead of welcoming their departure and using the opportunity to fill their seats with pro-Corbyn loyalists, the wind was taken out of the leadership's sails. I understand that McDonnell was applying pressure to Corbyn, alongside his protégé Owen Jones, to appease the PLP. For his part, Jones apparently issued a public statement against me because he didn't feel that he could *"stay silent"*. Perhaps Jones felt compelled to attack me because he was taking counsel from various individuals and groups that I would describe as 'Zionist'. The likes of Jewdas (a self-styled radical Jewish group), Jon Lansman, Michael Segalov, Rhea Wolfson, and Rachel Shabi were seemingly whispering in his ears.

But if Formby had hoped that my suspension would give her some credit among the PLP, she would soon get a rude awakening. At the next PLP meeting, she was savaged by a group of rancorous Labour MPs who smelled blood in the water and were going to continue inflicting as much damage as possible.[6] One Jewish comrade said to me, *"The problem with Jeremy is that he is treating his friends as his enemies and his enemies as his friends"*. She was completely right.

Joining in the attacks against me, the Tribune Group of Labour MPs published an open letter to Jennie Formby, signed by 38 MPs calling on her to suspend me.[7] The list of signatories looked like a roll call of the PLP's mediocre no-marks, who strolled through their parliamentary career making very little meaningful impact. Most people had never heard of many of them, even in their own constituencies. The chair of the group, Clive Efford, had been an MP since 1997. He was typical of the time-servers in the PLP, who tend to keep their heads down, blow with the wind, and do whatever the whips tell them to do. The Tribune Group is basically a self-preservation society. But their plan to obtain some electoral advantage by publicly distancing themselves from me came badly unstuck. It carried no electoral dividend whatsoever. Six of the 38 Tribune group members who signed the letter still went on to lose their seats in the general election later that year.

Many of Labour's leading lights also joined in the scrum to land their own blows against me, including London Mayor Sadiq Khan and GMB leader Tim Roache.[8] It would probably be easier to list the senior labour movement figures who hadn't joined in the efforts to get me suspended! I don't particularly believe in karma but Roache, as I mentioned previously, subsequently had to resign from his own position amid allegations of sexual assault, cover up, and a 'casting couch' culture at the GMB.[9] That wasn't the poetic justice I was seeking, but it highlights why the democratisation of the labour movement is so important. These malpractices are only able to fester when the leadership becomes detached from the members they're supposed to represent.

No more 'journeys'

After PMQs, before I left Corbyn's office, Amy Jackson had told me that I needed to *"go on a journey like Naz Shah had"*. The phrase had become a euphemism for undergoing a political lobotomy. One was supposed to take some time out for 'reflection', genuflect before the Israel lobby, kiss the ring, beg for mercy, and eventually make a comeback.

Naz Shah had been suspended by the party in 2016 for a couple of Facebook posts prior to being elected as an MP in 2015. So, she had been at the centre of her own media storm nearly three years prior to mine. The difference, however, was that she was prepared to make a craven apology for posts that the media had labelled as 'antisemitic'. Her supposedly 'highly offensive' transgressions in 2014 were to share a graphic from the acclaimed Jewish academic Norman Finkelstein's website, and a quote from Dr Martin Luther King Jr. The website image showed an outline of the State of Israel, superimposed on a map of the US, with the headline, 'Solution for Israel-Palestine conflict – relocate Israel into United States'. Shah had added the comment *"problem solved"*.[10] That was a perfectly reasonable and moderate observation to make in the face of such brutality by the Israeli colonial regime. After all, the US contributes several billion USD every year towards the State of Israel's military, and billions more in loan guarantees.[11] As for the Dr MLK Jr quote Shah had shared, that was also misrepresented by the media. The quote was taken from his 'Letter from a Birmingham Jail', *"We should never forget that everything Adolf Hitler did in Germany was 'legal'"*, to which she added the hashtag *"#ApartheidIsrael"*. Apparently, this was 'antisemitic' because it compared the State of Israel to Nazi Germany. The simple point was that legality is not the same as morality. Just because an apartheid system is ostensibly 'legal' in the State of Israel does not excuse the evil of that system. To point this out was to supposedly be a 'Jew hater'.

There was no way that I was going to fold like a deck of cards as Shah had done in the face of a coordinated smear operation by the Zionist lobby. The statement she issued in April 2016 on the day that the story broke was straight out of the leader's office handbook on grovelling apologies:

> *"I deeply regret the hurt I have caused by comments made on social media before I was elected as an MP. I made these posts at the height of the Gaza conflict in 2014, when emotions were running high around the Middle East conflict. But that is no excuse for the offence I have given, for which I unreservedly apologise.*
>
> *"In recognition of that offence I have stepped down from my role as PPS to the Shadow Chancellor, John McDonnell. I will be seeking to expand my existing engagement and dialogue with Jewish community organisations, and will be stepping up my efforts to combat all forms of racism, including antisemitism".*[12]

I would have thought that that was enough humble pie to consume for one day. But, 24 hours after posting her apology on Twitter, she was on her feet in the House of Commons seeking permission from the Speaker to make a statement to apologise to MPs. She was clearly desperate to maintain her parliamentary career and seemed willing to subordinate her support for the Palestinian struggle to the goal of regaining the Labour whip. That appeared to trump any notion of self-respect or willingness to use her parliamentary platform to expose the racist settler-colonial ideology of the apartheid State of Israel. She told MPs:

> *"I wholeheartedly apologise to the House for the words that I used before I became a Member of Parliament. I accept and understand that the words that I used caused upset and hurt to the Jewish community, and I deeply regret that. Antisemitism is racism, full stop. ...*
>
> *"I am grateful, and very thankful, for the support and advice that I have received from many Jewish friends and colleagues, advice on which I intend to act. I truly regret what I did, and ... I sincerely hope – that the House will accept my profound apology".* [13]

The Speaker, John Bercow, seemed rather perplexed that she felt the need to use a point of order to put her apology on the record in the Commons. After her short statement, he simply said, *"The Honourable Lady has found an opportunity to apologise. I thank her for what she has said, and it will have been noted by the House. I think that that is all I should say on this occasion"*. It was humiliating nonsense, of course, but it had the desired effect. Three months later, she was re-admitted to the party and the whip was restored. But it was a degrading harbinger of just how bad things were going to get. It indicated to the Zionist lobby that they could exert considerable influence over the Labour Party and were being given enormous latitude to demean senior Labour figures.

When PMQs had finished, I made my way to my Westminster office to tell my team what had happened and to call my family and close friends. The Derby Labour Party agent, James Shires, had come down from Derby in the morning, and so we went for a coffee outside the parliamentary estate to avoid prying media eyes. We walked down Victoria Street to a Caffè Nero, which seemed far enough away to evade the attention of the corporate hacks. I didn't know it, but I was in for a pleasant surprise. When we got to the counter, the woman who was serving was incredibly supportive. *"Keep going, we're all behind you"*, she said. It was a beautiful experience to be so warmly welcomed by a working class woman who was a complete stranger, and it was a perfect antidote to the smear-fest to which I was being subjected. However, Paddy Tipping, a former Labour MP and the Nottinghamshire Police and Crime Commissioner at the time, was sitting at one of the tables. He provided a foil to her kindness and encouragement.

Both Shires and I knew him quite well, but he pointedly turned his back before I was able to greet him. The contrast between real people and right-wing politicians was perfectly encapsulated in that café on that fateful day.

Walking by on the other side

Later that afternoon, I arranged to meet Paul Mallet, a close confidante, to plan how I was going to respond to Formby's formal investigation. I was sitting inside the Red Lion pub on Parliament Street, where I had sat with Marc Wadsworth 10 months earlier before escorting him to his expulsion meeting, when I received a call from Karie Murphy. I went outside to take the call, escaping the din of the pub. Murphy informed me that Formby had now suspended me. The street was heaving with patrons of the pub who had taken their drinks outside. Whilst I was still speaking to Murphy, I spotted a camera crew and a reporter from Sky News walking through the crowd. As I continued my conversation, they started filming in my direction. When I finished the call, an insistent Sky News hack, Tom Rayner, began firing questions at me.

> *"Mr Williamson, could I have a response to your suspension from the Labour Party. What do you make of it? ... Were you surprised that you got suspended after being told earlier that you were just being investigated? ... Have you spoken to Jeremy Corbyn or Jennie Formby? ... Have you spoken to them? Do you have any further apology? Do you want to add to your apology because that wasn't enough for many people? ... John Mann ... said you were 'an enabler of antisemitism in the Labour Party' ... But people want to know why you made the comments in the first place?"*[14]

In response to each question, I simply repeated that I would work within the party's processes to clear my name. I began to walk away, but Rayner followed me down the street, with his camera crew in tow. I then realised that I still had a glass in my hand from the pub, so I politely said, *"Excuse me, I just need to take my glass back"*. But, still, he persisted after I doubled back, firing questions like a Gatling gun. *"Do you think you will become a Labour MP again? ... Do you think you'll be a Labour MP again? ... Have you been reassured by Jeremy Corbyn's office that you will be reinstated?"*.[15] I thought the only live audience to the encounter were the crowd of bemused drinkers outside the pub, who began heckling the hack for interrogating me. Shouts of *"Leave him alone"* and *"Let him have a drink"* permeated the afternoon air as the motormouth continued his verbal blitz. I later discovered that the entire encounter was being beamed live on TV.

The party had clearly briefed the media before telling me about my fate, which is a common tactic deployed by its partisan bureaucrats. A couple of hours after that unpleasant discovery, I was on my way to the SCG's weekly meeting in a committee room near Westminster Hall when I bumped into Laura Pidcock in Portcullis House. Pidcock was the SCG's co-chair, and she was visibly distressed by what had happened to me. We spoke for about five or six minutes, during which time she made it clear that she didn't think it would be appropriate for me to attend any SCG meetings whilst I was suspended on the grounds that it's *"the Socialist Campaign Group of **Labour** MPs and we need to protect Jeremy"*. She said, *"You probably think that's really unfair",* which I most certainly did, but she added, *"Why don't you think about it overnight?"*. I was crestfallen by Pidcock's remarks, although I didn't let on to her, as she was already upset about the whole thing. I'm not sure that the SCG applied the same strictures to Corbyn when he was later suspended! In any case, when we finished our conversation, she went on over to the SCG meeting and I went back to my office with my tail between my legs.

The bottom had just fallen out of my world and my closest parliamentary comrades were abandoning me. I sat on my own in my office staring at the walls adorned with images of socialist icons like Rosa Luxemburg, Che Guevara, and Salvador Allende. It dawned on me that many of the socialists who had inspired me had been killed because of the stands that they'd taken. My tribulations paled by comparison. The only thing that my detractors could do to me was assassinate my character, but they weren't about to take my life. It put my situation into perspective. I didn't need to sleep on Pidcock's comment; it was obvious that the SCG were deserting me in the vain hope that, in doing so, the media maelstrom would calm down. It was yet another futile capitulation to the Zionist lobby and the right-wing PLP.

No criticism of Israel allowed

In the evening of that Wednesday, I went to see Naz Shah. We met at her London home, as she did not want to risk being seen speaking to me in a public location. When she was suspended in 2016, she had been the Parliamentary Private Secretary to John McDonnell. Her social media posts were revealed by the far-right blog *Guido Fawkes*.[16] The site freely admits that it was originally established *"purely to make mischief at the expense of politicians and for the founding author's own self-gratification"*.[17] Despite its dubious origins and grubby intentions, *Guido Fawkes* is given credibility by the mainstream media. Its dirt-digging dive into Shah's Facebook timeline was splashed across every national newspaper and broadcast channel in the country.

The fake furore by media commentators and politicians contrasted sharply with their comparatively muted response to Israel's 'Operation Protective Edge' offensive against Gaza, which occurred seven weeks after her original social media 'transgressions'. But, in the corporate media's newsrooms, their perverted priorities meant that Shah's impromptu interventions on social media merited more attention than Israel slaughtering men, women, and children in Gaza. Corbyn's response to the baying mob calling for her head was typically lame. He nourished the mindless media narrative, and he issued a completely counterproductive statement. He claimed, *"What Naz Shah did was offensive and unacceptable"*. But he must have known it was only offensive and unacceptable to Zionist racists.

When I spoke to Shah in her front room, she told me that she now realised what she had said *"was antisemitic"*. As I listened to her explain the political contortions she had gone through, I was reminded of the last scene in the classic 1970s film *One Flew Over the Cuckoo's Nest*. That was where the main character, Randle McMurphy, who had provided free-spirited resistance to Nurse Ratched's harsh hospital regime, ended up being lobotomised to shut him up. Shah's fate was comparable, except she had willingly submitted to the metaphorical lobotomy, which meant surrendering to the Zionist lobby to save her parliamentary career. That was not a path that I was prepared to tread. The day after I'd spoken to Shah, I tweeted the following message of thanks to the grassroots supporters who had been in touch to express their solidarity:

> *"I want to thank grassroots Labour Party members and supporters from the bottom of my heart for the incredible solidarity you have shown me over the last 48 hours. My message is this: Keep your eyes on the prize and hold on because #ChangeIsComing".*

The next time I saw Shah in the Commons, she asked why I had posted that message. She sounded exasperated with me and said that the Community Security Trust (CST), who were operating like some kind of Orwellian thought police were unhappy about it.

It was reported as long ago as 2011 that the CST was linked to Israel's Mossad spy agency.[18] The one thought I had had when Shah told me they were displeased with me was, *"Who the hell do they think they are?"*. However, I contained my irritation and pointed out that I had been asked to post something along those lines by Karie Murphy, who was concerned because members were threatening to resign over my suspension. At that point, I naïvely believed that the left could still prevail inside the Labour Party because we massively outnumbered the malcontents, and I wanted members to stay in the party.

It was the CST who had taken Shah on her 'journey' through their version of Room 101, where the thought police break 'thought-criminals' by coercing them into accepting the Zionist worldview without reservation. In evidence to the 2016 Home Affairs Select Committee inquiry into 'antisemitism', Mark Gardner from the CST said, *"I met Naz Shah and her contrition and confession of ignorance of the subject and her desire to learn and engage with the Jewish communities was exemplary"*.[19] I assume that the CST's hate for me was because, unlike Shah, I refused to be cowed by them. I guess 'thought criminals' like Jackie Walker, Tony Greenstein, and myself, who refuse to be 'politically rehabilitated', are deemed to be 'unpersons'. What I know for certain, though, is that every effort is deployed to drum people like us out of public life.

What I found surprising about the CST's involvement in the campaign against Corbyn is that it is, in fact, a registered charity, founded in 1994. And it receives huge sums from the public purse. Between 2015 and 2020 alone, it received government grants totalling almost £80 million *"to provide security measures at Jewish schools and synagogues"*.[20] Yet, despite its charitable status, the CST has arguably strayed well beyond that remit. It regularly disseminated disinformation against Corbyn personally, and the Labour Party in general, when he was leader. Lurid headlines were commonplace on its website, such as, *"Jeremy Corbyn and antisemitism: questions to answer"*.[21] On the day Corbyn was suspended in October 2020, another headline read, *"Report shows why British Jews' fear of Corbyn was not unfounded"*.[22] The CST even produced an absurd 52-page report entitled, *"Engine of Hate: the online networks behind the Labour Party's antisemitism crisis"*.[23] This nakedly biased and specious commentary by a supposed charity seems to violate the advice issued by the Charity Commission, which states that a charity *"must never support or oppose a particular political party"*.[24] Yet, no action has been taken against them. Compare this to the Charity Commission's treatment of huge swathes of Muslim charities, which were unfairly targeted under the regime of right-wing journalist, William Shawcross. Whilst Shawcross served as the Charity Commission's head, between 2012 and 2018, it launched sweeping investigations of Muslim charities, secretly labelling tens of them under the code *"extremism and radicalisation"*.[25] Real, state-sponsored Islamophobia was legitimised, whilst fake 'antisemitism' accusations were treated with the utmost seriousness.

My suspension from the party was initiated at the behest of a coterie of right-wing ideologues, Zionist extremists, and anti-Corbyn bureaucrats. Jeremy Corbyn, as leader of the party, could and should have stopped it. Corbyn's advisers should have never facilitated it. And my 'comrades' in the SCG could have immediately and forcefully spoken out against it. Just as I had sacrificed political capital to defend many of them and our socialist cause on innumerable occasions, they could have spent some of theirs to defend me. They refused. It was an utter betrayal.

CHAPTER FOURTEEN

"THE SILENCE OF OUR FRIENDS"

One of the most hurtful aspects of the whole sorry affair of my suspension was the absence of solidarity from supposed parliamentary comrades. On the day I was suspended, Jeremy Corbyn sent me a message just before midnight saying that he hoped I was alright and asked, *"When would be a good time to call?"*. I responded by saying that I'd cancelled all my appointments, so he could call any time the following day. The call never came. A few days later, Corbyn was assaulted outside a North London mosque. I sent a brief goodwill message and urged him to keep safe. He replied saying that we needed to keep each other safe, and he said he was looking forward to talking to me the following day. Again, no call came.

The only members of the Socialist Campaign Group (SCG) who made any attempt to offer proactive support were Laura Smith and Richard Burgon. Both of them kept in regular contact, but Smith was the most supportive. She told me that she had repeatedly urged the SCG to issue a collective solidarity statement, but that there was never sufficient support to do so. Significantly, at the last SCG meeting I'd attended the week before I was suspended, Smith had said that the SCG must do more to protect me. She said it wasn't fair that all the opprobrium was being directed at me. She wanted a discussion on what the SCG was going to do about it. But it was decided that there wasn't time to discuss it, and Burgon said it would be put higher on the agenda the following week. I later met with Laura Smith, just before the parliamentary summer recess, in an obscure pub in North London, to avoid the prying eyes of corporate media hacks. We spoke about the pitiful reaction of the SCG to my predicament, but I was encouraged when Smith said that she and one or two others were going to *"break cover"* soon and speak publicly in my support. She had previously said, *"I feel like a bag of shit for not publicly supporting you Chris, but the truth is I'm scared to do so on my own"*. However, for whatever reason, neither Smith nor anyone else in the SCG ever did break cover.

My spirits were lifted, however, by the outpouring of solidarity from grassroots members all over the country. The weekend following my suspension was the first of numerous soul-stirring experiences. I was sent some photographs from an anti-austerity rally in Haverfordwest, Pembrokeshire. The campaigners there had made placards with the slogan *"Solidarity with Chris Williamson"*. They were also asking participants to pose for a photo, holding another placard saying *"#IStandWithChrisWilliamson because..."*, with people filling in their own reasons. I was also encouraged to see the #IStandWithChrisWilliamson hashtag trending on Twitter.

From "burn neoliberalism" to burn Williamson

Despite the outpouring of support, I was feeling depressed and disconsolate in the immediate aftermath of my suspension. The fantastic solidarity from grassroots members was juxtaposed with the vitriol from right-wing MPs and the sound of silence from the SCG. So, the day after being suspended, it was comforting to receive a sympathetic text from the Norwich MP Clive Lewis, who I considered to be a friend. Lewis was one of only two MPs, the other one being Keith Vaz, who had previously joined me in offering support to Marc Wadsworth.

I remember strongly defending Lewis after he was criticised in 2017 for a comment that he posted on Twitter following the appalling Grenfell tragedy.[1] Lewis was justifiably angry about the way in which successive governments had embraced neoliberalism, resulting in safety standards being compromised by initiatives like compulsory competitive tendering and excessive deregulation. He posted a picture of the burned-out Grenfell Tower and wrote, *"Burn neoliberalism, not people"*.[2] After I had leapt to his defence on the BBC's *Daily Politics* programme, Lewis sent me a message thanking me for my support. He said BBC presenters were *"used to Labour MPs running away from anything controversial"*. He added that my intervention on his behalf, *"Made [him] giddy with happiness"*. But, a year-and-a-half later, there was no reciprocation of the solidarity that I had given him.

It was Oscar Wilde who said, *"True friends stab you in the front"* and that is what it felt like when I received a follow-up message from Lewis 12 hours later. He said I was *"calling it wrong"* on Judeophobia and suggested that we should have a chat about my approach. He claimed that many Jewish comrades were *"hurt"* by what I was doing. I had a feeling that Lewis was being taken in by the lobotomisation drive. After all, he had previously been cited in the Al Jazeera documentary, 'The Lobby', that exposed the pernicious influence of the Israel lobby inside the Labour Party. In that documentary, the Jewish Labour Movement chair at the time, Jeremy Newmark had boasted about being able to turn Lewis. *"Just to get Clive Lewis, as one of Corbyn's key lieutenants, onto an openly Zionist JLM platform took a lot of heavy lifting"*, Newmark had said.[3] The documentary then showed footage of Lewis speaking at a JLM fringe meeting at the Labour Party conference. The broadcast notes that his appearance there was viewed as a tactical victory of the JLM. It was reported that Momentum passed a motion of censure against Lewis for attending that meeting.[4] Newmark was pleased by this development and said, *"It's created a bit of division within Momentum"*.[5]

When I responded to Lewis, I enquired whether the Jewish comrades to whom he was referring were *"hurt"* by what I was actually doing, or what other people were saying I was doing. I stressed that all I had done was to point out that the Labour Party was an anti-racist party. I reminded him that that included standing with the Jewish community in Cable Street against Oswald Mosley's fascists and being the backbone of the Anti-Nazi League, of which I was a member in the 1970s. To simply challenge the false narrative against Labour shouldn't be a cause of offence, and I couldn't understand why people would be *"hurt"* by me pointing out Labour's anti-racist record.

Lewis then sent me a message from someone who he said was *"a well-known Jewish member of the left who supports JC [and] was on his original campaign"*. But the message just repeated the hackneyed talking points that the JLM and other assorted smear merchants had been circulating. This unidentified correspondent asserted that, *"Chris Williamson has a pattern of behaviour of causing offence"*. According to Lewis's nameless source, I was guilty of *"offensive comments"* and was *"boosting others doing so, including those suspended from the party and a hardcore Holocaust revisionist"*. They also claimed, *"Many Jewish Labour members support Jeremy Corbyn, so it is simply untrue – not to mention hurtful – to cast their real concerns about antisemitism as being about trying to scupper his leadership"*.

The most disappointing thing about Lewis's reaction was that he took this unnamed flimflammer's claptrap at face value. I shouldn't have been surprised, though, as his previous dalliance with the JLM demonstrated that he was susceptible to Zionist propaganda. Perhaps the most contemptible complaint made by Lewis's source was the claim that I was *"boosting"* an alleged *"hardcore Holocaust revisionist"*. This was a reference to my retweet of a post on 17 February 2019 by someone who was talking about the dire situation in Venezuela thanks to the imposition of US sanctions. The tweet included a video of Venezuelan president, Nicolás Maduro, and it included an extract of what he'd said.[6] The synthetic hullabaloo arising from my retweet illustrated the resources that were being devoted to portraying me in the worst possible light. The most absurd thing is that the carefully choreographed chagrin didn't even relate to that tweet! It was an attack on the person who posted it because of another tweet she'd published over nine months earlier. People had rummaged through her tweets in order to find something, anything, with which to attack me, and she was accused of holocaust denial because of an earlier tweet she'd posted. She strenuously denied the accusation. Nevertheless, she found her name being dragged through the mud in the pages of national publications because I had committed the crime of retweeting her. The reputational impact of these nefarious tactics on third parties was seen as legitimate collateral damage in the effort to silence outspoken supporters of Corbyn and his policy agenda. The twisted logic that my detractors were applying would mean that, before sharing anything on social media, I would first have to establish the originator had never posted anything that could be considered offensive in their entire lives. The strictures they were applying to me were clearly absurd, but they were embraced by Labour's right-wing bureaucrats and were being cited by my friend Clive Lewis, which was discomfiting to say the least.

When I next saw Lewis in the Commons, he said he wanted to arrange a meeting with me and some Jewish comrades, including *Guardian* journalist Rachel Shabi. Funnily enough, Shabi had come up to Derby North to cover my election campaign in 2017, and she subsequently rode on Corbyn's coat tails to establish herself as a somewhat left-wing mainstream voice, akin to Owen Jones. Lewis insisted that they supported Corbyn but had been *"hurt"* by me. I said I was happy to sit down with anyone, as I wanted to find out what they found so upsetting about the positions I had taken. All I had done was defend left-wing, anti-Zionist Jews and others who had been falsely accused of 'antisemitism' and stand up to those who were making false accusations. I strongly suspected that their complaints related to my forthright criticism of Israel, but I didn't get the chance to find out because Lewis never arranged the meeting.

As an aside, I did meet the Jewish representative on Derby's Multi Faith Centre, which I had helped to establish when I was a councillor. She was concerned about what she had read about me after I was suspended. Following a long discussion, she seemed to acknowledge that the positions I had taken on Israel, on championing the Palestinian struggle, and on supporting people falsely accused of 'antisemitism', were all perfectly legitimate and certainly not offensive.

A few weeks before I was temporarily reinstated to the party, I had been invited to speak at a protest in Norwich about the Tories' roll-out of Universal Credit. This was Lewis's backyard, and he was due to speak. But just before the demonstration was scheduled to take place, Lewis gave his apologies. I do not know whether that was to avoid sharing a platform with me whilst I was suspended but, either way, he didn't turn up. He subsequently sent me a message saying he hoped it went well, thanked me for coming down to Norwich, and said that the campaigners appreciated my appearance at the rally.

We didn't interact much in the following couple of months, and he was silent when I was reinstated, and then unlawfully re-suspended, within a 48-hour period. The next thing he did wounded me still further. I had shared a videoclip of Amol Rajan and Matthew Wright talking about the impact of class in Britain, and how the ruling class impose insurmountable barriers to prevent working class liberation.[7] I said:

> *"The time is long overdue for a return to class politics. New Labour focussed on identity politics and largely disregarded class. Consequently working class communities have been continuously screwed by the Establishment for the last 40 years".*[8]

Lewis then publicly rebuked me with a lamentable statement on Twitter that deliberately misrepresented what I was saying, referring to it as *"divisive crap"*.[9] He implied that I was suggesting that the campaigns to liberate women, LGBT+, black, and disabled people were the cause of the problems experienced by the 'white working class'. That was the opposite of what I was saying.

Lewis had helped to reinforce the efforts to portray me as a bigot, as did his concluding public remark, saying, *"Sounds like your journey to the darkside is now complete"*. For Lewis to indulge in such a distorted characterisation, particularly at a time when the vultures were circling, was unforgiveable. When I messaged him to say how disappointed I was, he was completely unapologetic and simply reiterated his public remarks. I don't know whether he was being deliberately obtuse, but he sent me a long diatribe posing a false dichotomy between class struggle and fighting for oppressed groups in society. What he failed to grasp is that one without the other is pointless. But that wasn't how he saw it. When I pointed out it was *him* who had referred to the 'white working class', not me, his response was surreal. He said, *"You didn't have to say the words"*. What he meant was that his obtuse interpretation was all that counted. He then patronisingly asserted, *"I'm not sure how you dig yourself out of this hole – but then to begin to do that you have to acknowledge you're in one. I'm not sure you do?"*. Labour activist, Guy Matthews, had summed up the point I was making in a brilliant short video that was released two months before this exchange with Lewis. Matthews was challenging UKIP's claims to represent working class interests and said, *"The working class is the working class, regardless of skin colour"*.[10] I found it hard to believe that Lewis was implying that I was indulging in some sort of dog-whistle politics. It was offensive in the extreme. How ironic, I thought, that Lewis had scolded me for the alleged *"hurt"* I had caused, yet he was perfectly happy to make gratuitously offensive public statements about me. It seemed my feelings didn't matter.

I was also baffled by Lewis's wilfully ahistorical analysis. New Labour's disregard for working class communities saw precarious employment, in-work poverty, and inequality grow exponentially on their watch. They stigmatised social security claimants, too. How could he ignore that fact and head off into an alternative reality? He was espousing full-on Zionist apologia and comparing the racism experienced by Black and Asian communities to 'antisemitism' in Britain. He said:

> *"Jewish people have ... been here many times before. They know the signs ... I now know why Zionism exists. I get it. I abhor the price it's come at for the Palestinian people but do you know what, for the first time I really get it".*

It was obvious that Lewis had completely lost the plot and it was thoroughly depressing to listen to him talk like that. He had obviously been brainwashed and, despite his passing remark about his concern about the price being paid by the Palestinian people, he was still prepared to regurgitate this racist guff. It seems Lewis didn't abhor the price being paid by the Palestinian people as much as he cared about securing his parliamentary career. If he genuinely 'got it', he would have been outraged that Palestinian people are forced to pay any price at all for wanting to live in their own homeland. Jews like Tony Greenstein, who is the son of a Rabbi who fought Oswald Moseley's fascists, take an entirely different view to Lewis. Greenstein says:

> *"Anti-Semitism is not a form of racism and it hasn't been for well over half a century. There is no evidence that Jews are subject to discrimination or singled out for violence. Ipso facto anti-Semitism is no longer a form of racism. Anti-Semitism of course persists as a form of prejudice and should be condemned on that basis but ... it is necessary to distinguish between ideas, attitudes, prejudices – which are all subjective and 'not provable' – and the objective acting out of such prejudice – in discriminatory acts, physical violence, institutional bias. It is because Jews*

> *don't experience racism that Tory Ministers, the Labour Right and the Tory press are concerned about 'anti-Semitism'."*[11]

Lewis had failed to listen to the views of anti-Zionist Jews. As a result, he ended up effectively backing an apartheid regime that is even worse than the one in South Africa that the ANC eventually defeated.

The anti-Corbyn campaign ramps up

Not long after being suspended, I decided to give Parliament a wide berth for a couple of weeks. When I did return, to participate in one of the interminable Brexit votes, I couldn't see a single friendly face in the Commons chamber, and I was ostracised by the Labour MPs sitting on the benches. I decided to make my way into the division lobby to await the vote, so that I could make an early exit. As I walked through the door, I was confronted by the sight of Ruth Smeeth and another right-wing Labour MP Stella Creasy, sitting opposite the entrance like a couple of gruesome gargoyles. As I passed them by, Smeeth snarled *"antisemite!"*. I was already feeling on edge, so Smeeth's slanderous stage whisper nearly sent me over. The red mist momentarily came down and I immediately spun round ready to give her a righteous earbashing, but I managed to compose myself. I just gave her and Creasy a withering look. They both looked shocked that I had reacted, which is typical of bullies who are used to harassing people with impunity. This type of encounter was repeated over and over again until I eventually left Parliament later that year.

As a consequence of my suspension, the party democratisation campaign in which I had been engaged came to a shuddering halt. Over the next four months, I had to cancel more than 20 nationwide speaking engagements, a twice-monthly guest slot on TalkRadio, and an appearance on BBC's *Have I Got News for You*. The smear merchants had succeeded in 'cancelling' me. Grassroots party members no longer had anyone within the PLP who was willing to fight their corner. Certainly, no other MP was making arguments for open selection and direct democracy to determine party policy. With no whipping boy at his side, Corbyn found himself under even greater siege.

The Novara clown posse

Key figures in Momentum, *Novara Media*, and soft left commentators, who had previously strongly supported me, played the role of useful idiots for the malevolent vested interests who were hellbent on derailing the Corbyn project.

Until they began to 'melt' like the very 'slugs' they had once denounced, *Novara Media* had been an important voice for the Corbyn project. So, it was a bitter blow when two of their prominent presenters turned on me. In April 2019, James Martin who is a supporter from Chester, took to social media to urge Michael Walker, *Novara's TyskySour* host, to back me, but he refused. Martin had posted a tweet saying that *"both of us know that Chris Williamson did or said nothing wrong or antisemitic, so why didn't you and* Novara *stand with him against the manufactured smears and witch-hunt?"*.[12] Walker responded by saying, *"That's where we disagree"*. I sent him a private message asking, *"Which part of my speech in Sheffield was, in your opinion, anti-Semitic, Michael?"*. He replied, *"I don't think any of it was antisemitic, and have never said so"*, even though that was the clear implication of his response to Martin. Walker went on to say:

> *"members have become (understandably) dismissive of allegations of AS – that dismissiveness needs to be tempered not encouraged. You encouraged it. I have also found numerous of your actions difficult to justify ... You've consistently been, at best, incredibly irresponsible in a moment when it only damaged the left".*

The exchange continued until he said, *"There is a narrative among the grassroots that you have been thrown to the wolves for defending Jeremy. I think you were suspended because of your own actions and will continue to say so"*. I was taken aback by Walker's overweening arrogance. I suggested that we should meet up to have a face-to-face conversation. He didn't respond. A few months later, in July 2019, he was at it again, publicly denigrating me on social media.[13] I renewed my invitation to meet him, only to receive an extraordinarily haughty response. *"We disagree Chris. You've been irresponsible and damaging to the movement. I have no real incli-*

nation to rebuild bridges", he said. Yet only a couple of years later, after Corbyn had been destroyed in a similar way to me, Walker's commentary began to see a marked shift,[14] making the kind of statements which he had previously suggested were *"damaging to the movement"*. In April 2022, he even tweeted in response to an interview with Keir Starmer in the *Jewish Chronicle*, *"It's funny how taboo it was [under Corbyn] to suggest the antisemitism row had anything to do with Israel..."*.[15] But he didn't acknowledge that it was precisely because of people like him that it was a *"taboo"*. It seems that he is unwilling to admit his previous credulity.

A co-founder of *Novara Media*, Aaron Bastani, had been working as my Communications Officer when I was originally suspended, although he bailed out soon afterwards. Nevertheless, he at least had the decency not to descend to the spiteful statements made by the likes of Walker and *Novara's* senior editor, Ash Sarkar, who had also joined in the feeding frenzy.[16] In fact, Bastani sent me a WhatsApp message saying that he had spoken to them both about their tweets, which he said were *"out of line"*. He attempted to make excuses for Walker's social media outbursts by saying, *"He's young Chris"* and reminded me that Walker *"wanted Jeremy Corbyn to stand down in March 2017"*. However, Bastani's attempt to censure the pair had little to no impact on either of them. Sarkar was at it again after I had been reinstated at the end of June 2019. She doubled down on her earlier perfidious intervention by challenging the decision to reinstate me, which contributed to the pressure on Formby, who then unlawfully re-suspended me two days later. Sarkar had happily shared a platform with me to defend Corbyn at an Intelligence Squared event five months before I was suspended.[17] And she introduced me in glowing terms at the Trafalgar Square rally against Donald Trump in July 2018:

> *"I am so happy to introduce our next speaker. He is a tireless fighter on behalf of working people up and down the country. He is the Derby North bad man. The one and only Chris Williamson MP!".* [18]

But it seems, in her eyes, I'd gone from hero to zero in just over six months. So much for the contrived mouthful she gave to Piers Morgan on ITV's *Good Morning Britain* on 12 July 2018, two days before the Trafalgar Square rally, when she said, *"I'm a communist, you idiot"*.[19] Her subsequent behaviour suggests that this was just a publicity stunt. Her actions proved that she was no communist. She was a shallow, self-serving liberal, as was her *Novara* compatriot Walker, who had laughably labelled himself a *"class war social democrat"*, whatever on Earth that means! The pair of them, it seems to me, had relished the mainstream media attention they'd been receiving until then. They'd both become regular talking heads, and Walker had even done a segment on *BBC Newsnight*. Disassociating themselves from me was evidently their way of keeping their noses clean. By contrast, although Bastani had resigned his role in my Westminster team as soon as the sharks were circling, he continued to post relatively supportive statements on social media.[20] In the end, what did their lack of solidarity get them? After Corbyn resigned in April 2020, they lost the mainstream glorification that they previously enjoyed. They had helped to destroy me for a mere 15 minutes of fame.

Even the likes of Richard Seymour contributed to the misrepresentation. Seymour positions himself as a cerebral left-wing commentator, unaffected by the right-wing agenda to undermine socialist voices. Yet in his 'hot take' the day after I was suspended, Seymour repeated the lie that I had said Labour had been *"too apologetic"* about 'antisemitism'.[21] He then added that my remark was *"at best a crass blurring of the issues"*.[22] Reinforcing his claim to intellectual political correctness, he went on to say, *"What, after all, is 'too apologetic' about racism? It strikes a horrible note, whatever was intended"*.[23] Had Seymour bothered with a cursory examination of my actual remarks, it would have been obvious to him that I was referring to the party being too apologetic *about its record in tackling anti-Semitism*. Seymour's 'hot take' was little better than the rubbish in the corporate media. The condescending tone of this armchair socialist was illustrated by the passage where he said that I had:

> *"organised events up and down the country to debate the big issues facing the movement. In so doing, however, he has a tendency with his loose cannon style to snarl up an already knotted argument.*[24]

But it was only a *"knotted argument"* because of commentators like Seymour buying into the disinformation campaign deployed by the very political vested interests he claimed to eschew. It proved what Malcolm X once said, *"The media have the power to make the innocent guilty and to make the guilty innocent"*.

Which Side Are You On?

To my surprise, it wasn't too long until Billy Bragg, someone I had once respected, began to attack me. I know that Owen Jones had spoken to Bragg at the 2019 Glastonbury Festival, a few days before he shared his eccentric views with the world. Maybe his encounter with Jones prompted him to publicly deride me. What we do know is that Jones is the darling of the 'optics left', or 'weathercocks' as Tony Benn used to call them, and his political judgement is prone to outlandish flights of fancy. Bragg had come under fire from grassroots Labour supporters for comments he'd made about me, which prompted him to publish a long, rambling diatribe, in which he compared me to Carl Benjamin (also known as 'Sargon of Akkad'), a UKIP member who'd made a rape 'joke'.[25]

Bragg said, *"While it is true that CW's words do not contravene the IHRA working definition of anti-semitism, they do express a shocking disregard for Jewish sensitivities"*. His point was that, even though I hadn't been Judeophobic, people shouldn't take *"a purely legalistic reading"* of my comments, because my *"insensitive statements"* could play a role in *"normalising ... abusive behaviour"*. He then compared me to Carl Benjamin, who tweeted to Jess Phillips in 2016, *"I wouldn't even rape you"*. Bragg said that Benjamin's *"supporters brushed away complains* [sic] *by arguing that he never said he was going to rape her"*. *"Technically, they were right"*, Bragg said, but the *"insensitive nature"* of Benjamin's comments had later derailed UKIP's campaigning. As you can already see, Bragg was comparing apples to oranges, making ridiculous leaps of logic. But he continued.

Bragg claimed that the fact Labour had suspended me for a 'pattern of behaviour' *"implie[d] that it was [Chris's] disregard for Jewish sensitivities rather than an outright expression of anti-semitism that caused him to be investigated"*. He concluded his absurd spiel by saying:

> "Like Benjamin's rape comment, it sent a message that [Chris] doesn't care what the victims of abuse think. Given the Labour Party's proud tradition of standing up for the rights of victims, such an insensitive attitude should not be tolerated."

Bragg's rant was totally outrageous. He was comparing comments that I had made in support of anti-Zionist Jews and other supporters of Palestine to a disgusting comment about rape. It was clear that he wasn't interested in the rights and wrongs of the issue, either. He was concerned about *"insensitivity"* and how my comments might affect Labour's campaigning.

I had previously been an admirer of Bragg's and I had seen him perform on a number of occasions. His solidarity with the miners during the 1984–85 strike, and the Red Wedge[26] initiative that he was instrumental in establishing in the mid-1980s, were highly commendable endeavours to combat injustice. I recall playing his version of Pete Seeger's 'Which Side Are You On?' over loudspeakers fixed to my car roof during the 1989 local government dispute, when strike-breakers were habitually crossing our picket line. I saw Bragg as a comrade, and I felt a real affinity towards him, especially when he came out in support of Corbyn's leadership bid in 2015. So, I was dismayed to see someone I had lionised for over three decades joining in the coordinated denigration of my reputation. He was repeating the downright lie that I had said Labour had been 'too apologetic' about Judeophobia. How could he not see that he was being used to drive another nail into the coffin of the Corbyn project?! The Establishment are past masters at the divide-and-rule routine, and Bragg was just the latest example of how the unified coalition behind the Corbyn surge was being systematically shattered, shard by shard.

Rather than engaging in a public Twitter spat, I wrote to Bragg to request a meeting. In my letter, I emphasised that the accusations against me were as preposterous as they were offensive, and I offered to send him a detailed rebuttal in confidence. I explained that I was being singled out for supporting left-wing Jews in the party, welcoming the departure of right-wing MPs like Joan Ryan, and for campaigning to make Labour MPs accountable to grassroots members. Bragg refused to meet me, and he tried to justify his joining in with the brouhaha by blaming my supporters for his outbursts. Apparently, he felt compelled to attack me because my supporters *"were not satisfied with [his] silence and demanded a statement of solidarity"*. He ridiculously described their social media criticisms as *"punishment beatings"*. In his response to my letter, he conceded that I had not made any Judeophobic remarks. But he said that Labour had to *"rebuild its relationship with those elements of the Jewish community who are distressed by the language used by some vocal advocates of the Palestinian cause who are Labour members"*. He claimed that I had hindered that process. The *"elements of the Jewish community"* to whom he referred were Zionist elements. In other words, racists and zealots. My view was that the party should not be rebuilding any relationships with people who support the dispossession of Palestinians from their land by settler colonialists. Labour should have been expelling them, instead. Zionism is inconsistent with Labour's values, or at least it should be.

It was clear from Bragg's response that he was very firmly in the 'optics left' camp. He even told me that *"perception trumps intention"*. According to Bragg's warped logic, the only thing that matters *"in a time of social media"* is not what you actually say, but whether what you say offends anyone. The fact that I was offended by Bragg's public statements about me meant that he had fallen foul of his own ordinance, but that inconsistency was lost on him. More importantly, however, what Bragg was advocating meant giving carte blanche to bad faith actors to take out anyone who threatened the status quo. Rather than admit that he was wrong, Bragg claimed victim status and fell back on illogical defences.

Copies of my full exchange with Billy Bragg can be viewed on the 'Ten Years Hard Labour' website. Please scan this QR code.

For all of Bragg's revolutionary rabble-rousing songs, when we had a chance of real revolutionary change, he gave succour to those who were working to demolish it. It's all very well bleating on about socialism on stage. It helps to sell his records. But if that isn't backed up by concrete actions, one has to wonder: 'Which Side Are You On?', Bragg?

"THE SILENCE OF OUR FRIENDS"

Dr Martin Luther King Jr once said, *"In the end, we will remember not the words of our enemies, but the silence of our friends."* Some of my old friends had now, it seemed, become my enemies. But there were still many people who purported to support me. And yet, they stood silent.

The betrayal I faced on all fronts, from Jeremy Corbyn to members of the SCG – people to whom I had shown ceaseless loyalty, and for whom I had sacrificed my own political capital in defending – was painful. I was hurt that, not only had they thrown me to the wolves and refused to defend me, but that, in some cases, they were actively making my life worse. I wasn't credulous about the nature of politics before this. I knew it was a dog-eat-dog world. But the cravenness, the abandonment, the nastiness was at a level I had never experienced before. It floored me.

CHAPTER FIFTEEN

A KAFKAESQUE NIGHTMARE

After my secret evening rendezvous with Naz Shah on the day I was suspended, I was shown a highly critical exchange between a former close member of my team and a senior figure in Momentum. It was another 'Et tu, Brute?' moment, as I had treated this individual like a son. But he was close to the 'optics left' crew before joining my team, and he was obviously still influenced by them. So, by the time I was on the train back home to Derby, I was feeling punch-drunk. I took two phone calls from Tony Greenstein and Jackie Walker's partner, Graham Bash. Both were pessimistic about me being reinstated and suggested that I should consider a speaking tour to build support. With the benefit of hindsight, I should have taken their advice instead of complying with the Labour Party's Kafkaesque disciplinary procedures. But I was in a state of shock and I refused to believe, after 43 years of dedicated service to the party, that I would be thrown to the wolves.

A few days after I was suspended, my constituency office was vandalised by a Conservative councillor. He seemed to think the media storm had given him immunity, because he brazenly posted his handiwork on social media.[1] I also received a number of serious death threats through the post and over the phone. It felt like being under siege from hostile forces. The complete absence of any solidarity from senior figures in the party left me feeling vulnerable and bereft. My entire adult life had been defined by the Labour Party. The prospect of being excommunicated and placed outside of the 'Labour family' was inconceivable to me.

When I received the formal letter from Formby notifying me that she'd suspended me, she claimed that a large number of complaints had been received about my conduct. Two weeks earlier, she had told me in a meeting that she received more complaints about me than every other member of the Labour Party put together. She acknowledged in her letter that each individual complaint *"may have resulted in no action"*. But she went on to claim that *"taken together they add up to a pattern of behaviour that may bring the party into disrepute"*. She then asserted that, in our meeting, she had warned me *"about the damaging effect of this pattern of behaviour on Jewish communities and on the Labour Party's efforts to rebuild trust with those communities"*. That was a flat out lie. In fact, two weeks previously, she had admitted that the complaints were nonsense. I strongly suspect that she included this passage to cover her back so that if/when her letter got into the public domain, she could say that she had challenged me beforehand. It illustrated just how far a former 'ally' was prepared to cave-in to the aggressive Zionist lobby. As if to rub salt into my wounds, she suggested that I could contact my GP for support with my *"mental health and wellbeing"*, and she even recommended contacting the Samaritans. She said that *"they offer a safe place for anyone to talk any time they like, in their own way – about whatever's getting to them"*. This was another back-covering sop after what had happened to Carl Serjeant, a senior Labour member of the Senedd Cymru, who took his own life in November 2017 after being suspended following anonymous allegations of inappropriate behaviour. The party was subsequently criticised for not offering him any pastoral care.[2]

To see this document please scan this QR code.

I didn't receive any communication detailing what the allegations were until several weeks later but, when it did eventually arrive, the accusations against me were pitiful. I thought that, if that's the best Formby could do, her grounds for suspending me were clearly illegitimate. My detailed response to those allegations is included in the Appendix of this book. The heartless way in which the Labour machine treats its members is completely unacceptable. Contrary to what I previously thought when Theresa May labelled the Conservative Party 'the nasty party', the Labour Party is just as bad, if not worse.

XXXXX [Redacted] XXXXX

Following receipt of my suspension letter, I made a Data Subject Access Request (DSAR) to obtain copies of the *"large number of complaints"* to which Formby had referred. I requested everything the party held on file about me from May 2015, when I'd previously lost my seat. I wanted to find out if Formby had been telling the truth about the supposed sea of complaints against me. However, the party was determined to keep me in the dark. They failed to comply with the statutory time limit for responding. In the end, time had dragged on so long that I asked my solicitors to make representations. By the time I received a detailed response, the December 2019 general election had come and gone. I was no longer an MP, and they were still holding out on providing the information I'd requested. The party informed me that they were applying the *"excessive exemption available to data controllers"* under data protection legislation. They claimed that there were in the region of 50,000 separate pieces of information about me!

The very limited information they did disclose can be viewed through the QR code below. Much of it was redacted, but there was an interesting email exchange from 26 February 2019 between Jennie Formby and someone whose name is redacted. She referred to the meeting we had, at which Karie Murphy was in attendance. At one point, she claimed:

> *"[Williamson is] campaigning against the democratically determined rules of the party. However, he seemed completely uninterested and wasn't really prepared to engage; I got the impression he thought we had no right to speak to him in this way."*

The imperiousness of that statement exemplifies how Formby's stewardship of the party's bureaucracy was completely incompatible with the creation of an empowered democratic mass party. The only dissent she was prepared to brook was from right-wing Zionists like Ruth Smeeth, Margaret Hodge, Tom Watson, et al. The *"democratically determined rules of the party"* are not immutable. If they were, members would never be allowed to propose and campaign for rule changes. Perhaps Formby believes rule changes should only be made by party elites. As for her *"impression"* that I thought she and Murphy had no right to speak to me the way they did... damn right! They most certainly did not have the right to demand that I stop talking to grassroots activists, cease campaigning for greater democracy, and discontinue speaking up for members subjected to the party's deleterious disciplinary processes.

To see these documents please scan this QR code.

Formby's words also betrayed a striking level of ignorance about the party's traditions. One of the founding principles of the labour movement is solidarity. Yet, to Formby, who came from a senior trade union background, solidarity seemed like an alien concept. Before he became leader, Corbyn was renowned for his willingness to express solidarity with party members who were being unfairly treated by the overbearing party machine. In the July 1982 edition of *London Labour Briefing*, he opposed expulsions of members of Militant from the party. He was also the provisional convenor of the Defeat the Witch-Hunt Campaign, the address for which was Corbyn's home.[1] Furthermore, Tony Benn opposed the expulsion of George Galloway in 2003 and spoke publicly about his disapproval of the move to eject him.[2] Both Benn and Corbyn were *"campaigning against the democratically determined rules of the party"*. Moreover, they were guilty of a *"pattern of behaviour"* for consistently opposing the direction of the party under Kinnock, Blair, and Brown. Had Formby been general secretary back then, would she have suspended them for these acts of solidarity? Her position was preposterous and unworthy of a general secretary who was hailed upon appointment as a great left-winger and Corbyn supporter.

There was another email on the same date that was almost entirely redacted, but there was at least one revealing passage that the censors allowed through. It read, *"Chris Williamson has become very close to JVL and takes their advice without questioning or interrogating it very much"*. It is true that I was close to Jewish Voice for Labour (JVL), precisely because it was a pro-Corbyn pressure group and a counterweight to the Zionist JLM. But the assumption that I took their advice without questioning or interrogation was pure supposition based on no evidence whatsoever. Meanwhile, the party leadership, including Corbyn and the bureaucracy, bent over backwards for the hostile JLM and indulged their every whim, designed to destroy the Corbyn project.

In another internal email dated 27 February 2019, the correspondent, whose name was redacted, agreed with Formby that:

> *"it is inappropriate for a Labour MP to help facilitate a member in the middle of a disciplinary process in campaigning against our democratically agreed processes ... this is clearly unacceptable for a Labour MP and cannot go unchallenged".*

But what I was doing was no different to what Corbyn, Benn, and many others had done with no sanction from the party! It was yet another example of rank hypocrisy, not least because right-wing Labour MPs were constantly intervening in the disciplinary process to demand that left-wing members be suspended and expelled.[3] These people were true bureaucrats, through and through. These sacred 'processes' of theirs had been, by and large, created under the right-wing leaderships of Kinnock and Blair. Why, for crying out loud, were they resistant to changing them?! It was absurd. But this was the true nature of the non-existent 'radicalism' of the Corbyn era. They never wanted to transform the party, they just wanted to manage the machinery themselves. It was idiotic and, ultimately, it proved fatal to both Corbynism and their own political careers.

Chalk and cheese – applying the Rule Book

My suspension illustrated the incredible double standards that the party was applying. For example, the former Labour MP Louise Ellman, a dyed-in-the-wool Zionist, invited Campaign4Truth to Parliament on 23 November 2017. This organisation is linked to the Jewish Defence League (JDL), a far-right terrorist group that was founded by Meir Kahane, an Islamophobic, anti-Arab, genocide advocate and far-right Rabbi, as well as a former member of the Israeli Knesset. How was it that I was repeatedly taken to task for sharing platforms with and/or supporting longstanding anti-racist activists, some of whom were Jewish and who had been accused of Judeophobia, yet Ellman received no sanction? Whilst I was pilloried, Ellman was given *carte blanche* to bring the party into disrepute and could do no wrong in the eyes of its bureaucracy. It seemed that the attitude of Labour's disciplinary agents was that it was fine to hang out with Islamophobes like Melanie Phillips, and far-right groups, but woe betide anyone expressing solidarity with anti-racist socialists.

Many of Ellman's media appearances were also inappropriate. She told the *World at One* programme on BBC Radio 4, on 28 February 2019, that *"anti-Semitism is thriving under Jeremy Corbyn's leadership"*. She added, *"It will be very difficult to tell people to vote for Jeremy to be Prime Minister unless he changes in a very radical way"*. She claimed that 'antisemitism' was *"endemic"* and *"widespread"* in the Labour Party, but what she meant by this only became clear when she explained what she understood by the term 'antisemitism'. This included her complaint about being held to account by party members who were concerned about her being vice chair of Labour Friends of Israel. But it wasn't 'antisemitic' to call on her to explain why she was defending a foreign government that was hostile to a Corbyn-led Labour Party. She described her local members as *"obsessive"* for questioning her political choices in defending Israel when it disregards international law, commits war crimes, and administers an apartheid system. Ellman claimed in the same interview that *"deep-rooted hostility to the whole concept of Zionism ... is part of the left-wing's antisemitism"*. It was complete balderdash. Members should be able to hold their MPs to account without being accused of bigotry. As was generally the case, anti-Zionism was conflated with 'antisemitism.

The previous day, Dame Margaret Hodge also appeared on the *World at One* to bring pressure on the party to suspend me. Coincidentally, this pressure corresponded with the release of a prominent United Nations Independent Commission of Inquiry report on 28 February 2019. The Inquiry found that Israeli soldiers had intentionally fired on Palestinian civilians during the 2018 Great March of Return, committing war crimes as they killed 189 people on that peaceful march. The release of this report would have been a landmark press event in the calendar of the Israeli Embassy, which works extremely closely with Labour Friends of Israel as was shown in Al Jazeera's documentary 'The Lobby'. A consequence of my suspension coinciding with the release of this UN report was that it helped to shift the corporate media's attention in Britain away from Israeli war crimes. *World at One* featured interviews about my case with Hodge and Ellman for two consecutive days, but it had no major segments on the UN's report.

A hostile environment

I was never enamoured by the trappings of the Westminster bubble. I had previously suggested that it be converted into a museum of democracy, and that we could move Parliament to the north of England.[4] Nye Bevan's assessment of the place is apposite, particularly for anyone who is sent there to represent the interests of the working class. Regrettably, the overwhelming majority of the present cohort of Labour MPs have been elected under false pretences. Bevan wrote about his first impressions as an MP from a working class background in his 1952 book *In Place of Fear*, which perfectly described how I felt when I was first elected:

> *"[The New MP's] first impression is that he is in church. The vaulted roofs and stained-glass windows, the rows of statues of great statesmen of the past, the echoing halls, the soft-footed attendants and the whispered conversation, contrast depressingly with the crowded meetings and the clang and clash of hot opinions he has just left behind in his election campaign. Here he is, a tribune of the people, coming to make his voice heard in the seats of power. Instead, it seems he is expected to worship; and the most conservative of all religions – ancestor worship.*

> *"The first thing he should bear in mind is that these were not his ancestors. His forebears had no part in the past, the accumulated dust of which now muffles his own footfalls. His forefathers were tending sheep or ploughing the land, or serving the statesmen whose names he sees written on the walls around him, or whose*

portraits look down upon him in the long corridors. It is not the past of his people that extends in colourful pageantry before his eyes. They were shut out from all this; were forbidden to take part in the dramatic scenes depicted in these frescoes. In him his people are there for the first time, and the history he will make will not be merely an episode in the story he is now reading. It must be wholly different; as different as is the social status which he now brings with him.

"To preserve the keen edge of his critical judgment he will find that he must adopt an attitude of scepticism amounting almost to cynicism, for Parliamentary procedure neglects nothing which might soften the acerbities of his class feelings. In one sense the House of Commons is the most unrepresentative of representative assemblies. It is an elaborate conspiracy to prevent the real clash of opinion which exists outside from finding an appropriate echo within its walls. It is a social shock absorber placed between privilege and the pressure of popular discontent."[5]

If anything, the situation in the House of Commons is now even worse than what it was when Bevan said it was *"the most unrepresentative of representative assemblies"*. Modern day MPs are obsessed with parliamentary parlour games rather than the issues that affect people's daily lives. They revel in the archaic parlance and customs. A showcase for democracy it certainly is not.

After I was suspended, the suffocating ambience, stultifying procedures, and hostility that was directed towards me by right-wing MPs made the trip to the Palace of Westminster on Monday mornings even more irksome and unappealing. Any and every opportunity was taken by the coterie of contemptibles that make up the bulk of the PLP to make life uncomfortable. Snide *sotto voce* remarks in the division lobbies and corridors were a daily occurrence. On one occasion, I was awaiting the outcome of a division in the Commons chamber when Corbyn passed by and said, *"Hello comrade"* and patted me on the back, prompting banner headlines the following day. *"Jeremy Corbyn is embroiled in fresh anti-Semitism storm after being accused of calling Labour MP suspended over row a 'comrade'"*, howled the *Daily Mail*.[6] Meanwhile, the *Jewish Chronicle* ran with, *"Jeremy Corbyn called*

'Jew-baiter' MP Chris Williamson 'comrade'", with a subheading proclaiming, *"He patted the suspended MP on the back on meeting him earlier this week"*.[7] Shock, horror! The level of hyperbole seemed to suggest that patting me on the back should be treated like a capital offence.

The former MP for Dudley North, Ian Austin, now Lord Austin, who had quit Labour by this point, told the *Mail on Sunday*, *"If any more proof were needed that the Labour leader couldn't care less about eradicating anti-Jewish prejudice in his party, this is it"*. Lord Austin, of all people, is in no position to claim any moral high ground, or to even comment on the question of 'prejudice', because his bigotry is on the record. When he was still a Labour MP, he called for routine fingerprinting of immigrants,[8] reductions in their already parsimonious social security entitlement,[9] and to make public housing off limits for them.[10]

Two months after I was initially suspended, I discovered that a three-person NEC Antisemitism Panel had been scheduled to consider my case. It never went ahead, however, because the Unite representative, Jim Kennedy, recused himself because he knew me. Jon Lansman, who was on the same panel, also knew me, but he had no such concerns about a conflict of interest, even though he had posted a hostile statement on social media about me in December 2018.[11] The failure to conclude the matter in early April 2019 was yet another demoralising blow, but I still clung to the forlorn possibility that I would be reinstated. I had hoped to throw myself into campaigning for Labour in the local elections the following month, just as I'd done in every previous local election since 1977, but the ongoing suspension made that virtually impossible.

However, party members in the Derbyshire Dales CLP were very supportive and urged me to join them on the campaign trail. So, I spent some enjoyable time with solid comrades in the beautiful Derbyshire countryside knocking on doors in Matlock and Wirksworth. It felt like old times. I remember campaigning on the same streets in a hard fought and vibrant parliamentary by-election back in 1986. The singer-songwriter Billy Bragg had come up to Derbyshire to support the candidate and staged an impromptu concert for activists and supporters. Little did I know back then that, 33 years later, I would find myself at odds with him and my own party. Nevertheless, it really cheered me up being back in the saddle, particularly as I was helping to elect a brilliant socialist candidate and a credit to the labour movement, Elisa McDonagh. These moments of joy, sadly, would always be brief.

Bringing out the big guns

On 28 May 2019, the Equality and Human Rights Commission (EHRC) succumbed to pressure from two anti-Corbyn Zionist groups to launch an *"investigation to determine whether the Labour Party had "unlawfully discriminated against, harassed, or victimised people because they're Jewish"*. It was the first time that the EHRC would be investigating a major political party, having only previously investigated the far-right British National Party. The organisations that had triggered the investigations were the self-styled Jewish Labour Movement (JLM) and the so-called Campaign Against Antisemitism (CAA). As I mentioned in a previous chapter, the JLM was only re-founded in 2015 to combat Jeremy Corbyn after being moribund for many years.[12] In fact, former JLM chair, Jeremy Newmark, is on record talking about reviving the JLM just after Corbyn was first elected as Labour leader. He said that *"a bunch of us sat in a coffee shop in Golders Green"* in order to *"talk about re-forming the JLM to do something with it"*.[13] As for the CAA, they have received funding from a pro-Israel charity called the Anglo-Jewish Association. The fact that the complainants were hostile, partisan organisations with an axe to grind was just swept under the carpet. Interestingly, ultra-Zionist Lord John Mann, the former right-wing Labour MP, claimed he had raised money for this assault on the Labour Party's reputation. Speaking at a meeting of the American Jewish Committee Global Forum in June 2019, he said *"in my own political party, I raised the money for the legal action that's gone now to a full human rights commission investigation into institutional antisemitism"*.[14]

In the statement announcing their inquiry, the EHRC said its investigation would seek to determine:

1. *"whether unlawful acts have been committed by the Party and/or its employees and/or its agents*

2. *"whether the Party has responded to complaints of unlawful acts in a lawful, efficient and effective manner".*

The EHRC had allowed itself to be instrumentalised as a political weapon in the battle to bring down and destroy the anti-imperialist Corbyn project. Of course, the announcement generated overblown headlines in the corporate media and hypercritical handwringing by the PLP detractors. The bad faith actors who had fabricated the 'antisemitism crisis' that gave the EHRC the excuse to mount the inquiry fell on the news like a pack of hungry hounds. They used it to disingenuously claim it was a vindication of what they had been saying all along, although the reality was very different. But the very fact that the EHRC had opened an investigation at all meant that the pressure to ensure I was not reinstated was ratcheted up several notches. The truth was that the pressure against anti-Zionists in the party as a whole was now overbearing. The failure to push back against the smears – as many, including myself, had predicted – had meant that the campaign of demonisation finally reached the point of no return. It would only get worse and worse from there.

CHAPTER SIXTEEN

RANK COWARDICE

After the first NEC Antisemitism Panel (part of a sub-committee of the NEC) had been convened to hear my case, and then dispersed, I would have to wait another three months before having my case heard. The people sitting on the panel that eventually considered the accusations against me were Labour MPs Keith Vaz and Sir George Howarth, as well as members' representative Huda Elmi. The three of them received 'independent' advice from a barrister, whose recommendation was to keep me out. The panel met at the end of June 2019, and, against the party bureaucracy's advice, it decided to reinstate me with a warning, by two votes to one. Vaz and Elmi had voted in my favour. The dissenting voice was inevitably Howarth, a right-winger who had previously urged the PLP to adopt the 'illustrative' examples that accompany the IHRA Working Definition of Antisemitism, at a time when the NEC was resisting doing so. I was one of a tiny handful of MPs who had spoken against Howarth's proposal when he raised it at a meeting of the PLP.

True to form, the media were notified of the result before I was. So, the first I knew about it was when I received a call from a hack at the *Times*, asking for my reaction. This was followed by a barrage of other calls from journalists. I told them all that they were telling me something that had not been communicated to me. The fact that I found out about my suspension being lifted from a journalist was yet another indictment of the party's dysfunctional and discriminatory bureaucracy. It afforded privileges to a media apparatus that wanted to crush Jeremy Corbyn's supporters.

When it became clear that my membership really had been fully restored, I arranged to meet my solicitors at Bindmans LLP, Jamie Potter and Liz McGlone, the following week. I was not prepared to accept a warning because I had done nothing wrong. In any event, the warning was merely a sop to my tormentors. But that plan soon came to an end, as I was overtaken by events. Under pressure by the unholy trinity of right-wing Labour MPs, reactionary media hacks, and Zionist zealots, Formby crumbled once again by reimposing the suspension. Two weeks went by before I received any formal notification, which came in the form of a curt letter from the Governance and Legal Unit declaring that the decision *"cannot safely stand"*.

To see this document please scan this QR code.

The pressure on the party to overturn the NEC panel's decision to reinstate me had been intense. Keith Vaz, who had argued for my reinstatement, ended up being turned. Initially, Vaz had been quite supportive. Not long after I was first suspended, he had told me in the Commons division lobby that I was the best placed candidate to retain Derby North in any forthcoming general election. He also told me that his CLP Executive Committee had written to Formby to admonish her for suspending me in the first place, and to demand my immediate reinstatement. But, after he voted to reinstate me, he began having his arm twisted to change his mind. He said he wanted to recant and came up with a cock and bull story about undergoing medical treatment when he was asked to decide my fate:

> *"The disciplinary ... process needs to be fair to all and to be seen to be fair and all must be treated equally and no favour should be shown to anyone. In my view, having served on the NEC for 15 years I consider the decisions the panel made yesterday cannot stand".* [1]

Then, in a flimsy attempt to give the impression that his change of heart wasn't just about my case, he added, *"In order to ensure complete integrity of the process either a new panel should be convened or all the cases from yesterday should be referred to the Disputes Committee for reconsideration"*.[2] The man had mutated into an invertebrate. Not only did he go against the very clear statements he had made to me in person, he undermined his own integrity. He debased himself at the behest of my detractors.

Hysterics

The hysteria that ensued over that 48-hour period following my reinstatement was truly extraordinary. Commenting on my re-suspension, *Media Lens*, a British left-wing media analysis website, picked up on an article written by a blogger known as 'Jewish Dissident', who juxtaposed my treatment with that of Boris Johnson's. The blogger wrote:

> *"Whether one agrees with Chris or not, it's hard to think of a single comparable instance where an innocuous comment of this sort has led to such a risible media circus, or to such a sustained campaign of personal and political vilification.*
>
> *"The treatment of good old Boris, our next Prime Minister, makes for an interesting contrast. The man who is apparently destined to lead our country has a clear track record of actual, as opposed to bogus, racism and bigotry. He's the man who has talked about 'watermelon smiles' and piccaninnies', described women as 'hot totty', professed his inability to distinguish between burka-clad women and letter boxes, and derided gay men as 'bumboys'.*
>
> *"Every single one of Johnson's vile, bigoted comments has been allowed to pass by the media and the Westminster establishment. Because, after all, it's just 'good old Boris' talking."*[3]

As if to prove that point, the future Prime Minister took to Twitter to join in the media melee. Johnson's tweet read, *"Shameful that Labour have reinstated this key Corbyn ally back into their party after his appalling remarks. We must never allow these apologists for anti-Semitism anywhere near government"*.[4] But, unlike Johnson, I have never made any Judeophobic comments in my life, whereas he actually wrote a book, *Seventy-Two Virgins*,[5] in which he indulges in horrible anti-Jewish stereotypes.

My cause was not assisted when Corbyn was asked to comment about my suspension being lifted. Rather than welcoming my return to the fold and saying how much he was looking forward to working alongside me again, he disowned the decision. He told reporters:

"I wasn't involved in the decision at all. It was an independent panel set up through the [NEC]. They examined the case and decided to admit him back in, albeit with a reprimand. They went through the case. They interviewed him [they did not]. They went through the case in great detail, and the three of them on the panel made that decision. We deal with antisemitism very, very seriously. There is no place for antisemitism in our society, and obviously not in our party as well. And anyone who makes antisemitic remarks, can expect to be, at the very least, reprimanded". [6]

Why was Corbyn incapable of issuing an unequivocal statement in my defence? It's not as if he hadn't done so previously. On 31 January 2019, the month before I was initially suspended, Corbyn had told a reporter from the *Derby Telegraph*:

"Chris Williamson is a very good, very effective Labour MP. He's a very strong anti-racist campaigner. He is not antisemitic in any way." [7]

Yet, months later, when his support would have really counted, he wouldn't repeat his earlier statement. I suspect that Corbyn had been advised to adopt this approach by his worse than useless advisers. However, if he said that of his own volition, I would be even more disappointed in him. Had he embraced the conclusion of the panel and welcomed me back, he would have had his strongest advocate inside and outside the PLP, and Jennie Formby would have been unlikely to overrule him. By failing to show any proper leadership in response to the decision he encouraged my enemies, who were also his enemies, to kick up a stink. And kick up a stink they did. To make matters worse, Corbyn's misguided comment that *"anyone who makes antisemitic remarks, can expect to be, at the very least, reprimanded"*, implied that was why I had been reprimanded. But I most certainly had not said anything remotely 'antisemitic' and the party hadn't even accused me of that. Consequently, Corbyn's remarks could not have been any worse had he openly condemned me.

Corbyn had provided an opportunity for Tom Watson to demand that my case be reopened, and he made the most of his chance to stick the knife in. In his hyperbolic response to Sky

News, Watson claimed *"everyone"* was *"shocked"* by the decision,[8] which was plainly not true. The vast majority of people who took any interest in this matter were delighted. The only people who were shocked were dreadful reactionaries in the PLP like Watson, the Zionist lobby, and the right-wing corporate media. It was the usual suspects who were at it again. All of these revolting characters were the same people who were inveterately opposed to Corbyn, like Jess Phillips, who said she would *"knife [Corbyn] in the front"*.[9] She couldn't wait to give her two pennies' worth. Speaking to the corporate press, she made a completely false assertion that I was guilty of *"a litany of offensive behaviour towards the Jewish community and those fighting antisemitism"*.[10] She also disingenuously claimed that it was *"a matter of principle about racism, about the Labour Party being the party of equality, the party that is anti-racist"*.[11] Of course, the truth was rather different. It was just another attempt to undermine Corbyn's leadership. Phillips and the other right-wing assailants were trying to give the impression of widespread hostility towards me. But the reality was that the sum total of those who opposed my readmission only constituted a tiny number of individuals.

Moreover, in an unparalleled move, around 70 Labour members of staff signed a letter, dated 27 June 2019, to Jennie Formby, calling for a review of the decision to lift my suspension back in June.[12] They dishonestly claimed that:

> *"The decision to readmit Chris Williamson MP into the party will help to create an environment where Jewish and non-Jewish employees, who care deeply about fighting antisemitism, are made to feel unwelcome by his presence whilst at work."*[13]

It was an outlandishly preposterous assertion that anyone would feel unwelcome in the Labour Party after my suspension had been lifted. I am also informed that many of those who signed the letter did not, in fact, work for the Labour Party, but for right-wing Labour MPs. As with all the Orwellian *blackwhite* propaganda during this period, the truth was the very opposite of what they were saying. The only people being made to feel *"unwelcome"* in the party were anti-racist socialists, who genuinely did *"care deeply about fighting antisemitism"*, as opposed to the con artists who were weaponising it for political purposes.

Instead of feeding this political puffery with ill-judged statements, Corbyn and the SCG, should have dismissed it out of hand. These were irrelevant malcontents who were trying to undermine efforts to bring about an end to austerity at home and subvert the attempts to stop Britain's involvement in foreign wars. But it wasn't to be.

Treachery in all corners

In the wake of my re-admission to the party, another attack was mounted against me by the Board of Deputies of British Jews (BoD). The BoD's dogmatism was personified by their former chief executive, Gillian Merron, who penned an opinion piece for the *Independent* claiming my *"reprieve [was] a disgraceful step backwards in Labour's half-baked 'fight' against antisemitism."*[14] Strangely, I had known Gillian, or 'Gilly' as we used to call her, long before she was elected to Parliament in 1997. In fact, we go back almost 40 years. I worked with her in the 1980s. We were welfare rights officers for Derbyshire County Council before she obtained employment with the National Union of Public Employees, for which I was also a lay official. We regularly campaigned for the Labour Party side by side. We used to socialise together, too. And she even holidayed with my late wife, Lonny, which included travelling with her to Cuba in 1990.

She has come a long way since then and now sits in the House of Lords, after being nominated by Sir Keir Starmer at the end of 2020. But Gilly was in no position to criticise anyone. Her record in Parliament was abysmal. Her low points included voting to impoverish the poorest families in Britain[15] and supporting the illegal and murderous 2003 invasion of Iraq.[16] To add insult to injury, she voted to scrap lone parent benefit just two weeks before Christmas in 1997. Furthermore, in the aftermath of the MPs expenses scandal in 2009, she repaid over £6,000.[17] Despite losing her parliamentary seat in 2010, she hit the headlines in 2012 when it was revealed that she was renting a London apartment to the Labour MP Lilian Greenwood.[18] She was then criticised in 2019 for making a profit of almost a quarter of a million pounds on the sale of a property, purchased with parliamentary expenses, that she sold in 2013.[19] Despite her wretched parliamentary record, it was still very wounding to read something like that from someone who I used to know quite well. Gilly's ranting article for the *Independent* contained no legitimate criticism of me. She was just swimming in the gutter with the rest of the smear merchants. She must have known that her vile op-ed was full of lies, yet she still put her name to it. It was a truly despicable thing to do. If Lonny were still alive, she would have been absolutely disgusted by Gilly's treachery. But as I was discovering, Gilly's betrayal was just one of many.

The Lansman factor

Following my reinstatement, I had posted a tweet thanking my supporters for their goodwill messages. Jon Lansman, at that time a director of the Momentum company, posted a tweet objecting to my celebratory tone. I had, he said, not shown *"one iota of contrition"*, and he concluded his tweet by saying, *"He has to go"*.[20] It's no mystery why Lansman wanted me out. Whilst he now laughably claims to have renounced his Zionism, Lansman, in my view, remains one. He shares all the typical hallmarks. In a 2016 interview with the *Jewish Chronicle*, Lansman admitted that, as a young man, he worked on a kibbutz in An-Naqab (the so-called 'Negev'). In so doing, Lansman had contributed, in his own small way, to the ongoing colonisation efforts that had earlier seen An-Naqab's indigenous Palestinian population killed, expelled, and displaced. He also said, *"I have Zionist friends in the party. ... Why should Israel supporters not have a place in Labour? Of course they should"*.[21] In June 2018, he was even shameless enough to visit the State of Israel. He gave a talk in Tal Abib (the garrison city that Zionists call 'Tel Aviv' is largely built on the ashes of Palestinian villages) on 'Corbyn, Labour, Israel, Palestine'.[22] Lansman had also made derogatory remarks about the pro-Corbyn group, Jewish Voice for Labour (JVL). He is on record saying that *"neither the vast majority of individual members of JVL nor the organization itself can be said to be part of the Jewish community"*.[23] Not only did he welcome Zionists into the party and visit the State of Israel, but he also assisted the Jewish Labour Movement in policing who was 'the right kind of Jew' in the party. Two months after his tweet about me, the *Electronic Intifada* reported that Lansman had been plotting to replace Jeremy Corbyn with John McDonnell, although McDonnell had apparently told him to *"fuck off"* after being approached with the idea.[24]

Looking back, it is truly astonishing that Lansman enjoyed the status that he did during the Corbyn years. Despite supposedly not being a Zionist, he is a proponent of 'bi-nationalism',[25] which is a particularly insidious Zionist position that is usually advocated by Zionist entryists into the socialist movement. Bi-nationalists argue that European colonists, who ethnically cleansed Palestine and their progeny, should have 'equal rights' with the people that they colonised. In this fairy tale vision, all should live in peace and harmony together, coloniser and colonised. It's a perverse tradition that has allowed racists to pose as peacemakers. In my view, Lansman is, and remains, an apologist for Zionism and the monster it created in the form of the world's last apartheid state.

During the Corbyn years, it seems that Lansman coasted off the credibility he had earned from working on Tony Benn's deputy leadership campaign in 1981. I am reliably informed, however, that Lansman significantly exaggerated his role in that campaign. Someone else who played an important part in organising support for Benn in Scotland shared with me that Lansman had once whined about always having to buy Benn cups of tea.

Intriguingly, later on in the day of my re-admission to the party, Ben Folley from the leader's office sent me a message using the same term that Lansman had used:

> *"Jeremy has asked if you would put out a message of contrition and seeking to reach out to those who have been offended by some of your comments which led to the disciplinary case. I've just seen your thank you tweet to supporters. A follow up tweet could do as Jeremy suggests. We need to attempt to close down the furore in the PLP today and a goodwill message could help."*

When I eventually spoke to Folley, I was annoyed that the leader's office was dancing to Lansman's tune. I told him in no uncertain terms that there was no way I was issuing *"a message of contrition"*. I certainly wasn't going to be dictated to by Lansman's dead hand. Such a statement from me, I argued, would enflame rather than close down the PLP furore. It would represent a concession and would, therefore, be weaponised. That is precisely what had happened with the statement I'd made, at the request of Corbyn's staff, following the Sheffield rally in February 2019. As far as I was concerned, anyone claiming offence because I opposed the State of Israel's oppression of Palestinians, or because I defended left-wing Jews and other grassroots members who were being slandered, could take a running jump.

Like father, like son

Next up was Seb Corbyn, Jeremy's son, who worked for John McDonnell. He had requested an urgent face-to-face meeting with me to discuss the frenetic situation. Our meeting was arranged in an anonymous room in some obscure corridor that I had never previously seen, deep inside the recesses of the Palace of Westminster. The location for our clandestine engagement was reminiscent of a scene from a John le Carré spy drama. I liked Seb, and he had always been very supportive of me. He was keen to tell me that *"my Dad didn't sell you out"*, but he also tried to persuade me to issue another statement. He said it could be along the lines of what I had said to Afshin Rattansi on his *Going Underground* programme on RT.[26] Rattansi had put to me some obnoxious comments from Amanda Bowman, Vice President of the Board of Deputies of British Jews. I had responded, in vain, by saying:

> *"I deprecate all forms of bigotry and racism and I will continue to fight it in all its forms, wherever I see it. I would like to work in tandem with the Board of Deputies to drive out bigotry and racism from our country ... And we should be allies, not enemies, in that sense."*

Those comments had, plainly, fallen on deaf ears. So, I again pushed back against Seb, calling his suggestion a hare-brained idea. But he insisted that they *"needed something"*. They clearly viewed our enemies like a pack of hungry wolves who could be appeased by throwing some meat their way. They didn't realise that they would simply want more, until they finally became tired of toying with us and decided to dig their teeth directly into our flesh. Seb told me that McDonnell felt it was important. McDonnell's credulity left me flabbergasted. I wondered about what planet he was living on. He was talking like he had just awoken from a four-year-long coma. I pleaded with Seb to take a step back and to look at the evidence. It was impossible to appease the Israel lobby and the assorted right-wing saboteurs. It was a political civil war to the death for the soul of the Labour Party and, unless the leadership began fighting back, it was doomed. In desperation, Seb offered to draft something for my consideration. I was willing to read anything he prepared, but I insisted that there was no way I would apologise, not least because it was me that was owed an apology for being outrageously traduced. However, Seb never sent me a draft statement, probably because Jennie Formby had already wielded the knife before he had time to prepare anything.

After my suspension had been lifted, Tom Watson and Diana Johnson started gathering signatures for a PLP motion calling for the whip to be withdrawn. But before Formby gave in to the baying mob, John McDonnell contacted me. His advice was to *"apologise again and again"*. This was typical of McDonnell. He suggested I should offer to meet any MPs or NEC members who felt offended by anything I'd said and urged me to seek a meeting with the Board of Deputies and Jewish Leadership Council. He was in denial about a tactic that had spectacularly failed time and time again. I told him there was no way I was prepared to do any of those things, not least because the evidence of the previous four years proved that it would not work. I had complied with the restrictive confidentiality clause in the party's disciplinary procedures, while all the time the party's bureaucrats were briefing the media against me. My reputation was being dragged through the gutter, and not one member of the SCG had publicly defended me. I said it was *his* solidarity that I needed now, not adverse advice, and I asked him to issue a supportive statement immediately and to then defend me in the media. Unsurprisingly, he did neither.

Seeking solidarity from my peers

The lack of meaningful support from anyone in or around the leader's office was probably best explained by a comment from one of Corbyn's most senior advisers. I was told by an impeccable source that this adviser had said, *"Chris Williamson is not the hill to die on"*. This arrogant indifference personified the praxis of the predominantly rich kids who staffed Corbyn's office. They bleated on about socialism, but they comprehensively failed to put their rhetoric into practice. Socialism was a fascinating hobby, rather than a way of life, for these guileless political strategists. They proved to be clueless when it came to responding to the hostile forces ranged against Corbyn and the burgeoning grassroots movement he had inspired. Contrary to the impression created by the right-wing and liberal commentariat, it wasn't a red flag that flew above Corbyn's office on the parliamentary estate. It was a white one.

Whilst the party's deputy leader Tom Watson was gathering signatures for a vindictive motion to have the whip withdrawn from me, I contacted eight members of the SCG to ask for their support. I set up a group chat on WhatsApp, and I sent the following message:

> *"Hi Comrades – You may be aware that the haters are planning to table a motion at the PLP to remove the whip from me for a year. As socialists I know we believe in solidarity and I am therefore asking if you are planning to, or would be willing to publish a collective supportive statement for me. There is massive support from grassroots members, but people are increasingly asking, where is the public support from socialist MPs to counter the haters. There may be other MPs like Dennis [Skinner], who would be willing to sign such a statement, so if you could get them to add their support as well that would be great.*

I didn't include the joint chair of the SCG, Lloyd Russell-Moyle, in that circulation list, for reasons that will become apparent later on. For now, suffice it to say that he suffers from Solidarity Deficit Syndrome. However, as I was soon to discover, Russell-Moyle's affliction had gripped the entire membership of the SCG.

Grahame Morris responded almost immediately to say he was supportive of a collective statement. He said that *"they are smarting from your democracy tour"* (a reference to my Democracy Roadshow), but the response from most of the others was lukewarm. Two of them, Ian Lavery and Danielle Rowley, didn't even respond. The previous day, the Lincoln MP, Karen Lee, had posted a tweet welcoming the decision to reinstate me, saying, *"Absolutely chuffed to bits with this news. A principled kind man, who has worked so hard for the Labour Party & his constituency. Great to have him back on board"*.[27] But then the mob got to work, and Lee was viciously lambasted for daring to back me publicly. The vitriol was so intense that she was coerced into issuing an apology. So, on the same day she issued a statement welcoming my return, she released another one:

> *"My apology: Chris is a colleague and was particularly helpful when I succeeded him as Labour's fire minister. I deleted my hastily written post because I did not address the sensitivity of his case. I abhor antisemitism in all its forms and I will redouble my efforts to support the Jewish community across the UK. I apologise for any offence I have caused.*[28]

So, Lee was clearly nervous about showing any support. In response to my WhatsApp message, she said, *"They are vicious and relentless, I've had an awful couple of days for supporting Chris, am hardly using my phone & deleted both twitter and FB apps from my phone. Absolute bullies"*. I responded to Lee's message, empathising with her predicament:

> *"I understand Karen. My daughter received a call from her ex to say 'your Dad's a racist'. This is a civil war comrades and only one side can win. Tactical withdrawals have to come to an end at some point. The Soviet Union stood and fought back against the Nazis at Moscow. We have metaphorically retreated well past Moscow and we're now on the east coast of the USSR. Any further retreats and we'll be drowning in the Sea of Okhotsk".*

I didn't realise at the time just how prophetic my Sea of Okhotsk metaphor would turn out to be. Lee is a decent woman and I appreciate why she backtracked. She was picked off because she was isolated. I blame the lack of leadership by Corbyn and his team, as well as John McDonnell. Tony Greenstein had once described McDonnell as a *"Stafford Cripps re-tread"*, but said he was *"worse than Stafford Cripps"* because Cripps at least *"had a backbone"*.[29] The Corbyn leadership utterly failed to stand up to the PLP's bully-boy tactics, and they bowed down to the fanatical Zionist lobby. Corbyn and McDonnell should have been the first to fulsomely welcome my reinstatement instead of leaving it to others. That they cowered in the shadows whilst Karen Lee was being denounced only proved their poor judgement, and it was another example of the political necrotising fasciitis that afflicted the leadership's response to the sham 'antisemitism crisis'. Lee was upset and embarrassed for backing down, and she followed up her previous message by saying:

> *"I can only begin to guess what you've been through Chris. Trolls have piled on me (& that's been just a couple of days) both local and national journo's calling & texting my private number. My office pressured me to apologise and I'm sorry but I felt so bullied I caved in. It's a cesspit. My daughter is really distressed about it all – I think that is the worst bit. Have come off social media for a bit. I'm so sorry to have weakened, I hope you can understand if not approve."*

Karen Lee should never have been put in that position. She stood up whilst everyone else kept their heads down. The other responses to my plea for solidarity were to say that I needed a 'strategy'. Richard Burgon said:

> *"You need a fully worked out practical strategy to secure your continued membership of the PLP. There are many procedural, legal and process issues to be analysed and considered as part of that".*

It wasn't convincing. It seemed like Burgon and the others wanted to kick the issue into the long grass. Dan Carden did at least acknowledge that there was *"an all-out assault taking place"* and went on to say, *"As a collective we need to fight back"*, but the collective fightback never materialised. Burgon and Laura Pidcock wanted to continue the discussion via Signal, a more secure instant messaging app. It seems they were nervous about anyone discovering they were even talking to me. As far as most of the PLP were concerned, I was persona non grata, and heaven help anyone with the audacity to speak to a political pariah – an 'unperson'. When we resumed the discussion on Signal, I suggested that any 'strategy' needed to include a collective statement of support to demonstrate that I am not isolated and have some support within the PLP. But Burgon bemoaned, *"What can 10 MPs do against a hundred?"*. That was one of the most dispiriting responses during that tragic tale. It underpins why the SCG is so ineffectual and useless. Whereas the Independent Group – seven MPs at the time – had launched a kamikaze attack against the Corbyn leadership in defence of Blairism, these characters couldn't even issue a statement of support for me.

The melting of Lloyd Russell-Moyle

On 1 July 2019, three days after my failure to obtain a solidarity statement from the SCG, the group's joint chair, Lloyd Russell-Moyle, spoke to Emma Barnett on BBC Radio 5 Live. It was one of the most pusillanimous performances I have ever witnessed, a truly cringeworthy interview.[30] He started badly and then got worse. Barnett asked him if he thought I had behaved *"antisemitically"*. He said, *"I wouldn't make that judgement, I would say that he has behaved foolishly in some of the stuff that he's said, and whether that's antisemitic or not, that is for people who are either Jewish or the [NEC] panel"*.[31] Barnett then interrupted him:

> *"No, it's not, I can call out racism and I'm not black. You spend, I'm sure, many of your days doing that on behalf of people. Why on Earth do you have to be Jewish in order to identify antisemitism? On an intellectual level, that falls foul on every level"*.[32]

Russell-Moyle started to melt. Barnett then asserted that I had retweeted or approved of many 'antisemitic' remarks on social media, which was an unadulterated lie. To reinforce her point, she gave four examples of my alleged 'antisemitism'. But even a mischief-making bad faith actor would struggle to justify Barnett's grandstanding averment that they illustrated any form of Judeophobia, because the truth is there wasn't a scintilla of Judeophobia in any of them.

The first example she gave was that I had spoken at one of Jackie Walker's performances of *The Lynching*, but she failed to mention that Walker is herself Jewish. The second was my support for Pete Willsman's re-election to Labour's NEC. He was being monstered after being surreptitiously recorded at an NEC meeting saying that some of those making accusations about 'antisemitism' were Trump supporters. The third was about me quoting people in the Jewish community complaining about what they described as the weaponisation of Judeophobia. And in the fourth example she repeated the lie that I had said the Labour Party had been 'too apologetic' about Judeophobia. But instead of rebutting Barnett's groundless slurs, which she had self-evidently failed to substantiate with her so-called examples, Russell-Moyle completely crumbled and agreed that the examples she gave were indeed 'antisemitic'.

It is important to emphasise that both in the case of Jackie Walker and Pete Willsman, they were secretly recorded in what were supposed to be closed and privileged meetings. In Walker's case it was explicitly portrayed as a safe space to allow members to explore and discuss a sensitive topic. This revealed the unprincipled and deeply unethical tactics used by right-wing Zionists inside the Labour Party, who resorted to taping private meetings in order to lure people into saying something that they could later misuse against them.

Falconer's foul falsifications

One of the other malcontents and bullies who was sticking in the knife was Lord Charles Falconer, Tony Blair's old flatmate. For some idiotic reason, Falconer had been welcomed into the fold by Corbyn. Falconer had initially been appointed Shadow Lord Chancellor by Corbyn in 2015 (later resigning as part of the 2016 coup). In February 2019, a few days before I was originally suspended, Corbyn had made the strategically incomprehensible decision to ask him to oversee Labour's handling of the fictional 'antisemitism crisis'. No doubt the out-of-touch whizz kids in Corbyn's office thought it was an inspired move. But, in the real world, it was an irrational idea that was bound to end in tears. Why would Corbyn ask someone who was emphatically opposed to his leadership to supervise the investigation into an issue that had been massively overstated to explicitly undermine his position? It made no sense, and it was indicative of the capitulation culture that had taken hold since the heady days of the unexpected advance that was made at the 2017 election.

I had known Falconer for some years. He has a country retreat in Nottinghamshire, not too far away from where I live in Derby. We had shared platforms at East Midlands Regional Labour Party events going back nearly 20 years. So, when he effectively accused me of being a racist, Nazi apologist on the *Jeremy Vine Show* on BBC Radio 2, he must have known that he was indulging in a calculated smear. For someone who is a Queen's Counsel, he has a cavalier attitude towards due process.

Later on in 2019, Falconer used an opinion piece in the *Guardian* to twist the knife. He repeated the same hackneyed defamation to claim that I had said Labour was being 'too apologetic' about Judeophobia:

> *"A disciplinary process that regards antisemitism as an appalling evil that has to be rooted out could not have concluded that the correct way to deal with Chris Williamson was let him back into the party with a reprimand – and without referring the case to a full disciplinary hearing – despite his claims that Labour had been "too apologetic" about antisemitism in the party. The process which produced that result must have been interfered with – or isn't worth the paper it is printed on".* [33]

But Falconer surpassed his malignant *Guardian* musings when he appeared on the *Jeremy Vine Show* the same week to discuss 'antisemitism in the Labour Party'. Jeremy Vine asked Falconer what I was supposed to have done wrong. He said he would give three examples but cited only two. In the first example, he quoted a remark he attributed to Gilad Atzmon about the Holocaust, saying, *"The Germans had responded because the Jews had declared war on Germany"*. Falconer then boldly asserted, *"And Chris Williamson supported that".* He must have known I had done no such thing. If he did, then he was consciously repeating a diabolical lie to smear me. If he didn't, then he had no business making such a reprehensible accusation. He then went on to say I had:

> "arranged a meeting in the Houses of Parliament in support of Jackie Walker who had been expelled from the Labour Party for a number of remarks that had brought the party into disrepute, including saying the Jews were largely responsible for the slave trade". [34]

This was yet another misrepresentation of both Walker's status in the party, and, more importantly, of what she had said. Moreover, the example he cited was actually thrown out by the party when she had initially been reinstated. Walker was subsequently suspended again in September 2016 following malicious allegations regarding remarks she had made about the definition of 'antisemitism' that had been covertly recorded. She had not, therefore, been expelled when Falconer spoke to Jeremy Vine. As a senior barrister overseeing the handling of Labour's fictional 'antisemitism crisis', he had no business making damnatory remarks about Walker on national radio. He would be held in contempt of court were he to publicly make derogatory comments like that about a defendant in a live legal case.

I wrote to Falconer the week after his mud-slinging stunt on BBC Radio 2 to tell him he had got his facts wrong. I concluded the letter by asking him to accept that my actions were entirely honourable and driven by a desire to ensure people are treated fairly and with respect. As expected, he didn't even acknowledge my missive, let alone offer a reasoned reply. But two-and-a-half months later, I saw him walking along the Brighton seafront at the 2019 Labour Party conference. He looked panic-stricken when he saw me. He was aghast, as I got closer, when I asked whether he had received my letter. He said he had done. But when I told him I'd not received a reply, he quickened his pace whilst stuttering and stammering some inarticulate waffle, before practically running away to avoid having a conversation with me.

To see this document please scan this QR code.

Falconer's response bore all the hallmarks of a bully who, when confronted about their actions, invariably fold like a deckchair on Brighton beach. Falconer was happy to cast aspersions from the safety of a BBC studio or as part of a parliamentary mob, but he was unable to justify his actions when he came face-to-face with his victim. Falconer's reaction also bolstered my view that Corbyn's appeasement strategy was misconceived.

Accountability as 'mob rule'

Grassroots Labour Party members from all over the country were on the warpath about the PLP's inexcusable antics. Many of the Labour MPs who had joined in the frenzied efforts to get me re-suspended were taken to task by their CLPs. Some faced calls for votes of no confidence and trigger ballots, meaning that members could potentially replace them as candidates in the subsequent general election. This gave rise to sanctimonious shrieks from Tom Watson, of all people, complaining about *"reprehensible bullying"* and *"mob rule"*.[35] His self-righteous remarks illustrated the spectacular capacity for breath-taking double standards by the Westminster village people. Watson was a renowned bully. In fact, he was described as *"a vile and obnoxious bully"* by members of Labour's NEC.[36] He had a reputation as a manipulative and divisive fixer, stretching back years. Former Blairite MP, Denis MacShane, described Watson as *"a cynical old fixer"* who *"was at the heart of trying to destabilise Tony Blair"*.[37] So, it was a bit rich for Watson to complain about *"bullying"* and *"mob rule"*. It was an unambiguous example of projection. Everything he was falsely accusing members of doing he was guilty of doing himself. And he was doing it in the full glare of wall-to-wall publicity.

One of the most illogical complaints about members holding these rogue MPs to account was that one of them, Ellie Reeves, was pregnant. This prompted Harriet Harman to write to the NEC to demand that pregnant Labour MPs should not face re-selection.[38] It was a truly astonishing intervention. Harman wanted to place pregnant MPs above criticism. In her view, it didn't matter how awful they were; they were untouchable. She even resorted to moral blackmail, warning of a *"justified outcry"* if an MP going through a selection process miscarried. But according to Harman's warped logic, sitting MPs who were pregnant should be given a bye when a general election was called. It was, of course, total nonsense, and it offended against all the principles of democracy. It was a classic dead cat strategy. The furore that was generated also got Ellie Reeves off the hook as the vote of no confidence against her was withdrawn.[39] Miriam Mirwitch, the chair of Young Labour at the time, joined in the debate by conflating the role of a worker with that of an MP. She said, *"MPs who are pregnant or on maternity leave should be automatically reselected. It's wrong when bosses sack workers who are pregnant or on maternity leave. The same applies to MPs"*.[40] But the same did not apply. MPs are elected representatives who should be accountable and subject to democratic procedures. If MPs want the same employment rights as workers, then they should get real jobs. This really goes to the heart of the matter. For these MPs, sitting in Parliament is a career rather than a vocation. Given how lucrative parliamentary work is, they will do anything to hang on to their positions. This makes them highly ineffective at bringing about the socialist change that many grassroots activists crave.

The leader's office once again facilitated the agents provocateurs with a pathetic and unhelpful intervention. As usual, they came down on the side of the scoundrels who didn't just want to oust me, but who also wanted to destroy Corbyn and obliterate the Labour Left. Corbyn's team made it known that Corbyn did not support the motion and his office put pressure on Lewisham West CLP to ensure local members were unable to vote on a trigger ballot or a no confidence motion against Reeves. They even wrote to the PLP to say that pregnant MPs should be exempt from re-selection processes for the next general election.[41] Speaking afterwards about being reprieved, Reeves said:

"I was really pleased to receive a message from [the leader's office] this morning saying the leader has stated he does not support the

no confidence vote. This was the support I was hoping for when I contacted them about it".[42]

Corbyn had, only months earlier, done the same for the Blairite Luciana Berger before she resigned from the party. It made no impression on her whatsoever. This was another example of Corbyn following an appeasement strategy even after it had demonstrably failed. Berger still went on to claim that the party was *"institutionally anti-Semitic"*.[43] She also said, *"People are just appalled and terrified, genuinely very, very concerned about what the future holds with ... Corbyn as Prime Minister"*.[44] The tragedy is that Corbyn's kind-heartedness enabled them to repeatedly play him as a fool, and his advisers served as doormats on which they wiped their jackboots.

Ermine clad clique

Before being suspended, I had repeatedly warned that the gutless responses to Corbyn's enemies was only strengthening their resolve to destroy us. But Corbyn, his office, and the SCG were behaving like rabbits caught in the headlights. Consequently, on 17 July 2019, less than three weeks after Corbyn and the SCG had failed to resist the calls to re-suspend me, 67 so-called 'Labour' peers took out a full-page attack ad against Corbyn in the *Guardian*. It was an unprecedented move, designed to do maximum damage, yet there were no consequences for these miscreant members of the House of Lords.

Corbyn, and the panoply of losers who comprised his team and 'allies', had provoked this situation through their own cowardice. The heading on their Lordships' dishonest advertorial stated, *"The Labour Party welcomes everyone* irrespective of race, creed, age, gender identity, or sexual orientation. (*except, it seems, Jews)"*. That subheading sat above a bold banner headline pronouncing, *"This is your legacy Mr Corbyn"*. The statement itself was a tissue of lies, innuendos, and half-truths. It claimed that Labour was *"no longer a safe place for all members and supporters"*, that Corbyn had allowed a *"toxic culture ... to divide our movement"* and that Corbyn hadn't *"opened [his] eyes"* to what was happening. It also asserted that Labour's *"staff shielded antisemitic conduct* *from the party's disciplinary rules"* and that Corbyn was *"presiding over the most shaming period in Labour's history"*. It concluded by saying to Corbyn, *"You have failed to defend our party's anti-racist values. You have therefore failed the test of leadership"*.[45]

Their Lordships' claims were utter drivel. Statistics had already been produced to prove that their claims were false. Corbyn had done more to stand up to racism and bigotry than all 67 of their Lordships put together. They were the ones dividing the movement by refusing to accept the democratic will of the membership and doing everything in their power to undermine Corbyn. But they were not going to let facts get in the way of a good old-fashioned smear.

As for their Lordships' claim about thousands of party members resigning, the Labour Party had become the biggest political party in Western Europe under Corbyn's leadership. No doubt some people did leave; there is always churn in any political movement. Some were undoubtedly opposed to Labour adopting a socialist and anti-imperialist programme. But their Lordships were misreporting the reality of the situation in another disreputable attempt to overstate and weaponise Judeophobia.

The mistake of Corbyn's leadership was not in failing to indulge the bogus assertions of bitter malcontents, like their Lordships, but in failing to stand up to them. He failed that test again in response to this despicable attack ad. Instead of withdrawing the whip, his reaction was a lame comment. A Labour spokesperson said that their Lordships were *"hostile to Jeremy Corbyn's politics"*, adding that the claims were *"false and misleading"*. The spokesperson also pointed out that *"disciplinary procedures relate to about 0.06% of members"*.[46]

And where was Jennie Formby? Why didn't she take any disciplinary action against the recalcitrant 67 who had unquestionably brought the party into disrepute? After all, she was supposed to be the custodian of the party's Rule Book. But it seems that there is one rule for some and another for everyone else. To put it another way, Formby discriminated against left-wing grassroots members and high-profile figures who challenged the false narrative against the party, whilst giving right-wingers free rein to do as they pleased.

CHAPTER SEVENTEEN

FIGHTING BACK

I had played ball with the party during the time immediately after my suspension. I had hoped that Jeremy Corbyn, his team, and the SCG would all finally see sense. There was a momentary, faint glimmer of this when my suspension was finally lifted. But their cowardice and betrayal led me right back to square one. After being re-suspended, I decided I would need to go on the offensive. I was no longer going to sit quietly and bide my time.

Whilst my supposed allies among the leadership prevaricated, grassroots support for me was building. Tina Werkmann did an incredible job as secretary of Labour Against the Witch-Hunt (LAW) in urging CLPs to pass motions in support of my reinstatement and in countering Jennie Formby's efforts to suppress solidarity motions.[1] Formby had written to CLP secretaries throughout the country advising them that solidarity motions regarding disciplinary cases were *"not competent business"*.[2] There was a heavy undertone that there would be consequences for any CLP who defied her diktat. However, there was no constitutional impediment to doing so, and numerous CLPs passed supportive motions in spite of her. But many other CLPs, including my own, were deterred.

I was particularly disappointed by the failure of solidarity from the delegates to my own CLP, especially the new chair, Elaine Dean. She had only recently taken over from Sarah Russell, who was working as my constituency office manager at the time. I was shocked by Dean's willingness to throw me under the bus. She had previously sent me an effusive private message, telling me that I was *"a brilliant MP and councillor"* and *"you are neither racist nor anti-Semitic and I've said this to everyone"*. She also offered to provide a *"sworn statement or affidavit that [I'm] not racist or anti-Semitic"*. But when I asked her to make a public statement to that effect, she refused (although, before I was re-suspended, she said she had written to Formby to express her support for me). It seems that, as the weeks went on, the disinformation about me had had an effect on her attitude. I was told that there was a big row at a Derby North CLP meeting where an attempt was made to pass a motion demanding my reinstatement, which Dean had ruled out of order.

Lee Garratt, a good local comrade who attended that meeting, was so irate that he stormed out in disgust, loudly complaining about what he described as an abject betrayal and a gerrymandered political fix. Like a lot of constituencies, there was an old guard in Derby North and Derby South CLPs, who whinged and moaned about the Corbyn revolution. They were hostile towards new members flooding into the party who were inspired by Jeremy Corbyn, and they resented it when 'Corbynistas' turned up at party meetings. I had organised campaign sessions in Derby nearly every week for over 20 years, but I rarely, if ever, saw any of those curmudgeons interacting with voters on the doorstep and in the community. Where many of them could be seen, however, was at Margaret Beckett's Derby South CLP annual constituency dinners and the afternoon soirees she hosted at her Derby home. They enjoyed wining and dining, but they would never do the hard graft required to win elections. One of those influential curmudgeons was Margaret's late husband, Leo Beckett. He was particularly aggrieved about Corbyn winning the leadership. When I attended one of Margaret's luncheons at her Derby home, shortly after the leadership election, Leo was contemptuous about the new leader. I remember him pouring scorn on Corbyn and saying, *"He's never taken a sensible position in his life"*. But what exactly did Leo mean by a *"sensible position"*? Opposing war? Campaigning for peace? Rejecting cuts to social security? Objecting to privatisation? Condemning tuition fees? Resisting imperialism? Are these not the kinds of things that everyone in the Labour Party should have been doing? Leo's objections to Corbyn reminded me of Harold Wilson's jibe about Tony Benn in 1981 when he said he *"immatures with age"*.[3] But as Benn said back then, *"I know why they call us names. It's because they dare not face our arguments"*.[4] History was repeating itself.

Meanwhile, as Derby North's CLP delegates dithered, grassroots members in Derby and everywhere else were forthright in their condemnation of my treatment. Tina Werkmann organised a big LAW demonstration outside Labour's headquarters to lobby a meeting of the NEC to demand my reinstatement.

She also garnered high-profile endorsements from celebrities and Labour movement icons. The comedian, writer, and actress Francesca Martinez was also incredibly supportive and went out of her way to obtain VIP backing for me. A few months before I was suspended, Martinez had interviewed me on stage at Conway Hall in London, for a JC4PM event in front of an enthusiastic and supportive audience.[5]

But despite the grassroots and high-profile support, Formby's bureaucracy was unmoved. After Formby's unlawful decision to reimpose my suspension, I started a crowdfunding campaign to mount a High Court challenge to preserve my membership of the party I joined when I was still a teenager. I knew that legal action was prohibitively expensive, but I felt that I had no choice. A group of my advisers established the 'Campaign for Chris Williamson' and started fundraising in earnest. We then met with my legal team, Jamie Potter and Liz McGlone, at Bindmans LLP. Much to the chagrin of the PLP and other assorted opponents, the response from supporters was incredible. It was a huge financial risk to engage in litigation against the party's bureaucracy, because money was no object to them, whereas I had no savings and still had a mortgage to service. The consequences of defeat would have left me with a six-figure legal bill. But the solidarity from grassroots members was incredibly heart-warming and, at times, emotionally overwhelming. It soon became clear that any legal costs would be covered by thousands of individual donations.

Thus, the legal war of attrition began. People were taking sides over my case which was fast becoming a cause célèbre, prompting well known public figures to nail their colours to the mast. In my corner were stars like Roger Waters, Miriam Margolyes, Professor Noam Chomsky, Alexei Sayle, Francesca Martinez, Lowkey, Dr Yanis Varoufakis, Dr Norman Finkelstein, and Ken Loach. Professor Ilan Pappé even recorded a video in my support.[6] The opposite corner had the likes of Rachel Riley, James O'Brien, Tracy-Ann Oberman, Owen Jones, David Baddiel, and Billy Bragg.

On 27 June 2019, the *Guardian* published a letter from over 100 prominent members of the Jewish community in my support.[7] The letter eloquently countered the bile being thrown at me, by unequivocally vouching for my credentials:

> "We the undersigned, all Jews, are writing in support of Chris Williamson MP and to register our dismay at the recent letter organised by Tom Watson and signed by PLP and [House of Lords] members calling for his suspension. ...
>
> "Chris Williamson did not say that the party had been 'too apologetic about antisemitism' as has been widely misreported. He correctly stated that the Labour Party has done more than any other party to combat the scourge of antisemitism and that therefore its stance should be less apologetic. Such attacks on Jeremy Corbyn's supporters aim to undermine not only the Labour Party's leadership but also all pro-Palestinian members.
>
> "The mass media have ignored the huge support for Chris both within and beyond the Labour Party. Support that includes many Jews. The Party needs people like him with the energy and determination to fight for social justice. As anti-racist Jews we regard Chris as our ally: he stands as we do with the oppressed rather than the oppressor. It should also be noted that he has a longer record of campaigning against racism and fascism than most of his detractors.
>
> "The Chakrabarti Report recommended that the party's disciplinary procedures respect due process, favour education over expulsion and promote a culture of free speech yet this has been abandoned in practice. We ask the Labour Party to reinstate Chris Williamson and cease persecuting such members on false allegations of antisemitism."

Those who had been carefully constructing the fake storyline about an 'antisemitism crisis' in the Labour Party went apoplectic when the letter was published and piled on to the newspaper. The credibility of some of the signatories was called into question. Hope Not Hate (HNH) – which has Ruth Smeeth on its board, and which has received funding through the Home Office's Building a Stronger Britain Together programme[8] – took to Twitter to inform the world that they'd complained:

> *"The person who signed the letter with HNH next to their name had absolutely no authority to do so, and the* Guardian *have removed our name at our request. Our position on Chris Williamson is and has always been clear..."*

The tawdry tactics paid off. By the next day, the *Guardian* had deleted the letter from its website and replaced it with a message saying, *"This letter was taken down on 9 July 2019 pending investigation"*.[9] When the letter was scrubbed from the *Guardian's* website, it popped up all over the place in other online publications, and it was probably seen by more people as a consequence. The signatories to the letter included Leah Levane and Jenny Manson of Jewish Voice for Labour and such Jewish panjandrums as Noam Chomsky, Norman Finkelstein, Ed Asner, and Richard Falk.

Whilst the heat against me was clearly intensifying in response to my decision to stop laying low, I was no longer feeling forlorn. The Mexican revolutionary hero, Emiliano Zapata, is often attributed as saying, *"It is better to live on your feet than to die on your knees"*. That couldn't more accurately sum up how I felt. I was determined to fight back rather than cower in some vain hope that the situation would eventually resolve itself. I was standing tall, and my supporters were becoming ever-more vocal in my defence. It was obvious that this change of posture was the right thing to do.

CHAPTER EIGHTEEN

TOTAL WAR

In 2019, I used the summer months to embark on another speaking tour, as I'd done in 2018 on the Democracy Roadshow. Just as my previous tour had riled-up the PLP and media hordes, this one would have the same effect, except on a much greater scale. This time, I would not only be speaking about politics, but I would also be aiming to buttress my legal fundraising campaign against the Labour Party, which had already been going well.

Unlike in 2018, Labour members were restrained from inviting me to formal constituency party meetings, thanks to a diktat issued by Jennie Formby. So, party members made ingenious alternative arrangements to get around the Labour straitjacket. I was also invited to address various trades councils up and down the country. After a few meetings had taken place successfully, I announced a sequel to the Democracy Roadshow, again speaking alongside Tosh McDonald. After that, we were flooded with requests to speak. To make the new Democracy Roadshow official, we made another promo video.[1] But, instead of using Tosh's Harley-Davidson motorbikes, as we'd done in our 2018 video, we hired a 1964 Ford Mustang Convertible. The colour was a stunning candy apple red. We had great fun. The backing track for the promo video was Canned Heat's pulsating 'On the Road Again'. The only trouble was that it was an overcast day when we'd hired the Mustang, and it rained a lot. Perhaps something could be said here about pathetic fallacy. The day embodied the state of the Labour Party. Yet, thanks to the tech wizardry of Ammar Kazmi, who filmed and edited the video, the final product looked like it had been shot on a beautiful English summer's day. Every meeting at which I spoke held a collection to go towards the legal fund, and thousands of pounds were raised on the road that summer.

In addition to the Democracy Roadshow sequel, I had also received a number of invitations from Labour members to speak about Modern Monetary Theory (MMT) and its possible application in the creation of a democratic, socialist economy. That wasn't a topic to stir the cancel culture creatures, you might think. But you would be wrong. They tried the usual dirty tricks of pressuring venues, warning Labour members about possible disciplinary action for attending my seminars, and even threatening staff at potential meeting places. But it was all to no avail. Not a single meeting was cancelled. In fact, when I spoke in Harlow, the former Labour MP, Stan Newens, made a very public point about attending, and he insisted on having a photograph taken with me. It was an uplifting moment for which I was incredibly grateful. I couldn't help thinking that, if only the MPs in the SCG had an ounce of Newens's steadfastness and sense of solidarity, we could have delivered a knockout blow against the reprobates. Sadly, Newens has since passed away, on 2 March 2021, aged 91. He had represented the movement with great distinction during his life. He served as a Labour MP from 1964 to 1970 and 1974 to 1983, and he was a Member of the European Parliament from 1984 to 1999. A few years before he died, he wrote an excellent autobiography, *In Quest of a Fairer Society*,[2] about his life in politics. I have a treasured copy in my bookcase that was personally signed by Newens when he came to promote it in Derby in May 2016.

Al fresco meeting beats Brighton bullies

My MMT seminar in Brighton saw right-wingers and the Zionist lobby going to extraordinary lengths to stop it from taking place. Their hate-filled campaign of harassment and intimidation resulted in three venues cancelling the bookings made by Greg Hadfield, who was organising the event. He told me that the proprietors had been subjected to what he described as *"intolerable pressure, including foul-mouthed abuse and threats, online, by telephone, and in person"*. The threatening behaviour was so severe that Sussex Police even said that they could not guarantee my safety.

The Brighton saga started when I was due to speak at the city's Brighthelm Centre on 7 August 2019. We were all set for what promised to be a stimulating meeting and *Guardian* cartoonist, Steve Bell, who lives near Hadfield, had donated two signed prints of a cartoon that the *Guardian* had refused to publish. The first one depicted Tom Watson as 'FATBERG SLIM, THE ANTISEMITE

FINDER GENERAL'. The second one was of the Israeli Prime Minister, Benjamin Netanyahu, sitting in front of the fireplace in 10 Downing Street with Razan al-Najjar on fire in the log burner. Al-Najjar was a young medic who'd been killed by Israeli snipers at the Gaza prison fence. Hadfield was planning to raffle them off at the meeting to help raise funds to cover the cost of the room hire. We had no idea that this plan would soon be upended.

Hadfield publicised the event on 23 July 2019 and, within 24 hours, more than 100 people had registered to attend. But no sooner had the event been publicised than it was cancelled. The day after, he received a curt email simply saying, *"Brighthelm cannot accept your booking for Thursday 7th August, this has now been cancelled on our database"*. They referred him to the hire agreement which states, *"Brighthelm reserves the right to stop or close any event without notice or compensation should it breach any UK Law, endanger or cause offence to other centre users or members of the staff or public"*. The implication was that a riotous affair had been planned, which was plainly ridiculous. Apparently the self-styled 'Sussex Jewish Representative Council' had complained and issued the following statement:

> *"This is a crass publicity stunt by someone, twice suspended from the Labour Party, looking for attention. ... As if that weren't insulting and disrespectful enough, the host thinks it is appropriate to auction signed copies of a cartoon that the* Guardian *refused to print due to concerns about its content. Our city and our community has experienced enough antisemitism."*

Later that same day, we also discovered that the ultra-Blairite MP, Peter Kyle, who represented an adjoining constituency to the one where the Brighthelm Centre is located, had also complained. In a statement to the *Argus* newspaper, Kyle said:

> *"I believe the meeting has been cancelled due to the room no longer being made available for them to use. I made my views known – our city should not be a welcoming place for people who bait the Jewish community or sow seeds of division. My office contacted them earlier to express my concerns ... I'm pleased the*

> Brighthelm have acted so sensitively and responsibly, they are a credit to our community."[3]

A journalist at the *Argus*, Jody Doherty-Cove, sent me a copy of Kyle's statement and asked for my comment. I said:

> "The grotesque slurs that Peter Kyle and others have levelled against me are truly despicable. I have a long and proud record of fighting racism, which has always involved standing up for every oppressed and marginalised group in society, including Jewish people.
>
> "When Peter Kyle was still in nappies, I was an active member of the Anti-Nazi League, physically confronting foul racists and anti-Semites in the National Front.
>
> "And under my leadership, I ensured that Derby City Council was one of the first local authorities in the country to establish an annual Holocaust Memorial Day commemoration.
>
> "The cancellation of this meeting venue has chilling implications for free speech. I was due to speak about democratising the economy. Peter Kyle needs to explain why he thinks it is acceptable to censor such a discussion."[4]

Hadfield then made enquiries about holding the meeting at Brighton's Friends Meeting House, but he opted instead for the Holiday Inn, which could accommodate a bigger audience. Registrations for the event had already exceeded 200. When this became public knowledge, the website was flooded with a litany of fake registrations, which included numerous vulgar pseudonyms. But their gratuitousness wasn't going to stop the seminar from proceeding.

However, fake registrations weren't the only trick that the opposition had up their sleeve, and their odious operation began to take a more sinister turn. There was an orchestrated social media campaign against the Holiday Inn and threats of a worldwide boycott if they allowed me to speak at a gathering on their premises. The zealots didn't stop there, either. Staff at the hotel had to endure numerous abusive phone calls. But the worst was still yet to come. Two men went to the hotel and threatened the reception staff that there would be *"consequences"* if the hotel went ahead with the meeting. And we know only too well the kind of disruption of which some Zionist extremists are capable. It will be recalled that they made bomb threats at the 2018 Labour Party conference to stop the screening of *WitchHunt*, a film about Jackie Walker's mistreatment. I understand that one member of staff felt so unsettled by the abuse she had received that she didn't come into work the next day. The pressure that the Zionist extremists had exerted had its intended effect and, two days before I was due to speak, the Holiday Inn cancelled. They said, *"We cannot allow our guests and employees to be put at potential harm"*.

Hadfield then approached the Friends Meeting House again, who agreed to accept the booking. But this replacement was deliberately not publicised. We agreed to keep it under wraps to try to prevent a repetition of what had happened with the Holiday Inn and the Brighthelm Centre. So, it was agreed to ask attendees to rendezvous at another location, where Hadfield would meet them before walking them down to the venue. However, less than six hours before I was due to speak, the Friends Meeting House also cancelled. Sussex Police had told them that, if the meeting went ahead, they would be unable to guarantee the safety of attendees and staff, although they apparently did not instruct them to cancel. The intervention by the police prompted the outside security company used by Friends Meeting House to pull out, saying they did not have the resources to deal with the situation.

I was about an hour's drive away from Brighton when Hadfield called to tell me what had happened. He explained that the only remaining option was to have an al fresco assembly. He informed me about what the police had said about my personal safety, and he was prepared for me to pull out at that eleventh hour. When the far-right blog *Guido Fawkes* heard about the third cancellation, they were jubilant. *"Williamson's Brighton Block"*, screamed a presumptuous graphic they'd created.[5] But there was no chance that I was going to give the haters the victory that they craved. I said that, come hell or high water, I was going to make my speech that evening.

In the end, the meeting was a huge success, with well over 150 people in attendance at Regency Square on Brighton's seafront. Thankfully, Hadfield had a contingency plan. He had obtained an outside public address system, so I had no difficulty making myself heard. Meanwhile, for all their bluster, the Zionist censors could only muster a half-dozen people, which included a bedraggled ragtag and bobtail of right-wing Labour Party malcontents. They cut a pathetic spectacle as they tried to intimidate the attendees by photographing them as they entered the square. I didn't even see them until afterwards, as I had entered the square through its underground car park.

After I finished my speech, I sat down on the retaining wall in the middle of Regency Square. A young woman took up the microphone and began to give a rousing speech to the attendees. At that point, I was approached from behind by a menacing-looking, burly character, who insisted that he wanted to *"talk"* to me. He was the only Zionist thug who had dared to venture onto the square, whilst the rest stood by the perimeter. Whilst I was sat down, he stood directly behind me, with his boots level with my lower back. I maintained my composure, and I told him that I'd be happy to speak with him, just as soon as the event had finished. But he aggressively demanded that I speak to him immediately. At that point, Ammar Kazmi, who'd accompanied me to the rally, intervened. He stood up and got eye-level with the intimidator. Hadfield then joined his side. Given the way that the Board of Deputies and right-wing Labour Party figures had generated such a febrile atmosphere, I thought that the guy might physically attack me, perhaps with a knife or a gun. In view of what had happened to Jo Cox MP, who was shot dead by a right-wing extremist in 2016, my heart was beating ten to the dozen, and my imagination was running wild. But I need not have worried. Kazmi and Hadfield had faced him down, and they were soon joined by other attendees who surrounded the brawny bully. Eventually, he fled the scene.

The speeches continued with Hadfield operating an open mic system to give people the opportunity to say a few words. It was then that an incredibly moving moment occurred. A Jewish woman, who was the daughter of two Holocaust survivors, asked Hadfield if she could address the audience. She spoke eloquently about her support for me and then asked if every Jewish person in attendance would stand by my side, next to a poster that said, 'Reinstate Chris Williamson'. She then asked them if they would take a group picture with me. It was a truly wonderful gesture, which brought a lump to my throat and tears to my eyes. The video of that interaction, and the photograph that was taken, were widely shared on social media. But the purity of that moment of unalloyed love and solidarity was sullied by the Labour Party's broken bureaucracy. They used that beautiful instant as one of the spurious reasons to impose a third suspension against me, just before the High Court hearing. In the warped minds of those Labour Party functionaries, some of those in attendance were the 'wrong kind of Jew'.

Trade unionist warmth, from Tolpuddle to Durham

The previous month, in June 2019, I attended the Durham Miners' Gala, as well as the Tolpuddle Martyrs' Festival in Dorset. I was made to feel incredibly welcome at both events, where the support from those in attendance was virtually unanimous.

At the Durham Miners' Gala, it was a fabulous feeling to be so well-received at the biggest annual expression of working class solidarity in the country. I had been asked by labour movement hero John Dunn to march behind the banner of the Orgreave Truth and Justice Campaign. It was a gorgeous sunny day as we wound our way through Durham's picturesque streets that were lined with thousands of people watching the parade of trade union and other labour movement banners pass by. As we neared the iconic County Hotel, where senior labour movement figures always wait on the balcony, looking over the march, Dunn began a chant of *"Reinstate Chris Williamson"*. The reaction of the crowd was remarkable. It was another one of many humbling moments that I experienced that year. ASLEF president Tosh McDonald and film director Ken Loach were joining in the cheers from the hotel balcony. Standing alongside them were Labour MPs Emily Thornberry and Rebecca Long-Bailey. They were less than thrilled to see me, and they were clearly not amused by the crowd's reaction. They looked like they had just swallowed a wasp.

Later on, at Tolpuddle, Cathy Augustine, vice chair of the Labour Representation Committee, had made some 'Campaign for Chris Williamson' T-shirts. She and a number of others were wearing them at the event. As well as a display of solidarity, it proved to be an excellent marketing effort, as numerous donations were made to my legal crowdfunder as a consequence. I spoke to representatives of most of the trade unions who were there, and they were universally supportive. I met with the general secretary and president of the Bakers' Union, Ronnie Draper and Ian Hodson, who were absolutely solid in their support.

Outside of SW1 in London, in which I was always encircled by out-of-touch malcontents, so many real people were on my side. It kept me feeling buoyant.

Drama at Peterloo

After the events in Durham and Tolpuddle, Alan Davies of the *Word* newspaper, contacted me on behalf of the Manchester Trades Council. They wanted to invite me to be the keynote speaker at the bicentenary of the Peterloo Massacre. The massacre was a brutal suppression of working class aspiration in 1819, which inspired Percy Shelley to write his celebrated poem *The Masque of Anarchy*. I was bowled over to be asked to speak at such a prestigious event. But, as the date drew closer and I was advertised as the keynote speaker, the usual suspects got to work with their threadbare smears, threats, and intimidation. There were even warnings of violence, and the organising committee were so concerned about my safety that arrangements were made to meet me some distance from where the rally was due to take place on Albert Square. I was then escorted to the rally with four bodyguards surrounding me. It all seemed rather surreal that such extreme safety precautions were deemed necessary. In the end, there was no need for minders. The reception could not have been friendlier (although I accept that it only takes one extremist to cause mayhem!).

Two centuries before, vested interests in the Establishment had wanted to stop Henry Hunt, a radical speaker who was campaigning for parliamentary reform, from addressing a crowd at the same location. Hunt was advocating for civil rights, including free speech and democracy. This is what precipitated the massacre that we were due to commemorate. Some people in Manchester's labour movement were even labelling me as a twenty-first century Henry Hunt because of my campaigns for greater democracy and the efforts being made to silence me. But my opponents weren't able to call on the local yeomanry this time, as the disreputable William Hulton had done two centuries earlier. Nevertheless, they still went to great lengths to disrupt the commemoration when Manchester Trades Council refused to withdraw the invitation. An emergency motion that was tabled at the Trades Council to cancel my appearance was decisively defeated. Manchester City Council even cordoned off parts of the square to try to limit attendance and they withdrew an agreement to provide a power supply for the public address system on the day. The Manchester-based *Jewish Telegraph* were gloating. *"Electric shock for Williamson"*, shrieked their front-page headline.[6] A Labour spokesperson allegedly told the *Jewish Telegraph* that no Labour MPs would be speaking because, *"It would be utter career suicide for them to do so. Williamson is toxic"*.[7] The leadership of some local trade unions withdrew their sponsorship of, and their speakers at, the event because of my attendance.

Julie Ward, who was a Labour MEP at the time, was scheduled to speak. But with a week to go, she wrote to Manchester Trades Council to say that if she had known I would be speaking, she would have politely declined the invitation. She warned of unintended consequences and collateral damage if I were allowed to address the rally. But Manchester Trades Council demonstrated their commitment to the principles of democracy, free speech, and solidarity by rejecting these siren voices, and I am incredibly grateful to them for their support. I am particularly thankful to Alan Davies and Stefan Cholewka for the camaraderie they displayed, even though they were put under enormous pressure. The SCG would have done well to take a leaf out of their book.

The vitriol and hyperbole had reached new levels, but it made very little impact on grassroots trade unionists and Labour Party members. Despite all the logistical obstacles that were erected, the day went incredibly well. The FBU provided an excellent public address system from their converted fire engine, which doubled-up as the platform for speakers. And, despite the Labour council's best endeavours to limit attendance, thousands squeezed into the available space in the square. I was greeted by loud cheers and thunderous applause when Alan Davies introduced me, and I used my speech to talk about my passion for justice, equality, and solidarity. I also spoke about my unwavering support for Jeremy Corbyn:

> *"We have a socialist leader of the Labour Party, probably for the first time since Keir Hardie. And it will be through our strength of purpose, our mass movement, that we will ensure that we carry Jeremy Corbyn across the threshold of 10 Downing Street and sustain him when he gets there."*

I concluded my speech by quoting the final verse of Shelley's seminal poem:

> *"Rise like Lions after slumber*
> *In unvanquishable number –*
> *Shake your chains to earth like dew*
> *Which in sleep had fallen on you –*
> *Ye are many – they are few."*

Shelley's words couldn't have been more apposite in the circumstances. After I had spoken from the platform, I spent the rest of the day shaking hands with well-wishers and posing for selfies with people. The actor, author, stand-up comedian, television presenter, and former recording artist Alexei Sayle had even travelled to Manchester to show his solidarity with me. The enthusiasm for the political message I was advocating was immense. I was hopeful that the grassroots support I was still enjoying would give Corbyn and the SCG the confidence to break their apparent *omertà* and come out swinging against the right-wing mischief-makers.

Zionist zealots swarm the University of Nottingham

The vitriol I faced was incessant. In October 2019, I found myself embroiled in yet another trumped-up 'antisemitism' controversy. I had been asked to speak to students at the University of

Nottingham by the former East Midlands BBC political editor, John Hess, who is an honorary professor in politics there. It was an annual slot I had filled for Hess for a couple of years. Needless to say, my previous lectures had been uneventful. But not this year. The Zionist trolls were out in force, making baseless denunciations about me and putting pressure on the university to cancel my appearance.

The uproar began after the university issued a statement about my upcoming lecture. It said, *"The Centre for British Politics (CBP) is delighted to be inviting Chris Williamson, Labour MP for Derby North to deliver a talk at the School of Politics and International Relations"*. Soon after, an organised lobbying effort was made by the pro-Israel Union of Jewish Students. Three days before the scheduled seminar, the UJS campaigns organiser, Daniel Kosky, misinformed the *Nottingham Post* that I supposedly had *"a consistent history of Jew-baiting and defending antisemitism"*.[8] He said the UJS were calling for *"the event to be cancelled immediately."*[9] In response to the pressure, the university issued a shoddy statement. Whilst they rightly refused to cancel the lecture, they simultaneously disparaged me. The opening two paragraphs were particularly egregious:

> *"The University of Nottingham does not in any way condone the actions and statements of Mr Chris Williamson MP that led to his suspension from the Labour Party and condemns any form of intolerance to religious belief of any kind. While we have no reason to believe that he will break the law when speaking on our campus, the University will monitor Mr Williamson's actions closely and intervene were there to be any speech that might be considered unlawful."*[10]

Break the law? Unlawful speech? What an outrageous insinuation to make about a serving MP with absolutely no history of doing either of those things! For a prestigious seat of learning to allow itself to be pushed around and manipulated by a group that supports a racist, settler-colonial ideology, demonstrated just how pervasive the phoney 'antisemitism' narrative had become. The lecture itself took place amid tight security. The UJS had organised a demonstration that was joined by a handful of students, which suggested that they had overestimated their support on campus. However, that didn't stop the media from giving them a platform unwarranted by their tiny contingent. A number of the UJS extremists infiltrated the lecture theatre. One pro-Israel zealot, Joshua Lee, tried to disrupt my presentation with a tirade of verbal abuse. He barked a longwinded diatribe, which concluded by saying, *"Are you the most unlucky anti-racism campaigner or are you just an outright liar?"*.

Joshua Lee is an interesting case-study. His activities reveal how pro-Israel campaigners on university campuses are able to pose as aggrieved 'Jewish students' who apparently have no ulterior motives and whose attacks deserve to be treated with poignancy and reflection. This is the standard modus operandi for the State of Israel's student pawns, in whom it invests unspeakable amounts of time, resources and finances to train. Another good example of the growing trend of pro-Israel militancy on British university campuses is the case of Edward Isaacs, a student at the University of Bristol. He successfully campaigned to have Professor David Miller sacked in October 2021 for his factually accurate and evidence-based comments on Zionism.[11] Isaacs was assisted in his crusade by right-wing scribblers like Sabrina Miller of *Guido Fawkes* and small-time hacks like Ben Bloch. Both Isaacs and Lee have links to Israeli politicians. Isaacs has served as an intern in the State of Israel for the Deputy Mayor of Jerusalem,[12] and I understand that he had claimed to be personally aggrieved by Professor Miller's astute comments (a common *hasbara* tactic).

Just months before Lee launched his tirade against me, according to his own LinkedIn profile, he had been engaged heavily in pro-Israel work, including within the Zionist state itself.[13] I don't believe it would be a stretch to say that Lee is a dyed-in-the-wool Zionist and a pro-Israel lobbyist.

Between July 2018 and August 2019, Lee held a Fellowship at the Committee for Accuracy in Middle East Reporting in America (CAMERA), a pro-Israel 'media monitoring' outfit that was set up in 1982 *"to respond to* The Washington Post's *coverage of Israel's Lebanon incursion"*.[14] During the Zionist invasion of Lebanon in 1982, under the command of the late war criminal Ariel Sharon, the Israel Occupation Forces paved the way for far-right Christian militias tied to the Kataeb Party (also known as the Phalanges) to brutally massacre, torture, and rape thousands of unarmed Palestinians in the Sabra and Shatila refugee camps. Over two days, the Phalanges created a bloodbath, armed with knives, axes, and hatchets. During the assault on the camps, the Israelis blocked the exits and provided logistical support to the Phalanges. Whilst the calamity of Sabra and Shatila was only one of numerous slaughters perpetrated against the Palestinian and Lebanese peoples during the invasion and subsequent occupation, it became one of the most notorious outrages. It was against the backdrop of such evil that Israel lobbyists, like those involved in CAMERA, embarked on their Israel advocacy, or *hasbara*.

Just like another familiar Israel lobby group – the self-styled 'Campaign Against Antisemitism' – CAMERA owes its beginnings to supposedly biased news reporting about atrocities committed by the State of Israel. In other words, it began as an anti-Palestinian whitewashing operation, designed to pressure media outlets into downplaying or removing content that informed the world about the plight of the Israeli regime's victims. Since its inception, CAMERA has worked to attack the BDS movement,[15] claimed that Israeli war crimes were not really war crimes,[16] and has focussed particular attention on the Zionist state's global war on university campuses. It even has a wing called 'CAMERA on Campus'.[17] During his time at CAMERA, Lee claims to have, *"Achieved publications in International news outlets"* and to have led *"seminars on Independent Press Standards Organisation regulations of UK media reporting"*.[18]

Moreover, between June 2019 and August 2019, Lee spent time in Jerusalem on Masa Israel Journey's six-week Summer Leadership Incubator. Masa was conceived by the self-same Ariel Sharon in 2004, when he was Prime Minister of Israel. The group offers young and budding Zionists generous grants towards participating in its programmes within the Zionist state, subsidising their stay *"with housing, insurance, visa, program placement, and more"* as *"a gift of the Government of Israel"*.[19] Masa has boasted of training sometimes over 10,000 people per year.[20] At Masa, Lee claims to have learned *"Adaptive Leadership theory and techniques"* designed by Ronald Heifetz.[21]

Heifetz is a pro-Israel *"leadership guru"*[22] and co-author of the book *Leadership on the Line*, in which the leadership of former

Israeli general and Prime Minister Yitzhak Rabin is repeatedly praised.[23] Rabin – absurdly, glorified as a 'peacemaker' by Zionists and the ignorant – was a key figure in the ethnic cleansing of historic Palestine alongside figures like David Ben-Gurion.[24] In 1988, during his time as Israeli Defence Minister, Rabin even ordered the Israel Occupation Forces to *"break the bones"* of Palestinians during the First Intifada.[25] Such were the leadership 'skills' of the 'peacemaker' Rabin!

According to Masa, its *"Vision"* is to create, *"Agile, courageous and creative Israel-connected adults"*, with a *"Mission"* of serving as *"a robust and integrated pipeline; cultivating and supporting leadership that builds Jewish communal capacity"*.[26] It hopes that those it has incubated will go on to use *"their informal authority to make a difference in Jewish life"*.[27] Masa is but one group among many, like Birthright Israel, which exist to indoctrinate Jewish students from around the world to support Zionism during all-expenses-paid trips to Israel.

During his time in Jerusalem, Lee also worked as a Research Intern for the Jerusalem Institute for Strategy and Security (JISS).[28] JISS, as its name suggests, is a conservative think-tank, that crafts security policy. It is staffed by Israeli military personnel and former advisors to senior Israeli politicians.[29] Lee says that he spent time *"formulating reports and analysis into diplomatic relations"* as well as *"briefing international diplomatic delegations and military officials, drawn from the National Security Council"*.[30] It seems that Lee is not only a dedicated supporter of the State of Israel, but that he also belongs to its most fervently reactionary, right-wing, anti-Palestinian traditions.

This is just a glimpse into some of Joshua Lee's background. Significantly, all of what I subsequently discovered about him had occurred before he arrived at my lecture to deliver his tirade, where he insinuated that I was a racist and an 'antisemite'. Lee is not an exception; there are many like him on campuses all over the land. Their fanatical pro-Israel apologia and *hasbara* are enthusiastically made into causes célèbre in news articles that mollycoddle these menaces as if *they* were the victims!

After Lee's rant, John Hess tried to bring some sobriety back to the session. But I was in no mood to let someone who I considered to be an ethno-supremacist get away with sullying my reputation as an anti-racism campaigner. I explained my track record to the students in the audience. I described how, as an apprentice bricklayer in the 1970s, I risked my personal safety on a number of occasions to challenge casual racism, which was widespread on building sites back then. I also pointed out that I was an active member of the Anti-Nazi League in the 1970s, challenging the racist National Front on the streets. My record on actively opposing racism stands any examination, and, as I pointed out, *"I have the scars to prove it, so don't come here and accuse me of being an 'antisemite' or a racist, it's an absolute slur"*.

The Zionist zealot's display made no impression on most of the 100 or so students in the hall, other than the handful who had already bought into pro-Israel propaganda. But the UJS's influence on campuses across the country is having a pernicious impact, particularly as their Zionist ideology is backed by the leadership of all the UK's major political parties.

My enemies were mobilising against me on all fronts. They called on their allies and their cells of lobbyists, and they applied untold pressure on everyone. They were not only mercilessly trying to smear me and assassinate my character, but they were also attacking those around me. They didn't just want to stop me from speaking at meetings and rallies. They wanted to obliterate me from existence. It was total war, and they neither had regard to the consequences of their actions nor to the people who were needlessly caught in the crossfire.

CHAPTER NINETEEN

THE FIX

In early September 2019, my court hearing was fast approaching. But I was still on the road as part of my sequel to the Democracy Roadshow. I travelled to Belfast with Ammar Kazmi at the invitation of Phil Kelly to speak at a Cuba Solidarity meeting. Kelly is a great comrade and an outstanding socialist spokesperson in the north of Ireland. He joined the Labour Party shortly after Corbyn was elected leader. Prior to the meeting, Kelly took Kazmi and I to see the sites. Alongside Kelly's brother, Aaron, we visited the Falls Road to look at the murals before stopping at Sinn Féin's art and craft shop, which is adorned with a large mural of Irish Republican legend Bobby Sands. The Sinn Féin staff made a big fuss of me. It was uplifting to speak with people who genuinely cared about social justice and opposing imperialism. It certainly stood in sharp contrast to Labour Party staff back in England, who were doing their utmost to undermine me and to destroy my parliamentary platform. At the meeting later that evening, I was given an incredibly warm reception by the audience. It was followed by long discussions into the night in the pub afterwards.

The following morning, Kelly had arranged for me to meet the workers who were staging a sit-in at Belfast's iconic Harland and Wolff shipyard, which had been earmarked for closure. To my surprise, they were all aware of my case and were incredibly supportive. It was a genuinely humbling encounter. They were threatened with losing their livelihoods and the closure of a workplace that had provided secure employment for generations, yet they wanted to express their solidarity with *me*, before speaking about their own precarious position!

Before we left for home, we were given the incredible honour of a guided tour of the Áras Uí Chonghaile (the James Connolly Visitor Centre) by Séanna Walsh, a Sinn Féin councillor. Walsh had been a Republican prisoner for 20 years. It was an inspiring experience to hear him speak about the life and struggles of the legendary socialist and Irish rebel James Connolly, who fought and was martyred for the cause of Irish independence. Listening to Walsh certainly put my trials and tribulations into perspective.

After returning to England, I continued on the Democracy Roadshow alongside Tosh McDonald, speaking to more enthusiastic audiences. The appetite for greater democracy in the party remained undimmed. I was still convinced that I could beat the suspension and resume my place in the party, to which I had devoted my life as a dedicated activist every year since I joined in 1976. Then, on 10 September 2019 I received the party's skeleton argument (their legal response) for the forthcoming High Court hearing. It came alongside a witness statement from the party's in-house lawyer, Thomas Gardiner. I was gobsmacked to see that they referred to the Democracy Roadshow (which was entirely irrelevant to my legal challenge). However, it confirmed what Labour MP Karl Turner had told me earlier. In July 2019, I received a phone call from Turner. He was one of the few MPs who'd stayed in touch with me after I had been suspended and then re-suspended. He told me that he had overheard a conversation in the Commons Tea Room between a number of Labour MPs who were talking about my case. He informed me that they had said, *"We want Williamson expelled as payback for the Democracy Roadshow"*. The documents I received from the party confirmed to me what I had suspected all along, and what had been corroborated by Turner: the campaign against me had nothing to do with 'antisemitism'.

On 11 September 2019, the night before the High Court hearing, I was given a morale-boosting send-off at a Democracy Roadshow meeting in Rochdale. But I still didn't sleep much that night. I was confident about the strength of my case, but the judicial system is inevitably something of a lottery, and the chances of victory can often depend on the judge who hears the case. I already knew that the courts were reluctant to intervene in the internal affairs of political parties, and I was concerned that my case could flounder on that point. It was an anxious time.

Formby adopts a war footing

After Boris Johnson became the new Tory Prime Minister in July 2019, speculation had been rife about an early general election, so I decided to seek an expedited hearing. But Formby instructed the party's lawyers to resist my request, resulting in three preliminary hearings wherein the party's legal representatives argued that there was no evidence an early general election might take place. They insisted that the Fixed-term Parliaments Act 2011 meant that the election could not be held until 2022. Their application was rejected on every occasion. On the third try, at the beginning of September 2019, not only did the judge throw out their application, but he also set a date for the full hearing. This clearly spooked the party's bureaucrats because, within 36 hours, just six days before the full hearing was scheduled, I received a letter from the party claiming that new allegations had been made, necessitating a further suspension (on top of my other one). I was informed that I would remain suspended *"irrespective of what may be determined in relation to any previous allegations of misconduct for which you are suspended"*. This was, in my view, a contrived manoeuvre by the party's apparatchiks to subvert the outcome of the High Court hearing in case it went in my favour. It was a dirty trick.

To see this document please scan this QR code.

Despite Formby's efforts to get the hearing postponed, the hearing eventually took place on 12 September 2019. I arrived early at the Royal Courts of Justice in London, and I was greeted by a former member of my staff, Ammar Kazmi, who was an undergraduate law student at the time and had come to watch from the public gallery. He was suited and booted, dressed in his typically sharp way. A BBC journalist, Tony Roe, recorded a video of us both entering the imposing Victorian Gothic building and posted it on Twitter. The herd of haters was quick to pounce on us, promoting conspiracies that Kazmi was acting as my barrister! It was another demonstration of how these malcontents would find any opportunity to attack me and anyone associated with me.

The court's fading décor suggests that it had seen better days. The courtroom itself had a shabby chic quality about it. In fact, the narrow wooden benches were decidedly uncomfortable. The hearing went on all day. The Labour Party had instructed a QC, Rachel Crasnow, to defend their position. I was represented by Aileen McColgan (who was made a QC a year later), and the judge was Mr Justice Pepperall. The courtroom battle that ensued was between the two advocates. No witnesses were called to give evidence. I sat behind my solicitor Jamie Potter, who in turn sat behind McColgan.

Before McColgan began making her submissions, Crasnow raised a gratuitous objection about the presence of a journalist from *PA Media*, Sam Tobin. The poor kid had a baby face and he looked hapless when confronted with such an unwarranted attack, until he stood up and gave a spirited and eloquent defence as to why he should be allowed to stay in the courtroom. Pepperall then put the onus on Crasnow to justify excluding Tobin, which she failed to do, and so he was allowed to stay.

McColgan then set out my case, until her submissions were interrupted by a fire alarm. Thankfully, the hearing resumed soon afterwards. I had asked the court to not only rule on my re-suspension from the party in June 2019, but also to rule on the further suspension imposed a few days before the hearing. The bloody-minded Labour bureaucrats hoped that, if they could keep my suspension in place, they could stop me from being a parliamentary candidate in the event of an early general election.

Then, in the afternoon, it was Crasnow's turn. During her submissions, I was busily scribbling notes for my solicitor to pass on to McColgan, because so much of what Crasnow was saying was completely inaccurate. She had the audacity to argue that I had benefitted from my suspension because it had raised my profile. She even suggested that the definitive letter that was issued to me in June 2019, notifying me of the NEC panel's decision to reinstate me, was only *"preliminary"* and had no binding effect. On occasions, the judge's body language during Crasnow's submissions suggested that he wasn't really buying her arguments. As Crasnow set out the party's tortuous and fanciful case, he often looked incredulous, which gave me hope that I might succeed in overturning both my re-suspension and my new, third suspension.

When all the submissions had concluded, Pepperall reserved his judgment, which meant another anxious wait. I had hoped to get a positive decision in time for the 2019 Labour Party conference. After the hearing, myself and the supporters who'd joined me in the public gallery went back to Elleanne Green's rooftop garden to celebrate what we hoped would be the conclusion of the legal machinations. Elleanne is another Jewish comrade who had been treated abominably by the party. She had her good name dragged through the gutter over yet more bogus 'antisemitism' claims. Her real crime, though, as far as her antagonists were concerned, was that she was a supporter of Jeremy Corbyn and had published pro-Palestinian posts on Facebook.

Conference antics

In the interval between the conclusion of the court hearing and the judgment being handed down, the Labour Party conference was looming. I had been invited to speak at numerous fringe meetings during the conference in Brighton that year, but I had hoped to be inside the official conference centre, too. Suspended party members were not allowed into the conference complex. I was waiting with bated breath for the judgment, but it didn't arrive in time. So, I was limited to the outskirts.

However, even my attendance at fringe meetings was considered beyond the pale for the right-wing and Zionist ultras who had colonised the PLP. Ruth Smeeth, a former spin doctor for BICOM, was incensed about me being in Brighton. She fumed, *"No one in the Labour Party should be sharing a platform with members who are suspended in relation to antisemitism ... nor should he be turning up to wind everyone up"*.[1] A frustrated Wes Streeting – who had earlier coordinated the parliamentary lynch mob against the black rights campaigner, journalist, and filmmaker, Marc Wadsworth – joined in with his own invective. He foamed, *"It beggars belief that people are still willing to give Chris Williamson a platform given his conduct"*. They must have realised that their efforts to obliterate me into non-existence had failed. Streeting was obviously exasperated when he added, *"As he is suspended from the Labour Party he should not be speaking at events at our conference"*.[2] But Streeting and his chums were about to get a rude awakening. I wasn't going to be stopped by the outbursts of an obnoxious bunch of right-wing careerists. When I was approached by the media for my reaction to these complaints, I left them in no doubt that I would not be deterred. I reiterated that I would be speaking at numerous conference fringe events and said:

> "It's a tragedy that a tiny but noisy minority of party members want to trash the spirit of the Human Rights Act. It's one of Labour's greatest achievements. Maybe these malcontents have forgotten that Labour enshrined freedom of expression into British law nearly 21 years ago. If these mischief-makers are genuinely interested in winning the next election, they should pipe down and devote their energies to exposing the Tories and promoting a common sense socialist programme. That's the way to beat Boris Johnson, rather than attempting to censor the voices of people like me who speak for the overwhelming bulk of party members and the vast majority of Labour supporters."

My attendance at the conference fringe was enthusiastically received by conference delegates and casual visitors alike. However, the right-wing wreckers and Zionist attack dogs did their level best to prevent any events, at which I was due to speak, from going ahead. Their principal method was targeting the proprietors of the venues. They also put pressure on anyone who was due to appear alongside me. They did have some success with this approach. I was due to share a platform with the distinguished MMT economist, Bill Mitchell, to discuss the macroeconomics behind a Green New Deal, and the importance of understanding MMT in restructuring the economy to address the climate crisis. But the minister at the Dorset Gardens Methodist Church, where the meeting was hosted, was leaned on, and he said that the church would not be available if I were one of the speakers. The Gower Institute for Modern Money Studies, who were sponsoring the seminar, appealed to the church to reconsider without success. So, I was dropped from the agenda. We were not going to be defeated by this setback, though. Mitchell was determined to speak alongside me in Brighton that week and said he would do an open-air meeting if necessary. But two outstanding activists in Brighton, Greg Hadfield and Becky Massey, had a better plan of action. They had been working on securing an alternative location to host a series of fringe events because of the impact that the cancel culture tactics were having on the availability of premises. Hadfield even made enquiries about hiring a marquee to obviate the problem caused by proprietors being intimidated into cancelling bookings. But, in the end, the stunning Rialto Theatre was made available to us during conference week. That meant that the aborted MMT meeting, at which Mitchell and I were going to speak, was able to proceed with a packed out, standing room only audience and an overspill room.

The Rialto was an invaluable resource that week, hosting numerous discussions and film screenings that otherwise would not have happened, including a book launch at Waterstones that was cancelled at the last minute.[3] The book, *Bad News for Labour*,[4] was a compilation of essays examining the facts behind the allegations of 'antisemitism' in the Labour Party. But, once again, pressure was applied to stop those inconvenient truths from being given a platform. Despite their best efforts to suppress the truth, however, the book launch went ahead with minimal disruption, because the Rialto is just up the road from Waterstones!

I had also been invited by Crispin Flintoff to speak at his Stand Up for Labour gig. But he had to drop me from the schedule as the venue threatened to rescind his booking, and some of the performers threatened to pull out if I appeared in the advertising. Whilst I was no longer on the flyers advertising the event, Flintoff asked me to come along, anyway. On the night in question, I had addressed an incredible LAW meeting at the Mercure Hotel alongside Ken Livingstone, Jackie Walker, Asa Winstanley, and others in front of a euphoric audience. They had given me numerous prolonged standing ovations, which was tremendously energising. But I wasn't sure what reception I would receive as I walked through the door of Brighton's comedy club. No one, other than Flintoff, knew I would be speaking. I felt a sense of trepidation as I stood at the back of the dimly lit club waiting for Flintoff to call me up onto the stage. I wondered if any Zionist thugs would be in the audience. Would Flintoff's announcement be met with howls of protests? Was this ruse going to fall flat on its face?

Then, the moment of truth arrived. Flintoff, who was the MC for the evening, was back on stage in his sequined jacket, speaking to the audience, *"I think Chris Williamson is in tonight. Shall I ask him up onto the stage to say a few words?"*. I momentarily winced as he said it, but my apprehension evaporated when I heard the roar of approval from the sold-out auditorium. As I walked from the back of the hall to the stage, I found myself being given another standing ovation. Flintoff gave me a high stool, similar to the one used by the late, great Dave Allen. I sat there briefly staring into the blackness of the club, unable to see the audience because the lights were so intense, listening to disembodied voices from different parts of the room shouting things like, *"We love you, Chris!"*, *"Don't let the bastards grind you down!"*, and *"We're with you, Chris!"*. When I finished my speech, I was mobbed by well-wishers who wanted to shake my hand. I remember a middle-aged couple coming up to me to say it was their wedding anniversary and how much they would love to have their photograph taken with me to mark the occasion. It was yet another one of countless gratifying interactions I had with rank-and-file members throughout the week. The disparity between the attitude of the upper echelons of the party, and ordinary grassroots members could not have been starker. It reinforced my view that Corbyn had made a lethal mistake in not clearing out the fifth columnists embedded in the party machine, and in not publicly backing my campaign to implement open selection.

Julian Assange inspires the masses

On the Saturday after conference, I attended a rally outside HM Belmarsh Prison to protest about Julian Assange's ongoing detention. His only 'crime' was to expose war crimes and the abuse of state and corporate power. For that, the US was seeking to extradite him, where he would face a prison term of 175 years! At the rally, I had the honour of meeting Assange's father, John Shipton, and we got on well. Later in the year, I was due to accompany him to speak at the Italian Parliament. Unfortunately, a couple of days before I was due to fly out, the 2019 general election was called, and so I was sadly unable to attend.

On 3 October 2019, I was back in the north of Ireland again, this time to speak at an 'Imperialism on Trial' event in Derry. I joined an esteemed panel of speakers to discuss Julian Assange's plight and to call for his freedom. The others who addressed the meeting at Derry's Playhouse Theatre included Irish MEPs Clare Daly and Mick Wallace, former UK Ambassador Peter Ford, and former Icelandic minister Ögmundur Jónasson. At the end of the meeting, Greg Sharkey, who had organised the meeting, announced that all of the speakers were donating their fees to my legal fighting fund. It was yet another indication that, despite the best endeavours of various vested interests who wanted to force me out of my position as a British MP, I still enjoyed solidarity from great comrades.

What I found peculiar was that I seemed to be the only MP regularly speaking out about the outrageous treatment to which Assange was being subjected. For example, when I tabled an Early Day Motion (EDM) in the House of Commons on 30 September 2019, only four other MPs signed it, namely Grahame Morris, Kelvin Hopkins, Ann Clwyd, and Ronnie Campbell. My EDM (Number 2746): condemned Assange's ongoing imprisonment, opposed attempts to extradite him to the US, and called on the British government to release him. Why were so few MPs willing to challenge what was being done to Assange in our name? I had grown weary listening to MPs pontificating about how much they supported freedom of speech and civil liberties in other countries, but who were markedly mute when it came to Assange. If these parliamentarians genuinely believed in the concept of free speech and civil liberties, that EDM would have had hundreds of signatures, not just five. It was yet one more example of the Westminster bubble merchants speaking with forked tongue. It showed that the imperialist instincts that have dishonoured the British Parliament for centuries were alive and kicking, on both sides of the so-called 'political divide'.

The truth is, there is no discernible divide in British politics, particularly when it comes to international policy. These parliamentarians love nothing better than puffing out their chests and lecturing the world with their 'do as we say, not as we do' rhetoric. Even Corbyn was distinctly quiet about this scandal. He'd only made one statement, when Assange was forcibly dragged from the Ecuadorian Embassy by police officers from Scotland Yard. Shadow Home Secretary Diane Abbott, and Shadow Justice Secretary Richard Burgon, also managed to muster a reaction with statements on Twitter. But, after that, they were mute. As for most other Labour MPs, they disgracefully joined in the smears against Assange and called for him to be extradited to Sweden to face allegations of sexual assault. This was a pretext that would see him extradited from Sweden to the US.

Assange's treatment was another reminder of just how utterly unfit for purpose Britain's political class really is. Most of our parliamentarians just act as a mouthpiece for the status quo, whilst indulging in pathetic parliamentary parlour games.

After the 2019 general election, I was pleased to see Corbyn speaking out more about Assange's case, and it was good that John McDonnell went to visit him at Belmarsh. But they should have done that when it counted: when they were both still in positions of influence. Assange's treatment by the British state can only be described as inhuman. The principles for which he stands should be embraced by any progressive political movement. Yet, under Corbyn's leadership, Assange was shunned. They clearly didn't want to invoke the ire of the corporate media. The behaviour of many of Assange's fellow journalists had been utterly contemptible, with many of them mocking Assange's plight. Before he was imprisoned at Belmarsh, they had said nothing about the shocking revelations that the CIA were plotting to kidnap and assassinate him.[5] Apparently, Mike Pompeo, who was the CIA Director at the time, wanted revenge after WikiLeaks published the Vault 7 files in 2017.[6] This was the largest leak in CIA history.[7] It revealed how British spy agencies had held workshops with the CIA to find ways to hack into the household devices of every British citizen.[8] The corporate media's failure to report on that affair, and the CIA's subsequent assassination plan, was a truly astonishing abdication of responsibility. Rather than defending the most effective investigative journalist in the world, the corporate media hacks perpetuated the smears against him.

Nils Melzer, the UN's Special Rapporteur on Torture, took up Assange's case, but he admitted that he was sceptical when Assange first appealed to his office for protection:

"Like most of the public, I'd been subconsciously poisoned by the relentless smear campaign, which had been disseminated

over the years. So it took a second knock on my door, to get my reluctant attention.

"But once I looked into the facts of this case, what I found filled me with repulsion and disbelief. In the end, it finally dawned on me that I'd been blinded by propaganda and that Assange had been systematically slandered, to divert attention from the crimes he exposed.

"Once he'd been dehumanised through isolation, ridicule and shame just like the witches we used to burn at the stake it was easy to deprive him of his most fundamental rights, without provoking public outrage worldwide."

Given the corporate media's shameful treatment of Julian Assange, it is little wonder that their coverage of the Corbyn project was so diabolical.

CHAPTER TWENTY

JUDGMENT DAY

The handing down of the judgment for the legal case that I'd brought against the Labour Party took place at the High Court in Birmingham, sitting in the Birmingham Civil Justice Centre. It couldn't have been a more different setting than the Royal Courts of Justice. Whilst the latter is in dire need of refurbishment, the former has a modern, minimalist design.

The court building was crawling with corporate media hacks, including Liz Bates, who had started the furore that led to my suspension, when she misreported my speech in Sheffield nine months earlier. Bates ended up failing upwards, rewarded for misrepresenting my remarks. She left her position at the *Yorkshire Post* and moved on to Channel 4 News, where she became a political correspondent. I am told by some media insiders that Bates secured her current job on the back of her delusory 'scoop'. How on Earth what she did could be described as a 'scoop' is beyond me. She had viewed a video that was freely available on a public Facebook page, and then posted a highly selective excerpt with a sensationalised caption. That isn't exactly Bernstein and Woodward. And she has practically admitted as such, calling the ease with which the 'scoop' fell into her lap an example of *"modern journalism"*.[1] Same old hackery, more like.

Bates was invited by BBC Radio 4 a week after I was suspended, on 6 March 2019, to discuss her fiction on the *Media Show*.[2] She was introduced and interviewed by Amol Rajan, who restated the calumny for which I had been suspended (that I had supposedly said Labour had been *"too apologetic over the issue of antisemitism"*). Outrageously, Bates told Rajan that I had *"a bit of a history of doing things that are pretty provocative towards the Jewish community"* and suggested that my speech had prompted a *"natural uprising"* of MPs against me. She was joined in the studio by Richard Ferrer from *Jewish News,* who said, *"Before the* Yorkshire Post *came along we thought we had the Chris Williamson scoop"*. This was a reference to my booking of a room in Parliament to show the film *WitchHunt* that focussed on the mistreatment of

Jackie Walker. Neither Ferrer nor Bates thought it relevant to mention Walker's Jewish heritage. Ferrer went on to say, *"Chris Williamson is Corbyn's outrider ... he's somebody with a long rap sheet, he's somebody who's been poking and jibing and toying with the Jewish community for a long time"*.

I'm inclined to give Rajan the benefit of the doubt about his description of me; I suspect it was just a case of lazy journalism on his part. But Bates and Ferrer were making dishonest accusations. The whole thing goes to show how 'journalists' can use 'antisemitism' smears to further their own careers and to generate clicks online.

When I saw Bates at the High Court in Birmingham, she was either oblivious or simply couldn't care less about the damage she had done. As soon as she saw me, she came over with a big beaming smile, as if she was a long-lost friend. She began asking questions. I didn't actually recognise her at first, until Ammar Kazmi whispered in my ear. I told her that I'd be making a formal statement outside the court afterwards. The sheer effrontery of these media hacks is quite something. They seem to adopt the same moral code as the mafia for their mercenary behaviour, that it's nothing personal, it's just business. But that's a cheap justification. It's morally bankrupt.

Bittersweet vindication

In his judgment in the *Williamson MP v Formby* case,[3] Mr Justice Pepperall found that the Labour Party's decision to re-suspend me was so unfair as to be unlawful. As a result, the re-suspension could not stand. That had the effect of quashing most of the specious allegations against me, thereby preventing the Labour Party's bureaucrats from referring them to the party's kangaroo court, otherwise known as the National Constitutional Committee.

Pepperall's judgment vindicated much of what I had been saying. He recognised the arbitrary nature of the power exercised by the party's bureaucrats when he said that *"the evidence indicates that in practice the [party's] rules are not strictly followed"*. As for Keith Vaz laughably raising *"issues about his health once colleagues reacted vociferously to the [NEC] panel's decision"*, Pepperall said:

> *"The evidence on this issue is unsatisfactory ... It would be surprising if, as an experienced Parliamentarian, Mr Vaz: a) had taken part in an important meeting if he felt himself unfit to do so; and b) then failed clearly to make that point in his subsequent email."*

Pepperall also rejected the arguments of the Labour Party's barrister, Rachel Crasnow QC, about supposed *"political interference"* in my case. I would argue that there *had* been political interference against me, but it certainly wasn't interference in my favour, as Crasnow had suggested.

Moreover, one of the most revealing and significant statements Pepperall made was that *"it is not ... difficult to infer that the true reason for the decision [to re-suspend me] was that [NEC] members were influenced by the ferocity of the outcry following the June decision [to re-admit me]"*. Crasnow had argued that it *was* appropriate for the party to take account of the political outcry surrounding my case. Pepperall disagreed:

> *"the NEC should decide cases fairly and impartially in accordance with the rules and evidence; and not be influenced by how its decisions are seen by others. Internal and press reaction to a decision are not of themselves proper grounds for reopening a case that was not otherwise procedurally unfair or obviously wrong."*

However, whilst Pepperall gave the party no quarter in many ways, I believe that he cut the party's Machiavellian mandarins far too much slack in his determination on the third suspension. It was plain as a pikestaff to anyone with a modicum of political acumen that I was being fitted up. Anonymous administrators had been waging an all-out assault on freedom of speech, anti-imperialism, and grassroots democracy inside the party. I was seen as a crucial totemic scalp, to send a signal to anyone else who was considering whether to speak out. Of course, Pepperall may have also had a weather eye on the turbulent media coverage of my case. There would have been total hysteria had he ruled the third suspension unlawful, too. We had already seen the *Daily Mail*, on 4 November 2016, labelling judges *"Enemies of the People"*. It was an infamous headline, printed after three High Court justices had ruled that the government couldn't unilaterally trigger the Brexit process without the consent of Parliament. If those sorts of attacks were in Pepperall's mind, I would find it hard to blame him for not wanting to become the target of the Israel lobby's ire. He decided that:

> *"While the Labour Party is no longer able lawfully to pursue the original disciplinary case against Mr Williamson, that does not afford him immunity from any subsequent disciplinary action. Accordingly, the NEC is entitled to investigate and process any new allegations made against Mr Williamson and the court should not lightly interfere in the Party's decisions to investigate or to re-suspend him pending such investigation. Equally, it should not micro-manage the disciplinary process."*

He concluded by saying:

> *"In any event, a [simplified] Part 8 hearing [procedure] conducted by legal argument upon the papers is not a suitable vehicle to enquire into the Labour Party's motives in bringing this second case against Mr Williamson."*

I had won 90 per cent of the case, but I was still suspended from the party. The judgment was a curate's egg.

Facing the media hounds

After Pepperall had handed down his judgment, I prepared myself to face the gaggle of cameras waiting in the street. I had worked on a statement the previous evening. Ammar Kazmi, Paul Mallet, and I then made some final tweaks in a side room before going outside. But, in their ensuing accounts, the corporate media focussed on the fact that the judge didn't throw out the hastily-cobbled-together third suspension that was imposed at the eleventh hour. All their headlines proclaimed that I had 'lost' my High Court battle with the party. They all quoted a Labour Party spokesperson, who said, *"The court has upheld Chris Williamson's suspension from the party"*, but that was a highly partial interpretation. The reality was that the court did two things. First, it ruled that the party had acted unlawfully in re-suspending me, which was the substantive part of the verdict. Second, the court did not want to intervene in fresh allegations that had been made less than a week before the High Court hearing took place. But those nuances were lost, perhaps deliberately, on the media hacks. By contrast, progressive publications like the *Canary*, the *Electronic Intifada*, and the *Skwawkbox* – which are ironically decried as being 'fake news' outlets by the legacy media – were the only ones to provide an accurate summary of what had happened.

Meanwhile, Rachel Crasnow QC was hailed in the *Times* as the 'Lawyer of the Week'. In a typically misleading article, the rag claimed that she had *"successfully defended the Labour Party against an application for an injunction by Chris Williamson"*.[4] But, back in the real world, her excellent lawyering would end up leaving her client, the Labour Party, forking out huge sums for my legal costs. That *Times* piece showed that the corporate media were celebrating what they saw as a defeat for the left. As far as they were concerned, it was another one down.

At that point, however, the arrangement of the costs hadn't yet been decided. The party was, true to form, being obstructive. Astonishingly, they wanted me to pay 60 per cent of *their* costs! So, I was left with another anxious wait, as the matter was left to be decided at yet another hearing. The costs hearing was held after Prime Minister Boris Johnson had called the December 2019 general election, so I was unable to attend. I remember waiting anxiously for Jamie Potter's call that day. When he did call, it was an enormous relief. The judge had awarded me 100 per cent of my legal fees up to 5 September 2019. On top of that, for the period between 6 and 12 September 2019 (between the issuing of the third suspension and the court hearing), he ordered the party to pay 30 per cent of my costs. The result revealed the arrogance of the party's bureaucrats, who treated the High Court as if it were an extension of their own dodgy procedures. Thankfully, Mr Justice Pepperall was having none of it. It is a travesty that, for left-wing activists to get justice from the so-called 'party of the workers', they sometimes have to go through the bourgeois courts.

The aftermath

Following the High Court ruling, grassroots members were up in arms about the dirty tricks that had been played by the party's hierarchy to keep me suspended. I received another outpouring of solidarity from Labour supporters across the country. Yet, the Socialist Campaign Group of Labour MPs still maintained what seemed like a vow of silence on the issue.

I spoke to my solicitors at Bindmans about what legal remedies might be available to force the party's hand but, the reality was, I required a political solution. That meant Corbyn needed to exert some influence to overcome the barriers that were being erected by Jennie Formby. She had sanctioned the latest suspension based on allegations that were even more ludicrous than the original ones. If Corbyn spoke out in my support, he would be able to carry the NEC with him and put Formby back in her box. But was he prepared to do that, I wondered? The support was there from the grassroots. Sure, it would have caused one hell of a stink with the Zionist lobby and the right-wing dominated PLP, but they were out to destroy Corbyn, anyway. He had nothing to lose. I wasn't sure, however, whether he had been persuaded that my demise was acceptable collateral damage in a misguided strategy to win any forthcoming election.

I messaged Corbyn on the day that the judgment was handed down to say that I would like to discuss the implications as a matter of urgency. I wanted to get my situation resolved quietly for the good of the party. I received no response. The following day, I sent him a copy of my video statement, responding to the outcome of the judgment,[5] but he remained uncommunicative. I also messaged Corbyn's communications director, Seumas Milne, who said that he would call me the following day. He didn't.

This went on for several days. There were repeated promises to get in touch, which then failed to materialise. I did eventually receive a call from Milne when I was back home in Derby, upstairs in my study. He said that he wanted to *"open a dialogue"* and have an *"off the record conversation"*. He told me that Corbyn would like me back in the party, and that he wanted me to stand in the next general election, whenever it came. But the discussion went downhill from there because the terms were unacceptable. Milne essentially wanted me to grovel in public, but I made it clear that there was no way I would debase myself like that again. I had already apologised in February 2019. I reminded Milne that the High Court judge had said that the party had acted unlawfully. The party owed me an apology. But this was lost on him. He just wanted me to beg. I told him that Corbyn should publicly back me, but he insisted that he wouldn't do that. He repeatedly said, *"I can tell you're pissed off"*. Damn right, I was! I had been hung out to dry and all Milne could say was, *"It's all about the numbers"* on the NEC. Despite there supposedly having been a narrow left-wing majority on the NEC from mid-2018 onwards, the reality was that it was a fragile alliance. The NEC had the power to waive the latest ill-conceived suspension, not Corbyn. But Corbyn was a member of the NEC, and he could have influenced those *"numbers"* by publicly supporting me. My conversation with Milne was unproductive and fractious. The numpties in Corbyn's office had learnt nothing from the previous few years. They were one-trick ponies, whose only strategy was to appease and capitulate to hostile forces. Milne was getting increasingly irritable after half an hour or so of talking twaddle, and he eventually complained that he hadn't eaten his dinner. That was like a red rag to a bull. I was infuriated by his insensitivity. My future was on the line and my reputation was being trashed whilst supposedly senior comrades behaved like the three wise monkeys. And all Milne could think about was his bloody stomach! *"Okay"*, I said, *"The dialogue is open, go and get your dinner"*. I hung up. I went downstairs and told my partner Maggie that I was being deserted yet again.

The left's capitulation was like using a faulty satnav to traverse the so-called 'parliamentary road to socialism'. It seems that a large section of the left had become so intoxicated with the thought of 'power' that they could think of nothing else. But this begs the question: if they were prepared to ditch their principles and their most loyal comrades in the pursuit of power, what else would they have done had they attained it? What Faustian pact were they prepared to make with the Establishment? Thanks to their foolish short-sightedness and deep-dyed disloyalty, we will never know.

CHAPTER TWENTY-ONE

TURKEYS VOTING FOR CHRISTMAS

Towards the end of 2019, speculation was growing about the possibility of an early general election. Boris Johnson had already tried and failed to obtain the two-thirds majority necessary to hold one, as stipulated by the (now-repealed) Fixed-term Parliaments Act 2011. But that wasn't going to stop him for long. If he ended up getting his way, it would mean having an election in the middle of December. That seemed absolutely bonkers to me. I didn't think the PLP would be daft enough to vote for that, because it would make street campaigning all but impossible.

However, I underestimated the PLP's propensity for stupidity. They were bounced into voting for it when the SNP said that they'd do so if Johnson were to put it to a vote again. Even so, Labour still had a sufficient number of MPs to frustrate any new attempt to hold an election in the run-up to the New Year. Nevertheless, like turkeys voting for Christmas, they all trooped in behind the Tories when the time came. The vote took place on 29 October 2019 and it was carried by 438 votes to 20. The last time there had been a December election was in 1923, when Labour returned just 142 seats, with the Tories winning 344 and the Liberals 115. I feared a similar outcome for the Labour Party in this election.

Campaigning in winter is miserable at the best of times but, when the stakes were so high, it was an abdication of responsibility. One of Labour's secret weapons in the 2017 general election was the buzz created by the quantity and visibility of activists on the streets. That was not going to happen on freezing cold nights when it was getting dark at around 4:30pm. Coupled with the terrible timing was the party's commitment to hold a second referendum on EU membership, which hung like a millstone around the necks of Labour candidates in 'Leave' constituencies. The party was effectively gift-wrapping a giant majority for Boris Johnson as an early Christmas present.

It was a crass decision to allow the Conservatives to determine the timing and the battleground that best suited their interests, although we now know that many on Labour's side wanted Labour to lose. It was a price worth paying in their eyes as they knew it would finally lay the Corbyn project to rest. As Labour MPs strolled into the Aye lobby, the election became a *fait accompli*. Johnson was inevitably going to achieve the requisite two-thirds majority. So, I made the decision to vote for it. I wanted to avoid giving the depraved PLP another opportunity to make mischief about my motivations. At that point, to have voted against would have been futile, anyway.

After the vote was concluded, I sat in the Aye lobby responding to some emails on my phone when Harriet Harman walked by. Around 10 or 20 seconds later she came back to say, *"I didn't want to walk past you without saying anything. I am so sorry about the way things have turned out"*. She then recounted how she had spoken at my constituency dinner in 2010 at the Roundhouse in Derby. She seemed genuinely regretful, even though she had signed the Tribune Group letter back in February 2019 that had called for my Labour membership to be suspended and the whip removed. Whether she was truly penitent or just embarrassed is a moot point. She certainly didn't publicly verbalise that she was sorry about the way things turned out. I said, *"You make it sound like this is the end, Harriet, when it's actually a new beginning"*. At that point in time, I was still hoping against hope that I would be the Labour candidate for Derby North in the election.

False promises

Later that same evening, my spirits were lifted when I bumped into Corbyn just outside the Commons chamber. We were both unaccompanied and this was the first time I'd had a chance to speak to him on his own since Formby suspended me eight months earlier. His opening gambit was that he was going to *"sort it"* to enable me to stand as Labour's candidate in the 2019 general election. He said that he'd ensured the NEC would endorse me at their meeting the following week. I thanked him profusely for what was an enormous relief. I told him that I would look forward to working closely with him again. We then spoke for a few minutes about the prospects for the election, and I expressed my reservations about the timing. But Corbyn was bullish and optimistic. We were then disturbed by some other MPs walking towards the Commons chamber, so we curtailed our conversation and went our separate ways. I was elated that Corbyn was at last offering me some genuine support. I thought the nightmare was, at last, coming to an end.

Buoyed by my conversation with Corbyn, I called a few close comrades and arranged to meet Paul Mallet at London St Pancras Station before catching the train home that evening. Despite my optimism, Mallet was sceptical about Corbyn's assurances. But Corbyn was a man of integrity, I told myself. I could never imagine that he would let me down after making a promise to my face. Nevertheless, Mallet and I thought it would be helpful to discreetly lobby a few NEC members. The next day, I wrote a letter to Jennie Formby. I warned her that Labour was on course to lose Derby North. I reminded her of my long track record in local government, and my experience as a Corbyn ally in Parliament. I brought to her attention the result of the *Williamson MP v Formby* High Court case, in which the judge had called my re-suspension from the party in June 2019 *"unlawful"*. I also asked her to consider the personal implications for both myself and my staff if I were to be excluded, and the gross unfairness to which I had already been subjected. I concluded by saying that I didn't want to be *"an unnecessary distraction"* in the campaign and said:

> *"Fighting that election for Labour is where I can most effectively contribute my efforts too, rather than continuing to be embroiled in a legal challenge that is heart-breaking for me and a liability for the party".*

Formby didn't even do me the courtesy of an acknowledgement, let alone a reply. I ploughed ahead with preparations for the election, and I pulled together a team that weekend to plan the campaign. Steve Beckett from Laura Smith's CLP offered his support and joined our deliberations at my office. Beckett had been a great supporter of mine, and he'd wanted me to be the candidate in Crewe and Nantwich before Laura Smith was selected in 2017. We also considered the possibility of running an independent campaign if the unthinkable happened, notwithstanding Corbyn's assurance a few days earlier. But I was confident that the prospects of such an eventuality were remote.

The coup de grâce

A few days before the NEC meeting that was to determine my fate, I called Seumas Milne to find out what steps were being taken to ensure that the vote went the right way. He was very non-committal. I told him that removing me as the candidate would make it harder for the party to retain the seat, but he seemed unmoved. I said that, if I were forced out, I'd stand as an independent and run a strong campaign that would almost certainly deny the party the chance of holding the seat. Again, he seemed untroubled by that prospect. His attitude made me wonder whether Corbyn had told him that he was going to *"sort it"* or whether Milne knew something that I didn't. Either way, he was blasé about the prospect of losing a seat.

The next day, I fulfilled my last engagement as an MP when I travelled down to Windsor to speak to the local CLP. It was another morale-boosting encounter. Interestingly, many of the local members were critical of Corbyn for not standing up to his detractors. I explained that it wasn't his style, but I privately believed that they were absolutely right and were echoing what I had said behind closed doors to Corbyn and the SCG. The next day, I received a goodwill message from Karie Murphy, who told me that she was doing everything she could ahead of the NEC meeting. She said that Corbyn sent his solidarity, too. It reinforced my view that Corbyn would deliver on his assurance. I then heard from a party insider that an NEC Antisemitism Panel was considering my case that day. I hadn't been formally notified, but that was par for the course from the party's churlish bureaucrats. The full NEC meeting where my fate would finally be determined was due to take place the following day. The chances of retaining my parliamentary seat would turn on whether I was able to fight the election under the Labour banner. So, I worked with my team on some top lines that Corbyn could use at the NEC meeting, and I forwarded them to him at 7:55pm.

The next morning, I was pacing up and down in my constituency office, anxiously awaiting the NEC's decision. I was comforted by the knowledge that Corbyn was going to speak for me at the meeting. My team were in the office alongside me, and we were doing our best to remain positive. Their livelihoods were also on the line. Their jobs relied on me continuing as the MP. So, it was a shock when we switched on the TV to see Corbyn on the screen. He was on the campaign trail somewhere, taking questions from journalists. Coincidentally, at the very moment we tuned in, a reporter was asking him whether I should be allowed to stand as a Labour candidate. He gave a typical Corbyn reply, saying, *"I do not dictate to the party, I lead the party ... The NEC will come to its decision today"*.[1]

My immediate reaction was that it must have been a recording. But no. It was a live broadcast. I was flabbergasted. How could he let me down so badly? Only eight days previously, he had personally assured me that he'd *"sort it"* and, just 24 hours earlier, he was sending me his solidarity via Karie Murphy. But then he ducked the meeting! I tried to reassure my team that Corbyn had probably lobbied his allies on the NEC to back me, without him needing to be there himself. But, in my heart of hearts, I felt betrayed. Corbyn had a majority on the NEC and I am certain that if he'd had the courage to turn up to speak for me, he would have carried the room.

The NEC vote wasn't even close. Formby continued her vendetta against me and produced a report for the NEC in which she proposed that I be dropped as the Labour candidate. Her recommendation was carried by 20 votes to five. Her justification was that I was still subject to the groundless third suspension that she had imposed when she realised the High Court was likely to rule that she had acted unlawfully by re-suspending me in June 2019. It was an unscrupulous, Machiavellian tactic that typified the machine politics of the Labour Party. It was the very antithesis of what the Corbyn project was supposed to represent. Despite her professed support for Corbyn, Formby's period as general secretary did more damage to our attempts to build a grassroots movement than her predecessor Iain McNicol, who Corbyn had elevated to the House of Lords. That decision was yet another example of Corbyn treating his enemies as his friends while his friends were treated as his enemies.

The NEC members who backed me at the meeting were Ian Murray, who was the FBU delegate, and four constituency representatives – Yasmine Dar, Rachel Garnham, Ann Henderson, and Darren Williams. ASLEF general secretary Mick Whelan, also an NEC member, spoke in my support, but he left the meeting before the vote was taken. Dame Margaret Beckett, who I had known since she was first elected as the MP for Derby South in 1983, abstained, as did Claudia Webbe, who is supposedly a left-winger. I was told that Jon Lansman and the NEC's youth representative Lara McNeill spoke vociferously against me.

Seumas Milne called me a few minutes after I had already heard the news. He offered no commiserations or solidarity. He just said very coldly that *"we didn't have the numbers"*. He then handed the phone to Amy Jackson *"to explain"*. In what was an extremely emotional moment, her insensitive, cold-hearted comments were absolutely disgraceful. Her opening remarks were, *"You've alienated people who wanted to help"*. I thought her response was completely out of order and I told her that she was partly responsible for this unjustifiable shitshow. She had supported the disastrous supine response to the 'antisemitism' hoax being perpetrated by the Israel lobby and the right-wing rump that makes up most of the PLP. I was furious. The red mist had well and truly descended, and I hung up to avoid saying something I might have later regretted. I remember thinking, why had Corbyn surrounded himself with people who were so utterly out-of-touch with reality?

News then came through that Tom Watson had resigned as deputy leader and that he was standing down as an MP. Whilst he had a majority of 7,713, he was vulnerable because he'd been vehemently pro-Remain,[2] and his seat was in a pro-Leave area. George Galloway had also announced that he was going to stand against him, which would no doubt have taken at least a few thousand votes off Labour, if not more. Additionally, it seems that Watson had potentially been bribed with the offer of a peerage by Corbyn's office, in return for standing down. This appears to have been the strategy employed by the leader's office to get rid of Iain McNicol as general secretary in 2018. It was a stupid thing to do. Watson had been heavily criticised for misusing his parliamentary privilege to amplify Carl Beech, the fantasist who'd made up elaborate conspiracies about a VIP Westminster paedophile ring. Watson's peerage was ultimately rejected by the House of Lords vetting commission.[3] Clearly, a number of factors must have made Watson realise that his position was no longer tenable. But before standing down, he used his final act on Labour's NEC to deliver the death blow against me, bringing my time as a Labour MP to an abrupt halt. Nearly 44 years of devoted service to the party was unceremoniously flushed down the toilet.

At that point, I resolved to resign from the party and to fight the election as an independent.

Corbyn's wife, Laura Álvarez, rang me that evening after hearing about my decision. Laura had been supportive throughout my suspension and had spoken to me over the phone on several occasions. She said that she and Corbyn both loved me and wanted me to *"come back next year"*. She acknowledged that I had been targeted for supporting him. It was a nice gesture, but it was cold comfort for being dropped as the candidate. I knew it would be almost impossible to win as an independent contender, but I was going to give it my best shot. I told her that I felt obliged to stand to demonstrate to the party's broken bureaucracy that there had to be consequences for their deplorable behaviour.

When I checked my laptop before going home, I saw that the party had emailed a formal letter to me to confirm the decision to throw me on the scrapheap. They had the gall to refer me to the Samaritans again, in case I needed support for my mental health and wellbeing as a result of their decision. I wasn't feeling suicidal. But, when I got home, I did feel pretty depressed. A big part of my identity had been stolen. The Labour Party had been my life. I reminisced about how excited and nervous I'd been when I was on the bus to attend my first branch meeting as a teenager. I remembered feeling that I had joined the adult world when I sat in the corner of that meeting room, listening to those strangers talking about issues that I didn't fully understand at the time. I had wanted to fight against injustice and decided that the best way to do that was through the Labour Party. I had thrown myself into being a dedicated activist and I quickly found myself being given jobs to do. I became the local Labour Party tote collector around the village of Shardlow, where I lived just outside of Derby. It used to take several hours to complete the round on foot. When I reached the small council estate of West End Drive, the kids playing in the street used to shout, *"The Labour man's here"*. But I was a 'Labour man' no more.

To see this document please scan this QR code.

It felt like a bereavement and the sense of loss was intensified because I had been discarded like I was nothing, simply for standing up for what I believed to be right. I had: tried to safeguard the party's reputation; defended the leader against all attacks; fought for an anti-imperialist international policy; and stood up for the rights of grassroots members. For that, I was viciously vilified and forsaken. Some of those who deserted me were the very people I had so vigorously defended, and some of them actively joined in the attacks. These erstwhile 'comrades' had either opted for a quiet life or had been duped.

We were engaged in a struggle for socialism and anti-imperialism. We were aiming to strike a blow against the military-industrial-complex and to create an ally for the Palestinian people on the UN Security Council. How could anyone of good conscience be neutral about a witch-hunt that was designed to sabotage those noble goals? It made me think about the quote attributed to Dante Alighieri, *"The hottest places in hell are reserved for those who, in times of great moral crisis, maintain their neutrality"*.

I had followed the examples of Jackie Walker, Marc Wadsworth, Ken Livingstone, Tony Greenstein, and others. I had stood by my principles, maintained my dignity, and I could look at myself in the mirror with a clear conscience. Whilst my heart was broken, I was still standing and ready to continue the fight against injustice, albeit no longer from within the Labour Party.

CHAPTER TWENTY-TWO

INDEPENDENCE

On Thursday 7 November 2019, the morning after I had resigned from the Labour Party, it really hit me that I was now outside of the Labour fold. I couldn't face going into my constituency office, so I spent the day at home licking my wounds. Steve Beckett, who had already volunteered to work on my campaign, got in touch to confirm that he would be my agent in the election. He was absolutely solid and speaking with him cheered me up. I then heard on the grapevine that Labour's NEC was going to parachute Tony Tinley, a local right-wing Unite officer, as Labour's parliamentary candidate in Derby North. The members of Derby North CLP weren't involved in the selection. Tinley had backed Owen Smith in the 2016 attempted coup against Corbyn. I was told that the announcement was going to be made the following Monday. So, I decided to draft a letter to Jennie Formby, urging the party not to field a candidate against me. Even as a non-Labour candidate, I would be promoting the values and policies advocated by Corbyn. I realised the chances of my proposal being accepted were close to zero, but I thought it was at least worth a try. As it turned out, my letter was ignored. I spent that weekend collecting signatures for my nomination papers, and I ended up being the only pro-Corbyn candidate on the ballot paper.

Assembling the election team

The chair of Harborough CLP, Dave Roberts, came over to offer his support. He had helped in my successful 2017 campaign and was keen to assist again. He had worked with Arthur Scargill to establish the Socialist Labour Party in 1996 and was disgusted by what had happened to me. George Galloway also invited me onto his TV programme that weekend, to talk about what had happened and my decision to go it alone. I had actually consulted Galloway about the possibility of standing as an independent before making the decision. I was interested in his perspective, as he had stood successfully against the Labour Party on two separate occasions, as well as losing on one occasion. Initially, he was sceptical. But, after we spoke about the pros and cons, we both thought it was worth doing. Galloway had been incredibly supportive of me from the moment I was suspended in February 2019, and he used his various platforms to highlight my case, repeatedly returning to it in his broadcasts. I told Galloway that I knew it was an uphill struggle and the odds were against me, but it was a fight that had to be had. I also knew that, whatever the outcome of the election in Derby North, this was just the beginning of the next chapter in the struggle.

Steve Beckett had booked himself into a hotel across the road from my office for the duration of the campaign, and we were getting offers of assistance from all over the country. The dreadful winter weather and dark nights meant that door-knocking in the evenings was out of the question. Without the benefit of the Labour Party's extensive voter database, we were also having to do everything from scratch. In addition to the absence of an organisational infrastructure, changes in electoral legislation meant that I could only describe myself as 'Independent' on the nomination paper rather than 'Independent Labour' or 'Independent Socialist'. This put me at a distinct disadvantage, because voters often only look at political parties on their ballot papers. But, despite these obvious stumbling blocks, I continued on, if only to give Labour's bureaucrats a bloody nose.

When Beckett and I went to the Council House in Derby to lodge my nomination forms, we bumped into the Mid Derbyshire Labour candidate and some of her supporters. They were incredibly sympathetic and were telling me how much they hoped I would win. It was a lovely moment and another reminder that the people behind the witch-hunt were in a minority.

We were a couple of weeks into my campaign, which was going well considering all the hurdles we had to negotiate, when I got the distressing news that Beckett had suffered a heart attack. He was incredibly stoic when I spoke to him over the phone, remaining cheerful and resolute. He was more concerned about leaving me *"in the lurch"*, as he put it, which was typical of his kind and considerate nature. Beckett had been really enthusiastic, putting in a huge effort to make my election operation as professional as possible. In that first fortnight, he was by my side each day, coming into the office at 8:00am and was still there when everyone else had left. I went to see him in hospital that evening, and he was full of praise for the health staff who had been looking after him. Listening to him speak, it was hard to believe that he'd had a heart attack earlier that day. He was still fretting about ensuring I had an agent and we agreed that I would ask Dave Roberts from Harborough if he would consider taking on the role.

When I contacted Roberts, he was more than happy to take over as my agent, and, like Beckett, he put in a herculean effort throughout the remainder of the campaign. As the close of nominations drew nearer, there were more appeals for the Labour Party to withdraw its candidate in Derby North. Tosh McDonald, the former ASLEF president, was one of the leading voices calling on Labour not to field a candidate against me. In a statement published in the *Morning Star*, he said that I had been *"a longstanding supporter of Jeremy Corbyn and Labour's socialist programme"*, and that:

> *"Given [Chris's] outstanding record of campaigning, his history of public service in Derby and his steadfast loyalty to the leadership, nominating an official Labour candidate could allow the Tories to capture the seat."*[1]

The day after Tosh's statement was published, there was a disappointing intervention by the executive committee of the Communist Party of Britain (CPB). They called on socialists, progressives, trade unionists, Greens, and Scottish and Welsh nationalists to vote Labour everywhere. The CPB's London district secretary, Steve Johnson, even *"urged a Labour vote in every constituency, including Derby North despite the outrageous suspension of "excellent" sitting MP Chris Williamson"*.[2] I had a good working relationship with local CPB members in Derby, and I'd cooperated with them on a range of different issues. The former CPB chair, Bill Greenshields, lives in Derby and we had an extended email exchange after I had been dropped as the official Labour candidate. Greenshields was supportive of me personally, but he tried to persuade me not to stand as an independent. He was worried that I would be criticised if I split the vote and let the Tories win. I stressed that I was the only pro-Corbyn candidate on the ballot paper and there had to be consequences for the dysfunctional, anti-democratic, and abusive Labour Party bureaucracy. Unfortunately, the CPB had invested far too many resources and hopes into the Corbyn project by this point. The CPB had managed to get some of its (allegedly 'former') members into senior positions in Labour's bureaucracy, most notable of which was Andrew Murray, who became a 'part-time consultant' in Corbyn's office.[3]

In the end, all the pleas for Labour to stand down in Derby North were denied, and Tony Tinley went into the contest with the party's blessing. To Labour's mandarins, whether he won or lost was immaterial, because either way it would mean one less pro-Corbyn MP in the House of Commons. In the meantime, in spite of increasingly inclement weather, we often had more people on the streets at weekends campaigning for me than the Labour Party. I was deeply touched by the level of commitment from people who travelled from all over the country to help put out leaflets and knock on doors for me. Many of them were still Labour Party members. The sense of solidarity and camaraderie during that campaign was immense. The fact that everyone who came to help knew I had little to no chance of winning didn't diminish their efforts, which were truly magnificent all the way through to polling day itself.

The clock strikes 10

On election day, a few of us sat around in the office awaiting the outcome of the exit poll at 10:00pm. When it finally arrived, it predicted a disastrous night for Labour. The party's saboteurs and external vested interests had triumphed. That result hammered the final nail in the coffin of the already ailing Corbyn project. In that moment, all the hopes and expectations that Corbyn had initially generated were shattered. The euphoria of him winning two leadership contests in 2015 and 2016, and leading the party in 2017 to its biggest vote share increase since 1945, evaporated. It was the bitterest of blows. The monumental tragedy was that Corbyn had been the architect of his own downfall, for reasons that I've already laid out repeatedly.

John McDonnell was at BBC Broadcasting House when the exit poll came through and said, *"Brexit dominated the election ... I think people are frustrated and want Brexit out of the way"*.[4] It was a remarkable comment because, only a few months previously, he'd said he wanted to campaign for Remain in a second EU referendum.[5] McDonnell's policy positioning, alongside other members of the SCG like Diane Abbott and Clive Lewis, had put Corbyn under enormous pressure to go along with the second referendum stupidity. Despite all of Corbyn's instincts screaming that this was wrong, he eventually caved in to their ridiculous demands.[6] This suited Corbyn's opponents because it was obviously going to play badly with the electorate, and it effectively sealed Labour's fate as the anti-democratic party that wanted to overturn the 'will of the British people'.

I had opposed calls for a second referendum from the very beginning, even though I had campaigned for Remain in 2016. At the last PLP meeting I attended, two days before Formby suspended me in February 2019, I had passionately argued that we should promise to deliver a 'People's Brexit' rather than the 'Bankers' Brexit' being offered by the Tories. I made the point that, in an election, we could argue that a Labour government, free from the shackles of the EU's state aid rules, could use the flexibility of our sovereign currency to lift the living standards of the 99 per cent. Our messaging could have chimed well with the successful 'Take Back Control' slogan of 2016. We could have promised that the British people under a Corbyn-led government would take back control of their own lives by eradicating poverty, eliminating precarious employment, and delivering affordable homes for everyone. The whole terms of the debate could have been turned on their head. Instead of being on the defensive over Brexit, Labour could have gone on the attack and been able to get a hearing for the social policies that the party was offering. But that opportunity was squandered. The malcontents got their way, aided and abetted by the likes of McDonnell. In 2017, we had come close to securing the levers of government to implement a transformative vision for Britain, but we were later betrayed.

What if?

I can't help but think that, if I had retained my seat in the 2015 general election, I would've been present at the fateful SCG meeting that selected a socialist candidate for the Labour leadership contest. Could I have been the left's standard-bearer in that battle? Would I have ruled myself out, like Diane Abbott, Ian Lavery, and John McDonnell did? By all accounts, Corbyn had been reluctant to stand when the SCG met in the small meeting room off Westminster Hall known as W3. In fact, when they first met to discuss the issue, they couldn't decide whether to even field a candidate. Some were fearful that a left candidate would be drubbed, which would weaken the left's influence. But Labour members, and the country at large, were chomping at the bit for an alternative to the right-wing run-of-the-mill candidates who had already put themselves forward, like Andy Burnham, Liz Kendall, Yvette Cooper, Mary Creagh, and Chuka Umunna.

So, it might have fallen to me to be the left's candidate. Given my popularity inside the PLP at that time, I don't think I would have encountered the difficulties that Corbyn did in obtaining the requisite number of nominations from Labour MPs. Could a Chris Williamson leadership challenge have won? Would the PLP have been any happier with me than they were with Corbyn? Could I have managed the obvious tensions between the PLP and the CLPs? These are impossible questions, but I nevertheless find myself speculating about the answers at times.

Corbyn obviously got a lot right, but his lack of prior leadership experience left him ill-prepared for the challenges that ended up confronting him. Of course, nothing could have adequately prepared anyone for the onslaught that Corbyn encountered, but I think my period as a council leader and a Shadow Minister would have allowed me to lead the party in a more clear-eyed way.

I appreciate that it is easy to talk about these things in hindsight. But many of the errors that Corbyn made were obvious at the time. Rather than defending himself, Corbyn turned the other cheek. Instead of asserting his authority, he stood on the sidelines, justifying his lack of basic leadership by saying, *"I'm not a dictator"*.[7] Rather than showing loyalty to his own foot soldiers, he allowed them to have their reputations ruined, and for them to be suspended, expelled, and shunned. Had I been leader, I would never have allowed the coterie of right-wing smear merchants, who were indulged by Corbyn, to have gained the upper hand. I would've defended myself, I would've ensured MPs followed the party line, and I would've protected and promoted socialist loyalists.

Corbyn himself has admitted that the movement he led *"didn't go far enough"*. In an interview with *Tribune* in late 2020, before he had been suspended from the Labour Party, Corbyn said:

> *"We didn't go far enough. We didn't go fast enough. ... What I wish we'd gone further on ... is changing the culture in which local parties operate. They have to be far more responsive to the community. ... [T]he party has to recognise that the media hostility to the Labour Party and the labour movement isn't going to go away. ... The only answer to that is communicating amongst ourselves".* [8]

What Corbyn didn't admit, however, was that these mistakes were totally avoidable. Alongside countless others across the country, I had been repeatedly calling for: grassroots members to be empowered; the party's structures to be changed wholesale; the PLP to be disciplined; the fake 'antisemitism crisis' and other smears to be exposed; and for the party to adopt a bolder economic prospectus, among many other things.

Would this have delivered a Labour government? It's hard to say. I'm sympathetic to the argument that, whatever we did, the might of the British Establishment would have gone into overdrive to keep a socialist Prime Minister out of 10 Downing Street. But even if we never made it into government, we could have advanced the cause of socialism in Britain, built-up a new generation of cadres, and made the Labour Party a truly socialist party. Instead, we took one step forward and two steps back. We reached the mountain top and glimpsed at the promised land, before being violently dragged back down again. The end result of Corbyn's leadership is that socialism has been delegitimised in Britain, younger generations feel apathetic and disillusioned, and Labour has been irreversibly placed into the hands of right-wing fanatics. The Corbyn project was an ill-fated mirage.

CHAPTER TWENTY-THREE

THE ROAD TO PERDITION

The outcome of the 2019 general election was even worse than most people had feared. The so-called 'Red Wall' was breached and previously solid Labour seats fell like ninepins to the Tories in the north of England. New Labour and Ed Miliband had already alienated Scottish voters. The modest 2017 recovery in Scotland was reversed, with Labour being all but wiped out north of the border, returning just one MP in 2019. For my part, I lost my deposit. The only silver lining on election night was that some of the worst, most ghastly quislings in the PLP also lost their seats. I must admit that I experienced a degree of schadenfreude when I saw the likes of Ruth Smeeth, Gareth Snell, and Anna Turley being given the boot. These characters should have never been Labour MPs in the first place. The reason party members were so excited about the Democracy Roadshows I'd ran in 2018 and 2019 was because people knew that electing a Corbyn-led Labour government with the existing PLP in place would have been a pyrrhic victory. Our anti-imperialist, socialist programme would have been sabotaged by right-wing Labour MPs from the get-go. These pampered parliamentarians knew they could ride roughshod over members' wishes with impunity, owing to the capitulations at the 2018 Labour Party conference.

Revolving doors

Many of the PLP malcontents who lost their seats in the 2019 general election quickly found lucrative employment outside of Parliament. For example, Ruth Smeeth, the former BICOM spin doctor who was one of the loudest exponents of the so-called 'antisemitism crisis', was appointed chief executive of the Index on Censorship.[1] The group claims that it *"campaigns for and defends free expression, promotes debate, and monitors threats to free speech worldwide"*.[2] Yet, they appointed someone who, when she was an MP, actively opposed debate inside the Labour Party and attempted to silence free speech. Maybe Smeeth had a

Damascene conversion between losing her seat in December 2019 and being appointed to her new role six months later. Luciana Berger, who left Change UK to join the Liberal Democrats, also found alternative employment with ease. She was appointed managing director of Advocacy and Public Affairs at the PR company Edelman UK.[3] The same month, Edelman hired Chuka Umunna, another Corbyn critic, as an executive director.[4] Seven months later, he jumped ship to take a high-paying post with the banking giant JP Morgan.[5]

Those who had destroyed our chances of achieving a fairer society under a Corbyn-led government had the assurance of a cushy lifestyle outside of Parliament, leaving everyone else to face the consequences of their actions.

Moving forwards

The election was undoubtedly a disaster. But the seats tally doesn't tell the whole story. In spite of the best efforts of the PLP saboteurs, 10,269,051 people still voted Labour in 2019. That's nearly a million more than Miliband achieved in 2015, over 1.6 million more than Gordon Brown secured in 2010, and nearly three quarters of a million more than Blair won in 2005. The fact that we'd won so many votes, but still lost so many seats, demonstrates how misplaced Tony Benn's optimism was following the result of the disastrous 1983 general election. Benn praised the fact that it was *"the first time since 1945 a political party with an openly socialist policy has received the support of eight and a half million votes"*.[6] Yet, now with over ten million votes in 2019, we faced the same situation. This proves that an anti-imperialist, socialist project cannot be delivered solely through electoral politics. The key to wresting control of our collective future is to build a genuine grassroots social movement.

The mechanisms don't exist inside the Labour Party for the grassroots to seize control. We had the opportunity to create those mechanisms under Corbyn, but that opportunity was wasted. Without open selection for parliamentary candidates there will never be a sufficient number of Labour MPs for a socialist candidate to reach the nominations threshold and get on the ballot in any future leadership contest. It is a moot point as to whether any such candidates even exist in the current PLP. The selection process for aspiring Labour MPs is now so tightly controlled by right-wing bureaucrats that the chances of anyone with views similar to Corbyn's becoming a Labour parliamentary candidate in the future are practically non-existent.

The idea that Labour could ever become a social movement has been blown apart by Sir Keir Starmer. Barely 10 months into his leadership, the baby steps that the party had been taking in this direction through the community organising unit (set up under Corbyn) was axed.[7] The notion of a genuine popular movement deeply rooted in communities was seen as an abomination by the party's aristocracy.

Labour's emphasis is, and always has been, on electoral politics. It is a sacrosanct constitutional obligation. Chapter 1, Clause 1 of the Labour Party's Rule Book stipulates that the party's *"purpose is to organise and maintain in Parliament ... a political Labour Party"* and to:

> *"bring together members and supporters who share its values to develop policies, make communities stronger through collective action and support, and promote the election of Labour Party representatives at all levels of the democratic process."*[8]

But representative democracy is in crisis, and the links that Labour once had in communities have all but disappeared. The 'politics' has been taken out of Labour politics – a process that was started by Neil Kinnock in the mid-1980s and accelerated by Tony Blair and Gordon Brown. The days of municipal socialism are long gone, replaced by managerialism. Some Labour councillors are still trying to use their local government platforms to make a real difference, but most are reduced to banalities like litter-picking photo opportunities that they can post on social media. There is little engagement with communities, and party members are expected to be content with being used as leafleting and canvassing fodder for local and national elections.

There is no serious effort by the Labour Party to build roots in communities. Ed Miliband made a half-hearted attempt to reverse that trend. Latterly, Corbyn talked more seriously about building a genuine social movement, and the formation of the community organising unit was a small, but important, statement of intent. However, even under Corbyn, the priority was still on electoral politics, and community organising was very much the poor relation. We have been conditioned to think that, if only we can elect decent representatives, our task will be complete. But the evidence from around the world, including our own experience with the Corbyn project and the Momentum initiative, suggests that solely relying on an electoral strategy inevitably leads to disappointment and failure.

The spread of Israeli colonisation

Jeremy Corbyn's abject failure to rebut, deconstruct, and expose the lies levelled against him about 'antisemitism' has had knock-on effects for the entire anti-imperialist left in Britain. Under Corbyn, the Labour Party effectively served as an incubator for the Israel lobby to battle-test their character assassination strategies. So, contrary to what many people perhaps expected, the hysteria didn't end when Corbyn stepped down as Labour leader in April 2020. Instead, it has snowballed, and these strategies are now being deployed apace to silence anti-Zionist voices well-beyond the Labour confines.

One of the areas to which pro-Israel zealots have turned their attention following the demise of the Corbyn project is university campuses. David Collier, who is *"regarded as being [one] of the most active and vocal proponents of the campaign against pro-Palestine activists and senior figures in the Labour Party"*,[9] posted a poll on Twitter on 17 February 2020. The tweet said, *"Corbynism was beaten back – but the force behind it is still out there spreading. Which sewer of antisemitism needs to be researched and exposed?"*. Collier provided four options, one of which was university campuses. The result of the poll showed that 58 per cent of respondents were in favour of attacking pro-Palestine activists in universities.[10]

The frantic atmosphere that these Zionist racists have created has seen once-prestigious seats of learning being bounced into adopting the discredited IHRA Working Definition of Antisemitism. In a letter to university vice-chancellors dated 9 October 2020, Tory Education Secretary Gavin Williamson (no relation) threatened to cut funding from any higher education establishment that failed to adopt the IHRA Working Definition.[11]

The Conservative Education Secretary seemed to be playing fast and loose with the Human Rights Act 1998. Article 10(1) of the Act enshrines the right to *"hold opinions and to receive and impart information and ideas without interference by public authority"*. This is reinforced by Section 6(a) of the Act, which states that, *"It is unlawful for a public authority to act in a way which is incompatible with a [European] Convention right"*. Yet, that is precisely what the Education Secretary was doing. Furthermore, Part IV, Section 43(1) of the Education (No 2) Act 1986 requires universities, polytechnics, and colleges to ensure that *"freedom of speech within the law is secured for members, students and employees of the establishment and for visiting speakers"*.

A group of eminent lawyers wrote an open letter to the *Guardian* in January 2021 to object to the government's attacks on free speech about Israel. They said Gavin Williamson *"was legally and morally wrong [in] October [2020] to instruct English universities to adopt and implement the IHRA"*. They were concerned that the IHRA Working Definition had *"been widely used to suppress or avoid criticism of the state of Israel"*.[12]

It would later become apparent that ministers were suffering from a significant bout of cognitive dissonance. Whilst flouting the existing legislation that protects free speech and academic freedom, they simultaneously introduced the Higher Education (Freedom of Speech) Bill to impose a duty on universities to safeguard free speech for their staff. It explicitly stated that academic staff should be free to *"question and test received wisdom, and ... put forward new ideas and controversial or unpopular opinions, without placing themselves at risk of being adversely affected"*.[13] Mysteriously, this effort would very quickly come to a shuddering halt.

In February 2021, a long-brewing campaign against academic David Miller, who was a Professor of Political Sociology at the University of Bristol, reached boiling point. Zionist ideologues, and their allies, launched an aggressive, concerted war to see Professor Miller dismissed. It reminded me of the huge noise that the Israel lobby had generated only two years earlier in February 2019, which saw me suspended from the Labour Party. They mobilised all of their cells embedded in lobbying groups, the media, and Parliament. Their efforts included a letter to Bristol's vice-chancellor, signed by over 100 parliamentarians, ludicrously accusing Professor Miller of *"inciting hatred against Jewish students"*. The so-called All-Party Parliamentary Group Against Antisemitism claimed that Professor Miller had brought the *"university into disrepute"*, and they insisted that the vice-chancellor *"must now act before any further damage is done"*.[14] They also accused the academics who had bravely and publicly supported Professor Miller of having *"disgraced"* their profession.[15]

Later on, the self-proclaimed champion of free speech in universities, Gavin Williamson, seemed to recant what he had previously been saying. In response to a question about Professor Miller from Tory MP Robert Halfon, who has reportedly taken £115,847.18 from pro-Israel sources in the form of funding and junkets since 2010,[16] Williamson said:

> *"I would never expect a university to tolerate racists and I would never expect a university to tolerate antisemitism. Where there is racism – whether that is manifested in antisemitic remarks – I would naturally expect there to be a proper and full employment procedure. I wouldn't expect any form of racism to be tolerated and I would expect those people who are committing antisemitism to be dismissed from the staff."*[17]

This campaign, which kept up momentum by repeatedly misusing parliamentary privilege and other avenues to further the State of Israel's agenda, was yet another example of the malicious tactics to which we have now become accustomed. After being investigated for months, Professor Miller was eventually sacked in October 2021 for the 'crime' of producing evidence-based critiques of Zionist ideology.[18] The university had wilted under pressure exerted by the assets and allies of hostile foreign governments. The State of Israel, and its counterparts in the regime of the United Arab Emirates, had had a target on Professor Miller's back for many years. They finally claimed the scalp they had been craving for so long.

In confirming Professor Miller's dismissal on 1 October 2021, a statement issued by the university confirmed that an independent investigation conducted by a Queen's Counsel had concluded *"that Professor Miller's comments did not constitute unlawful speech"*.[19] Despite that, the university stated, *"Professor Miller did not meet the standards of behaviour we expect from our staff and the University has concluded that Professor Miller's employment should be terminated with immediate effect"*.[20] Precisely what that *"standard of behaviour"* was supposed to be wasn't spelt out. However, it was clear that it meant surrendering the right to express any evidence-based critiques that exposed the realities of Zionism and the State of Israel.

Why was Professor Miller singled out? After all, he is an eminent academic and all his statements about Zionism and Israel were informed by painstaking research. But I believe *that* was precisely why he was unfairly targeted. He was exposing inconvenient truths, and not just about the State of Israel. Professor Miller is a founder of both Spinwatch and Powerbase. Spinwatch undertakes *"cutting-edge research into key social, political, environmental and health issues in the UK and Europe"*.[21] It investigates the public relations industry, looking at how corporate and government propaganda distort public debate and undermine democracy.[22] Powerbase provides *"a free guide to networks of power, lobbying, public relations, and the communications activities of governments and other interests"*. It aims to *"expose corporate capture, political spin, and lies"*.[23] Professor Miller is also the director of Left Legal Support Group Ltd, which oversees the Left Legal Fighting Fund that I founded in 2019 to assist casualties of the ongoing witch-hunts against socialists and anti-imperialists.

And, during all of this, where was the Socialist Campaign Group of Labour MPs (SCG)? They were either nowhere to be seen or they were joining in with the attacks. Take, for example, Lloyd Russell-Moyle, who had already lost all credibility after his lamentable interview with Emma Barnett about my case in 2019, in which he practically soiled himself. Yet, he managed to stoop to a new low as a member of the Higher Education (Freedom of Speech) Bill Committee. In a sneering contribution, he claimed:

> *"I was on a panel at one event where there was – I do not think he is even a professor – the Miller chap from Bristol, and I remember that at the end of the event I said I think what has been said here*

is a load of rubbish – I think I was more fruity in my language. I told my office at the time to write a letter to him to say that I would not sit on any more panels and would not host any events with him". [24]

However, it seems that Russell-Moyle wasn't just embellishing the truth. He was telling outright porkies. Russell-Moyle did host a Spinwatch meeting, alongside Diane Abbott, in a parliamentary committee room in March 2019, and he did leave early because there was a division in the Commons. But, contrary to his assertions, Russell-Moyle did not articulate any criticisms about the event and no letter from his office was ever received by Professor Miller. I suspect the real reason behind Russell-Moyle's outburst at the Bill Committee meeting was that the far-right sewage site *Guido Fawkes* had reported on the 2019 Spinwatch event. It had also published a photograph on social media of Russell-Moyle sitting next to Professor Miller.[25] I wouldn't be surprised if Russell-Moyle was simply trying to distance himself from the Spinwatch event in an act of self-preservation. It was dishonourable and cowardly.

Lloyd Russell-Moyle, along with the rest of the SCG, have demonstrated that they will defend neither free speech nor academic freedom. Some of them may even oppose these concepts. Their wretched failure to speak out about the treatment of Professor Miller throws their spinelessness into sharp relief. It begs the question, once again, what is the point of the SCG? Whenever their support is needed, they are nowhere to be seen.

CHAPTER TWENTY-FOUR

THE "ANTISEMITISM" AGENDA

The demise of the Corbyn project has echoes of a Shakespearian tragedy about it. The bogus 'Labour antisemitism crisis' that consumed the Corbyn leadership was stoked by a group of useful idiots who claimed to be enthusiastic Corbyn allies. These minor celebrities continually undermined him. Their positions weren't based on principle. It didn't matter what the rights and wrongs of any given issue were. Instead, they simply obsessed about whether something looked bad. How would it play out in front of the media hounds? It was all based on *"optics"*, a word that they frequently used. These pseudo-socialists – the 'optics left' – cheered on the witch-hunt against supposed 'antisemites', helping to bury any possibility of a transformational socialist government coming to power.

But it wasn't just the optics left to blame. Corbyn himself must take the lion's share of responsibility. Rather than rebutting the 'antisemitism' smears, he indulged them. He could never call a spade a spade. It meant that Corbyn was on the back foot from the very beginning of his leadership. His record as a lifelong anti-racist activist was brushed aside by an alliance of Zionist extremists and right-wing neoliberals. And he played right into their hands by taking their counterfeit complaints at face value. That he gave houseroom to the conspicuous 'antisemitism' calumny – perhaps out of fear of causing offence – sent a signal to many on the left that the hyperventilating hoaxers were on to something. After all, if Corbyn admitted that there was a 'problem', why shouldn't those who claimed to support him? This strategic miscalculation would prove to be fatal. Corbyn's opponents had played a masterstroke in political propaganda from which he'd never recover.

The 'antisemitism' smear was so cynical because it manipulated the instincts of the anti-racists who supported Corbyn. It feels deeply grotesque and uncomfortable, as an anti-racist, to be accused of being a racist. But, instead of calling the lies out for what they were, Corbyn and many of his supporters ploughed all their energies into a vain attempt to prove that they were not, in fact, racists. It's almost impossible to prove a negative, and it was a massive distraction from developing a programme for government. But grassroots members were engulfed by paranoia, and many more were pressurised into keeping their heads down. Criticisms of Israel, and support for Palestine, became muted. Much was lost as a result. Freedom of speech inside the Labour Party was all but annihilated, focus was shifted away from Corbyn's progressive socialist programme, and many of those who were targeted suffered mental ill-health, with some having their livelihoods, careers, and reputations destroyed.

And that was the whole point of the 'antisemitism' agenda. It was never about tackling prejudice against Jews. It was about smashing the pro-Palestine left, undermining the confidence of their convictions and the passion of their internationalist instincts. Of course, malicious cries of 'antisemitism' are nothing new, nor should it have been controversial to call them smears. And yet, it reached a point where even questioning the validity of 'antisemitism' accusations became a form of 'antisemitism' in itself (so-called 'denialism'). The use of 'antisemitism' accusations was called out, long ago, by none other than former Israeli government minister, Shulamit Aloni. In a 2002 *Democracy Now!* interview,[1] journalist Amy Goodman asked:

> *"Often, when there is dissent expressed ... against policies of the Israeli government, people ... are called 'antisemitic'. What is your response to that, as an Israeli Jew?"*

Aloni replied:

> *"Well, it's a trick. We always use it. ... it's very easy to blame people who criticise certain acts of the Israeli government as 'antisemitic' and to bring up the Holocaust and the suffering of the Jewish people. And that justifies everything we do to the Palestinians."*

Acres of column inches have been written about the 'Labour antisemitism crisis' by right-wing and notionally left-wing commentators alike. One of the loudest voices in the contrived controversy has been *Guardian* scribbler Owen Jones, the supreme leader of the optics left. Unfortunately, Jones is one of only a handful of individuals to have written in detail about the Corbyn project following its collapse. Until now, his tainted historicisation of the events of that time have not been extensively scrutinised. In his book *This Land*,[2] published in September 2020, he dedicated a full chapter to 'The Antisemitism Crisis'. Within it, he devoted six pages to an abusive tirade against me, referring to me as *"king"* of the *"cranks"*.[3] I don't intend to waste time correcting his fictitious account and puerile insults about my political record, but his commentary on 'antisemitism' must be challenged.

Jones's shameful portrayal about this tumultuous period is heavily reliant on interviews with former – often unnamed – staff in Corbyn's office. His interpretation of events doesn't differ much from mainstream accounts. He depicts a leader's office in disarray and a party whose disciplinary structures are incapable of grappling with a distinct *"left-wing antisemitism"*[4] that had apparently gained prominence as a result of a *"vacuum"* arising from Corbyn's *"lack of leadership"* on the issue.[5]

His version of events exonerates, or denies the existence of, the Israel lobby, whitewashes (and redwashes) Zionist colonisation, and fails to offer a critical or insightful analysis to his readers. One commentator aptly said that some of Jones's commentary *"could have been written by Shimon Peres"*.[6]

Anti-Semitism, 'antisemitism', and Judeophobia

It goes without saying that anti-Semitism exists. Anti-Semitism and Judeophobia, however, are not interchangeable terms. We must also discuss the more recent term 'antisemitism' (unhyphenated). I will return to that shortly.

Judeophobia – or hatred of Jews as Jews – has been longstanding in history, particularly in Europe. Blood libel, well-poisoning myths, the Rhineland massacres, the Edict of Expulsion, the Strasbourg massacre, the Spanish Inquisition, pogroms in Tsarist Russia. These all pre-dated the Holocaust, and they were predominantly driven by religious anti-Judaism.

The German term *antisemitismus* was popularised in 1879 by Wilhelm Marr, as a *"scientific construct based on racial theory"*.[7] The term was meant to sound 'scientific' to distinguish it from religious anti-Judaism. Anti-Semitic pseudo-science and hatred found its most horrific manifestation in the 1930s and 1940s under the Nazis. Jones correctly states that anti-Semitism resulted in the *"attempt to exterminate every single Jew on the European continent by industrialized, bureaucratic means"*.[8] Mercifully, thanks to the heroism of my Mam's and Dad's generation, the Nazi hordes were defeated, and anti-Semitic ideas rightfully became unacceptable and reviled throughout most of Europe.

In the twenty-first century, anti-Semitism is thankfully a relatively rare phenomenon, to which only a small number of genuine neo-Nazis subscribe. The term anti-Semitism, therefore, has become specious when applied to anti-Jewish prejudice in the modern day. The only meaningful contemporary term that describes hatred of Jews as Jews, and which is not imbued with Nazi pseudo-science and racialisation, is 'Judeophobia'. That is the term used by serious scholars of anti-Jewish animus, such as Professor David Engel[9] and Professor Jonathan Judaken.[10] As Professor Judaken explains:

> *"ancient Judeophobia ... was characterized by important contextual differences from the early Christian Judeophobia of the* Adversus Judaeos *tradition. This anti-Judaism was transformed by the era of the Crusades and the High Medieval period, when ... new fantasies about Jews ... emerged. Modern racism developed out of the theological heritage of the Spanish Inquisition, the conquest of the Americas, transatlantic slavery, Enlightenment systems of categorization, and the rise of nationalism in the wake of Napoleon. Post-Holocaust Judeophobia has taken new forms in a postcolonial era defined by globalization."*[11]

These *"new forms"* of Judeophobia today tend to manifest on a cultural, rather than a scientific or a religious, level. Despite these changing realities, the use of the term 'anti-Semitism' remains widespread. The weaponisation of anti-Semitism has been a longstanding feature of the State of Israel's propaganda efforts across the world. During and after the period of the 1973 Ramadan War, the state's Ministry of Foreign Affairs developed and promoted the concept of the 'New Anti-Semitism' in order to fight a growing anti-Zionist surge. Fears were growing among

Zionists that the State of Israel was losing the public relations battle in Europe and the United States. Abba Eban, then the State of Israel's Foreign Minister, said:

> *"One of the chief tasks of any dialogue with the Gentile world is to prove that the distinction between anti-Semitism and anti-Zionism is not a distinction at all. Anti-Zionism is merely the new anti-Semitism".*[12]

Since then, this 'New Anti-Semitism' – a concept specifically created to attack anti-Zionists – has continued to evolve. Part of that evolution has been the dropping of the hyphen and the capital S, creating the term 'antisemitism'. The term 'Semite' was originally intended to encapsulate both Jews and Arabs.[13] German anti-Semitism, whilst focussed against European Jews, was constructed on racist ethnography towards a 'Semitic' people. The eradication of the hyphen in the modern day is supposedly meant to be a rejection of the concept of the 'Semite'. But the true purpose of Zionists dropping the hyphen is part of a wider trend of historical revisionism, which seeks to disconnect Jewish and Muslim histories. In emphasising the historical meaningfulness of both Jews and Arabs being entwined under the 'Semite' umbrella, Professor Judaken underscores that:

> *"European self-constructions long depended upon a two-headed hydra: the Jew as the internal enemy, the theological enemy, and the Saracen, the Moor, the Arab, the Muslim, the Turk, or Islam itself as differing names that served as the external enemy, the political enemy."*[14]

On a theological level, *"anti-Jewish medieval myths, specifically host desecration and well-poisoning, ritual murder implicated Jews in a conspiracy against Christendom"*.[15] Whereas, on a political level, the various Islamic caliphates constituted a perpetual foreign enemy. These internal and external enemies of Christendom – Jews and Muslims – had their fates entangled at numerous points in history. For example, Professor Judaken explains that, during the Crusades, Jews were murdered by Christians on their way to fight the Saracens in Jerusalem. Furthermore, the Fourth

Lateran Council of 1215 mandated that Muslim clothing should be marked, alongside Jewish clothing. Additionally, during the Spanish Inquisition, Muslims were targeted alongside Jews. Following the Inquisition, *"90 percent of Jews lived under the crescent of Islam"*.[16] This combined 'Semitic' history *"was erased in the 1930s, around the time that another hyphenated construct, "Judeo-Christian," was popularized"*.[17] Professor Judaken highlights the important political implications of *"consciously"* maintaining the hyphen in 'anti-Semitism' today. He says that it:

> *"point[s] to the forgotten intersections and interactions between Jews and Muslims, while remarking upon the history of the myth of 'the Semite' that underpins the origins of the term ... The choice to hyphenate is particularly significant in a political frame where Jews and Muslims are often figured as perpetual enemies despite the historical scholarship that shows otherwise".*[18]

Zionist colonisation of Palestine has seen the propagation of ahistorical narratives about bad relations between Jews and Muslims. Zionist insistence on a 'New Antisemitism' (now unhyphenated), whose *"epicentre is Islamic"* (so-called 'Islamic antisemitism'),[19] forms part of a wider Islamophobic and anti-Arab strategy to delegitimise Palestinian resistance and to align Israel with the *"Judeo-Christian"* West in a *"clash of civilizations"*.[20]

So, 'antisemitism' is a propaganda term, designed to meld distinct periods of European anti-Jewish history into one, and to promote Islamophobic myths. Jones fully and openly commits to this propaganda, which is designed to impregnate the 'guilty' European consciousness with the original sin of 'centuries' of 'antisemitism'.

Additionally, Jones assists the State of Israel's diplomatic objectives by furthering 'New Antisemitism' talking points, encouraging the idea of a supposed *"left-wing antisemitism"*. According to Jones, this stems from a belief in *"shadowy individuals wielding sinister unaccountable power behind the scenes"*.[21] He uses the Rothschild conspiracy theory as an example. The Rothschild conspiracy was made notorious in Nazi Germany and, since that time, has been found predominantly among the political right, supported by the likes of David Icke. But Jones ignores this. He gives credence to the nonsensical arguments that leftists – as anti-elitists and anti-capitalists – are somehow innately vulnerable to supporting Judeophobic ideas. This vague concept of 'conspiracism' is what he presents as evidence of a peculiarly 'left-wing' form of 'antisemitism'. It is absurd and unconvincing.

The '2,000 years of hatred' myth

As well as supporting the State of Israel's propaganda about 'New Antisemitism', Jones supports the 'transhistorical' theory of Judeophobia. In essence, this seeks to connect all instances of Judeophobia into a single, unbroken chain, distilling anti-Jewish persecution from across the ages into a 'collective trauma' shared by every single Jewish person today. Jones says:

> *"Antisemitism is ingrained in all European societies. Two thousand years of blood libel, scapegoating, pogroms, expulsions and murder, culminating in an attempt to exterminate every single Jew on the European continent ... all this ensured that this very specific form of racism set down deep roots in many different cultures. ... Antisemitism is a shapeshifter: it appears in many different guises".* [22]

It is true that Judeophobia has manifested itself at various times over the past 2,000 years in Europe. But it has arisen in different ways, pursued for different reasons by different groups. Contrary to Jones's arguments, Judeophobia has not been a single *"shapeshifter"* transcending history. As Professor Judaken explains:

> *"What has endured are persisting myths, images, tropes, or fantasies about Jews developed over the long history of Christian anti-Judaism. ... [T]he ... forces ... that have periodically driven the revival of these persisting **myths are not the same in dissimilar contexts.** Consequently, different eruptions of Judeophobia **require different explanations.** For this reason, **cyclical eternalism**, like its twin, **transhistorical anti-Semitism**, does not advance our understanding (emphasis added)."* [23]

The idea that Jews will always be persecuted wherever they are ('cyclical eternalism') and the notion that the physical and mental harm of historical events is distilled into the consciousness of all Jews today ('transhistorical anti-Semitism') is simply unsustainable. The point of these ideas is to deliberately make Jewish people feel paranoid.

The engenderment of fear among Jews who live outside of the State of Israel is central to the modern Zionist project. It serves as a foundational justification for the state's very existence, and for the preservation of its character as a 'Jewish' ethnostate. Jones writes that, after the Holocaust, *"There appeared to be an incontestable need for a Jewish homeland"*.[24] The 'need', according to Zionists, is for the safety of Jewish people to be preserved within their own ethnically and religiously defined nation state. Zionists want Jewish people to believe that they will never have security unless they abandon their own countries and settle in occupied Palestine.

Zionists take advantage of every opportunity – and sometimes create their own opportunities – to encourage Jews to make *aliyah* to Palestine (in other words, to become colonists). Jones mentions *"Jews who fled Iraq in the mass exodus of 1951"*.[25] He implies that they fled because of 'antisemitism', as opposed to a Zionist false-flag operation. It has been argued by the anti-Zionist Iraqi Jewish author, Naeim Giladi – alongside many others – that the Baghdad bombings were perpetrated by Israeli agents:

> *"the Zionist movement in Iraq and the Israeli agents who ran it were prepared to do anything in order to achieve their goals. Their objective was to bring about the exodus of all Iraqi Jews before March 8, 1951, at any cost."*[26]

In more recent times, following an attack in Copenhagen that killed four Jewish people, the then Israeli Prime Minister, Benjamin Netanyahu, took the opportunity to say, *"Jews have been murdered again on European soil only because they were Jews. ... we say to Jews, to our brothers and sisters: Israel is your home"*.[27]

This constant fearmongering also seeks to provide a justification for Israel's Law of Return, which was passed by the Knesset in 1950. The law allows Jews from all over the world, who have never set foot in historic Palestine, to claim ownership of part of its land. Two years later, in 1952, the Knesset passed the Nationality Law, preventing Palestinians from returning to their homeland. It stipulates that a person who resided in Palestine immediately prior to the establishment of the State of Israel in 1948 is automatically regarded as a resident if they were registered as a resident before the enactment of the Nationality Law. It is drafted in that specific way to prevent Palestinians who fled their homeland during the 1947–48 campaign of ethnic cleansing, and returned 'illegally' thereafter, from obtaining citizenship.

Perpetuation of the 'collective trauma' myth helps to legitimise the establishment of the Zionist state in 1948 and to justify the continued colonisation by Zionists of Palestinian land. This Zionist propaganda should be challenged, not indulged. Jewish communities should be reassured that they *are* secure, and that they are, and will continue to be, welcome in their own countries of origin. The British left should say clearly that the place for British Jews is within Britain, not Palestine.

Whitewashing and redwashing Zionism

Jones uses his book to tell his readers that the *"imprecise usage of 'Zionism' and 'Zionist' in the West is deeply problematic, leaving it eviscerated of meaning"*.[28] This implies that Zionism is a nuanced, varied, and intangible philosophy that is too difficult for the vast majority of people to understand or legitimately criticise. Like many Zionist propagandists, Jones tries to cloak Zionism in a mirage of uncertainty. This is a common Zionist tactic that is used to shut down debate.

Jones's characterisations of Israel and its relationship with colonialism are as historically illiterate as they are politically Zionist. One must look only to the words of Theodor Herzl, the founder of modern Zionism, to see this evidenced in painfully explicit terms. In his book of 1896, *Der Judenstaat* (The Jewish State), Herzl explained that his appeal to European imperial powers to support the creation of a Jewish State would need to be explicitly couched in colonial language in order to *"make sense to them"*.[29]

Herzl presented Zionism as a civilising mission, carrying, as he put it, *"culture to the East"*. Moreover, he openly highlighted that Zionists would want their new state to *"create new trade routes – and none will be more interested in this than England with its Asiatic possessions. The shortest route to India lies through Palestine"*. Herzl continued by saying, *"And so I should think that here in England, the Zionist idea, which is a colonial one, should be easily and quickly understood"*.[30] The first wave ('First Aliyah') of Zionist colonists entering Palestine began in 1881. Herzl understood the importance of ever-increasing colonists arriving in Palestine to expropriate land from the indigenous population:

> *"We must expropriate gently the private property on the estates assigned to us. ... But ... the removal of the poor must be carried out discreetly and circumspectly. Let the owners of [real estate] believe that they are cheating us, selling us things for more than they are worth. But we are not going to sell them anything back. ... By the time the reshaping of world opinion in our favour has been completed, we shall be firmly established in our country ... The voluntary expropriation will be accomplished through our secret agents. ... We shall then sell only to Jews, and all real estate will be traded only among Jews."*[31]

In other words, according to Herzl, Zionism was a settler-colonial project which would create a civilised European outpost serving Western imperial interests, particularly those of England. Herzl wasn't the only Zionist leader with such ideas. In April 1905, at a talk in Manchester, Israel Zangwill said, *"[We] must be prepared .... to drive out by the sword the [Arab] tribes in possession ... or to grapple with the problem of a large alien population, mostly Mohammedan"*.[32] In 1941, David Ben-Gurion made clear, *"It is impossible to imagine general evacuation [of Palestinians from the land] without compulsion, and brutal compulsion"*.[33]

The creation of a Jewish ethnostate in Palestine, at the expense of the indigenous population, had therefore been on the cards since the 1880s. It was given further impetus by the Balfour Declaration of 1917. That same year, Ronald Storrs, the British military governor of Jerusalem, identified that the idea was to create a *"little loyal Jewish Ulster in a sea of potentially hostile Arabism"*.[34] In 1937, the Peel Commission proposed a partition plan. In the eyes of Zionist leaders Ben-Gurion and Chaim Weizmann, this constituted *"a stepping stone to some further expansion and the eventual takeover of the whole of Palestine"*.[35] Ben-Gurion was willing to accept a partitioned state *"on the basis that after we build a strong force following the establishment of the state, we will abolish the partition of the country and we will expand to the whole Land of Israel"*.[36] The council of the Jewish Agency responded to the Peel Commission by constituting a Population Transfer Committee, which would plan the compulsory transfer of Palestinians, to take place, as they put it, not *"by preaching 'sermons on the mount' but by machine-guns"*.[37]

That plan was put into action in 1948, when 750,000 Palestinians were expelled from their land in the Nakba ('catastrophe').[38] Many further thousands were killed by militant Labour Zionists like Ben-Gurion and his Haganah armed forces (which later became the Israel Occupation Forces) and by Zionist terror militias like Irgun and the Stern Gang.

It is astonishing, therefore, that Jones has sought to argue that this reality is *"fundamentally different from ... projects of European settler-colonialism"*.[39] Jones differentiates the latter by saying, *"In those horrors, Europeans arrived to plant their flags to claim land on behalf of their own states, while Israel's founders were fleeing the flags of their old nations"*. Even on its own terms, this isn't true for Jews who moved to historic Palestine outside of Nazi-occupied Europe before the 1930s and after 1945. Jones's understanding of settler-colonialism, moreover, is completely misconceived. The appropriate distinction is between non-settler forms of colonialism and settler-colonialism. In the former, as in the European allusion Jones makes, colonialists seek to subjugate indigenous people by force of arms and to create a system whereby the indigenous population themselves become part of the wider empire. Settler-colonialism, on the other hand, seeks to move settlers into a foreign land, generally displacing and supplanting the indigenous population. It is clear that the history of Palestine conforms to the latter model and that Jones has (deliberately or otherwise) wrongly defined settler-colonialism in order to exempt the State of Israel.

Commentator Oliver Eagleton has also rightly identified that Jones's *"Israel-for-beginners potted history"* *"contains no mention of the Nakba"* except for *"a passing reference"*.[40] That is to say,

Jones doesn't explain what the *"incontestable need for a Jewish homeland"* meant for Palestinians. As Eagleton further remarks, Jones's historicisation of the State of Israel *"is a rehearsal of liberal-Zionist hasbara that betray scant engagement with scholarship on the region"*.[41] For Jones, the humanitarian catastrophe that resulted from the foundation of the Zionist state is simply an afterthought.

Jones also portrays the State of Israel's founding as being uncontroversial, because *"the torchbearers of the Labour left – such as Tony Benn, Nye Bevan, Jennie Lee, Eric Heffer, Ian Mikardo and Michael Foot – were strong champions of the early Israeli state"*.[42] But that is no defence. As much as they might be *"torchbearers"*, those people were utterly wrong on this issue. The support given by the Labour Party to the establishment of the Zionist state was done in the full knowledge that it meant depopulating Palestine of its indigenous people. In fact, a motion submitted to the 1944 Labour Party conference was unambiguous about its support for a policy of ethnic cleansing. The motion read as follows:

> *"There is neither hope nor meaning in a 'Jewish National Home' unless, we are prepared to let Jews, if they wish, enter this tiny land [Palestine] in such numbers as to become a majority. ... [I]n Palestine [there] surely is a case ... to promote a stable settlement, for transfer of population.* **Let the Arabs be encouraged to move out as the Jews move in** *(emphasis added)."*[43]

Nothing can justify the humanitarian catastrophe that was created when the United Nations General Assembly approved the plan to partition Palestine in 1947. Labour's historical position is a source of shame, not pride. Yet, Jones legitimises the State of Israel's origins, saying that it only *"came to resemble a colonial occupier"* after An-Naksah (the 'Six-Day War') in 1967, with the *"original socialist principles"* of the state later *"jettisoned"* by the Likud Party.[44] This is a shocking remark to come out of the mouth of a so-called socialist like Jones. It is out-and-out redwashing of Zionist colonisation. Moreover, the *kibbutzim* agricultural collectives, which Jones praises as *"incubators of a new socialist society"*,[45] in reality:

"built exclusively Jewish settlements on Palestinian land and militantly guarded them. Kibbutzim have been ... presented as an ideal of socialist egalitarianism. [But they] ultimately helped entrench a racist and capitalist system of domination which continues to exploit and dispossess Palestinians to this very day."[46]

Jones takes the concept of 'Labour Zionism' at face value. Herzl and Ben-Gurion both fell within the tradition of Labour Zionism. Their 'socialism' was an explicitly colonial one. It relied on brute force, terror, and purposeful policies of depopulation and transfer. The State of Israel has never been – and can never be – a socialist country.

Misdiagnosing the problem

The undercurrent in Jones's entire analysis of the Labour Party's 'antisemitism crisis', is his complete misdiagnosis of the problem. He gets bogged down in statistics and processes, whilst glossing over the true motivations behind the ceaseless smear campaign against the party. In his view, the whole affair *"need never have happened"*.[47] This perception is profoundly naïve. Jones seems to think that the problem revolved around the party's failure to expel enough 'antisemites', delays in adopting the IHRA Working Definition's 'illustrative' examples, and Corbyn's failure to apologise enough.

In reality, the campaign against Corbyn and the Labour Left was not about the individual actions of the leader or any of his supporters. It was entirely motivated by the policy platform developed by the Corbyn leadership. A key pillar of Corbyn-era policy was a commitment to anti-imperialism as part of a genuinely ethical international policy. This meant recognising Palestine, potentially supporting the Boycott, Divestment, Sanctions (BDS) movement, and opposing Israeli apartheid and occupation, all of which were inimical to the interests of the State of Israel. Whilst Jones touches on these issues in his book, he fails to consider their importance. His analysis of the collapse in Jewish support for Labour under its former leader Ed Miliband,[48] who is himself Jewish, illustrates the point. Jones refers to former right-wing Labour MP Michael Dugher and Jewish actress Maureen Lipman, both of whom identified Miliband's decision to *"back a motion on Palestinian statehood"* in 2014 as the cause of the collapse in Jewish support.[49] Before the 2015 general election, the neoconservative *Spectator* magazine ran a headline saying, *"How Ed Miliband lost the Jewish vote"*.[50] Even under a Jewish leader, therefore, the party felt the ire of a section of Britain's Jewish community. It is not an insignificant detail that a majority of British Jews support Israel, to such an extent that merely recognising a Palestinian state, even without supporting BDS or going further, could invoke such a backlash. This is neither a Judeophobic nor a far-fetched observation.

The State of Israel's centrality to Labour's 'antisemitism crisis' was abundantly clear. Interventions against Corbyn were made by the State of Israel's UK Embassy under Mark Regev,[51] the Israeli Ministry of Strategic Affairs,[52] and even Benjamin Netanyahu.[53] Yet Jones, and others, repeatedly dismissed this reality as a 'crank' conspiracy theory. His apparent reluctance to acknowledge this reality results in him failing to explore some important issues. Take, for example, the case of Simon Morris, who was recommended as an adviser to the leader's office by Lord Michael Levy, a businessman who had been approached by Jeremy Corbyn's chief-of-staff, Karie Murphy. One of Morris's initial suggestions to Corbyn to help diffuse the 'crisis' was to *"visit Israel"* as a *"tangible sign ... recognising the state of Israel's right to exist"*.[54] Whilst Jones seems to acknowledge the fact that denying such a request was reasonable, he fails to probe it further.

As if that weren't enough evidence, the same suggestion was repeated in 2018, when Corbyn met the Board of Deputies of British Jews. Jones writes that, *"One [Deputy] asked Corbyn why he could never say anything positive about Israel – perhaps, praising its hospitals for treating Arabs and Jews alike"*.[55] Why was visiting the State of Israel, and praise for the racist state, being tied to the issue of combatting Judeophobia?

The IHRA calamity

Jones's description of the furore that erupted in response to the adoption of the IHRA Working Definition's 'illustrative' examples is one of the worst aspects of his analysis. He characterises the resistance to their adoption, in the face of widespread opposition from pro-Palestine advocates (including many Palestinians themselves), as *"choosing to die on the wrong hill"*.[56] Jones highlights some of the arguments that were made against adopting two of the IHRA's examples, but he essentially concludes that, as principled as it was for Corbyn to take a stand, it wasn't worth doing because it was already a *fait accompli*. In the words of one craven former Corbyn adviser, Andrew Fisher, attempting to refine the examples to accommodate a Palestinian perspective was *"just a fucking idiotic thing to do"*.[57] In quoting Fisher, Jones ultimately seems to agree that the silencing of pro-Palestinian voices was acceptable.

Recent history has shown that resisting the adoption of the IHRA Working Definition, alongside its 'illustrative' examples, was an important fight. Despite the repeated capitulations and betrayal of Palestinians, the war against the anti-Zionist left didn't stop after Corbyn's departure as Labour leader in April 2020. And there's no end in sight. That's precisely because Zionism is a maximalist ideology, which takes an all-guns-blazing approach to its opponents. Zionists pay no mind to concessions and apologies. On the contrary, surrendering has the effect of emboldening them to go further. This strategy succeeded in forcing the Corbyn leadership to capitulate on every major Palestine-related issue, aided and abetted by Owen Jones and the optics left. It also convinced vast swathes of the country that Corbyn was an 'antisemite'. It plagued, and ultimately helped to bury, Corbyn's leadership.

The truth is, under Corbyn, there was no emergence of a so-called 'left-wing antisemitism', and there was no special anti-Jewish problem affecting the Labour Party. What Jones and the optics left failed to come to terms with is the fact that Labour's 'antisemitism crisis' was cooked up by anti-Palestinian fanatics. They were determined to do whatever was necessary to destroy the prospects of an anti-imperialist government coming to power. If we are to prevent the socialist left from being defamed and stigmatised for a generation, we must push back against the false narratives that the likes of Owen Jones perpetuate.

CHAPTER TWENTY-FIVE

"IF YOU DON'T FIGHT, YOU WILL ALWAYS LOSE"

After I won my High Court case against the Labour Party in October 2019, and I recovered my legal costs, I ploughed all that money into establishing the Left Legal Fighting Fund. The Fighting Fund is an embracement of a counter-lawfare strategy. The idea is to build up a permanent organisation that can defend socialist and anti-imperialist activists who are under attack, as well as to level the playing field with our opponents. Serious efforts are ongoing to lock the left out of public life forever. The election of Jeremy Corbyn as Labour leader in 2015, and the party's huge advance under his leadership at the 2017 general election, sent a shudder down the Establishment's spine. That's why, even though Corbyn has been toppled, they are continuing to go to extreme lengths to bury us. Lawfare – the misuse of legal and quasi-legal procedures to attack political opponents – is one of an array of tactics that they're using.

Since I established the Fighting Fund, it has been used to successfully challenge the Labour Party, take on the EHRC, and defeat efforts to destroy people's livelihoods. It has also been used to arrange pro bono legal representation for Black Lives Matter activists who were harassed and targeted by the police in the summer of 2020, following the police murder of George Floyd in the United States. The successes of the Fighting Fund in these 'David and Goliath' battles should demonstrate that the road to success of the British left will be paved with determined struggles. As the late general secretary of the RMT union, Bob Crow, once said, *"If you fight, you won't always win, but if you don't fight, you will always lose"*. Unfortunately, many comrades in the British socialist movement have failed to grasp the threats that we face, and they continue to pin their hopes on the fantasy that they'll be gifted victory. Their feckless attitude reminds me of a point once made by another socialist and anti-imperialist hero, Thomas Sankara, that *"[the] slave alone will be responsible for his own misfortune if he harbours illusions in the dubious generosity of a master*.[1] We on the left must be prepared to become the masters of our own destiny.

Weaponising the EHRC

On 28 May 2019, the EHRC launched an investigation into the Labour Party following belligerent lobbying efforts by two anti-Corbyn and pro-Israel outfits, the Jewish Labour Movement and the Campaign Against Antisemitism. To many of us, the motivations were clear: this was an attempt by Zionists and other racists to weaponise Judeophobia in order to criminalise anti-Zionists. It also served another purpose, which was to help derail the Labour Party's pro-Palestinian leadership. I believe that this charade was intended to serve as a battering ram against Corbyn during a potential early election. The report, however, was long-delayed, and it failed to materialise before the general election in December 2019. The very fact that the investigation was even taking place served as a talking point for the anti-Palestinian racists who were smearing those involved in the Corbyn movement. The launch of the EHRC investigation is a classic example of lawfare tactics.

The EHRC had long been a discredited organisation, well before it was appropriated by Zionist lobby groups. When it was conceived under New Labour, it was supposed to be the chief enforcer of equality and non-discrimination laws in Great Britain. But it started as it meant to go on. Its first chair, Trevor Phillips, had headed up the Commission for Racial Equality (a predecessor of the EHRC). Phillips had criticised multiculturalism for supposedly *"sleepwalking"* Britain into segregation with *"fully fledged ghettos"*.[2] He was also close to a number of senior figures in the New Labour government, including Peter Mandelson, who was the best man at his wedding. After he came under ever-increasing pressure due to his tempestuous management style, which prompted questions about his suitability to remain in post at the Commission, Mandelson and Harriet Harman reportedly suggested giving him a seat in the House of Lords and a ministerial position.[3] Additionally, in 2017, the EHRC was accused of targeting black, Muslim, and disabled staff for compulsory redundancies.[4] Two former Commissioners said they had lost their positions at the Commission in 2012 because they were considered *"too loud and vocal"* about issues of race.[5] They were the only black and Muslim commissioners at the time, too.

The warning signs about the EHRC's partisan approach in respect of Judeophobia were apparent in September 2017, when the EHRC's chief executive Rebecca Hilsenrath issued a highly irregular statement saying, *"Anti-Semitism is racism and the Labour Party needs to do more to establish that it's not a racist party"*.[6] She singled out the Labour Party because of comments by members at a fringe meeting during the 2017 Labour Party conference. It was reported that some delegates had called for the Zionist JLM to be expelled from the party and had compared the Israeli regime to the Nazis because of their oppression of the Palestinian people. Neither of those statements is remotely anti-Semitic, and it was wholly inappropriate for Hilsenrath to make such an intervention. If anything, as the CEO of the equalities watchdog, she should have been taking Zionists to task, because Zionism is a demonstrably racist ideology. Meanwhile, despite calls by the Muslim Council of Britain for the EHRC to investigate widely reported allegations of Islamophobic and racist behaviour by Tory members, including Boris Johnson, Hilsenrath remained remarkably mute.

On 26 March 2020, I received a letter from the EHRC stating that a complaint about me was going to form part of their investigation into the Labour Party's handling of the fake 'anti-semitism crisis'. Only months later, in June 2020, they sent me a confidential copy of their draft report, in which they had named me and made a preliminary finding that I had *"contributed"* to the Labour Party's unlawful *"harassment"* based on Jewish race and religion. The dearth of evidence that they used to justify their preliminary finding against me clearly indicated that this was a crude attempt to achieve a premeditated outcome. It seemed clear that they knew what they wanted to say about me and had then cobbled together some 'evidence' to justify it. They had made this preliminary finding, even though I had sent their investigation team detailed submissions in my defence. When I received the draft report, I began a public crowdfunder so that my solicitors could go on the offensive. Within the space of 12 hours, I had already raised over £9,000, thanks to the incredible warmth and generosity of my supporters. Not long afterwards, that figure climbed even higher. My solicitors found serious legal flaws in the EHRC's draft report, which I cannot detail here due to a confidentiality directive. Suffice it to say, however, in my detailed submissions, I insisted that the EHRC must remove its unsustainable and baseless finding against me from its final report. I also warned them that, unless they did so, I would seek an injunction to prevent the report's publication.

Ultimately, the EHRC totally backed down. They removed their finding against me, and they also removed several other entire pages from the report. It demonstrated that, rather than cowering and pleading for mercy, the only logical posture to adopt was to get on the front foot. Notwithstanding this victory, I found it astonishing that I had even been placed in a position where I had to defend myself against a politically motivated quango that wanted to drag my reputation through the gutter. And they wanted to do it at the behest of the Israel lobby, no less. I issued a forthright statement on the day that the report was published, highlighting a number of these issues.[7]

In the end, the best that the EHRC could muster was to accuse two individuals of 'contributing' to the Labour Party's supposed harassment of Jews: former London Mayor Ken Livingstone and former borough councillor Pam Bromley. This was the sum total of a more than year-long investigation. Instead of challenging this threadbare, legally flawed report, Sir Keir Starmer's Labour Party accepted it in full. It suited their objective of further undermining Corbyn and the left. Since then, at the time of writing, the Left Legal Fighting Fund has been assisting Ken Livingstone and Pam Bromley with a judicial review against the EHRC. For Ken Livingstone to effectively be labelled by the party and the EHRC as a racist is a wicked and entirely unjustified opprobrium. Livingstone did more to advance the cause of anti-racism than any other senior politician in post-war history, particularly during his time as leader of the GLC and Mayor of London.

Pinning down Sir Keir Starmer

The publication of the EHRC report on 29 October 2020 was used as a pretext by Sir Keir Starmer to suspend Jeremy Corbyn.

Even though Corbyn had inspired millions and recruited hundreds of thousands of people to the Labour Party (wiping out its huge financial deficit in the process), he still suffered the same suspension indignity as I'd done under his leadership. After all was said and done, Corbyn's efforts to appease his persecutors counted for nothing. Even after an NEC panel reinstated him in November 2020, Sir Keir refused to restore the Labour whip, leaving him in a kind of twilight zone, as a Labour member but an independent MP. Were the knighted leader's actions guided by Niccolò Machiavelli's, *The Prince*?

> *"it should be noted that men must be either caressed or wiped out; because they will avenge minor injuries, but cannot do so for grave ones. Any harm done to a man must be of the kind that removes any fear of revenge."*[8]

That quote encapsulates the modus operandi of the right-wing New Labour remnants who now have complete control of the Labour Party. They are committed to the total and utter annihilation of any traces of the Corbyn project. I can only imagine what Keir Hardie would have made of his namesake, Sir Keir Starmer, replacing Corbyn as leader. I very much doubt that he would have approved of a knight of the realm leading the party that he founded to advance the cause of the working class. Unlike Sir Keir's servile monarchism, Keir Hardie was an outspoken republican who used his platform to attack the incongruous institution of the monarchy. The comparison between the two Keirs illustrates just how far the Labour Party has strayed from its original tenets.

The twenty-first century Keir was apparently knighted in recognition of his services to law and criminal justice, but there are serious questions that remain unanswered about his time as Director of Public Prosecutions (DPP), the head of the Crown Prosecution Service (CPS) in England and Wales. When he was elected Labour leader, investigative journalist Matt Kennard wrote an open letter to Sir Keir, posing five penetrating questions:

> *"1. Why did you meet the head of MI5, the domestic security service, for informal social drinks in April 2013, the year after you decided not to prosecute MI5 for its role in torture?*

"2. When and why did you join the Trilateral Commission and what does your membership of this intelligence-linked network entail?

"3. What did you discuss with then US Attorney General Eric Holder when you met him on 9 November 2011 in Washington DC, at a time you were handling the Julian Assange case as the public prosecutor?

"4. What role did you play in the Crown Prosecution Service's irregular handling of the Julian Assange case during your period as DPP?

"5. Why did you develop such a close relationship with the Times newspaper while you were the DPP and does this relationship still exist?"[9]

During Sir Keir's time as DPP, he repeatedly refused to prosecute intelligence personnel following allegations of complicity in torture. In a private session of the Intelligence and Security Committee (ISC), MI5 confessed that one of its officers interrogated Binyam Mohamed whilst he was detained in Karachi. Mohamed was held and tortured there for three months. But 'witness B' implausibly claimed that he did not observe any abuse and that no instances of abuse were mentioned by Binyam Mohamed. Furthermore, the ISC concluded that there was a reasonable probability that intelligence passed by MI5 to the US was used in the subsequent interrogation where he was tortured. Yet, in 2010, Sir Keir said that the CPS had advised the Metropolitan Police that there was insufficient evidence to prosecute witness B *"for any criminal offence arising from the interview of Binyam Mohamed in Pakistan on 17 May 2002"*.[10] In 2012, Sir Keir issued another statement in which he said that MI5 and MI6 agents would not face charges over the ill-treatment and torture of Binyam Mohamed, as well as another detainee in Afghanistan.

Sir Keir was also DPP when attempts were being made to extradite Julian Assange to Sweden to face allegations that had been made against him when he had sought asylum in the Ecuadorian Embassy. The CPS has admitted to destroying key emails relating to the Assange case[11] when Sir Keir was in charge, and they advised against the Swedish authorities interviewing Assange in the Ecuadorian Embassy. They even sent an email to the Swedish prosecutors, who were considering dropping the extradition proceedings against Assange, saying, *"Don't you dare get cold feet!!!"*. Political commentator and author Oliver Eagleton was absolutely right to describe Starmer as *"a servant of the British security state"*.[12] Starmer's pre-parliamentary record proves it, as do his actions since becoming an MP and, latterly, Labour leader.

Moreover, when Sir Keir completed the 2013/14 CPS Board Gifts and Hospitality Register, he left the financial value of the hospitality he received from Sir Jonathan Evans, then director-general of MI5, as *"Unknown"*. And he left the column blank where reasons for accepting gifts and/or hospitality are supposed to be provided. Interestingly, it was revealed by Eagleton that, the same week Sir Keir met with Evans, *"the CPS rejected crucial [Freedom of Information] requests relating to the [Assange] case"*.[13]

Additionally, Sir Keir is the only current MP to be a member of the Trilateral Commission, an organisation that describes itself as a *"discussion group"*[14] to *"foster closer cooperation"* between *"Western Europe, Japan, and North America"*.[15] It was established in 1973 by a bunch of liberal elites, headed by US billionaire and oligarch David Rockefeller. They were worried about what they described as an *"excess of democracy"*, the cure for which was *"a greater degree of moderation in democracy"*.[16] They said:

> *"the democratic surge of the 1960s was a general challenge to existing systems of authority public and private ... People no longer felt the same compulsion to obey those whom they had previously considered superior to themselves in age rank status expertise character or talents".*[17]

In much the same way, the Corbyn project represented an unacceptable renaissance of the 1960s *"democratic surge"* to petty despots like Sir Keir. Little wonder he wanted to sabotage it. Meanwhile, he continues to rub shoulders with the likes of Henry Kissinger in the Trilateral Commission, that mysterious international body whose meetings are strictly off-the-record and whose membership roll used to include notorious paedophile Jeffrey Epstein.[18]

I could fill pages upon pages with the grisly details of Starmer's record at the CPS. However, it suffices to quote a conclusion made by Oliver Eagleton, author of *The Starmer Project*, a book that presents a fascinating – if not infuriating – account of this history. Eagleton says, *"despite [Starmer's] overtures to the Labour Left in early 2020, Sir Keir's record shows his evolution into an unabashed authoritarian"*.[19] Going further, Eagleton explains that the Starmer project is *"purely restorationist: to unravel Corbyn's legacy and reestablish the Right's monopoly on power"*.[20] He defines the four tenets of Starmerism as follows:

> *"1 a 'values-led', non-antagonistic electoral strategy; 2 an unsparing crackdown on the Labour Left, seen as more dangerous than the Conservatives; 3 an Atlanticist– authoritarian disposition, combining intervention abroad with repression at home; and 4 a return to neoliberal economic precepts, overseen by Blairite leftovers."*[21]

In light of these revelations, and with such clear articulations of what Starmerism means, it should be abundantly clear that Sir Keir – and the acolytes of the regime that will eventually succeed him – are political enemies of the left. There is nothing good that can be salvaged from the Labour Party. It must be opposed.

The post-Corbyn fightback

Despite the best efforts of Labour's right-wing imposters to crush those who supported Corbyn, the embers are still smouldering. Activists, most of whom have left or been expelled from Labour, are fighting back through various initiatives like Resist, the Trade Unionist and Socialist Coalition, the Socialist Labour Network, and the Left Legal Fighting Fund. However, within Labour itself, the New Labour cuckoos who colonised the party under Tony Blair have now well and truly subjugated it. They immediately took over the general-secretaryship and the NEC, and they instituted a raft of rule changes at the 2021 party conference. Without any levers to evict these charlatans, the prospects of a socialist, anti-imperialist programme ever being formally embraced by the party in opposition, let alone in government, are now close to zero.

Another kick in the teeth is that the post-Corbyn Labour regime is making use of the anti-democratic and Orwellian procedures created under Corbyn's leadership. In August 2021, Jennie Formby posted an extraordinary statement on Twitter. It was in response to a wave of expulsions following Labour's proscription of four left-wing groups in July 2021, and the subsequent purge of Labour Party members who were previously associated with them. She said, *"I cannot see how expelling members for being 'guilty by association' in any way makes Labour more electable"*.[22] However, guilt-by-association is precisely why she suspended me and so many others under her regime. In fact, many of the McCarthyite rules that Labour's new bureaucracy has used to attack grassroots members were first enacted under Formby. In late November 2020, after a wave of motions were moved at local Labour meetings against Corbyn's suspension, Labour's general secretary David Evans said that such motions should be *"ruled out of order"*.[23] But it was Formby who introduced this rule in March 2019, after numerous CLPs were passing motions in support of me following my suspension. She issued a diktat, saying that local members couldn't discuss *"individual disciplinary cases"*.[24] Maybe Formby had learnt that her readiness to throw people under the bus was both non-strategic and morally wrong. If not, Formby's apparent volte-face can only be explained as sheer hypocrisy.

The impostors behind the witch-hunt, who incessantly squealed about Jeremy Corbyn and his political prospectus being an electoral liability, masterminded historic lows for the party. The Chesham and Amersham by-election on 17 June 2021, for example, saw Labour utterly crushed, obtaining just 622 votes. That amounted to 1.6 per cent of the total votes cast. The two elections that took place in that constituency under Corbyn's leadership saw 11,374 voting Labour in 2017 and 7,166 in 2019. The same quack soothsayers oversaw lost ground in Hartlepool, a seat that had always been Labour. In the by-election on 7 May 2021, the party was trounced. Completing a hat-trick of humiliations, the Batley and Spen by-election on 1 July 2021 saw Labour just scraping over the line, with a pitiful majority of 323. In other words, Labour's vote-share collapsed from 55.5 per cent in 2017 to just 35.3 per cent in the 2021 by-election. That didn't stop Sir Keir hailing the result as *"a fantastic victory"* and declaring *"Labour is back!"*. But if the Batley and Spen result were to be repeated across Britain in a general election, the Conservatives would *increase* their parliamentary majority by around 100.[25] It was a similar picture in the Erdington by-election on 3 March 2022, where Labour held on to the seat, but with its lowest vote since 1923.

In their desperation to hold Batley and Spen, Labour resorted to numerous dirty tricks. Fearful of the impact being made by the insurgent contender, George Galloway, who was standing for the Workers Party, the Labour council removed all his posters from lampposts in the constituency a few days before the polls opened. Furthermore, Labour activists were captured on video damaging Workers Party public address equipment, whilst Labour councillors were filmed tearing down Workers Party posters on private property. Royal Mail also impeded the Workers Party campaign. They initially agreed to deliver a Workers Party election communication in the early part of the campaign, but they then refused to take delivery of the leaflet from the printers at their sorting office. In the end, an alternative distributor had to be found. But the worst aspect of Labour's campaign was its gross and unjustifiable deployment of Islamophobia. The party insinuated that the reason so many Muslims in the constituency had turned away from Labour was because they were 'antisemitic' and 'homophobic'.[26] A party official reportedly said:

> *"We're haemorrhaging votes among Muslim voters, and the reason for that is what [party leader Keir Starmer] has been doing on antisemitism. Nobody really wants to talk about it, but that's the main factor. He challenged Corbyn on it, and there's been a backlash among certain sections of the community."*[27]

In a cynical and haphazard attempt to regain the favour of Muslim voters, Sir Keir raised the issue of Palestinian statehood in a single question at PMQs on 9 June 2021. Labour activists also distributed a leaflet to Muslim voters showing Boris Johnson with India's Hindu-supremacist and Islamophobic Prime Minister, Narendra Modi, with the strapline, *"Don't risk a Tory MP who is not on your side"*.[28] It was typical British imperial divide-and-rule stratagem.

I campaigned for the Workers Party in the by-election, and I was struck by just how popular Galloway was with the Muslim communities who lived there. When I was outside recording a video about the campaign, some young Muslim kids were curious about what I was doing. One of them came over to me to ask, *"Are you George Galloway?"*. When I said I wasn't, but that I was supporting him, they were delighted, and they asked if they could watch. A group of Muslim teenagers then gathered around, but they seemed hostile, perhaps thinking that I was a journalist recording some propaganda on their patch. When I explained that I was there to back Galloway, they immediately showed their warmth and gave me a loud cheer. Their support was unsurprising, given Galloway's long history of opposing Western aggression against Muslim-majority countries. On another occasion, when I was canvassing on a council estate in the constituency, people from at least half a dozen households said that they liked Galloway after seeing him on Celebrity Big Brother in 2006. That reaction from working class voters illustrated just how out-of-touch the metropolitan elites really were. They had routinely used Galloway's Celebrity Big Brother appearance to undermine his credibility, but they never mentioned that he used it to raise tens of thousands of pounds for medical aid in Gaza, and they ignored all the people that had watched, and liked, the show.

Labour used every underhanded tactic imaginable to stop Galloway from re-gaining a parliamentary platform, and they succeeded. Nevertheless, the Workers Party achieved a substantial 22 per cent of the votes cast. The atmosphere in the Workers Party camp reminded me of my successful 2017 election campaign. Everybody was energetic and determined to make a beneficial impact. They took time to speak at length with voters and they managed to knock on every door in the constituency. Most importantly, they demonstrated that the false Labour 'god' could bleed. If a performance like the one in Batley and Spen could be repeated in marginal seats across the land, it would drive a stake through the heart of the vampirical Labour machine. In that regard, the example of the London borough of Tower Hamlets should serve as an inspiration. Prior to the May 2022 local elections, Labour held the borough's mayoralty and 40 out of a total of 45 seats on the local council. However, a new left-wing party called 'Aspire'

– led by Lutfur Rahman – took them both out of Labour's hands. Rahman beat Labour's John Biggs for the mayoralty and Aspire won a majority on the council. Rahman had previously been the borough's independent Mayor, but he was ousted in 2015 by an election court judge on spurious and, I believe, racially-motivated claims of 'electoral fraud'. Tower Hamlets has the highest proportion of Muslims of any English local authority, and a large ethnic minority population. It has frequently been targeted by the far-right, facilitated by the Labour Party. After Batley and Spen, Tower Hamlets proved that not only can Muslim communities, who've been abused by Labour, fight back but they can also win.

Whilst the Workers Party was mounting an electoral challenge to the amoral Labour crusaders, the Left Legal Fighting Fund and Labour Activists for Justice joined together to open another front in the High Court on 17 June 2021. The case of *Neslen and others v Evans*[29] involved eight Labour activists – the High Court 8 – who'd been left languishing in limbo (in some cases, for several years) after being unfairly targeted for disciplinary action on account of their pro-Palestine activism. The High Court 8 argued that Labour, through its dodgy procedures, had broken its contract with them under the party's Rule Book. They wanted to achieve three Declarations from the court, ensuring that Labour would:

> *"(1) adhere to the principles of natural justice and procedural fairness, (2) respond to the findings of unfairness contained in [the 2020] EHRC Report on 'Labour antisemitism', and (3) refrain from giving the impression that party members are under more stringent confidentiality requirements than they really are."*[30]

In spite of numerous gross calumnies, the EHRC had made some half-decent recommendations in its 2020 report in favour of *respondents* (the people who have to answer complaints made against them). The High Court 8, rather creatively, used the EHRC report against the party, which had, until then, been using it as a blunt instrument against the left. Despite Sir Keir promising on live television that he would implement those recommendations,[31] the party argued in court that it hadn't, contrary to what it had said, promised to create an independent complaints system. Instead, it merely needed to introduce an air of independence into the current one. Moreover, the party had used a secret Antisemitism Code of Conduct, judging the High Court 8 against standards they'd never seen. Disappointingly, Mr Justice Butcher refused to grant those Declarations and awarded Labour its costs.

The outcome of that case reiterated the difficulties faced by grassroots members in challenging the party's bureaucracy. The party has large resources, whereas most ordinary members have access to only limited funds. The legal action, however, did at least bounce the party into publishing its previously secret Antisemitism Code of Conduct. The party also confessed in open court that the reason they had not previously published the code was because it would have been *"politically incendiary"*. The legal action also forced the party to capitulate on five cases. The High Court 8 was originally supposed to be the High Court 13, but Labour re-admitted the other five before the hearing took place. Ultimately, the case underscored that Labour is a law unto itself. Butcher's ruling has given Labour's hierarchy carte blanche to abuse grassroots members with complete impunity.

Diana Neslen, one of the three Jewish claimants among the High Court 8, said that it was *"a pyrrhic victory because it shows the Labour Party has learned nothing on how to treat its members"*. I agree. But the cold hard truth is that Labour is beyond reform and its bureaucrats have no desire to treat grassroots members better.

The case of the High Court 8 highlighted that the first element of Bob Crow's maxim must also be borne in mind, *"If you fight, you won't always win"*. That doesn't make the fight unimportant. It just means that you must pick yourself up again and fight some more. That is the spirit we must embrace in confronting the Labour menace. Whilst big court cases are probably an unlikely avenue to challenge Labour in the near future, there are other ways to make Labour bureaucrats sweat. It's becoming apparent that Labour, under its ruinous right-wing stewardship, is facing financial difficulties.[32] Alongside an exodus of members (and their membership subscriptions), trade unions are withdrawing funding or disaffiliating altogether. As a result, Labour has had to massively cut down its staff numbers.[33] We must work to deepen Labour's contradictions through a multi-pronged strategy. That way, we'll be able to clear the road for other vehicles – parliamentary and extra-parliamentary – to take Labour's place.

CHAPTER TWENTY-SIX

MAKING THE REVOLUTION

I understand why, despite the constant kicks in the teeth, many people continue to cling to the Labour Party. After all, I devoted 44 years of my life to it. I know all about the so-called 'Labour family'. I understand the emotional attachment. But Labour is not a family. It is a political party that is only as good as the political programme that it offers, and, failing that, it is only as good as it can be made to become. Labour, however, cannot be reformed.

In truth, the writing was on the wall during the Corbyn years. Despite the intransigence and sense of entitlement of the PLP and the right-wing party Establishment, I had continued to hold on to my Labourist illusions. But, for all the supposed left-wing strength under Corbyn, it wasn't enough to transform the party. After assuming the leadership, Sir Keir Starmer quickly reverted the party to type, irrevocably delivering it into the hands of the neoliberal war machine, irrespective of whomever may succeed him. The prospect of a Labour government no longer strikes fear into the hearts of wealthy corporate elites, arms dealers, neocons, NATO leaders, and brutal regimes around the world. They know that a Labour government would mean business as usual.

A colonial and imperialist endeavour

The Labour Party is a victim of state capture. Much of its international policy is now effectively dictated by the State of Israel. Sir Keir won the Labour leadership in 2020 with the backing of the Zionist state's supporters and lobbyists.

During the 2019-20 leadership campaign, Sir Keir was repeatedly asked to disclose the names of his big donors, but he refused to do so.[1] It remained a mystery how he was the only candidate able to afford to send a direct mailing to all Labour members with an A3 poster bearing an image of his face, something which must have cost an inordinate amount of money. It was later revealed that he received a huge £50,000 donation from Sir Trevor Chinn, an executive committee member of the pro-Israel lobby group BICOM.[2] Sir Keir also prostrated himself, like the other two leadership candidates, before supporters of settler-colonialism. In a leadership hustings with the Zionist JLM, he said, *"I understand and I sympathise and I support Zionism"*.[3] He also signed a list of 10 pledges from the Board of Deputies of British Jews. Those included a McCarthyistic vow to expel people who profess support for Labour members who are under disciplinary action, and a promise to only *"engage with the Jewish community via its main representative groups"* (meaning Zionist groups).[4] In other words, Sir Keir demonstrated, even before being elected Labour leader, that he would be a safe pair of hands to enact the State of Israel's interests.

Labour's unqualified support for Zionism means that it will never again lift a finger to support Palestine. But it is even worse than that. In January 2021, it was revealed that the party had welcomed into its bureaucracy a 'former' Israeli spy, Assaf Kaplan, to work as Labour's 'Social Listening and Organising Manager'. By his own admission, we know that Kaplan worked for Unit 8200 for nearly five years. That unit conducts cyberwarfare operations and uses blackmail tactics against Palestinians.[5] It wouldn't be unreasonable to suggest that Kaplan's role in the party may extend beyond his official job description. Precisely what Kaplan might be doing for the Labour Party, we do not know.

In November 2021, Sir Keir addressed Labour Friends of Israel's annual lunch, where he explicitly condemned anti-Zionism, saying, *"Anti-Zionist antisemitism is the antithesis of the Labour tradition: It denies the Jewish people alone a right to self-determination"*.[6] At that same meeting, he attacked the BDS movement and endorsed the Zionist *terra nullius* myth, that Zionist colonists had *"made the desert flower"*.[7] The Decolonize Palestine project has this to say about that racist Israeli propaganda:

> *"According to this myth, Palestine was a neglected bleak desert, and that only after the arrival of the Zionist colonists with their ingenuity was it "redeemed" and made prosperous and blooming with life. This ... plays on Orientalist tropes about the east, framing it as a desolate, backwards and uncared for land. Land that under the right circumstances, and cultivated by the "right" civilized people, could bloom into a green paradise. ... [T]his ...*

amounts to nothing more than Greenwashing settler colonialism. It simply exists to try and show why the Zionist settlers are more deserving of the land than Palestinians, who had supposedly neglected it."[8]

The new paradigm that Sir Keir imposed on the party was on display again in January 2022, when he *"warmly"* welcomed Tory defector Christian Wakeford into the Labour fold, to loud cheers from the PLP.[9] Wakeford had been an officer of Conservative Friends of Israel (CFI) and, in February 2020, he declared a donation for a CFI-funded trip to the Zionist state, valued at £2,300.[10] At the time of his defection, he remained vice chair of the Britain-Israel All-Party Parliamentary Group.[11] All this, which is only the tip of the iceberg, shows that Labour's trajectory is to become ever-more anti-Palestinian. In early April 2022, Starmer – glorified by his supporters for being a former 'human rights lawyer' – told Jake Wallis Simons of the *Jewish Chronicle* that he didn't believe that Israel is an apartheid state.[12] The finding of apartheid was made by numerous liberal human rights groups in 2021, such as Human Rights Watch, B'Tselem, and Amnesty International. In the same article, Wallis Simons revealingly stated, *"The heart of Labour's difficulties with Jews lies in its feelings towards Israel"*.[13] It is clear that Labour now serves as an extension of the State of Israel's propaganda and lobbying operations in Britain.

Sir Keir also gave Labour's unconditional backing to NATO, which is a bellicose, expansionist, militarist alliance that should have been disbanded following the collapse of the Soviet Union in 1991. As part of his masturbatory, warmongering delirium, Sir Keir said that he believed Britain's entering into NATO was on a par with the creation of the NHS.[14] He went to extreme lengths to defend the group. When 11 members of the SCG signed a Stop the War Coalition statement on 18 February 2022 that was mildly critical of NATO in relation to its escalation of the Ukraine crisis,[15] Sir Keir ordered them to remove their names. In another spineless retreat, the 11 cowards failed to stand by the principles that they claimed to uphold, and they tamely withdrew their signatures. A party spokesperson said, *"With Keir Starmer's leadership there will never be any confusion about whose side Labour is on – Britain,*

NATO, freedom and democracy – and every Labour MP now understands that."[16]

The MPs who backed down were Diane Abbott, Tahir Ali, Apsana Begum, Richard Burgon, Ian Lavery, John McDonnell, Ian Mearns, Bell Ribeiro-Addy, Zarah Sultana, Mick Whitley, and Beth Winter. Sir Keir's cynical use of the Ukraine crisis as a political weapon to hammer left-wing members was unprecedented in Labour's history. Never before, not even under Tony Blair, had Labour MPs been so publicly humiliated for promoting peace. In April 2022, Sir Keir rubbed salt in the wound by suggesting that Corbyn wouldn't regain the whip unless he distanced himself from Stop the War, affirming Labour's *"unshakable support for NATO"*.[17]

Endless expulsions

Meanwhile, in addition to the suspensions and expulsions of longstanding socialists with a lifetime of standing up to racism and opposing imperialism, Labour's right-wing officialdom added the proscription of entire groups to their armoury. In July 2021, the party's NEC rubber-stamped a proposal to proscribe four left-wing caucuses.[18] Labour Against the Witch-hunt, Labour in Exile Network, Resist (which I helped to establish), and Socialist Appeal were all banned by the party. Anyone found to be associated with any of those bodies was expelled. With apparently no sense of irony, a Labour spokesperson said:

> *"Labour is a broad, welcoming and democratic party and we are committed to ensuring it stays that way. The NEC has decided that these organisations are not compatible with Labour's rules or our aims and values."*[19]

The comment was a great example of Orwellian *newspeak* and *doublethink*, which is typical of the party's pronouncements. The NEC also agreed to root out other factions deemed incompatible with Labour's aims and values.[20] In March 2022, the NEC banned a further three groups, including Labour Left Alliance and the Socialist Labour Network.[21] A new NEC panel was established to oversee such McCarthyite processes. It is guided by even fewer principles of natural justice than were applied by the notorious House Committee on Un-American Activities in the 1950s to denounce left-wing US citizens. In fact, the 2022 edition of Labour's Rule Book saw the addition of a clause that brazenly states, *"Neither the principles of natural justice nor the provisions of fairness ... shall apply to the termination of party membership"*.[22]

After nearly losing control of the Labour Party when Jeremy Corbyn was elected leader, the appetite of the party's upper echelons for suspensions, expulsions, and proscriptions became insatiable. Ken Loach – the nation's foremost socialist filmmaker whose classics include *Cathy Come Home*, *Kes* and *I, Daniel Blake* – was expelled in August 2021. Announcing his expulsion, he said:

> *"Labour HQ finally decided I'm not fit to be a member of their party, as I will not disown those already expelled ... I am proud to stand with the good friends and comrades victimised by the purge ... Starmer and his clique will never lead a party of the people. We are many, they are few".*[23]

It took Sir Keir less than two years to drive the party to the verge of bankruptcy as a consequence of a mass exodus of party members and the withdrawal of trade union funding.[24] But Shadow Chancellor Rachel Reeves was elated. She told the *Financial Times* that, *"Membership in my constituency is falling and that's a good thing. [They] should never have joined the Labour Party. They never shared our values"*.[25] Reeves also blamed the party's parlous financial position on Corbyn, even though it was his leadership that had eliminated the party's debts. According to the party's 2020 annual report, when Corbyn stepped down as leader, Labour had more than £27 million in its bank accounts, including £13.5 million in reserves.[26]

Forever war against Corbynism

One could be forgiven for wondering why the New Labour revivalists are seeking to smash the Labour Left, even after consolidating total control over the party. But that is to misunderstand the nature of the challenge confronting the left in Britain today. We face an all-out assault by reactionary forces. They believe that, in order to ensure that nothing like the Corbyn project can ever arise again, mere victory isn't enough. That's why they are hell-bent on atomising us, devouring us until we no longer exist. They aren't simply content on seeing Corbyn thrown out of the PLP; they want him out of Parliament. They don't just want leftists expelled from the Labour Party; they want them ostracised from public debate. They don't just want to secure their power now; they want to secure it forever, no matter who is leader of the party. This has been aptly dubbed a *"forever war"* against the left.[27]

Unfortunately, too many on the Labour Left have not yet understood the nature of the threat in front of them. One wonders what more it could possibly take for them to finally open their eyes, but we must be prepared to consider the possibility that they'll never understand. That includes the 'leading lights' of the Corbyn era. Against the backdrop of Sir Keir's plans to expel hundreds upon hundreds of socialists, all that John McDonnell could say was that it was *"Standard Blairite fare"*.[28] Meanwhile, Jeremy Corbyn said that it was *"divisive"*.[29] Sir Keir must have been quaking in his jackboots! Whilst he flaunted his desire to crush the last vestiges of socialism and anti-imperialism inside the Labour Party, the Labour Left was impotent to respond. Their 'stay and fight' mantra quickly turned into 'stay and keep your head down'.

Then there are those, equally delusional, who extol Labour's Marxist antecedents. But they are whistling in the wind. They sometimes quote Lenin to rationalise their positions, but they misunderstand what the great man said. He justified membership of the Labour Party as a means to an end, and as something that should be taken up by socialists only for as long as it serves those ends. He said:

> *"we favour affiliation insofar as the Labour Party permits sufficient freedom of criticism. ... In such circumstances it would be highly erroneous for the best revolutionary elements not to do everything possible to remain in such a party. Let the ... social-traitors ... expel you. That will have an excellent effect upon the mass of the British workers."*[30]

In other words, if Labour permits free speech, and socialists can make use of that by pushing forward a revolutionary agenda and denouncing *"social-traitors"*, then by all means be a member. If, in the course of carrying out those activities, one is expelled, then that's a good thing. But the problem is that Labour, in the modern day, doesn't permit free speech or criticism, certainly not of the kind that Lenin had envisaged. Expulsions from Labour also don't contribute to revolutionary feelings among workers, because Labour is now utterly detached from its trade unionist origins.

Despite having some Marxist history, Marxists were never a major component of the Labour Party, nor was Labour ever a socialist party. Those who run Labour today are embarrassed by its previous minority Marxist elements. The fact that the Labour Party under Clement Attlee republished the *Communist Manifesto* in 1948 to celebrate its centenary means absolutely nothing to Labour's right-wing zealots. They have an ideological and, in some instances, a pecuniary,[31] interest in maintaining the neoliberal, pro-war status quo. As early as 1953, Labour's general secretary, the late Morgan Phillips, told the Socialist International Conference in Copenhagen that Labour owed more to Methodism than Marxism.[32] And in the twenty-first century, senior Labour figures seem to be more interested in the ideas of Milton Friedman and Friedrich Hayek than of Marx and Engels.

We will overcome

Since Jeremy Corbyn's departure as Labour leader in April 2020, Labour has been thoroughly exposed as an integral part of Britain's reactionary Establishment. We deserve so much more than that. It's misplaced to blindly support a party that prioritises the interests of corporate capitalism and the military-industrial-complex over working class interests at home and liberation struggles abroad. The maleficent New Labour ghost continues to haunt the party, and any strategy to rebuild from the ruins of the Corbyn project must ensure that the strategic mistakes of Corbyn's leadership are not repeated. As the academic and filmmaker Mike Wayne has convincingly argued, *"After Corbyn, the left in Labour needs to try something new, something different;*

something intellectually and politically post-Labour".[33] More of the same isn't going to cut it.

Therefore, our task must be to build an alternative to the Labour Party in order to confront the challenges posed by the climate crisis, inequality, poverty, perpetual war, and empire. All of these challenges can be overcome, but it won't be Labour that delivers salvation. The wasted energies being exerted in a hapless fight against the Labour Establishment – a fight that has already been lost – would be more productively spent elsewhere. There is much to do. The change required is more fundamental than simply creating another political party. The British left has tried that strategy countless times before, to no avail. The very basis of our representative democracy has been degraded by successive governments. To succeed, we also need to campaign for a new model of democracy, one that truly empowers the people rather than the oligarchs. To help achieve this, we need to build up a cadre of selfless and accountable representatives. The aim must be to construct a participatory system of democracy to undo the current self-serving culture that has infested Westminster. One task, therefore, is to pour resources into political education, creating avenues to build-up and support professional activists who are in touch with their communities. There is no reason, with all the resources at their disposal, why our trade unions cannot play a central role in this. But, to repeat a question that Lenin posed over 120 years ago: *"what does political education mean?"*. He continued:

> *"Is it sufficient to confine oneself to the propaganda of working class hostility to autocracy? Of course not. It is not enough to explain to the workers that they are politically oppressed ... Advantage must be taken of every concrete example of this oppression for the purpose of agitation."*[34]

In modern day Britain, we should be exposing all the ills of our current society to draw as many people into the movement as possible: inertia in response to the climate emergency; the unaffordable cost of living; police brutality; Islamophobia, anti-blackness, and other forms of racism; the mistreatment of disabled people and sexual minorities; violence against women; the mental ill-health epidemic; state corruption; hostility towards refugees and asylum seekers; the crisis in education; the destruction of the National Health Service and social care infrastructure; imperialism and war, among so many other things. These are all problems that we must raise continually, in addition to the wider economic struggle. And we should seek to highlight particular examples of the British state's cruelty and barbarity, which inspire righteous outrage and encourage people to fight for their liberation. To the extent that we have so far failed in this task *"we must"*, as Lenin quite rightly said, *"blame ourselves, our remoteness from the mass movement ... for being unable as yet to organise a wide, striking, and rapid exposure of these despicable outrages"*.[35] It's easy to blame people for being 'thick'. It's more difficult to engage in introspection, to recognise our mistakes, and to learn from the light of experience. But that's the only way that we'll get out of the dreary post-Corbyn rut in which we now find ourselves.

Currently, the British left is dogged by short-termism. We want to have a ready-made alternative available *today*. We want to be able to head down to the polls to cast a vote for our preferred party *today*. We want to see the capitalist-imperialist oligarchy in Britain toppled *today*. And so, we are distracted by a series of unfulfilled desires. But we must look to 10 years from now, if not longer. How, in that time, can we build a genuine grassroots social movement? This is not a question that I alone can answer. It is a question to which we must all devote our brain power.

To start confronting the challenges ahead of us, we must not be complacent. The victory of socialism will *not* simply be 'a matter of time'. Dr Martin Luther King Jr once highlighted *"the strangely irrational notion that there is something in the very flow of time that will inevitably cure all ills. Actually, time itself is neutral; it can be used either destructively or constructively"*.[36] We have an obligation to actively use the time we have in a constructive manner. Socialists and anti-imperialists – including those who have remained inside the Labour Party following the demise of the Corbyn project – must come together to help raise the nation's political consciousness. We would do well to learn from Ernesto 'Che' Guevara, who explained the process of achieving victory at a gathering of workers in Cuba in 1961, not long before armed US-backed mercenaries were decisively crushed during the Bay of Pigs invasion. He said, *"victory is won: by preparing the people, by strengthening their revolutionary consciousness, by establishing unity, confronting each and every attempt at aggression"*.[37]

The political duopoly in Britain has been broken before, when the Labour Party supplanted the Liberals as the main challenge to the Conservative Party a hundred years ago. More recently, Labour was annihilated as an electoral force in Scotland by the SNP. This can be replicated across the country. But it will be, I suspect, a gradual process.

What are some practical steps that we can take? We can organise in our trade unions to help democratise them and free them from their Labourist bondage. We can attend protests and engage in direct action, inspiring people to shout, fight, and resist. We can mount counter-lawfare strategies to protect our movement and go after those who seek to crush us. We can build electoral alliances in strategic areas of the country to help smash Labour's crumbling hegemony. We can also maintain a 'bread and roses' agenda, encouraging social gatherings in which we combine art, literature, and music with political bonding. In short, we can utilise every possible avenue available to us in order to make gains and to increase consciousness.

To defend our people, and to win for our movement, we must all embrace such revolutionary zeal. The problems we have as a movement are not simply strategic, they are attitudinal. We must cast off our mental shackles. As Nye Bevan once said, *"The opportunity for power is not enough if the will to seize it is absent"*.[38] There are some encouraging signs that people are starting to recognise that the timidity of the Corbyn project was its undoing. People are beginning to understand that tinkering around the edges isn't good enough. However, we still have a long way to go.

My plea to socialists everywhere is to reflect critically on our past errors, to come to terms with the bleak situation that we now face, and to find common cause with each other. To win, we must *want* to seize victory with both hands, and we must work ceaselessly to achieve it. The fightback starts now.

¡Hasta la victoria siempre!
Until victory, always!

APPENDIX

RESPONSE TO FIRST SUSPENSION ALLEGATIONS – 16 APRIL 2019

Below is my detailed response to the Labour Party's initial 38 investigation questions, which followed my suspension from the party on 27 February 2019. I submitted it on the day of the deadline, 16 April 2019.

. . .

Introduction

I set out my responses to the Investigation Questions below. I confirm I have made a Data Subject Access Request to secure copies of the *"large number of complaints"* that are referred to in your letter dated 27 February 2019. These *"complaints"* allegedly *"add up to a pattern of behaviour that may bring the [Labour] Party (the Party) into disrepute."* Without sight of these, I am precluded from fully defending the allegations against me, or assessing their validity and veracity. I have co-operated and respond as fully as possible based on the limited information that has been provided.

I have been a Labour Party member for a continuous period of 43 years. For seven of those years, I have been a Labour Member of Parliament. For three of those years, I was a Shadow Minister. I was a Labour councillor for 20 years and served twice as Leader of a Labour council. Before this and throughout my period in office, I have been a committed and loyal activist. This loyalty has extended to remaining in the Party and defending its values even when these have been let down by various leaders over the past four decades. My commitment has never been in question and my loyalty has never wavered, whether Labour has been in government or in opposition, or whether the left or right wing of the Party has been in the ascendancy.

In 2010, I contested Derby North for the Labour Party and won against the odds after a hard-fought campaign. In 2017, I secured the seat for the Labour Party again standing on a platform of supporting Jeremy Corbyn's vision to govern for the many, not the few. I was reported to be the candidate whose values most closely aligned with Corbyn's nationally and my campaign locally was perceived as a 'test case for Corbynism'. In 2014, I was recognised as the most loyal Labour MP in Parliament by the Parliamentary Internet, Communications and Technology Forum. I am proud to represent my Party and fight for its Leader, a man of honour whose leadership has already transformed our political landscape and under whose premiership the principles we stand for would be realised – taking millions out of poverty; addressing our housing and homelessness crises; saving our NHS and schools from stealth privatisation and a race to the bottom in standards; an ethical foreign policy and a transformation of the relationship between citizen and state.

WitchHunt screening – 4th March 2019

1. **Did you book a room in Parliament for 4th March 2019 to screen a film entitled 'WitchHunt'?**
Yes.

2. **Please explain your understanding of the film.**
WitchHunt is the story of the black Jewish anti-racism trainer and activist Jackie Walker, who was suspended and subsequently expelled from the Labour Party as a result of a three-year organised campaign of pressure on the Party and its complaints system. The film shows that this campaign primarily targets Jewish Labour Party members and those in the Party deemed to be most closely aligned with Jeremy Corbyn. It is a tale that highlights the personal struggle and pain caused to ordinary Labour Party members as a result of this campaign. I had already seen the film and did not intend to attend the screening.

Jewish Labour Party members and organisations involved in making the film, (including but not limited to Jewish Voice for Labour [JVL]), have been systematically harassed by those leading the organised campaign of pressure on the Party, its complaints team and its Leader.

In 2018, on the fringes of the Labour Party Conference in Liverpool, JVL was threatened that the screening it had organised of an earlier biographical film about Jackie Walker's history of anti-racism would be bombed.[1] In undercover footage published by Al Jazeera in 2017, former Israeli Embassy operative and Jewish Labour Movement National Director Ella Rose said of Jackie Walker, *"I saw Jackie Walker on Saturday and thought: You know what? I could take her – she's like 5'2" and tiny"*.[2]

In 2018, at a rally organised by the Board of Deputies of British Jews to campaign against Jeremy Corbyn's leadership of the Party, right-wing and far-right protesters associated with the Board of Deputies rally crossed over to a counter-protest where they harassed elderly Jewish women supporters of Jeremy, calling out *"kapo"* and claiming these Jewish women would be *"first into the ovens"* under a Labour government. One young Jewish man was reduced to tears after being told to *"go back to the ghetto"*.[3] At this rally, Labour MPs unwittingly stood among far-right extremists who wore symbols associated with anti-Palestinian terrorism and the violent, racist Kahanist movement (formally banned in Israel and regarded as a terrorist organisation by Israel's allies). Some of those extremists wore t-shirts bearing the image of Menachem Begin – who masterminded the terrorist bombing of Jerusalem's King David Hotel in 1946 which killed 91 people – and later served two terms as Israeli Prime Minister.

On 4 September 2018, Jewish Labour Party members gathered in large numbers to protest outside Party headquarters against the adoption of the examples contained in the International Holocaust Remembrance Alliance (IHRA) definition of anti-Semitism by the Party – led by JVL. A small counter-demonstration in support of the Labour Party adopting the IHRA examples was almost exclusively attended by known far-right activists.

On the same day as this protest, I received a stream of abuse over a megaphone from Damon Lenszner outside the Party's headquarters while attempting to give media interviews outlining the position of the majority of Party members I have spoken to across the country towards the IHRA examples. Mr Lenszner repeatedly screamed *"Labour fascist"* and described me as "at the top table, eating the scum off Corbyn's plate". The incident was recorded on camera. I note that Mr Lenszner and Jonathan Hoffman, who is former vice-chair of the Zionist Federation, were recently issued with warrants after they failed to appear at Westminster Magistrates' Court. Mr Lenszner was charged with assault by beating and Mr Hoffman with common assault and using threatening words and behaviour under Section Four of the Public Order Act.

In my view the Party has been institutionally absent in the defence of Jewish socialists while abuse against them is normalised by extremist groups.

The apparently targeted, organised campaign of malicious and vexatious complaints which disproportionately targets left-wing Jewish Party members addressed by the film is, in my experience deplored by the membership at large. This campaign has been supported by some in the Parliamentary Labour Party (PLP) in good faith because they are unaware of the links between this campaign and far-right ideology. This is, in my view, due to a major gap in the Party's political education offering on the origins and nature of the war for Palestine and how that conflict affects contemporary politics, including in the UK.

The Party must address these problems in order to protect left-wing Jewish members and fight anti-Semitism. It is patronising and insulting to assume that pro-Israel groups speak for Jewish members or British Jews in general. Left-wing Jewish members tell me they regard this monopoly on opinion as anti-Semitic because it inaccurately and unfairly equates Jewish identity with support for a political ideology they regard as racist. The relationship between the organised campaign of harassment targeting our Jewish members and the far-right is also a national security issue – both in respect of domestic extremism and foreign interference in our democracy.

To better understand the international dimensions of the far-right's role and motivations and to contextualise the national security issues at stake, I encourage NEC members to read a recent article entitled 'Why the new nationalists love Israel' by the *Financial Times* columnist Gideon Rachman on the subject of Israel's cultivation of far-right alliances across Europe. Mr Rachman is by no means a man of the Left and writes from a perspective that is supportive of Israel, and yet he observes that: *"These days, Europe's far-right is far more hostile to Muslims than Jews, and that Islamophobia often translates into support for Israel."*[4]

3. Please explain why you booked a room in Parliament to screen this film.

WitchHunt is an account of the systematic abuse, threats of violence and centralised, industrial-scale online harassment faced by Jewish supporters of Jeremy Corbyn's leadership. I was not scheduled to give a talk or to be present at the event but I believed it to be essential that the film ought to be shown in Parliament, in a secure environment for our internationalist socialist Jewish members, whereas outside Parliament they are routinely harassed by far-right street thugs and others, resulting in a bomb threat at Conference 2018 as mentioned above. I was merely a facilitator in respect of the prospective screening of the film.

An underlying argument of the film is that if those orchestrating the campaign against our members and the Party Leader cannot prevent Labour winning the next general election, they intend to ensure a Labour government cannot make any substantive changes to foreign or domestic security policy, thus neutralising the supposed 'threat' posed by Jeremy's leadership. In contrast, I perceive Jeremy's leadership to be the best prospect for millions of the most vulnerable in our society to reclaim their dignity after nine punishing years of Conservative rule.

As a Labour Party member of 43 years and a Labour MP supportive of Jeremy Corbyn's leadership, I believe it is essential that parliamentary colleagues, Party members and the public should understand the origins and nature of the campaign against the Party, and specifically against Jeremy's leadership. I see that this film is a valuable teaching resource about the ongoing campaign against Jeremy's leadership and the Party as a whole.

4. Do you have anything else you think the Party should know about this screening?

I was contacted by Jewish members of the Party to ask whether I would be able to host the screening in Parliament.

The film is an important learning resource for Labour Party members of all ranks. For more context on my decision to support the screening of this film in Parliament and so as to better acquaint themselves with the origins and nature of the campaign against allies of the Party Leader, NEC members should watch the film and can do so here: https://witchhuntfilm.org/.

Sheffield Momentum meeting – 23rd February 2019 – Item 1

5. Did you speak at a meeting of Sheffield Momentum on the 23rd February 2019?
Yes.

6. During this meeting did you say, *"The Party ... is being demonised as a racist bigoted party ... I think the Party's response has been partly responsible ... we've backed off on too much, we've given too much ground, we've been too apologetic"*? If so, please explain what you meant when you said this.

I used some of those words but they were not delivered as presented above.

The selective and highly misleading quote above is without context and appears to have been provided maliciously and vexatiously by a third party with the deliberate intention of my words being misconstrued. The NEC's investigation process should be neutral, beyond reproach and should not rely on politically motivated briefing campaigns by third parties motivated against the Party and its Leader.

As a serving MP or as a Party member, I reasonably expect the Party to conduct its own basic research regarding alleged misconduct before imposing a disciplinary sanction as serious as suspension, particularly when it is attached to charge of anti-Semitism and the consequential reputational damage I have and continue to endure.

If the Party fails in this basic duty of clarifying and verifying allegations made by malicious and vexatious third parties before imposing suspension (as is the case here), I have justifiable reason to doubt the transparency, robustness and fairness of the disciplinary process, and question whether the actions taken against me have been in the interests of the Party and the public.

For the avoidance of doubt, and by way of accurate disclosure, a transcript of the relevant part of my speech in Sheffield is provided below.

"We are not a racist party, are we? We're not an anti-Semitic party. We are the Party that stood up to racism throughout our entire history. It was Labour, and Jeremy's mam, standing shoul-

der-to-shoulder with the Jewish community in Cable Street fighting Oswald Mosley's fascists. It was Labour that was the backbone of the Anti-Nazi League in the 1970s when we confronted the anti-Semites, the racists, the Islamophobes on the streets and we defeated those fascists, didn't we? And now we – Jeremy, me and others – are being accused of being bigots, of being anti-Semites. And it's almost as we're living within the pages of George Orwell's 1984. You know the Party that's done more to stand up to racism is now being demonised as a racist, bigoted party.

And I've got to say I think our Party's response has been partly responsible for that. Because in my opinion – I never have, I've got to say – we've backed off far too much, we've given too much ground, we've been too apologetic. What have we got to apologise for? For being an anti-racist party? And we've done more to actually address the scourge of anti-Semitism than any other political party. Any other political party. And yet we are being traduced. And grassroots members are being traduced. And I'm not going to stand up and tolerate that in any way shape or form and whenever I get the opportunity [inaudible] I will not allow these people to slag off decent, hard-working, socialist members of our Party. I'm just not going do it because it's an absolute bloody travesty what they're saying about Party members."

7. **During this meeting, did you claim to have sung 'Celebration' outside the office of Joan Ryan MP after she resigned from the Party. If so, please explain what you meant when you said this.**

No. In a light-hearted interview with the *New Statesman*'s Kevin Maguire, I stated that I had sung 'Celebration' inside my office which was opposite Ms Ryan's office. She would not have heard me. I did not sing 'outside the office' of Ms Ryan. I cannot claim that I was disappointed when Ms Ryan left the Party and believe that those sentiments are shared by the overwhelming majority of Labour Party members.

Joan Ryan is no longer a Labour Party MP or a member of the Party. The majority of the active members of Enfield North CLP appear to be deeply grateful for this. She lost a no confidence vote called by members of her CLP – an extraordinary step for members to take – in September 2018.[5]

Her response was to describe members of her own CLP as *"Trots Stalinists Communists and assorted hard left"* [sic] on Twitter and to claim that she had no confidence in them.[6] Ms Ryan's conceited behaviour and disregard for members clearly brought the Party into disrepute under Rule 2.1.8 and undermined members' confidence in the Party's procedures, as well as damaging the standing of Parliament and MPs at a time when we needed to do more to connect with those we represent.

Ms Ryan's comments constituted a direct and public attack on Party members by a then Labour Party MP and were a clear breach of the Party's Code of Conduct: Social Media Policy. Disappointingly, no action was taken by the Party, which highlights the inconsistent and haphazard way in which the Party implements disciplinary action.

> **Joan Ryan MP** ✓
> @joanryanEnfield
>
> So lost 92 to 94 votes hardly decisive victory and it never occurred to me that Trots Stalinists Communists and assorted hard left would gave confidence in me. I have none in them.
>
> 3:17 PM - 6 Sep 2018

The vote of no confidence in Ms Ryan was preceded by a growing discontent among members in Enfield specifically relating to anti-black racism locally, and anti-Palestinian racism stemming from her chairmanship of Labour Friends of Israel.

The *Skwawkbox* reported extensively in 2018 on the controversial deselection of all black councillors in Enfield – a borough where one in five residents is black – and what Labour Party members locally believed to be the cause.[7]

Local Labour Party members had also consistently expressed their outrage at findings by Al Jazeera relating to Ms Ryan in their 2017 documentary 'The Lobby'. As well as being caught on camera fabricating allegations of anti-Semitism against a Party member[8][9] – an especially gross form of misconduct and abuse of power for an MP – Ms Ryan was also found discussing at Conference 2016 a £1 million+ fund provided by the State of Israel with disgraced Israeli official Shai Masot,[10] who separately had plotted to "take down" a sitting Foreign Office minister on behalf of the State of Israel. Masot was immediately recalled to Israel to be disciplined once his government became aware of the documentary but Ms Ryan faced no censure from the Labour Party.

Following the broadcast of this documentary, Jeremy Corbyn wrote to the Prime Minister: *"This is clearly a national security issue. It is only [on the basis of an investigation] that Parliament and the public will be reassured that such activities will not be tolerated by your government."*[11] Shadow Foreign Secretary Emily Thornberry called Masot's behaviour *"improper interference"* in our democracy.[12] Both Jeremy and Emily were absolutely right to demand a government inquiry into a subversion campaign targeted both at our Party and the Foreign Office. However, the Party did not discipline Ms Ryan.

Given that Ms Ryan defected to a pro-austerity, pro-war group of MPs organised not as a party but as a private company,[13] my comments in Sheffield – specifically that Ms Ryan *"left the Labour Party years ago, to be honest"* – have shown to be true.

It is a gross failing of the Party's disciplinary regime that Ms Ryan was allowed to leave the Party of her own volition even after her own CLP had deemed her unfit to represent the Party and she had been exposed as conspiring with a foreign official. Since leaving the Party, she has gone on to speak at the American-Israel Public Affairs Committee (AIPAC) Conference, which was boycotted by mainstream Democratic Party presidential candidates. I understand Ms Ryan was invited there to attack the Labour Party and its Leader and did so fulsomely.[14] The Labour Party has not responded.

Below is the assessment of the new Vice Chair for Membership in Enfield North CLP of our Party's rise in popularity locally since Ms Ryan defected,[15] and an interaction with a local resident who suggests they are now much more inclined to vote Labour after Ms Ryan's defection:[16]

> **Ed Poole**
> @edwardpoole1975
>
> Just been out on the doorstep in Enfield North for the first time since our MP left the Labour Party. Many people telling us they will now vote Labour because she's left! #TIG
>
> 5:58 AM - 14 Apr 2019
>
> 803 Retweets 2,182 Likes
>
> ⎯⎯⎯
>
> **Adam McGibbon** @AdamMcGibbon · 7h
> Replying to @edwardpoole1975
> You haven't canvassed me, but I live in Enfield North and *never, ever* would have voted for Joan Ryan. Open to the prospect of voting Labour here in future GE's now.
>
> **Ed Poole** @edwardpoole1975 · 6h
> Sorry about that. There are tens of thousands of residences in Enfield North and on a day like yesterday we got through about 600. Many of those were out. We will try and get round everyone at least once. But I'm happy to answer any questions on here too.
>
> **Adam McGibbon** @AdamMcGibbon · 6h
> Oh no, not complaining about not being canvassed at all! Just pointing out that your thesis, that a large number of voters who would never vote for Joan Ryan are now open to the prospect of vote Labour, is probably correct, and I'm one of them! :)
>
> **Ed Poole** @edwardpoole1975 · 6h
> Brilliant to hear! Thank you.

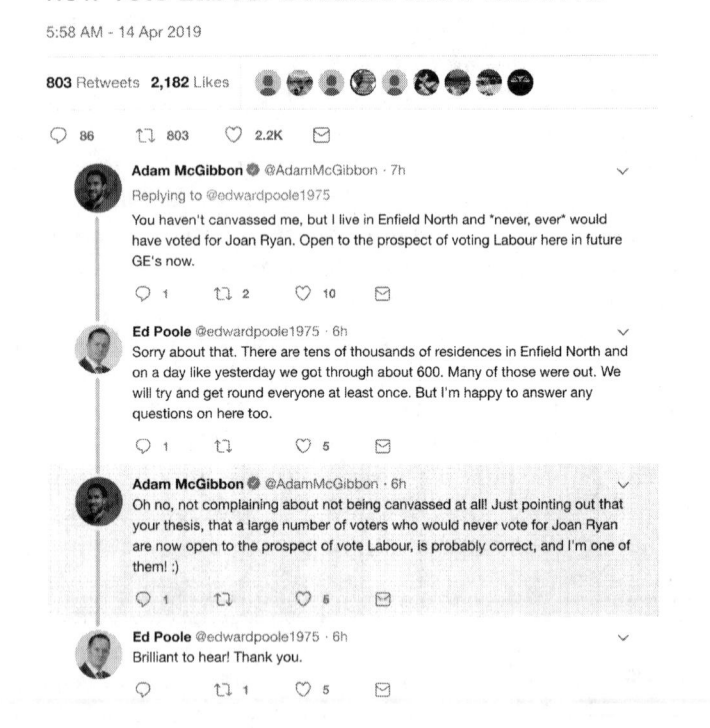

8. Is there anything else you think the Party should know about this meeting?

No, but I think it is important for the Party to understand that in 2012 I had spoken in support of Ms Ryan at a local fundraising meeting. Over time, however, our views became irreparably disparate.

APPENDIX

Gilad Atzmon Petition – 21st December 2018 – Items 2 and 3

9. Did you sign a petition entitled 'Hands Off Gilad Atzmon'? If so, please explain why you signed this petition.

I did not sign the petition and contacted Change.org to express my surprise after a Twitter user posted a screenshot of the petition page showing my name as a signatory. I have received confirmation from Change.org that my *"account does not show [your] signature in this petition."*

I note that the picture in Item 2 purporting to be a screenshot of the petition page showing my signature was posted on 21 December 2018 to Twitter by the Conservative candidate for Odd Down Ward in Bath & North East Somerset Council, Alastair Thompson.[17] The picture he tweeted corresponds exactly with that shown in Item 2.

10. Please explain the reason for posting the tweet in Item 3.
See below.

11. Please explain your understanding of the Gilad Atzmon petition.

I was told by a Party member in Islington that the Town Hall had been lobbied to prevent Mr Atzmon, an accomplished and award winning saxophonist, from playing there. I had never heard of Mr Atzmon and was unaware of his political, theological and cultural views. I was told in good faith by a trusted activist that Mr Atzmon was a former Israeli soldier who espoused pro-Palestinian views and was being censored on that basis. This appeared unjust and entirely plausible given the climate of fear encouraged by the growing number of malicious campaigns designed to shut down free speech on Palestine.

As a token of support, I tweeted a link to the petition which **automated** the wording of the tweet in Item 3. Within a couple of minutes, a deeply knowledgeable Party member and pro-Palestinian activist called me to ask if I was aware of all of Mr Atzmon's views. I was not and I confirmed the same. He told me that Mr Atzmon's ideas on 'Jewishness' racially characterise Jews; that Mr Atzmon had made Judeophobic remarks so extreme they could incite violence; and that the Palestinian solidarity movements of Britain had long dissociated from and denounced Mr Atzmon for these reasons. He also pointed me to articles that had been written by Palestinian advocates arguing that Mr Atzmon's views were dangerous.

On this advice, **I reacted promptly and deleted the tweet within twelve minutes of originally posting it.** As detailed above, I also contacted Change.org in respect of Item 2, a screenshot purporting to prove my signature of the petition. It has been confirmed that there is no *"indication that the screenshot was taken from the aforementioned petition"*. I tweeted a full apology which said:

"APOLOGY

"Earlier today I tweeted a petition about an Islington Council ban against The Blockheads performing with their chosen line-up. The Council has blocked jazz musician Gilad Atzmon from playing with the group. Since then I've learned that Atzmon, a former Israeli soldier, is not confined to the jazz world. I am told that in various blogs and in speeches he has adopted anti-Semitic language.

"I wasn't aware of this until after I tweeted the petition. As soon as I was informed, I deleted the tweet. I've always condemned all forms of racism, including anti-Semitism, and strongly dis-associate myself from Atzmon's anti-Semitic views. I therefore apologise for tweeting this petition and any distress or offence it may have caused."

12. Is there anything else you think the Party should know about this tweet?

The incident led me to consider even more carefully than before my chosen associates and the importance of taking sound and considered advice from well-informed sources. I take my responsibility to my constituents and to the Party very seriously as I have clearly demonstrated.

The fact that I did not sign the petition itself and that Change.org have confirmed this leads me to question how a screenshot could appear alleging that I had signed the petition.

APPENDIX

It is known, for example, that those who are co-ordinating the malicious and vexatious campaign to malign Labour Party members and allies of Jeremy Corbyn have resorted to editing screenshots in their pursuit of their targets, as well as creating fake social media accounts posing as Labour Party members in order to post comments and content that would put these fake characters in breach of the Party's Rule 2.1.8 and Code of Conduct: Social Media Policy, with the objective of bringing negative media attention to the Party.

A particularly disturbing element of this campaign has been an effort to invent fake online personas that are Muslim who then post anti-Semitic content.[18] There are serious questions to be addressed about the Islamophobia driving this campaign.

Board of Deputies Tweet – 27th October 2018 – Item 4

13. Please explain the reason for posting the tweet in Item 4.

'Blow me down with a feather' is an expression of surprise. The article in the tweet refers to an anonymous community leader within the Board of Deputies of British Jews (BoD) accusing the BoD president Marie van der Zyl of using an *"anti-Semitic trope"*. The *Jewish Chronicle* reported:[19]

> *"[A] senior communal source was highly critical of Mrs van der Zyl's latest remarks, telling the JC:* "In what world do you use the words 'Jewish community' and 'power' in the same sentence?"

> *"The community has spent months highlighting antisemitic tropes and then the President of the Board of Deputies herself says Jews have power which they learn how to use. I don't know what's worse – that this was a spur of the moment comment or that it was actually planned? The Board is more worried about their positioning than getting the right answer."*

14. Were you aware of the Pittsburgh synagogue shooting when you posted this tweet?

No.

15. Is there anything else you think the Party should know about this tweet?

My expression of surprise that the BoD president could be accused by another senior communal leader within the BoD of harbouring anti-Semitic ideas highlights the extent of confusion and disagreement in contemporary political discourse about what constitutes anti-Semitism.

As a social movement and a party with many Jewish members, the Labour Party has an important responsibility in this discourse so that anti-Semitism is defined in a way that protects Jews and does not allow for malicious and vexatious claims to distort the meaning of anti-Semitism, which would lead to British Jews becoming more vulnerable in the long-term.

Vanessa Beeley Tweet – 19th August 2018 – Item 5

16. Please explain the reason for posting the tweet in Item 5.

I was a guest speaker at the Beautiful Days Festival 2018. The Festival is organised by the rock band The Levellers. The Rebel Tent hosted political discussions on climate change, foreign policy, prospects for the Labour Party and LGBT rights. One of these discussions was entitled 'Syria – What is to be done?' and featured a discussion between the former British ambassador to Syria, Peter Ford, with the activist Peter Tatchell.

I had been a panellist on the previous panel, entitled 'A New Politics from the Left', discussing the Labour Party's rapid progress and its future under the leadership of Jeremy Corbyn. I decided to stay in the tent to hear the discussion on Syria and joined the audience.

During the discussion on Syria, Vanessa Beeley made an impressive contribution from the floor, speaking with authority and eloquence of her own substantial reporting experience in Syria. She also made the case against military intervention in the conflict. Her arguments that day most closely represented the Labour Party's position.

We met briefly towards the end of the event and I sent the tweet as a courtesy acknowledging that we had met. It is very common to use social media to 'tag' or acknowledge people who you meet in professional circles.

17. Please explain your understanding of who Vanessa Beeley is.

Vanessa Beeley is a reporter and researcher who writes for 21stcenturywire.com and has reported extensively from Syria. She was a finalist for the 2017 Martha Gellhorn Prize for Journalism.

18. Is there anything else you think the Party should know about this tweet?

No.

Justice4Marc Manchester Meeting – 30th May 2018

19. Did you speak at a Justice4Marc meeting in Manchester on 30th May 2018?

Yes.

20. During the meeting, did you say *"that's why certain dark forces are using their power, using their contacts in the media in order to undermine this project"*? If so, what did you mean by this?

I have attached the full transcript of the speech for contextual purposes. I urge NEC members to consult the transcript to fully understand the argument I was making in support of the Party and Jeremy's leadership.

Since late 2015, there has been an organised campaign of pressure targeting the Party, the Leader and the complaints system with the objective of ending Jeremy's leadership. This has taken many forms and emanated from a variety of sources.

Examples include (1) the *"improper interference"* in our democracy by a hostile foreign government referenced by Emily Thornberry in a letter to the Foreign Affairs Committee; (2) the Integrity Initiative – a taxpayer-funded information warfare campaign targeting the Labour Party, commissioned by the Foreign and Commonwealth Office (FCO), managed by British former military intelligence officials and outsourced to organisations such as Bellingcat, which has recently dedicated a full-time researcher to smearing Jeremy Corbyn and the Party;[20] and (3) Labour MPs opposed to Jeremy's leadership habitually bringing the Party into disrepute by briefing against the Leader's Office, leaking and co-ordinating personal attacks against Jeremy.

The first two are extremely serious national security matters and the latter is a disciplinary issue the Party should deal with.

I was deeply dismayed to be one of the few Labour MPs raising questions in Parliament over the Integrity Initiative's promotion of anti-Labour Party messages, which were paid for by the Foreign Office. Such a brazen, state-directed attack on our Party flies in the face of all democratic convention and seriously compromises the integrity of our press.

In respect of the PLP, Party members do not understand why, for example, when Dame Margaret Hodge called Jeremy a *"fucking antisemite and racist"* in the House of Commons in July 2018,[21] this was not met with any penalty or serious disciplinary sanction. There is also widespread dismay that Dame Margaret Hodge has recorded confidential conversations with the Party Leader and leaked material to the press – most recently to the *Sunday Times* last Sunday – and has faced no penalty or serious disciplinary sanction. Her behaviour has been described by the Party Leader as a *"total breach of trust"*.[22] I fully agree with his view.

Members have also described to me their lack of faith in the Party's disciplinary system given that Ian Austin MP faced no penalty or serious disciplinary sanction after he repeatedly screamed abuse at the Party's chair Ian Lavery MP and told the Leader to *"shut up and sit down"* in Parliament while Jeremy was at the despatch box giving a statement on the Chilcot Report and the UK's involvement in the invasion of Iraq. Mr Austin brought the Party into disrepute not only through his public abuse of the Leader but by disgracing a solemn moment during which the public would expect decorum to be maintained as the Party Leader commented on the thousands of tragic deaths during the invasion and the war that followed.

Both Mr Austin and Dame Margaret Hodge received warning letters, after which Mr Austin publicly and repeatedly refused to apologise for his conduct.

21. Who do you understand dark forces to refer to?

See above.

There are a range of 'forces' that seek to undermine the Party in co-ordination with tax-exiled newspaper owners who see the

Labour Party's promise to govern for the many, not the few as a threat to their interests.

The consequences of this campaign to undermine Jeremy's leadership have been covered extensively in a paper by academics at the London School of Economics and Political Science entitled 'Journalistic Representations of Jeremy Corbyn in the British Press: From Watchdog to Attack Dog' and academics at Birkbeck, University of London working with the Media Reform Coalition of Goldsmiths, University of London. The 2016 paper produced by the Birkbeck and Media Reform Coalition team at the height of a supposed crisis in the Labour Party was entitled, 'Should he stay or should he go? Television and Online news coverage of the Labour Party in crisis'. The Media Reform Coalition and Aston University's Dr Tom Mills has written extensively on the subject of how distorted media portrayals of Jeremy Corbyn and his allies have affected the Party, such as in a 2017 article for the *Conversation* entitled 'Media bias against Jeremy Corbyn shows how politicised reporting has become'. The article summarises some of the academic and other research on this subject up until that point and can be read here.

Four years of incessantly hostile media coverage have laid the ground for serious and generalised violent radicalisation against the Left. We have already lost one colleague to a horrific act of violence. More recently, the growing size of far-right rallies and the normalisation of far-right rhetoric should be a serious cause of alarm for the Party and its members. This has not occurred in a vacuum.

A senior serving general threatened in the *Sunday Times* in September 2015 that the armed forces would take *"direct action"* to prevent a Corbyn government implementing defence reforms.[23] In the same piece, intelligence officials threatened they would withhold crucial intelligence from Jeremy and his Cabinet in the event of a Labour election victory. Then came the fabricated Czech spy stories. More recently, former MI6 chief Sir Richard Dearlove has in October last year[24] and February this year briefed the *Sunday Times* and *Mail on Sunday* respectively against the Leader's Office. In September, sitting MI5 chief Andrew Parker did the same with the *Sunday Times*.[25]

This demonisation of Jeremy personally, his staff and MPs who support his policy agenda is organised, co-ordinated and emanates from **multiple** sources, within British and from various foreign governments. It has culminated in the shocking footage of 3rd Parachute Regiment troops using Jeremy's image as target practice in Afghanistan and the *Times* running a recent front-page promoting the idea of a 'strongman' taking charge of our democracy.[26]

The Party must not be naïve about the scale of the challenge facing it. Party members and those deemed either politically or personally close to Jeremy are the primary targets of this campaign. The Party has weakened its position in facing down this challenge: firstly by failing to recognise the sources of this campaign and secondly by failing to implement a consistent standard in its disciplinary approach towards Party members and MPs.

This is particularly pertinent in light of findings in the LSE paper mentioned above, which states, *"the British media has systematically attacked Jeremy Corbyn ever since he came to national prominence in the summer of 2015"*[27] and research by the Media Reform Coalition which states that:

> *"BBC correspondents tended to ascribe militancy and aggression exclusively to Jeremy Corbyn and his supporters rather than Labour rebels, in spite of the fact that the leadership was, throughout this period (2016), largely on the defensive in responding to attacks and accusations by rebel MPs".* [28]

Both reports are essential context for NEC members in assessing how my public comments have been persistently and maliciously misconstrued.

I note also that a 2016 YouGov poll found that 77 per cent of Labour members and 69 per cent of Labour voters believed that the mainstream media had been deliberately biasing coverage to portray Jeremy in a negative light.[29] Jeremy's allies and supporters in the Party, of which I am one, have obviously faced similar treatment and the complaints presented here should be viewed in light of that organised campaign as well as the campaign's effects on those who have been susceptible to its influence while acting in good faith.

22. During this meeting, did you say *"Some people might find it a bit difficult to show solidarity with Marc, for fear of being ... you know ... implicated and criticised and demonised"*? If so, what did you mean by this?

In the face of an orchestrated campaign of intimidation as described above, it is obviously difficult for Party members to defend those who have been unfairly targeted. Breaking those bonds of solidarity is a key objective of the campaign against our Party and its Leader. I have always been a strong advocate for solidarity within the Party and it remains a key focus of my work.

23. During this meeting, did you say *"anti-Semitism is being weaponised and I think some people have weaponised it and I agree with that, that's pretty clear"*? If so, what did you mean by this?

I did but it is of the utmost importance for the context to be understood and in particular the words that immediately preceded this line in my speech:

> *"So, it's good to see that Jennie Formby, who I've got the utmost confidence in, she's a great trade unionist, a great supporter of Jeremy Corbyn, and she will be, I think, a wonderful, and is already proving to be a great general secretary of the party.*
>
> *"So she is bringing these new procedures in and there will be time limited processes; going to depoliticise the whole affair, which I think is also important because I know many people in the Jewish community have said to me, and it's been put at my door as if I've coined the phrase, and I haven't, it was people in the Jewish community who've said to me that anti-Semitism was being weaponised."*

The idea of the 'weaponisation' of anti-Semitism is not one I originated. It has a long precedent among historians of Jewish political thought and among historians of Israel. I first encountered the phrase in a statement by the Jewish Socialists' Group relating to the Labour Party dated 28 April 2016, which stated:

> *"Accusations of antisemitism are currently being weaponised to attack the Jeremy Corbyn-led Labour party with claims that*

Labour has a "problem" of antisemitism. This is despite Corbyn's longstanding record of actively opposing fascism and all forms of racism, and being a firm a supporter of the rights of refugees and of human rights globally." [30]

I encourage all NEC members to read the statement, which expresses the sentiments of many left-wing Jewish Labour Party members whose voices are drowned out by the organised campaign to malign and marginalise them.

The words 'weaponise' and 'weaponisation' are used repeatedly by various sources in condemning allegations of anti-Semitism that are maliciously and vexatiously used by political opponents of Jeremy Corbyn and the Labour Party.[31]

I believe that bad faith accusations are being made against allies of the Party Leader in a bid to undermine his position. It is also the case that the Party's refusal to clearly identify the source of these politically motivated allegations as a malicious and co-ordinated campaign, which is part of the process of *"improper interference in our democratic politics by other states"* identified by Emily Thornberry in 2017, has allowed members to face trial by media.

The Party's encouragement and/or lack of action in relation to this trial by media, such as by breaching members' confidentiality and leaking details of disciplinary cases to hostile press, has led to increasing politicisation of anti-Semitism by opponents of the Party's mainstream and popular manifesto plan to transform our society.

Three examples are particularly instructive in demonstrating how the Party has facilitated and/or failed to take appropriate action in relation to malicious accusations and the politicisation of anti-Semitism. Firstly, that of Chuka Umunna, who said in a statement in October 2016 (reproduced in full on *LabourList*)[32] following the publication of the Home Affairs Select Committee report on anti-Semitism:

"Some have suggested that there is institutional anti-Semitism across the whole of the Labour Party – this is not a view I share, not least because I have not seen one incident of anti-Semitism in almost 20 years of activism within my local Labour Party in

Lambeth. However, we would be putting our heads in the sand if we denied the existence of anti-Semitism amongst a minority in our wider Labour family – this is something our movement has a solemn duty to root out if we are to remain true to the principles we were founded to promote and protect."

These are sentiments I wholeheartedly agree with. That Chuka Umunna MP was then able to accuse the Party of 'institutional anti-Semitism' less than two years later[33] as he made preparations to leave it is not exclusively an act of opportunism. It is also a failure of the Labour Party to articulate clearly and with authority the origins and cause of the outsized media attention on both genuine and unfounded claims of anti-Semitism among its members.

Recent assertions by Siobhan McDonagh MP on the Today programme that anti-capitalism is anti-Semitism[34] and Margaret Hodge MP on Channel 4 News that anti-Zionism is anti-Semitism[35] are stark evidence that accusations of anti-Semitism are being weaponised (i.e. used) to demonise internationalist socialism.

The Party's lack of a coherent understanding of what constitutes anti-Semitism and its refusal to call out such political instrumentalisation of anti-Semitism by opponents of the Leader puts Jews at risk. Ms McDonagh's and Dame Margaret Hodge's comments were met with scorn by the public – the risk, therefore, is that **genuine** anti-Semitism is not taken seriously enough. This would endanger British Jews and cannot be allowed to happen.

It is important for the Party to note that I have also repeatedly been the subject of weaponised allegations. The clearest example of this was the response by several organisations when I signed the Holocaust Educational Trust's Book of Commitment in Parliament, offering my sympathy and solidarity to Holocaust survivors. I wrote:

"Hatred and bigotry led to the unimaginable horrors of the Holocaust. We must never forget and always strive to build a better, peaceful and compassionate world through love and solidarity."

There can be no possible interpretation of those words that could be reasonably construed as anti-Semitic. Such a suggestion would obviously be malicious and vexatious. Yet my contribution to the Book of Commitment and a photograph I tweeted of me signing the Book was met by the Jewish Leadership Council with *"disgust"* and described as a *"smokescreen"*; by the Board of Deputies with an accusation of *"hypocrisy"*; and by the Holocaust Educational Trust as *"repulsive"*.[36] Given that I have been absolute and vigorous in condemning anti-Semitism, I have to question how anyone acting in good faith could arrive at such conclusions and whether concerns over anti-Semitism are indeed the motivation for such a response.

It is important to note also that the Holocaust Educational Trust took the photograph I tweeted of me signing the Book of Commitment and shared the photograph with me. The organisation did not, at the time I was signing the Book of Commitment, object to my doing so. This also leads me to ask which third party prevailed upon the organisation to issue an aggressive condemnation of me and with what intention. This malicious politicisation of solidarity with Holocaust survivors does not appear to have originated from the Holocaust Educational Trust but does fit a pattern of weaponisation of anti-Semitism for other political ends.

24. Is there anything else you think the Party should know about this event?

Marc Wadsworth is a black anti-racism campaigner with a long track record of educating others and fighting fascism on the frontline. He was an adviser to the family of Stephen Lawrence in the aftermath of Stephen's murder by racist thugs and was responsible for introducing the family to Nelson Mandela. I attended the event to support his reinstatement as a Labour Party member (offering solidarity) after he was, in my view the victim of a malicious, politically motivated and unfounded accusation of anti-Semitism.

It is important to note that in the same speech, I supported the progress the Party has been making both in attempting to clarify what constitutes anti-Semitism and in improving its disciplinary processes. I refer you to paragraphs 47–51 of my speech, which are quoted below:

> *"And indeed, were the Chakrabarti recommendations implemented prior to Marc's absurd disciplinary hearing ... well it wouldn't have even got to a hearing would it?*
>
> *"It would have been simply thrown out. So, it's good to see we are making progress because we should not tolerate, and nobody is suggesting that we should tolerate anti-Semitism or any form of bigotry. Of course we're not suggesting that. And for people to try and imply that that is what we are suggesting, well that's another calumny as well, and we must not let that stand either."*

Marc Wadsworth Hearing 25th April 2018

25. Did you attend a demonstration outside the NCC hearing of Marc Wadsworth on 25th April 2018? If so, please explain your reason for attending.

No. I accompanied Marc Wadsworth into the NCC hearing.

26. Is there anything else you think the Party should know about this demonstration?

I attended Marc Wadsworth's hearing to give evidence in person. Labour MPs Keith Vaz and Clive Lewis submitted written evidence.

Peterborough Momentum Meeting – 17th March 2018 – Item 6

27. Did you speak at a meeting of Peterborough Momentum on 17th March 2018?

Yes.

28. During this meeting, did you say *"We've got these ridiculous suspensions and expulsions from the Party ... in the most grotesque and unfair way"*? If so, what did you mean by this?

Please refer to 20–23 above.

I note also the cases of Jean Fitzpatrick, Professor Moshé Machover and Glyn Secker, all of whom were placed under investigation in questionable and unfair circumstances. All were reinstated as members rapidly but confusion inside the Party about what constitutes anti-Semitism allowed them to be maliciously and vexatiously pursued, harming their reputations.

I note similarities between comments I made at the Peterborough meeting and page 18 of the Shami Chakrabarti Inquiry report:

> "I find it regrettable, to say the least, that some subjects of recent suspension and disciplinary process, under the Party's disciplinary procedures, found out about their suspensions and investigations as a result of media reporting rather than notice from the Party itself. Staff or elected officials should never feel it necessary (even during a pre-election media frenzy) – to operate a presumption of suspension. If anything, the presumption should be against interim suspension. The question should be about the seriousness of any immediate damage that the person subject to investigation might do to the Party if allowed to continue as a member in the meantime.
>
> "Indeed, if the principle of proportionality had been properly applied in recent times, I query whether so many people would ever have been suspended at all, rather than simply given notice that they were being investigated in relation to a complaint that their conduct had brought or was bringing the Party into disrepute."[37]

29. Is there anything else you think the Party should know about this meeting?

It was an upbeat meeting, characterised by camaraderie and optimism about the future of the Labour Party and the broader Left.

Guardian Article – 28th August 2017 – Item 7

30. Did you make the comments reported by the Guardian in Item 7?

Yes.

31. **Please explain what you meant by saying** *"I'm not saying it never ever happens but it is a really dirty, lowdown trick, particularly the antisemitism smears. Many people in the Jewish community are appalled by what they see as weaponisation of antisemitism for political ends".*

Please see 20–23 above.

Jewish communal groups such as Jewish Voice for Labour, the Jewish Socialists' Group, Jews for Justice for Palestinians, some Haredi communities as well as many individuals from across the British Jewish community have expressed deep concern about the **weaponisation** of anti-Semitism for political ends in relation to Jeremy Corbyn and the Labour Party. A selection of letters to the *Guardian* on the subject from just one day in August 2015 elicits a wide range of arguments supporting precisely this point.[38] I could quote many more Jewish members who agree. From my own conversations around the country, I know that this is the majority view within our Party.

An excerpt from Naomi Wayne's August 2015 letter to the *Guardian* on behalf of Jews for Justice for Palestinians captures the essence of the sentiment I hear around the country:

> *"We take no position regarding the Labour Party leadership contest. However, we deduce that the use – and serious abuse – of accusations of antisemitism and the like is evidence of panic that someone who stands up for Palestinian rights might end up leading a major British political party."*

32. **Please explain what you meant by** *"I think for all the talk of Venezuela and antisemitism and the latest thing is sexism now, Jeremy's overwhelming landslide victories in the leadership elections and the general election mean people have stopped listening to the smears".*

Please see 20–23 above.

Jeremy Corbyn is obviously not sexist. At the time I made those comments, he was being portrayed as such by those who are responsible for the organised and targeted campaign against him and his supporters. My comments refer to this attempt to smear Jeremy.

TalkRadio – 20th September 2017

33. Were you interviewed by Julia Hartley-Brewer on TalkRadio on 20th September 2017?
Yes.

34. During the interview, did you say *"I know some people have expressed anxiety and the abuse online is unacceptable, but that isn't from Labour Party members. There's no evidence as far as I'm aware [that] any of the abuse online is being perpetrated by them"*? If so, please explain what you meant by this.

As part of the organised campaign of pressure on the Party, its complaints team and its Leader, political opponents of the Leader have attempted to suggest that the Leader has fostered a climate of intimidation and abuse in our Party. Nothing could be further from the truth. The political instrumentalisation of anti-Semitism by opponents of the Labour Party and its Leader have led to the mischaracterisation of far-right abuse as emanating from Labour Party members. This is not the case.

Recent online targeted harassment of Luciana Berger MP, for example, has been led by the far-right group National Action. In October 2014, the Hitler-obsessed Garron Helm targeted Ms Berger. After he was jailed, the BNP rallied to his cause.[39] In December 2016, the neo-Nazi Joshua Bonehill-Paine was sentenced to two years in prison for his support of Mr Helm's harassment.[40] More recently, the Islamophobe John Nimmo was jailed for abusing Ms Berger.[41] In 2018, another Hitler-obsessed far-right thug, Jack Coulson, was jailed on suspicion of a threat to kill her.[42]

Yet Party members and MPs are under the wrong impression that Ms Berger was being abused by Labour members. When members and Party officials are not availed of the facts, they are unable to make sound judgements. I urge NEC officials to pay close attention to the facts and the political motivations underlying the co-ordinated campaign against political allies of the Leader.

35. What is your response to the allegation that your conduct may be or have been in breach of [Rule 2.1.8]?

APPENDIX

I categorically reject that I have breached Rule 2.1.8 of the Party's Rule Book. I have never and would never show hostility and/or prejudice to **any** person on the grounds of a protected characteristic. I am a committed and long-standing member of the Labour Party and have consistently sought to uphold its values and that of the Leader. I have campaigned tirelessly in support of the Party and its ethos and have never sought to bring the Party into disrepute. I am disappointed by the unsubstantiated nature of the allegations categorised in the letter of 27 February 2019 that have been provided in a vacuum, without context and/or prior investigation by the Party. The letter makes reference to *"a large number of complaints"* and *"a pattern of behaviour"* without justification. I have not been privy to the *"large number of complaints"* and therefore cannot fairly provide comment. I do not believe that the examples provided show a *"pattern of behaviour"* that brings the Party into disrepute and I have been able to provide meaningful and balanced responses that clearly show that I have acted in good faith at all times. I have provided various examples of other Party members that have publicly brought the Party into disrepute and that have not been sanctioned. I question why there is such disparity in the implementation of disciplinary action within the Party and in light of the above, I challenge my suspension and the allegations against me.

36. The Party's Code of Conduct: Social Media Policy states that *"treat all people with dignity and respect. This applies offline and online."* Do you think the posts in this pack are consistent with this policy?

I have not breached the Party's Code of Conduct: Social Media Policy (the Policy) and I treat all people with dignity and respect.

I have cited at 12 above that the incident in respect of Mr Atzmon has led me to think even more carefully about my associations and to take advice from well-informed sources. I stand by this and will continue to adopt this approach in the future.

37. Looking back at the evidence supplied with this letter, do you regret saying, posting or sharing any of this content?

I publicly apologised in respect of the tweet concerning Mr Atzmon which demonstrates I heeded the advice I received and

I took prompt action to remove the post immediately. I will continue to exercise care over my social media profile in the future.

38. Do you intend to post or share content of this nature again in the future?

I have never intended to post any content that would cause offence, show hostility to any person with a protected characteristic or bring the Party into disrepute. I would not intentionally do so in the future. I deplore any insinuation to the contrary.

Summary

I have been entirely honest and frank in my answers to the questions posed. I reiterate again that my suspension is onerous, unfounded and only seeks to ostracise me from a Party to whom I have been committed for 43 years. I am disappointed that the Party has not sought to thoroughly investigate the alleged complaints against me before taking action. I have highlighted that a number of the allegations are factually inaccurate or have been presented without context so as to misconstrue my words and/or intentions. The Party has shown, as demonstrated above, that it has failed to implement its own Rules and Code of Conduct consistently across its membership.

I request again that the suspension is lifted on the basis set out above. It is a draconian sanction that is having an adverse impact upon me, the Party and my vocation as an MP.

APPENDIX

RESPONSE TO THIRD SUSPENSION ALLEGATIONS – 5 SEPTEMBER 2019

Below is my response to a further set of 27 questions from the Labour Party's bureaucrats, after they imposed of a third suspension against me. I submitted my response on 5 September 2019.

. . .

1) Please see the evidence attached overleaf. The Party has reason to believe that these are your Facebook (Items 1 and 2), Twitter (Item 3), and email (Item 4) accounts. Can you confirm this is the case?

Yes.

2) The Party further has reason to believe that you posted or shared the statements contained in Items 1 through 4 yourself. Can you confirm this is the case? If not, each individual piece of evidence is numbered so please specify which of the pieces of evidence you are disputing posting or sharing?

Yes, I did post or share the statements contained in Items 1 through to 4.

Item 1

> Ken Underwood I'm not sure many people realise quite how radical is the mind-set of those born into the ruling class. It's exemplified imho in the huntin-shootin-fishin ethos. The only hint of that in this article is the reference to Northern Chemists.
> David Icke calls them reptilian shapeshifting vampire aliens which is only a marginal exaggeration.lol. Coldblooded, lying parasites who regard themselves as a different breed.
> That's why Jeremy Corbyn is such a contrast to them. He is good to the same degree that they are bad. People need to realise that. The wolves are dismayed to have a sheep leading the flock!
> 3y

> Chris Williamson We need to help people realise that Ken
> 3y

3) Please explain your understanding of the statement *"David Icke called [the ruling class] reptilian shapeshifting vampire aliens which is only a marginal exaggeration. Lol. Coldblooded, lying parasites who regard themselves as a different breed"?*

My understanding is that the Facebook user quoted was being hyperbolic or exaggerating for effect. This is clear from the context of the full statement.

4) By commenting *"We need to help people realise that Ken"* are you indicating agreement or support for the statement above? If not, please explain what you meant by this.

Mr Underwood said: *"I'm not sure many people **realise** quite how radical is the mind-set of those born into the ruling class. It's exemplified imho in the huntin-shootin-fishin ethos (my emphasis)."*

I responded: *"We need to help people **realise that** Ken (my emphasis)."*

Mr Underwood's comment was a reflection on the gap in empathy and compassion between the most privileged in our society and the working class. My brief reply was stating that the Labour Party needed to help the public understand the class critique that underlies its rhetoric and policies under Jeremy Corbyn's leadership.

Your omission of the material and substantive part of his statement; its replacement with a throwaway hyperbole which he clearly indicated was a humorous aside; and your subsequent insinuation about my meaning, are unfortunate examples of the bad faith that has characterised my experience with the Governance and Legal Unit since my suspension.

Item 2

5) Please explain your understanding of the statement *"Jackie's suspension is absurd – and a travesty. Worse still, it belittles the efforts of those who genuinely want to tackle anti-semitism rather than cynically use it as a political football"*?

Item 2 is a Facebook status authored by Red Labour, a socialist activist group founded by Ben Sellers. Mr Sellers worked on Jeremy Corbyn's campaign team as Jeremy contested the leadership. Since then, he has worked as a senior adviser to Shadow Business Secretary Laura Pidcock, a position he still holds.

I shared the status to my Facebook friends. I supported Jackie Walker for reasons set out in pp. 1–4 of my original submission in response to the first round of questions I received (16.04.19).

APPENDIX

> **Chris Williamson**
> 10 May 2016
>
> > **Red Labour**
> > 9 May 2016
> >
> > #Solidarity to Jackie Walker, lifelong anti-racist campaigner. Good on her for not taking this crap lying down:
> >
> > "Following the anti-Semitic allegations Ms Walker kept her head down- Labour were after all fighting elections and UK Tory PM David Cameron was looking for any 'dirt' and using it in the House of Commons by abusing his parliamentary privilege.
> >
> > But the elections are over and Jacqueline is now coming out fighting.
> >
> > Her partner, a man of Jewish faith, posted a "Personal statement re anti-Semitic allegations against the Labour Party" this weekend.
> >
> > And if you want to hear what Walker has to say on the allegations invite her to speak at your local Labour meetings.
> >
> > Opinion: We now appear to be in a 1950s type McCarthy witch-hunt era which means some in the Labour Party are too afraid to speak out and offer support, in some cases to people they have known for years and know to be anything but racist or anti-Semitic."
> >
> > Not us. Jackie's suspension is absurd - and a travesty. Worse still, it belittles the efforts of those who genuinely want to tackle anti-semitism rather than cynically use it as a political football:
> >
> > http://www.newtekjournalismukworld.com/.../jacqueline-walker-...

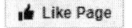

6) By sharing this statement are you indicating agreement or support?

Yes. I continue to support Jackie Walker, as I have set out above and in my previous statement.

I would like to add that Jackie Walker's suspension was lifted eighteen days after I shared this post, which suggests that at the time the Panel members agreed with me and Red Labour.

Item 3

7) Please explain why you thought it was appropriate to defend the comments made by Scott Nelson even though you had been informed of the content of those comments?

I did not defend the comments made by Scott Nelson. I was not aware of the full extent of them, and I then made the point that he had apologised for those comments. I believe we should have a space for people to apologise and make amends when they have done wrong. It is my understanding that Mr Nelson has now been re-admitted to the Labour Party.

Gideonomics @davessidekick · 1d
I'd respect you a lot more if you hadn't retweeted Socialist Voice, who says we should boycott Tesco and M&S cos they were set up by Jews

💬 5 🔁 1 ♡ 15

Chris Williamson MP ✓ @DerbyChrisW · 16h
I am sure he said no such thing. These smears are so wrong, please let's stand together to beat racism and replace of this abysmal Tory Govt with a Corbyn-led Labour Govt to build a society and an economy that works for the many not the few

💬 8 🔁 2 ♡ 1

Gideonomics @davessidekick · 16h
I couldn't agree more with the second bit but I'm afraid on the first bit..

[Screenshots of tweets by Scott Nelson @SocialistVoice:]

"...sh ancestors created those companies. ...e companies have Jewish blood. My ...stors were Irish, so I have Irish blood OfMancunia"
19 Dec 2015

"Pointing out the Jewish ancestors of Tesc M&S and the human rights abuses of workers abroad doesn't make me an antisemite @AriOfMancunia"
0:17 AM - 16 Dec 2015

"...ers abroad being exploited for 50p a ...y Jewish companies - but you'd rather ...lemn a tweet @rhys_ukipni ...omasEvansUKIP"
17 Dec 2015

"So condemning Jewish companies for p treatment of workers and barbaric war crimes makes me an antisemite? @garveyboy @AriOfMancunia"
9:08 AM - 19 Dec 2015

💬 3 🔁 2 ♡ 15

Chris Williamson MP ✓
@DerbyChrisW

Replying to @davessidekick and @carolynharris24

He repeatedly apologised for those comments. He is opposed to all forms of racism and bigotry and he never called for a boycott.
Please give him a chance.
Thank you.

01/04/2018, 23:24 from Derby, England

APPENDIX

8) Do you think your comments were appropriate given that a member of your own staff had reportedly described Mr Nelson's conduct as *"clearly... antisemitic"*.

I have never defended the comments that were made by Scott Nelson. Please see my response to question 7 above.

Item 4

> **From:** "WILLIAMSON, Chris" <chris.williamson.mp@parliament.uk>
> **Date:** 18 August 2018 at 15:42:23 BST
> **To:** Christine Edwards <christineedwards@btinternet.com>
> **Subject: RE: DAME MARGARET HODGE**
>
> Thanks for your email Christine
>
> I suggest you look at Norman Finkelstein's comments here: https://www.youtube.com/watch?v=xf5fOrutJfGQ
>
> Chris Williamson
> Tel: 01332 343261
> Tel: 0207 219 1687
>
> -----Original Message-----
> **From:** Christine Edwards <christineedwards@btinternet.com>
> **Sent:** 17 August 2018 22:06
> **To:** WILLIAMSON, Chris <chris.williamson.mp@parliament.uk>
> **Subject:** DAME MARGARET HODGE
>
> To Mr. Chris Williamson Labour MP
>
> I have been watching for some days as Labour leader Mr Jeremy Corbyn squirmed on the hook of lies regarding the laying of the wreath. Changing his recollection of events as proof of the events unfolded. We expect this level of lies and deceit from your leader I then read today your gross criticism of Dame Margaret Hodge. You say her point of view diminishes the seriousness of the issue. You missed out the sentence.....IN MY OPINION. You should be ashamed of yourself. You are a surface dweller only looking for your own glorification with no regard for history, the truth or facts. You will soon be forgotten.
> I personally admire Dame Margaret Hodge for saying what she did and the manner in which she said it. I am a Conservative voter and I must say I like seeing you dig your own grave in this despicable way.
> Christine Edwards. Worcestershire
>
> Sent from my iPad
>
> UK Parliament Disclaimer: This e-mail is confidential to the intended recipient. If you have received it in error, please notify the sender and delete it from your system. Any unauthorised use, disclosure, or copying is not permitted. This e-mail has been checked for viruses, but no liability is accepted for any damage caused by any virus transmitted by this e-mail. This e-mail address is not secure, is not encrypted and should not be used for sensitive data.

9) Please explain your understanding of the Norman Finkelstein video in Item 4.

Professor Finkelstein is one of the pre-eminent academic authorities on the political legacy of the Holocaust. In his book *The Holocaust Industry*, he explains at length and with great clarity that instrumentalisation of the Holocaust for political ends by advocates of Israel has harmed the fight against genuine antisemitism.

The video is an emotional plea by Professor Finkelstein, whose family were victims of Nazi war crimes, for the instrumentalisation of the Holocaust to cease in contemporary debates in the Labour Party, where this method is used to attack Jeremy Corbyn.

10) Please explain why you shared this video with a member of the public.

The email in Item 4 is an abusive message sent to me by a Conservative voter. Given the tenor of her communication, I did not see fit to engage her at length. Instead, I courteously pointed her to Professor Finkelstein's video because it most accurately surmises the views I hear from Labour Party members across the country who are concerned with fairness in the disciplinary process – especially Jewish members who are angered by the instrumentalisation that Professor Finkelstein describes.

11) Were you aware that the video stated that the video described Ms Hodge as *'cheapening and exploiting the memory of Jewish suffering'*; *'trivialising the memory of the Holocaust'*; and requesting that she should *'get the hell out of the Labour Party'*?

My understanding was that the video addressed the political instrumentalisation of the Holocaust, an issue which resides within Professor Finkelstein's expertise and which closely adheres to the themes he addresses in his book *The Holocaust Industry*.

12) Do you think it is appropriate to attack personally other members of the Party as done in this video?

Professor Finkelstein makes a range of political arguments about an emotive subject. It is for his critics to engage with those arguments. Professor Finkelstein's message reminds us there is no monopoly on Jewish opinion.

13) Do you think it is detrimental to the Party to share these sorts of comments about another Labour MP to a member of the public?

I did not attack Margaret Hodge. However, robust disagreement between members and challenging or critiquing members' viewpoints is an important part of engaging in politics. I have been the subject of baseless personal attacks, as is clear from the message I received that is at item 4 and the concerns I have previously raised with the Party about the attacks to which I have been subject directly from other Labour MPs. As far as I am aware, the Labour Party has done nothing about those attacks. Moreover, many other MPs and members of the Labour Party have been the subject of personal attacks from MPs and Labour

Party members, including Jeremy Corbyn, without any action being taken as a result.

Item 5

Chris Williamson Word interview 1

14) What is your knowledge of the membership status of the person interviewing you in this video?

I have no knowledge of the membership status of the person in that video.

15) Regarding the comments you made about freedom of speech in this video: do you believe that Labour Party members should be able to say things that are prejudicial and grossly detrimental to the Party without repercussion?

There are rightly limits to free speech in the law – particularly to prevent incitement and to protect minorities.

What constitutes speech that is 'prejudicial and grossly detrimental to the Party' is a matter of political interpretation. Labour Party members across the country express concern to me that the Party's current interpretation of this is draconian and lacks credibility because this clause has so often been used to target socialist members. When the disciplinary process is no longer seen as even-handed, fair and credible, the Party's ability to campaign on a platform of building a fair society and a fair economy are harmed.

Item 6

Chris Williamson interview 3
104 views

16) What is your knowledge of the membership status of the person interviewing you in this video?

I have no knowledge of the membership status the person in that video.

17) What is your understanding of Labour Against Zionist Islamophobic Racism (LAZIR)?

As far as I know, it is an activist group established this year.

18) Do you think that members of the Labour Party should *"naturally be working with LAZIR"*?

I have included a transcript of the conversation as Annex 1. I believe that Labour should work with a broad church of opinion in robust open debate, as set out above.

LAZIR campaigns against the IHRA definition of anti-Semitism and for a one-state solution in Palestine. These are not the current, official positions of the Labour Party.

Nor, for many decades, were support for racial equalities legislation or gay marriage official Labour Party positions, and activists advocating for these landmark reforms were sometimes perceived by the Party as unpalatable extremists or a liability. Political parties, including ours, are often the most conservative actors in the political process and usually the last institutions to catch up with the changes taking place around them. I believe open discussion about complex issues is important, and that the Labour movement should promote debate as opposed to shutting it down. To do otherwise leads to "never ending guilt by association", which was the subject of the discussion here and appears to be the basis of many of the allegations made against me.

19) Do you agree with the interviewer that allegations of *"transphobia"* or *"misogyny"* are *"all kinds of smears used to generate division in the movement"*?

The insinuation in the question is undeserving of a further response. My record is well-known. Please see the answer to the question I was asked at Annex 2.

20) Please explain what you meant by *"I don't think [trope] is a particularly helpful term"*?

The interviewer asked me to define a 'trope'. I could not do so with clarity and made that point. My response, transcribed in Annex 3 below, is self-explanatory. I suggested that most people we are trying to communicate with and engage as members or voters would, rightly, also struggle to define the term and we should avoid jargon in our political communication.

Item 7

> **Labour Against the Witchhunt**
> 14 July
>
> Durham Miners Gala, great event. We particularly liked Laura Pidcock talking about how outrageous it is "that people have fought for anti-racism all their lives are now being branded racists". Like Chris Williamson, of course, who came to visit us on our stall. We also handed out thousands of leaflets for the Appeal for a democratic Labour Left Alliance.

21) Why do you think it was appropriate to publicly defend and/or promote a person who has been expelled from the Labour Party for conduct that is prejudicial and grossly detrimental to the Party?

I have given a detailed response on pp. 1–4 of my original submission concerning my views of Ms Walker's suspension and expulsion and I will not re-state them here.

Item 8

Chris Williamson says he will be working to clear his name

22) Did you tell the Independent *"It's a tragedy that a tiny but noisy minority of party members want to trash the spirit of the Human Rights Act. It's one of Labour's greatest achievements. Maybe these malcontents have forgotten that Labour enshrined freedom of expression into British law nearly 21 years ago...If these mischief-makers are genuinely interest in winning the next election, they should pipe down and devote their energies to exposing the Tories and promoting a common sense socialist programme"?*

Yes.

23) Who did you intend the terms *"malcontents"* **and** *"mischief-makers"* **to refer to?**

This refers to members of the Parliamentary Labour Party who are opposed to Jeremy Corbyn's leadership and have attempted to prevent me from addressing public meetings around the country.

24) Please explain what you meant by *"they should pipe down"*?

I think my meaning is clear from the context. I meant that members of the Parliamentary Labour Party hostile to Jeremy's leadership should not prevent his supporters from communicating Labour's transformative socialist policy platform and should not prevent discussions on internal party democracy – the two issues I most commonly address in my public meetings around the country.

Item 9

> **Chris Williamson MP #GTTO** @DerbyChrisW · Aug 9
> Thank you @melaniekmelvin for recording this incredibly emotional moment from last night's open-air meeting in **Brighton**.
>
> **Melanie Outrider** @melaniekmelvin · Aug 8
> The moving moment at our meeting in Brighton when people of Jewish origin were called up by the daughter of Holocaust survivors to stand in solidarity with Chris. #IStandWithChrisWilliamson
> Show this thread
>
> 💬 40   🔁 220   ♡ 417   ⤴

25) Were you aware at the time that you shared a platform with her that Melanie Melvin was auto-excluded from the party in 2017 and that she has previously claimed that the *"Sarin gassing [in Syria] was filmed by the BBC at Pinewood on the orders of Mrs May and the Israeli lobby"* and that Diane Abbott *"could claim Jewish ancestry"* so that *"there'd be action"* taken against people who bully her on Twitter?

I did not share a platform with Melanie Melvin, and I do not know who she is beyond whatever interaction I may have had with her on Twitter.

It may be helpful to set out what happened at the meeting that took place in Brighton on 8 August 2019. The meeting was chaired by Greg Hadfield, and there were only two other invited speakers, which were myself and a woman who I had not met before but have since learned is called Asa Jansson.

After the three of us had spoken, the Chair allowed anyone in the audience who wanted to speak some time with the microphone. Several people came up to speak, one of whom was Tony

Greenstein. As far as I can recall, Ms Melvin did not speak at the event at all. If she did, she did not introduce herself.

Following the event, I shared a video that Ms Melvin had recorded of a Jewish woman – whose parents are Auschwitz survivors – calling Jewish members of the audience up to the top of the small slope on Regency Square to express solidarity with me. I had no input in any of this. However, I was touched by the support of many Jewish members who came to stand with me. One of those members of the audience was Tony Greenstein. As a politician, I interact in some way with hundreds and sometimes thousands of people every day at meetings and online. It is obviously unreasonable to expect an encyclopaedic knowledge of their biographies and membership status. Nor, in most instances, should such knowledge preclude interaction and debate.

26) Were you aware at the time that you shared a platform with him that Tony Greenstein was expelled from the Labour Party in 2018 for conduct that is prejudicial and/or grossly detrimental to the Party?

Whilst I was aware of Tony Greenstein's expulsion from the Labour Party, it is, as I have already outlined, incorrect to say that I shared a platform with him. I did not attend the event with any expectation that he would be there, or that he would speak at an open mic section of the event.

Nevertheless, as I have stated, what constitutes prejudicial or grossly detrimental conduct is a matter for political interpretation, especially when the disciplinary procedure is consistently used as a political instrument.

27) Do you think it is appropriate for a Labour Party member who is an MP to share a platform with people who have been expelled or auto-excluded from the Labour Party?

Please refer to my responses above. The Labour Party under Jeremy Corbyn is a mass political movement with a broad base. When the disciplinary process is used disproportionately and unfairly, it becomes difficult for any reasonable observer to determine whether expulsion from the Labour Party is a reflection on the individual or on the Party's procedures.

'Auto-expulsion' is a draconian measure for a mass movement that attempts to draw its supporters from a diverse social base, and that attempts to expand rather than contract that base. In my view, it is a measure incompatible with the Labour Party's rhetoric and policies under Jeremy Corbyn.

Further Questions

28) Rule 2.I.8 in the Party's rulebook states:
"No member of the Party shall engage in conduct which in the opinion of the NEC is prejudicial, or in any act which in the opinion of the NEC is grossly detrimental to the Party. The NEC and NCC shall take account of any codes of conduct currently in force and shall regard any incident which in their view might reasonably be seen to demonstrate hostility or prejudice based on age; disability; gender reassignment or identity; marriage and civil partnership; pregnancy and maternity; race; religion or belief; sex; or sexual orientation as conduct prejudicial to the Party: these shall include but not be limited to incidents involving racism, antisemitism, Islamophobia or otherwise racist language, sentiments, stereotypes or actions, sexual harassment, bullying or any form of intimidation towards another person on the basis of a protected characteristic as determined by the NEC, wherever it occurs, as conduct prejudicial to the Party. The disclosure of confidential information relating to the Party or to any other member, unless the disclosure is duly authorised or made pursuant to a legal obligation, shall also be considered conduct prejudicial to the Party."
What is your response to the allegation that your conduct may be or have been in breach of this rule?
I refer you to my submission of 16 April 2019 in which I made clear that I categorically reject breaching Rule 2.1.8 of the Party's Rulebook, and continue to do so in light of the questions put to me in your letter of 3 September 2019. I have never and would never show hostility and/or prejudice to any person on the grounds of a protected characteristic. I am a committed and long-standing member of the Labour Party and have consistently sought to uphold its values and that of the Leader. I have campaigned tirelessly

in support of the Party and its ethos and have never sought to bring the Party into disrepute.

I have been able to provide meaningful and balanced responses that clearly show that I have acted in good faith at all times. In light of the above, I challenge my suspension and the allegations against me.

29) The Party's Code of Conduct: Social Media Policy states that *"treat all people with dignity and respect. This applies offline and online"* **do you think the posts in this pack are consistent with this policy?**

I have not breached the Party's Code of Conduct: Social Media Policy (the Policy) and I treat all people with dignity and respect. Had the Party had serious concerns about my understanding of this, they should have communicated that to me at the time of these perceived breaches of that code, some of which took place in 2016.

30) Looking back at the evidence supplied with this letter, do you regret posting or sharing any of this content?

I always treat people with dignity and respect.

31) Do you intend to post or share content of this nature again in the future?

I will continue defending the Labour Party and its values.

ANNEXES

Annex 1

Interviewer: I asked you in the meeting – we didn't get into too much detail about it, probably because we were quite rushed out there – but I asked you about the role of 'internal pressure groups', they might call them, such as [Jewish Voice for Labour] and [Labour Against the Witch-Hunt]. And the way that there seems to be never-ending guilt-by-association there, and the guilt-by-association leading to internal splits between people that should naturally be working together. And I gave you three examples: the JVL grouping, the LAW grouping – best represented by, perhaps, Tony Greenstein – and the new LAZIR grouping, led by someone called Peter Gregson, as far as I can tell.

Do you think that it's important that we scrutinise these claims and force these groups back together? Because, essentially, the division that's occurring between them is actually leading to a huge amount of resentment in the movement and division there. I mean, do you think we can do more work in that regard?

Chris Williamson: Well, I think it's important to try and work in unity, if and when we can. I mean, obviously, in certain circumstances there's going to be differences of opinion, there's going to be potential splits, and I think having a debate is a healthy thing. You can have healthy disagreements, and that's the nature of democracy.

But I think it is incumbent upon us, really, to try and work together. This is one of the points I was making in a different context to the Parliamentary Labour Party [meeting] a few weeks – or months, now it is – ago, where I was making the case that: 'Look, we're all Labour Party MPs, we all joined the Party – I would like to think – and stood for Parliament to try and promote social justice, an ethical foreign policy, and so on. And, yeah, we're going to have differences of opinion but let's try and find ways of working together'.

So, it's not always going to be possible, and we have to be realistic about that. But I think, wherever we can, all of us, it's incumbent upon us, to do our best to try and work together because that old labour movement maxim about 'Unity is Strength' is absolutely apposite, really. And whenever we are falling out with each other, we're letting, essentially, the Establishment, the powers that be, those that really do wield power in the country – we're letting them off the hook.

Annex 2

Interviewer: Obviously, there's been a lot of debate. And I'm keen to push this further than just the big, public issue of anti-Semitism. I'm keen to push it into real realms and territory of the deal with, say, transphobia and misogyny as well. Because these are all kinds of smears that are used to generate division in the movement. And I don't know if it's deliberate or accidental or what it is. But what do you think the role of definitions are in this, and how important do you think they are?

Chris Williamson: Well, I mean, I think for some people they are important. But, for me, I would just refer back to, I think, a comment that Jeremy [Corbyn] was making the other day, talking about – I don't think he was talking specifically about the point that you've raised – but he was making the distinction between 'tolerance' and 'respect'. And he said it's not just about tolerating different people, backgrounds, faiths, whatever – it's about respecting people. And I think if we can embrace that notion of respect, I think that would take us a long way down the road of moving the movement on and avoiding some of these unseemly fall-outs that we've seen, which has scarred the movement over the last two years.

Interviewer: So, I mean, would it be correct to characterise you as somebody who thinks that definitions aren't really that substantially important?

Chris Williamson: [Sighs audibly] I mean, I don't know whether I've thought about it that deeply. To be honest with you, my view is that we should respect people, we shouldn't judge people, and I think if you can have a kind of non-judgemental attitude and you can respect people, then I think that will carry you a long way in terms of avoiding some of the difficulties that we've found ourselves in over the last few years or so.

Interviewer: Well, non-judgemental is a little bit of a step back from what the movement has to do, isn't it? Doesn't the movement, at some point, have to say, 'This person's crossed a line' in some cases?

Chris Williamson: Well, maybe, yeah, true. As I say, there will be certain circumstances. But, I mean, people who join the movement, you'd generally like to think they are like-minded people. They join because they want to fight for social justice, they want to bring about an ethical foreign policy on the international stage.

But, yes, sometimes people potentially do step over the line; that is why you have rules in the Party to deal with that. But they should be used sparingly, in my view, and not be the first port of call to suggest that people be expelled or whatever. Because sometimes people articulate in certain ways that it's more through ignorance, really, than malice.

And I think this notion of trying to understand and then trying to work with people – and to have a collective, supportive approach, rather than judging people and calling people out in that very overt way sometimes. Particularly with social media these days, there's this sense of quick-to-judge and dogpile and demonise people when they may have made a foolish comment – and it's fine to call them out for that – but work with people, try and help people to grow!

I remember speaking to a young person, who's very active in the Labour Party now, but they were saying – coming from a working-class background – and they were saying, initially, when they first started taking an interest in things, they were initially attracted by the kind of far-right rhetoric. And it was only through talking to others, and there was a local Labour councillor who got involved with the local boxing club where he was a member and started some of the political discussions and raising consciousness that he realised the error of his ways.

But if you were to just demonise that individual, we may have lost him forever. And he's a great man – I wouldn't name the guy – but he's a hugely important figure, in my opinion, in his own constituency and has made a massive contribution. And there'll be thousands of people, millions of people potentially, like that out there. We need to be building this movement in all its diversity and bringing people in, rather than trying to keep people out.

Annex 3

Chris Williamson: I think there are a range of probable definitions [for a 'trope']; I don't want to necessarily hazard my own. I know it's a term that's used. I don't think it's a particularly helpful term, to be honest with you. And I think if you spoke to a lot of people throughout the country – working class, middle class, you name it – if you speak to a range of different people, I think a lot of people would be not quite sure what that is, either. And so, I think it's really important that we're clear with our language and we don't use jargoney terms.

NOTES

CHAPTER ONE – THE STARTING GUN

1 Conor Burns, 'Margaret Thatcher's greatest achievement: New Labour' (11 April 2008) *Conservative Home* <https://archive.ph/fWZU3> [Accessed March 2022].

2 Hansard, 'Debate on the Address, Volume 510' *UK Parliament* (25 May 2010) <https://archive.ph/DLRax> and <https://archive.ph/Aw9NV> [Accessed April 2022].

3 Kevin Schofield, 'Fifteen former Labour MPs take out newspaper advert urging voters to reject Jeremy Corbyn' *Politics Home* (10 December 2019) <https://archive.ph/0Up9C > [Accessed April 2022].

4 Wikipedia, '2010 Labour Party leadership election (UK)' *Wikipedia* <https://archive.ph/2G06E> [Accessed April 2022].

5 Patrick Wintour, Hugh Muir and Rowena Mason, 'Diane Abbott sacked by Ed Miliband in Labour reshuffle' *Guardian* (8 October 2013) <https://archive.ph/7TInl> [Accessed March 2022].

6 Richard Murphy, 'Michael Meacher MP discusses his Bill for a stronger UK GAAR in International Tax Review' *Tax Research UK* (19 September 2012) <https://archive.ph/GVBFI> [Accessed April 2022].

7 BBC News, 'Ex-Home Secretary Johnson is named shadow chancellor' *BBC News* (8 October 2010) <https://archive.ph/W5U9> [Accessed March 2022].

8 International Monetary Fund, 'World Economic Outlook: Coping with High Debt and Sluggish Growth' *IMF* (October 2012) <http://web.archive.org/web/20220306090818/https://www.imf.org/en/Publications/WEO/Issues/2016/12/31/Coping-with-High-Debt-and-Sluggish-Growth> [Accessed March 2022].

9 Nichola Watt, Patrick Wintour and Vikram Dodd, 'Alan Johnson resigns as shadow chancellor' *Guardian* (21 January 2011) <https://archive.ph/j7xd5> [Accessed April 2022].

10 Hansard, 'Comprehensive Spending Review, Volume 516' *UK Parliament* (20 October 2010) <https://archive.ph/2FfDy> [Accessed April 2022].

11 BBC News, 'Ex-Home Secretary Johnson is named shadow chancellor' *BBC News* (18 January 2012) <https://archive.ph/0ctht> [Accessed April 2022].

12 Tony Bonsignore, 'I was wrong to let the banks off the leash, Gordon Brown admits' *Citywire* (14 April 2010) <https://archive.ph/i26Ki> [Accessed April 2022].

13 David Blanchflower, 'The choice is yours – Balls and Bernanke, or Slasher' *New Statesman* (2 September 2010) <https://archive.ph/OWpdO> [Accessed April 2022].

14 Nigel Morris, 'Miliband turns his fire on the Chancellor for cutting "too far and too fast"' *Independent* (24 March 2011) <https://archive.ph/Hk24B> [Accessed April 2022].

15 Channel 4 News, 'Miliband defends policy on public sector pay' *Channel 4 News* (17 January 2012) <https://archive.ph/lSmH1> [Accessed April 2022].

16 Roisin O'Connor, 'Rachel Reeves says Labour does not want to represent people out of work' *Independent* (17 March 2015) < https://archive.ph/s2G64 > [Accessed March 2022].

17 Patrick Wintour, 'Labour commits to abolishing bedroom tax' *Guardian* (20 September 2013) <https://archive.ph/2chit> [Accessed April 2022].

18 Wendy Wilson, 'Housing Benefit: under-occupation in the private rented sector' (4887 House of Commons Library Briefing Paper) (9 June 2017), p. 3.

19 Hansard, 'Orders of the Day, Volume 149' *UK Parliament* (21 March 1989) <https://archive.ph/BbNkY> [Accessed April 2022].

20 Labour Party, 'For the Many Not the Few: The Labour Party Manifesto 2017' (Labour Party 2017), p. 62.

21 House of Commons, 'Register of Members' Financial Interests' *Stationery Office* (13 January 2012) <http://web.archive.org/web/20210918182325/https://publications.parliament.uk/pa/cm/cmregmem/1782/1782.pdf> [Accessed April 2022].

NOTES

22 James Ball and Harry Davies, 'Labour received £600,000 of advice from PwC to help form tax policy' *Guardian* (12 November 2014) <https://archive.ph/s1xIt> [Accessed April 2022].

23 Tom Warren and Ted Jeory, 'Labour's mystery £600k donor Martin Taylor revealed as Mayfair hedge funder' *Bureau of Investigative Journalism* (20 March 2015) <https://archive.ph/KC9kk> [Accessed March 2022].

24 Solomon Hughes, '£276,000 a year for chairing ISS – the company that wouldn't pay its NHS cleaners on time' *Morning Star* (17 April 2020) <https://archive.ph/YoLkc> [Accessed April 2022].

25 Nicholas Watt, 'Ed Miliband brings in former ITV chief to review Labour structures' *Guardian* (1 August 2011) <https://archive.ph/3bpmY> [Accessed April 2022].

26 House of Lords, 'Lord Allen of Kensington' *UK Parliament* <https://archive.ph/FJ7jx> [Accessed April 2022].

27 Co-operative Party, 'Annual Conference 2013: Housing Policy Paper' *Cooperative Party* (2013) <http://web.archive.org/web/20211020033806/https://party.coop/publication/housing-2/> [Accessed March 2022].

28 Defend Council Housing, 'Hands off our homes: invest in council housing' *DCH* (September 2011) <http://web.archive.org/web/20210227081831/http://www.defendcouncilhousing.org.uk/dch/resources/DCHNewspaperSept2011.pdf> [Accessed April 2022].

29 Dave Hill, 'Ken Livingstone, private landlords and the "London living rent"' *Guardian* (15 December 2011) <https://archive.ph/ZArZO> [Accessed April 2022].

30 Jules Birch, 'Letting Go' *Inside Housing* (9 July 2012) <https://archive.ph/ZhIVs> [Accessed April 2022].

31 Robert Philpot (eds), *The Purple Book: A Progressive Future for Labour* (Biteback Publishing 2011).

32 Ibid, p. 200–214.

33 Michael Meacher, 'Be honest, Labour modernisers. These are failed Tory ideas' *Guardian* (20 September 2011) <https://archive.ph/Aoksr> [Accessed April 2022].

34 Peter Edwards, 'Labour donor Lord Sainsbury also funded Lib Dems as part of EU campaign' *LabourList* (26 August 2016) <https://archive.ph/h3C7W> [Accessed April 2022].

35 Solomon Hughes, 'How billionaire Lord Sainsbury bankrolled the birth of New Labour' *Morning Star* (1 September 2016) <https://archive.ph/lbB91> [Accessed April 2022].

36 Kayte Rath, 'New Labour group Progress rejects GMB union 'outlaw' threat' *BBC News* (15 June 2012) < https://archive.ph/mESUU> [Accessed March 2022].

CHAPTER TWO – NEW LABOUR'S GHOST

1 Vladimir Lenin, 'Lenin's Speech on Affiliation to the British Labour Party: The Second Congress of the Communist International – July 19-August 7, 1920' *Marxist* <https://archive.ph/QYE68> [Accessed March 2022].

2 Child Poverty Action Group, 'Welfare Reform Act 2012' *CPAG* (1 April 2012) <http://web.archive.org/web/20220120233536/https://cpag.org.uk/welfare-rights/resources/article/welfare-reform-act-2012> [Accessed April 2022].

3 Hansard, 'Immigration: Visitors, Volume 702' *UK Parliament* (25 June 2008) <https://archive.ph/x4gN2> [Accessed April 2022].

4 Shiv Malik, 'Graduate's Poundland victory leaves government work schemes in tatters' *Guardian* (12 February 2013) <https://archive.ph/0PAft> [Accessed April 2022].

5 Liam Byrne, 'The Jobseekers Bill is difficult for Labour – but I think we've made the right call' *LabourList* (21 March 2013) <https://archive.ph/iRyvC> [Accessed April 2022].

NOTES

6. Fire Brigades Union, 'Facing Reality – The need for a fully-funded fire and rescue service' *FBU* (June 2013) <http://web.archive.org/web/20220407023109/https://www.southwestfbu.com/sites/default/files/documents/9492%20FBU%20FACING%20REALITY%20LOW%20RES.pdf> [Accessed April 2022].
7. Barry Neild, 'Margaret Thatcher's death greeted with street parties in Brixton and Glasgow' *Guardian* (8 April 2013) <https://archive.ph/qS9IR> [Accessed April 2022].
8. Hansard, 'Tributes to Baroness Thatcher, Volume 560' *UK Parliament* (10 April 2013) <https://archive.ph/fqQpb> [Accessed April 2022].
9. Ibid.
10. Hansard, 'Firefighters (Industrial Action), Volume 517' *UK Parliament* (26 October 2010) <https://archive.ph/5rrae> [Accessed April 2022].
11. Victoria Richards, 'Ed Miliband condemns suggested strike action' *Sunday Times* (16 January 2011) <https://archive.ph/QqWDO> [Accessed March 2022].
12. BBC News, 'Ed Miliband: "These strikes are wrong"' *BBC News* (30 June 2011) <www.bbc.co.uk/news/av/uk-politics-13971770> [Accessed April 2022].
13. Patrick Wintour, 'Tom Watson resigns from shadow cabinet' *Guardian* (4 July 2013) <https://archive.ph/jdMIg> [Accessed April 2022].
14. Chris Williamson, 'Is this the next public service in line for Tory privatisation?' *LabourList* (25 March 2013) <https://archive.ph/RpRF8> [Accessed April 2022].
15. Chris Williamson, *Twitter* (20 December 2020) <https://archive.ph/L1qgT> [Accessed March 2022].
16. Guardian, 'Libya military action' *Guardian* (18 March 2011) <https://archive.ph/Ue7DR> [Accessed April 2022].
17. Amy Hamdy, 'Survey of ICT and Education in Africa: Libya Country Report' *infoDev* (June 2007) <http://web.archive.org/web/20220215111755/https://www.infodev.org/infodev-files/resource/InfodevDocuments_412.pdf> [Accessed April 2022], p. 2.
18. Datablog, 'Human development index: Equality matters if we are to reduce poverty' *Guardian* (4 November 2010) <https://archive.ph/un01A> [Accessed April 2022].
19. United Nations Development Programme, 'Human Development Report 2020 – The next frontier: Human development and the Anthropocene' (2020) <http://web.archive.org/web/20220330123421/https://hdr.undp.org/sites/default/files/hdr2020.pdf> [Accessed April 2022], p. 242.
20. Hansard, 'Iraq: Coalition Against ISIL, Volume 585' *UK Parliament* (26 September 2014) <https://archive.ph/E3PgG> [Accessed April 2022].
21. Hansard, 'Iraq: Coalition Against ISIL, Division 53' *UK Parliament* (26 September 2014) <https://archive.ph/rWqZE> [Accessed April 2022].
22. AFP, 'Iraqi fighters mourn comrades killed in US strikes' *France 24* (29 June 2021) <https://archive.ph/7prQh> [Accessed April 2022].

CHAPTER THREE – "RED ED"?

1. Paul Hunter, 'Winning back the 5 million – understanding the fragmentation of Labour's vote' *Smith Institute* (February 2011) <http://web.archive.org/web/20210225053353/http://www.smith-institute.org.uk/wp-content/uploads/2015/10/Winning-back-the-5-million.pdf> [Accessed March 2022].
2. Patrick Wintour and Tim Webb, 'Peter Mandelson abandons plan for part-privatisation of Royal Mail' *Guardian* (1 July 2009) <https://archive.ph/3MYsY> [Accessed April 2022].
3. Peter Kellner, 'Is rail nationalisation a vote-winner?' *YouGov* (21 September 2015) <https://archive.ph/ETzZX> [Accessed April 2022].
4. Rail Technology Magazine, 'Labour pledges franchising review in manifesto' *Rail Technology Magazine* (13 April 2015) <http://web.archive.org/web/20210629090507/https://www.railtechnologymagazine.com/Rail-News/labour-pledges-franchising-review-in-manifesto> [Accessed April 2022].

NOTES

5 Labour Party, 'Review of Education Structures, Functions and the Raising of Standards for All' (2014) <http://web.archive.org/web/20220123163450/https://www.yourbritain.org.uk/uploads/editor/files/Putting_Students_and_Parents_First.pdf> [Accessed April 2022].

6 Nicky Morgan, 'Educational excellence everywhere' *UK Government* (17 March 2016) <https://archive.ph/HfRCB> [Accessed April 2022].

7 BBC News, 'Tuition fees: Labour pledges maximum cap of £6,000' *BBC News* (25 September 2011) <https://archive.ph/E2Hz> [Accessed March 2022].

8 BBC News, 'PMQs: David Cameron criticises shadow chancellor Ed Balls' *BBC News* (30 March 2011) <https://archive.ph/t8tlz> [Accessed April 2022].

9 Board of Deputies of British Jews, 'The Board of Deputies launches its Ten Pledges for Labour leadership and deputy leadership candidates' *BoD* (13 January 2020) <https://archive.ph/IHISj> [Accessed March 2022].

10 BBC News, 'Ed Balls launches Twitter attack on ex MP Chris Williamson' *BBC News* (13 January 2020) <https://archive.ph/hK00S> [Accessed April 2022].

11 Tom Harris, 'Is Scotland on the right track? More or less…' *Third Avenue* (20 August 2018) <https://archive.ph/YnEFG> [Accessed April 2022].

12 Doug Bolton, 'Arnie Graf: Labour was so out of touch it 'didn't know a single worker on the minimum wage', says Miliband's former campaign adviser' *Independent* (4 August 2015) <https://archive.ph/f6TRt> [Accessed April 2022].

13 BBC Newsnight, 'Jeremy Corbyn makes his pitch for Labour leadership – BBC Newsnight' *YouTube* (8 June 2015) <www.youtube.com/watch?v=q-gJD6PvUOo> [Accessed April 2022].

14 Sky News, 'Ed Balls: I Hope To Toast Victory In Labour's 'Immigration' Mug" *Sky News* (31 March 2015) <http://web.archive.org/web/20201101011246/https://news.sky.com/video/ed-balls-i-hope-to-toast-victory-in-labours-immigration-mug-10365510> [Accessed April 2022].

15 BBC Newsnight, 'Ed Balls on Jeremy Corbyn, Owen Smith and the future of the Labour – BBC Newsnight' *YouTube* (22 September 2016) <www.youtube.com/watch?v=GGtHm7gTdnA> [Accessed April 2022].

16 Labour Party, 'A Better Future for Britain: The Labour Party Manifesto 2015' (Labour Party 2015), p. 14.

17 Ibid, p. 26.

18 Ibid, p. 25.

19 LabourList, '15 Labour MPs release statement calling for change in party policy direction' *LabourList* (26 January 2015) <https://archive.ph/E611K> [Accessed March 2022].

20 Labour Party, 'Ed Miliband – Leadership 2010' *YouTube* (14 July 2010) <www.youtube.com/watch?v=h-4fVGlj9F4> [Accessed April 2022].

21 Paul Goodman, 'CCHQ gets the result it wanted – Red Ed, the mouthpiece of the unions' *Conservative Home* (25 September 2010) <https://archive.ph/4rBZ1> [Accessed April 2022].

CHAPTER FOUR – A DISASTER WAITING TO HAPPEN

1 BBC News, 'Miliband comes to defence of squeezed middle' *BBC News* (26 November 2010) <https://archive.ph/U9NRB> [Accessed April 2022].

2 BBC News, 'The Big Tent' *BBC News* (28 September 1999) <https://archive.ph/xUwxZ> [Accessed April 2022].

3 BBC News, 'Profile: John Prescott' *BBC News* (27 August 2007) <https://archive.ph/odQno> [Accessed April 2022].

4 NatCen Social Research, 'Most people in Britain today regard themselves working class' *University of Oxford* (30 June 2016) <https://archive.ph/io5bd> [Accessed April 2022].

NOTES

5 Geoffrey Evans and Jonathan Mellon, 'The Re-shaping Of Class Voting' *British Election Study* (6 March 2020) <https://archive.ph/Dy2tr> [Accessed April 2022].

6 WalesOnline, 'Peter Hain: Labour can win next election by exploiting Lib Dem divisions' *WalesOnline* (28 September 2011) <https://archive.ph/0OjM3> [Accessed April 2022].

7 Bryn Morgan, 'General Election results, 7 June 2001' (01/54 House of Commons Library Research Paper) (18 June 2001) <https://web.archive.org/web/20220221062458/https://researchbriefings.files.parliament.uk/documents/RP01-54/RP01-54.pdf> [Accessed April 2022], p. 6 and p. 17.

8 BBC News, 'Election 2010: National Results' *BBC News* <https://archive.ph/LNa1> [Accessed April 2022].

9 Brian Wheeler, 'Ed Miliband tells Labour conference: We're the one-nation party' *BBC News* (2 October 2012) <https://archive.ph/cINMF> [Accessed April 2022].

10 Portland Communications, 'Labour Party Conference – the 35% strategy' *Portland Communications* (26 September 2014) <https://archive.ph/8fqFx> [Accessed April 2022].

11 Sky News, '#EdStone – Reaction To Labour's Election Pledges' *YouTube* (3 May 2015) <www.youtube.com/watch?v=cw0NOk3Hyqg> [Accessed September 2021].

12 George Eaton, 'Labour's manifesto: who's writing it and what happens next' *New Statesman* (2 February 2015) <https://archive.ph/rouO1> [Accessed April 2022].

13 Toby Helm, 'Jon Cruddas: this could be the greatest crisis the Labour party has ever faced' *Guardian* (16 May 2015) <https://archive.ph/XAwmT> [Accessed April 2022].

14 'Labour's campaign team gets a shake up' *LabourList* (3 July 2014) <https://archive.ph/5bSv6> [Accessed April 2022].

15 Patrick Wintour, 'Revealed: Labour party's general election campaign war room' *Guardian* (10 April 2015) <https://archive.ph/rj3Wn> [Accessed April 2022].

16 Kate Allen, 'Miliband's 'Edstone' turns into a £20,000 grave error for Labour' *Financial Times* (25 October 2016) <https://archive.ph/2sP0E> [Accessed April 2022].

17 Channel 4 News, 'Labour entryists: the left activists joining to back Corbyn' *Channel 4 News* (7 August 2015) <https://web.archive.org/web/20201215104641/www.channel4.com/news/corbyn-is-a-game-changer-for-the-left> [Accessed April 2022].

18 Common Decency, 'Home' *Common Decency* <https://archive.ph/CZ6Al> [Accessed April 2022].

CHAPTER FIVE – ATTACK OF THE GAMMONS

1 Jack Blanchard, 'Tony Blair begs Labour members whose heart is with Jeremy Corbyn to "get a transplant"' *Mirror* (22 July 2015) <https://archive.ph/9qztR> [Accessed April 2022].

2 Lisa Nandy, 'Labour cannot pick and choose what type of racism to confront' *Financial Times* (29 June 2019) <https://archive.ph/bh0Pv> [Accessed April 2022].

3 John Vidal, 'Michael Meacher: an environment minister who stood up for his beliefs' *Ecologist* (22 October 2015) <https://archive.ph/VusPZ> [Accessed April 2022].

4 Rosa Prince, 'Eric Pickles tells councils to stop "pleading poverty" and start spending £20 Billion in reserves' *Daily Telegraph* (26 December 2014) <https://archive.ph/Q5R9m> [Accessed April 2022].

5 BBC News, 'Derby school support staff deal collapses' *BBC News* (16 September 2017) <https://archive.ph/wFQNt> [Accessed April 2022].

6 Zena Hawley, 'Bitter dispute over fair pay that led to strike action and months of disruption for parents finally ends' *Derby Telegraph* (24 May 2018) <https://archive.ph/mZaCS> [Accessed April 2022].

7 Hansard, 'Petition, Volume 554' *UK Parliament* (28 November 2012) <https://archive.ph/kA7w8> [Accessed April 2022].

NOTES

8 Jeremy Corbyn, 'Defence Diversification' *Jeremy for Labour* (August 2015) <https://web.archive.org/web/20210309003440/https://d3n8a8pro7vhmx.cloudfront.net/jeremyforlabour/pages/111/attachments/original/1439209889/DefenceDiversification.pdf> [Accessed April 2022].

9 Nuclear Education Trust, 'Defence Diversification: International learning for Trident jobs' *Nuclear Education Trust* (June 2018) <https://web.archive.org/web/20220304125352/http://www.nucleareducationtrust.org/sites/default/files/NET%20Defence%20Diversification%20%20%20%20Report.pdf> [Accessed April 2022].

10 Brian Salisbury, 'Story of the Lucas Plan' *Lucas Plan* <https://archive.ph/jfJr5> [Accessed April 2022].

11 Aaron Bastani and Charlotte England, 'Tim Roache Resigned Amid Allegations of Sexual Assault, Cover up and a 'Casting Couch' Culture at GMB' *Novara Media* (1 May 2020) <https://archive.ph/ftLEx> [Accessed March 2022].

12 Luke Bailey, 'John Woodcock MP quits Labour Party, claiming sexual harassment investigation has been "manipulated"' *i-News* (18 July 2018) <https://archive.ph/M2KNc> [Accessed March 2022].

13 Rob Merrick, 'Boris Johnson orders probe into 'far-left hijacking' of Black Lives Matter and Extinction Rebellion' *Independent* (8 February 2021) <https://archive.ph/lj6ms> [Accessed March 2022].

CHAPTER SIX – A VERY AMATEURISH COUP

1 Iain Watson, 'Elections 2016: What Jeremy Corbyn has to do to survive' *BBC News* (5 April 2021) <https://archive.ph/5nr7H> [Accessed March 2022].

2 Jessica Elgot, 'EU referendum live' *Guardian* (13 June 2016) <https://archive.ph/qP8uh> [Accessed March 2022].

3 'Which way did you vote in the Brexit referendum?' *Statista Research Department* (24 June 2016) <https://archive.ph/eVEuF> [Accessed March 2022].

4 Nick Clark, 'Thousands demonstrate to support Corbyn' *Socialist Worker* (28 June 2016) <https://archive.ph/Zqc7T> [Accessed March 2022].

5 BBC News, 'Labour MPs pass no-confidence motion in Jeremy Corbyn' *BBC News* (28 June 2016) <https://archive.ph/ZNIYy> [Accessed April 2022].

6 Conor Pope, 'Heated PLP meeting spills out into Commons corridors' *LabourList* (27 June 2016) <https://archive.ph/C9sUH> [Accessed March 2022].

7 'The Parliamentary Labour Party has behaved abominably' *Morning Star* (18 July 2016) <https://archive.ph/UWP0L> [Accessed March 2022].

8 Kevin Maguire, 'Commons Confidential: Bring back our vegan brickie' *New Statesman* (29 May 2015) <https://archive.ph/HXG1x> [Accessed March 2022].

9 Karl Turner, *Twitter* (21 August 2016) <https://archive.ph/r1XIk> [Accessed March 2022].

10 Karl Turner, *Twitter* (21 August 2016) <https://archive.ph/TS5WH> [Accessed March 2022].

11 John Dunn, 'Owen, Owen Gone!' *Labour Briefing* (27 August 2016) <https://archive.ph/EfaMi> [Accessed March 2022].

12 Aaron Bastani, 'Labour Official Who Undermined Party and Mocked Staff Was in Running for General Secretary Under Starmer' *Novara Media* (17 April 2020) <https://archive.ph/7yCDQ> [Accessed March 2022].

13 Alex Nunns, *The Candidate: Jeremy Corbyn's Improbable Path to Power* (OR Books 2016), p. 323.

14 Stephen Bush, 'What Labour's plotters are thinking' *New Statesman* (26 June 2016) <https://archive.is/ikCp1> [Accessed March 2022].

15 Conor Pope, 'Shock victory in High Court as Labour members overturn January freeze date' *LabourList* (8 August 2016) <https://archive.ph/FI2EY> [Accessed March 2022].

NOTES

16 Ibid.

17 Julia Rampen, 'Labour wins bid to exclude 130,000 new members from the leadership contest' *New Statesman* (12 August 2016) <https://archive.ph/R5UFN> [Accessed March 2022].

18 Steve Walker, 'BBC figures show AT LEAST 121,000 ELIGIBLE voters denied their vote' *Skwawkbox* (21 September 2016) <https://archive.ph/gllO5> [Accessed March 2022].

19 Luke Morgan Britton, 'Labour Party suspend member over "inappropriate" Foo Fighters post' *NME* (26 August 2016) <https://archive.ph/5YTRB> [Accessed April 2022].

CHAPTER SEVEN – REALITY CHECK

1 'Tony Blair, 'My job was to build on some Thatcher policies' *BBC News* (8 April 2013) <https://archive.ph/Acow9> [Accessed April 2022].

2 Labour Party, 'Labour Party Manifesto 1974' *Archive of Labour Party Manifestos* <https://archive.ph/BSx2> [Accessed March 2022].

3 Bill Mitchell, 'The British Cabinet divides over the IMF negotiations in 1976' *Bilbo Blog* (8 June 2016) <https://archive.ph/fVsYT> [Accessed March 2022].

4 Ian Aitken, 'Bulldozer Healey tramples on left' *Guardian* (1 October 1976) <https://archive.ph/wUMel> [Accessed March 2022].

5 Joe Moran, 'Defining Moment: Denis Healey agrees to the demands of the IMF' *Financial Times* (4 September 2010) <https://archive.ph/fcPWG> [Accessed March 2022].

6 Ed Miliband – 'Ed Miliband – Leadership 2010' *YouTube* (14 July 2010) <www.youtube.com/watch?v=h-4fVGlj9F4> [Accessed March 2022].

7 Patrick Wintour, 'Andy Burnham apologises for Labour overspending before credit crunch' *Guardian* (13 July 2015) <https://archive.ph/keAPi> [Accessed March 2022].

8 Carlos García Hernández, 'Fiat Socialism' *Gower Initiative for Modern Money Studies* (1 March 2019) <https://archive.ph/WbYTt> [Accessed March 2022].

9 The MMT Podcast, 'Chris Williamson and Bill Mitchell: MMT And The Labour Party' *MMT Podcast* (September 2019) <https://web.archive.org/web/20220418073910/https://podcasts.apple.com/us/podcast/31-chris-williamson-bill-mitchell-mmt-labour-party/id1375093518?i=1000450947261> [Accessed March 2022].

10 John McDonnell, *Twitter* (31 May 2017) <https://archive.ph/OHNd4> [Accessed April 2022].

11 Susan Ratcliffe (eds), 'Margaret Thatcher 1925–2013' in *Oxford Essential Quotations* (4th edn, OUP 2016).

12 David Osland, 'Lord Sugar's promise to leave the UK if Corbyn is PM shows he is oblivious to the interests of the working class' *Independent* (15 December 2018) <https://archive.ph/qawad> [Accessed April 2022].

13 Richard Murphy, 'The political economy of People's Quantitative Easing' *Tax Research UK* (17 August 2015) <https://archive.ph/kEt20> [Accessed April 2022].

14 Stephanie Kelton, *The Deficit Myth: Modern Monetary Theory and How to Build a Better Economy* (Public Affairs 2020).

15 Bill Mitchell, 'A summary of my meeting with John McDonnell in London' *Bilbo Blog* (17 October 2018) <https://archive.ph/FOrkC> [Accessed April 2022].

16 Jonathan Reynolds, 'Why Labour doesn't support Modern Monetary Theory' *LabourList* (4 June 2019) <https://archive.ph/lopYJ> [Accessed April 2022].

17 Chris Williamson, 'The economic virtuous circle at the centre of MMT' *Morning Star* (7 June 2019) <https://archive.ph/oYoCQ> [Accessed April 2022].

18 Labour Party, 'Labour's Fiscal Credibility Rule 2018' *Labour Party* <https://web.archive.org/web/20220119202721/https://labour.org.uk/wp-content/uploads/2017/10/Fiscal-Credibility-Rule.pdf> [Accessed April 2022].

NOTES

19. Martin Wolf, 'Summer Books 2020' *Financial Times* (23 June 2020) <https://archive.ph/CgQIT> [Accessed April 2022].
20. Ned Sherrin, *Oxford Dictionary of Humorous Quotations* (4th edn, OUP 2008), p. 257.
21. Patrick Wintour, 'GMB leader says unions will support new voting system for Labour leader' *Guardian* (30 January 2014) <https://archive.ph/H3ofP> [Accessed April 2022].
22. BBC News, 'Labour presses on with ,one member, one vote' leadership reforms' *BBC News* (30 January 2014) <https://archive.ph/1pBuP> [Accessed April 2022].
23. Chris Wimpress, 'Eric Joyce MP Arrested After Headbutting A Tory During Commons Bar Fight' *HuffPost* (23 February 2012) <https://archive.ph/GZz8W> [Accessed April 2022].
24. Paul Cheston, 'Commons headbutt MP banned from all pubs in UK' *Evening Standard* (9 March 2012) <https://archive.ph/cW3Py> [Accessed April 2022].
25. Rajeev Syal, 'Falkirk Labour hopeful admits paying for mass recruitment to party' *Guardian* (13 November 2013) <https://archive.ph/2oriv> [Accessed April 2022].
26. Michael Settle, 'Miliband calls in police over union conduct in Falkirk seat' *Herald* (6 July 2013) <https://archive.ph/cz9x6> [Accessed April 2022].
27. Press Association, 'Falkirk ballot row: insufficient grounds for criminal inquiry, say police' *Guardian* (25 July 2013) <https://archive.ph/rt8Ma> [Accessed April 2022].
28. Ray Collins, 'Building A One Nation Labour Party: The Collins Review Into Labour Party Reform' *Labour Party* (February 2014) <https://web.archive.org/web/20210506193856/https://b.3cdn.net/labouruk/a84a677f479406989c_p0m6b5w60.pdf> [Accessed April 2022].
29. 'Ed Miliband speech on the union link – full text' *LabourList* (9 July 2013) <https://archive.ph/bYUTd> [Accessed April 2022].
30. Ray Collins, 'Building A One Nation Labour Party' (n 28).
31. Rowena Mason and Jessica Elgot, 'Peter Mandelson: I try to undermine Jeremy Corbyn "every single day"' *Guardian* (21 February 2017) <https://archive.ph/XfCPQ> [Accessed April 2022].
32. Ralph Miliband, *Parliamentary Socialism: A Study in the Politics of Labour* (first published 1961, Merlin Press 2009), p. 27.

CHAPTER EIGHT – MANUFACTURING A "CRISIS"

1. Asa Winstanley, '4 reasons the "anti-Semitism" attacks on Jeremy Corbyn are dishonest' *Electronic Intifada* (19 August 2015) <https://archive.ph/QR9Ga> [Accessed March 2022].
2. Jon Schwarz, 'New Labour Party Leader Jeremy Corbyn Faces Special Guilt-By-Association Standard' *Intercept* (12 September 2015) <https://archive.ph/cBhok> [Accessed March 2022].
3. BBC News, 'Jeremy Corbyn victory: Reaction in quotes' *BBC News* (12 September 2015) <https://archive.ph/4vXFc> [Accessed April 2022].
4. Editor, 'Co-Chair Of OULC Resigns Over Their Endorsement Of Israeli Apartheid Week' *Oxford Student* (15 February 2016) <https://archive.ph/XXgwG> [Accessed April 2022].
5. Aftab Ali, 'Oxford University Labour Club co-chair, Alex Chalmers, resigns amid anti-Semitism row' *Independent* (17 February 2016) <https://archive.ph/imnlQ> [Accessed March 2022].
6. Jamie Stern-Weiner, 'Jeremy Corbyn hasn't got an 'antisemitism problem. His opponents do' *Open Democracy* (27 April 2016) <https://archive.ph/PlrPr> [Accessed March 2022].]
7. Benjamin Salmon, Oxford University's Labour Club Accused Of "Having A Problem With Jews"' *HuffPost* (17 February 2016) <https://archive.ph/MVcg2> [Accessed April 2022].

NOTES

8 World Union of Jewish Students, 'Hasbara Handbook: Promoting Israel on Campus' *WUJS* (March 2002) <https://web.archive.org/web/20220127180357/https://www.middle-east-info.org/take/wujshasbara.pdf> [Accessed April 2022].

9 Paul Waugh, 'Fresh Row Over Labour Anti-Semitism Inquiry As Unite Official Raises Links To Labour Friends Of Israel' *HuffPost* (8 March 2016) <https://archive.ph/Q86OW> [Accessed May 2022].

10 Janet Royall, 'Allegations of anti-Semitism Oxford University Labour Club' *Labour Party* (May 2016) <https://web.archive.org/web/20201024032308/https://antisemitism.org/wp-content/uploads/2016/08/Royall-Report.pdf> [Accessed April 2022], p. 10.

11 Oxford Student, 'Oxford Labour Club Condemns Chris Williamson MP For Anti-Semitism' *Oxford Student* (23 December 2018) <https://archive.ph/cwosO> [Accessed April 2022].

12 Shami Chakrabarti, 'Report: The Shami Chakrabarti Inquiry' *Labour Party* (30 June 2016) <https://web.archive.org/web/20210830050821/https://labour.org.uk/wp-content/uploads/2017/10/Chakrabarti-Inquiry-Report-30June16.pdf> [Accessed April 2022], p. 2.

13 Ibid, p. 1.

14 Georgie Keate, 'Chakrabarti "ignored antisemitism problems"' *Times* (8 August 2016) <https://archive.ph/RdGpD> [Accessed April 2022].

15 Jewish Chronicle, 'Anger as Labour leader Jeremy Corbyn hands Shami Chakrabarti a peerage' *Jewish Chronicle* (4 August 2016) <https://archive.ph/fOvmR> [Accessed April 2022].

16 BBC News, 'Punctuation protest against far right trolls on Twitter' *BBC News* (8 June 2016) <https://archive.ph/NPKRm> [Accessed April 2022].

17 BBC News, 'Ken Livingstone: Jeremy Corbyn announces new investigation' *BBC News* (5 April 2017) <https://archive.ph/12boZ> [Accessed April 2022].

18 PR Week, 'Ex-Hoon adviser lands top lobbying role at EDS' *PR Week* (8 June 2006) <https://archive.ph/6RK8B> [Accessed April 2022].

19 Ibid.

20 'ATLAS Consortium proud to be chosen as preferred bidder by the Ministry of Defence for the Defence Information Infrastructure (Future) project' *Fujitsu Press Release* (2 March 2005) <https://archive.ph/QU6TQ> [Accessed April 2022].

21 Kenneth Gilpin, 'EDS Wins Record $7 Billion Contract for Navy Computer Network' *New York Times* (7 October 2000) <https://archive.ph/bk8fJ> [Accessed April 2022].

22 John-Paul Kamath, 'EDS wins $1 billion Shell IT contract' *Computer Weekly* (1 April 2008) <https://archive.ph/kBrfr> [Accessed April 2022].

23 Jamie Stern-Weiner, 'The American Jewish scholar behind Labour's 'antisemitism' scandal breaks his silence' *Open Democracy* (3 May 2016) <https://archive.ph/VlXod> [Accessed March 2022].

24 Michael Dugher, *Twitter* (28 May 2016) <https://archive.ph/Lkj5c> [Accessed March 2022].

25 Caroline Mortimer, 'Anti-Semitism row: Momentum organiser Jackie Walker readmitted to Labour party following racism allegations' *Independent* (28 May 2016) <https://archive.ph/edPAc> [Accessed March 2022].

26 Nicholas Mairs, 'Former Labour vice chair Michael Dugher to quit party over "institutional anti-Semitism"' *Politics Home* (17 February 2019) <https://archive.ph/ZrtXd> [Accessed April 2022].

27 Robert Philpot, 'Labour was "catastrophic" on Israel, says shadow cabinet member Michael Dugher' *Jewish Chronicle* (27 May 2015) <https://archive.ph/mgtaN> [Accessed March 2022].

28 Hansard, 'Palestine and Israel, Volume 586' *UK Parliament* (13 October 2014) <https://archive.ph/SNGFT> [Accessed April 2022].

NOTES

29 Labour Friends of Israel, 'LFI Vice Chair, Michael Dugher MP, gives keynote speech at "We Believe in Israel" Conference' *Labour Friends of Israel* (15 March 2015) <https://archive.ph/Se43E> [Accessed April 2022].

30 PR Week, 'Smeeth exits Sodexho for pro-Israel lobby group' *PR Week* (9 September 2005) <https://archive.ph/7jIt5> [Accessed April 2022].

31 Asa Winstanley, 'UK charity with Mossad links secretly denounced anti-Zionist Jews to government' *Electronic Intifada* (21 December 2011) <https://archive.ph/sb6Op> [Accessed April 2022].

32 Steve Walker, 'Video: for transparency, #MarcWadsworth's actual words re Ruth Smeeth' *Skwawkbox* (25 April 2018) <https://web.archive.org/web/20190419052122/https://skwawkbox.org/2018/04/25/video-for-transparency-marcwadsworths-actual-words-re-ruth-smeeth/> [Accessed April 2022].

33 Ibid.

34 Ibid.

35 Marc Wadsworth, 'A Long, Hard Fight For Justice' *Voice* (5 January 2012) <https://archive.ph/z2RwM> [Accessed April 2022].

36 Tom Marshall, 'Labour MP Ruth Smeeth storms out of anti-Semitism report launch "in tears"' *Evening Standard* (30 June 2016) <https://archive.ph/3QPYU> [Accessed April 2022].

37 UKPol, 'Ruth Smeeth – 2016 Statement on Chakrabarti Report' *UKPol* (30 June 2016) <https://archive.ph/96N24> [Accessed April 2022].

38 Cyril Chilson, 'The 2018 Expulsion of Cyril Chilson, a child of Holocaust survivors, says everything you need to know about the "antisemitism" witchhunt' *Labour Briefing* (10 July 2019) <https://archive.ph/DUMvc> [Accessed April 2022].

39 ITV News, 'Labour MPs march in support of Jewish colleague ahead of anti-Semitism hearing' *ITV News* (25 April 2018) <https://archive.ph/WZpL2> [Accessed April 2022].

40 Michiel Willems, 'Jewish Chronicle newspaper to compensate expelled Labour activist after false accusations' *City AM* (22 July 2021) <https://archive.ph/Wehra> [Accessed April 2022].

41 Stephen Lendman, '"Worse than Apartheid" – The Movement to Boycott Israel' *Pulse* (27 February 2009) <https://archive.ph/KUGvH> [Accessed April 2022].

42 HOPE not hate, 'The fight against antisemitism' *Facebook* (1 April 2019) <https://www.facebook.com/watch/?v=391419021698680> [Accessed April 2022].

43 UKPol, 'Gordon Brown – 2008 Speech in Israel' *UKPol* (2 October 2015) <https://archive.ph/KBXrl> [Accessed April 2022].

44 Peter Walker, 'Jeremy Corbyn rejects spy ‚smears' and takes on press critics' *Guardian* (20 February 2018) <https://archive.ph/reA59> [Accessed April 2022].

CHAPTER NINE – BACK INTO THE LION'S DEN

1 Anoosh Chakelian, 'Life as Labour's most pro-Jeremy Corbyn candidate in England's most marginal constituency' *New Statesman* (18 May 2017) <https://archive.ph/AHQBG> [Accessed April 2022].

2 BBC Two, 'Labour: The Summer that Changed Everything' *BBC iPlayer* (17 November 2017) <www.bbc.co.uk/programmes/p05nddg1> [Accessed April 2022].

3 Rowena Mason, 'MPs should have no say over who leads Labour, argues shadow minister' *Guardian* (28 August 2017) <https://archive.ph/tYPf2> [Accessed March 2022].

4 Lee Harpin, 'My "hope" over Corbyn' *Jewish Chronicle* (4 September 2017) <https://archive.ph/JM4Dz> [Accessed April 2022].

5 WikiLeaks, 'UK Political Snapshot: Gloomy Budget and A New Scandal Torpedo Brown's Poll Numbers' *WikiLeaks* (24 April 2009) <https://archive.ph/3BDQK> [Accessed April 2022].

NOTES

6 Asa Winstanley, 'UK Labour MP Ruth Smeeth was funded by Israel lobby' *Electronic Intifada* (6 December 2016) <https://archive.ph/ErSdS> [Accessed March 2022].

7 Uttoxeter Post, 'Labour chooses election fighter' *Uttoxeter Post* (28 November 2007) <https://web.archive.org/web/20150402153401/http://www.uttoxeteradvertiser.co.uk/Labour-chooses-election-fighter/story-21608686-detail/story.html> [Accessed April 2022].

8 Lee Harpin, 'Audit reports Newmark deceived JLC' *Jewish Chronicle* (8 February 2018) <https://archive.ph/tYUcr> [Accessed April 2022].

9 Lee Harpin, 'Newmark protests his innocence after police drop investigation' *Jewish Chronicle* (28 March 2019) <https://archive.ph/IAFV6> [Accessed April 2022].

10 Toby Helm, 'Jewish Labour Movement no longer backs own party' *Guardian* (8 December 2019) <https://archive.ph/xbxui> [Accessed April 2022].

11 *Fraser v University & College Union* [2014] UKEAT/0266/14/DM.

12 BBC News, 'Denis MacShane jailed for MP expenses fraud' *BBC News* (23 December 2013) <https://archive.ph/Cf2sk> [Accessed April 2022].

13 Channel 4 News, 'John Mann confronts Ken Livingstone over Hitler Zionist comments' *YouTube* (28 April 2016) <https://youtu.be/tJCzVV5eIg8> [Accessed April 2022].

14 BBC Radio London, 'Ken Livingstone: I've never heard anyone in Labour say anything antisemitic' *Guardian* (28 April 2016) <https://web.archive.org/web/20170406074524/https://www.theguardian.com/politics/video/2016/apr/28/ken-livingstone-naz-shaw-vanessa-feltz-labour-antisemitic-row-audio> [Accessed April 2022].

15 Yf'aat Weissm, 'The Transfer Agreement and the Boycott Movement' *Yad Vashem* <https://web.archive.org/web/20220125085723/https://www.yadvashem.org/odot_pdf/Microsoft%20Word%20-%203231.pdf> [Accessed April 2022].

16 Jessica Elgot and Anushka Asthana, 'Labour speaks out on Venezuela as pressure mounts on Corbyn' *Guardian* (3 August 2017) <https://archive.ph/ebdUy> [Accessed April 2022].

17 Ralph Miliband, *Parliamentary Socialism: A Study in the Politics of Labour* (first published 1961, Merlin Press 2009), p.101.

18 Alan Duncan, *In the Thick of It: The Private Diaries of a Minister* (HarperCollins 2021), p. 334.

19 Ibid, 356.

20 Steve Walker, 'Remember when Corbyn was mocked for floating women-only carriages?' *Skwawkbox* (21 August 2017) <https://archive.ph/hBVoZ> [Accessed April 2022].

21 Ibid.

22 BBC News, 'Derby North MP Chris Williamson mocked over women-only carriages' *BBC News* (23 August 2017) <https://archive.ph/nWmNl> [Accessed April 2022].

23 Steve Walker, 'Labour right goes into strawman-meltdown over women-only carriages' *Skwawkbox* (23 August 2017) <https://archive.ph/CQl1p> [Accessed April 2022].

24 Jess Phillips, 'This is how to keep women safe on trains...' *Guardian* (27 August 2017) <https://archive.ph/TPFgR> [Accessed April 2022].

25 Rachel Cooke, 'Jess Phillips: someone to believe in' *Guardian* (6 March 2016) <https://archive.ph/NgX8l> [Accessed April 2022].

26 Steve Walker, 'Phillips attacks Tories with second jobs. Here are her own extra-parliamentary activities' *Skwawkbox* (8 November 2021) <https://archive.ph/KSU2B> [Accessed April 2022].

27 Solomon Hughes, 'Moonlighting MPs bring Parliament into disrepute' *Morning Star* (27 July 2018) <https://archive.ph/SMNxW> [Accessed April 2022].

28 Rachael O'Connor, 'Labour MP Jess Phillips paid £15,000 to host one episode of Have I Got News For You' *Metro* (7 February 2022) <https://archive.ph/asIvL> [Accessed April 2022].

NOTES

29 Sky News, 'Keir Starmer accused of hypocrisy over Brexit law firm role' *Sky News* (25 July 2017) <https://archive.ph/x2umP> [Accessed April 2022].

30 Henry Goodwin, 'Guess who else eyed up a consultancy gig? Sir Keir Starmer' *London Economic* (9 November 2021) <https://archive.ph/hA4f1> [Accessed April 2022].

31 House of Commons, 'Register of Members' Financial Interests' (2 March 2020) <https://archive.ph/CiBfP> [Accessed April 2022].

32 House of Commons, 'Register of Members' Financial Interests' (23 August 2021) <https://archive.ph/jXTVk> and (6 September 2021) <https://archive.ph/Xsyx3> [Accessed April 2022].

33 Sky News, *Twitter* (8 November 2021) <http://web.archive.org/web/20220322105954/https://twitter.com/SkyNews/status/1457820419025690632> [Accessed March 2022].

34 Hansard, 'Engagements, Volume 450' *UK Parliament* (18 October 2006) <https://archive.ph/QTRpx> [Accessed April 2022].

35 Steve Walker, 'Austin tries Mann-style attack on Williamson Fails' *Skwawkbox* (7 September 2017) <https://archive.ph/NfcFf> [Accessed April 2022].

36 Samuel Osborne, 'Jeremy Corbyn told to ,sit down and shut up' in Commons as he criticises Iraq War after publication of Chilcot report' *Independent* (6 July 2016) <https://archive.ph/TNTNL> [Accessed April 2022].

37 Hansard, 'Report of the Iraq Inquiry, Volume 612' *UK Parliament* (6 July 2016) <https://archive.ph/LnPhI> [Accessed April 2022].

38 Ibid.

39 Ibid.

40 Jessica Elgot, 'Labour drops abusive conduct investigation into MP Ian Austin' *Guardian* (27 November 2018) <https://archive.ph/iZ1k8> [Accessed April 2022].

41 Richard Vaughan, 'Labour to discipline Margaret Hodge after calling Jeremy Corbyn a 'f***ing anti-semite'' *i News* (18 July 2018) <https://archive.ph/FcDD3> [Accessed April 2022].

42 Jessica Elgot, 'Labour ends action against Margaret Hodge in antisemitism row' *Guardian* (6 August 2018) <https://archive.ph/1l4yD> [Accessed April 2022].

43 Jessica Elgot, 'Labour drops abusive conduct investigation into MP Ian Austin' *Guardian* (27 November 2018) <https://archive.ph/iZ1k8> [Accessed April 2022].

44 Phil Miller, 'Ex-Labour MP Ian Austin becomes May's trade envoy to Israel' *Morning Star* (19 July 2019) <https://archive.ph/dMIhF> [Accessed April 2022].

CHAPTER TEN – "THOUGH COWARDS FLINCH AND TRAITORS SNEER"

1 Nick Cohen, '"Fake news": the far left's favourite new excuse' *Spectator* (27 September 2017) <https://archive.ph/TFpZ8> [Accessed April 2022].

2 Asley Cowburn, 'Jon Lansman: Momentum chair would 'understand' Labour leadership challenge if party loses general election' *Independent* (1 October 2016) <https://archive.ph/Or6WF> [Accessed April 2022].

3 Jewish Chronicle, 'Pressure grows on Labour as Momentum expected to "remove" Jackie Walker' *Jewish Chronicle* (30 September 2016) <https://archive.ph/emoXh> [Accessed April 2022].

4 Jessica Elgot, 'Momentum likely to oust Jackie Walker over Holocaust remarks' *Guardian* (29 September 2016) <https://archive.ph/gKr21> [Accessed April 2022].

5 BBC News, 'Labour suspends activist over alleged anti-Semitic comments' *BBC News* (5 May 2016) <https://archive.ph/MYnik> [Accessed April 2022].

6 Ben Chu, 'Labour Party members with anti-Semitic views should be banned for life, says John McDonnell' *Independent* (24 March 2016) <https://archive.ph/UY2B5> [Accessed April 2022].

7 Jon Stone, 'Labour has a 'serious' antisemitism problem, Lord Levy says' *Independent* (28 April 2016) <https://archive.ph/GoNdr> [Accessed April 2022].

366

NOTES

8 'Pointed polemic from suspended Labour activist' *Morning Star* (25 January 2018) <https://archive.ph/cooSe> [Accessed April 2022].

9 Jewish Agency for Israel, 'The Law of Return' *Jewish Agency for Israel* <https://archive.ph/EO79c> [Accessed April 2022.].

10 Grenfell Action Group, 'KCTMO – Playing with fire!' *Grenfell Action Group* (20 November 2016) <https://archive.ph/LAXdq> [Accessed April 2022].

11 Louis Emanuel, 'Martin Moore-Bick should resign as Grenfell Tower inquiry chief, says MP' *Times* (4 July 2019) <https://archive.ph/XUgME> [Accessed April 2022].

12 BBC News, 'Grenfell fire: MP calls for inquiry chairman to quit' *BBC News* (4 July 2019) <https://web.archive.org/web/20170808171416/http://www.bbc.com/news/uk-40491449> [Accessed April 2022].

13 Press Release, 'Grenfell Tower Press Release by leading BME organisations, lawyers & residents' *Black Activists Rising Against Cuts* (3 July 2017) <https://archive.ph/nSPQ9> [Accessed April 2022].

14 BBC Radio 5 Live, *Twitter* (5 July 2017) <https://twitter.com/bbc5live/status/882564823455846400> [Accessed October 2021].

15 *Nzolameso v City of Westminster* [2015] UKSC 22.

16 Press Association, 'Grenfell inquiry judge let council rehouse tenant 50 miles away' *Guardian* (29 June 2017) <https://archive.ph/UbVhp> [Accessed April 2022].

CHAPTER ELEVEN – FREE AGENT

1 Chris Williamson, 'Can Labour councils seize the initiative on fighting cuts?' *Morning Star* (4 November 2017) <https://archive.ph/tKrRV> [Accessed April 2022].

2 Paul Waugh, 'Double Council Taxes On Wealthy Homes, Shadow Minister Chris Williamson Urges Labour Town Halls' *HuffPost* (9 January 2018) <https://archive.ph/NRJ9s> [Accessed April 2022].

3 Wes Streeting, *Twitter* (11 January 2018) <https://archive.ph/EZG8e> [Accessed April 2022].

4 Heather Stewart, 'Junior Labour MPs in line for promotion after Corbyn ally quits frontbench' *Guardian* (11 January 2018) <https://archive.ph/0Emla> [Accessed March 2022].

5 BBC News, 'Labour's Chris Williamson denies being sacked over council tax call' *BBC News* (12 January 2018) <https://archive.ph/WEe6Z> [Accessed April 2022].

6 LabourList, '"Straight talking, honest politics" – Labour reveal first Corbyn focussed PPB' *LabourList* (1 October 2015) <https://archive.ph/77weC> [Accessed April 2022].

7 Lizzy Buchan, 'Chris Williamson: Corbyn ally quits Labour frontbench as shadow fire minister' *Independent* (11 January 2018) <https://archive.ph/84udk> [Accessed April 2022].

8 Labour Party, 'The Labour Party Democracy Review' *Labour Party* (6 November 2017) <http://web.archive.org/web/20220325104522/https://labour.org.uk/about/democracy-review-2017/> [Accessed April 2022].

9 LabourList, 'Revealed: The full contents of Labour's internal democracy review' *LabourList* (2 November 2017) <https://archive.ph/zeIwE> [Accessed April 2022].

10 Chris Williamson, 'Democracy is the most revolutionary thing in the world' *Morning Star* (11 July 2018) <https://archive.ph/FuGAO>[Accessed April 2022].

11 Lucy Powell, *Twitter* (6 August 2017) <https://archive.ph/9QkA3> [Accessed April 2022].

12 Chris Williamson, 'The Democracy Roadshow 2018' *YouTube* (9 July 2018) <https://www.youtube.com/watch?v=sHFNcg7Oc9E> [Accessed April 2022].

13 Matt Honeycombe-Foster, 'Corbyn ally Chris Williamson blasts back after Labour grandee accuses him of risking party split' *Politics Home* (27 August 2018) <https://archive.ph/HujAd> [Accessed April 2022].

NOTES

14 Barry Sheerman, *Twitter* (20 August 2018) <https://archive.ph/VnoJc> [Accessed April 2022].

15 BBC News, 'Chuka Umunna tells Jeremy Corbyn to "call off the dogs"' *BBC News* (8 September 2018) <https://archive.ph/ZOoUI> [Accessed April 2022].

16 Chuka Umunna, *Twitter* (14 September 2013) <https://archive.ph/rfqN8> [Accessed April 2022].

17 Neil Coyle, 'Williamson's Democracy Sideshow will only help the Tories' *House Magazine* (31 August 2018) <https://archive.ph/IPHFg> [Accessed April 2022].

18 Sienna Rodgers, 'Bermondsey Labour MP Neil Coyle's texts to Jeremy Corbyn revealed' *LabourList* (4 September 2020) <https://archive.ph/qMyFC> [Accessed April 2022].

19 Kate Proctor, 'Jeremy Corbyn faces criticism over 'groaning and hissing' entourage at meetings with MPs' *Evening Standard* (22 March 2017) <https://archive.ph/5k22x> [Accessed April 2022].

20 David Wooding, 'Labour's Shadow Cabinet Labour's top team blasted for woeful and "catastrophic" slump in number of questions asked in debates in the House of Commons' *Sun* (16 April 2017) <https://archive.ph/4in1Q> [Accessed April 2022].

21 Decca Aitkenhead, 'Neil Kinnock: "I'm bloody angry. Only anger is keeping me from falling into despair"' *Guardian* (8 July 2016) <https://archive.ph/Nb6gS> [Accessed April 2022].

CHAPTER TWELVE – BEGINNING OF THE END

1 Len McCluskey, *Always Red* (OR Books 2021), pp. 259-60.

2 Chris Williamson, 'The struggle for Labour Party democracy continues' *Morning Star* (26 September 2018) <https://archive.ph/0IpnJ> [Accessed March 2022].

3 Kevin Schofield, 'Len McCluskey and Chris Williamson in public spat amid Labour MP 'open selection' row' *Politics Home* (25 September 2018) <https://archive.ph/9Op9F> [Accessed March 2022].

4 Ibid.

5 Len McCluskey, 'Accusing Unite of "machine politics" undermines Jeremy Corbyn' *LabourList* (26 September 2018) <https://archive.ph/TRLUU> [Accessed March 2022].

6 Len McCluskey, *Always Red* (OR Books 2021), p. 260.

7 Ibid.

8 Dan Sabbagh, 'Labour adopts IHRA antisemitism definition in full' *Guardian* (4 September 2018) <https://archive.ph/1x3xC> [Accessed March 2022].

9 Dan Fisher, 'Split Between Britain, U.S. Seen as 'Inevitable': Foreign policy: The Conservative Party chairman fears that a 'less European' America will provide the wedge' *Los Angeles Times* (19 April 1990) <https://archive.ph/xVoW1> [Accessed April 2022].

10 Asa Winstanley, 'Jeremy Corbyn must stop pandering to Labour's Israel lobby' *Electronic Intifada* (28 March 2018) <https://archive.ph/8b8U1> [Accessed March 2022].

11 BBC News, 'Jewish leaders' letter and Jeremy Corbyn's reply' *BBC News* (26 March 2018) <https://archive.ph/kMXt2> [Accessed March 2022].

12 BBC News, 'Corbyn apologises for "hurt" caused by anti-Semitism in Labour' *BBC News* (26 March 2018) <https://archive.ph/eZftO> [Accessed April 2022].

13 Ewen MacAskill, 'Jeremy Corbyn's team targets Labour membership of 1 million' *Guardian* (27 September 2016) <https://archive.ph/Uzd7V> [Accessed March 2022].

14 Sienna Rodgers, 'Jennie Formby provides numbers on Labour antisemitism cases' *LabourList* (11 February 2019) <https://archive.ph/XQr5i> [Accessed March 2022].

15 'Labour's ruling body holds crunch anti-Semitism talks' *BBC News* (4 September 2018) <https://archive.ph/yQiqj> [Accessed March 2022].

NOTES

16 David Wilcock, 'Jeremy Corbyn ally Chris Williamson LOSES court battle to be reinstated in the Labour party after being suspended during the anti-Semitism scandal' *Daily Mail* (4 September 2018) <https://archive.ph/ZwhQm> [Accessed March 2022].

17 Asa Winstanley, 'Anti-Palestinian activists guilty of harassment' *Electronic Intifada* (19 June 2019) <https://archive.ph/Ic6ju> [Accessed March 2022].

18 Rosa Doherty, 'Ex-Zionist Federation vice-chair faces arrest warrant after failing to appear in court' *Jewish Chronicle* (26 March 2019) <https://archive.ph/PCdJz> [Accessed March 2022].

19 Kenneth Stern, 'Written Testimony of Kenneth S. Stern' (7 November 2017) <https://web.archive.org/web/20220127200518/https://www.jewishvoiceforlabour.org.uk/app/uploads/2018/08/Stern-Testimony-11.07.17.pdf> [Accessed March 2022].

20 Justin Cohen, 'Jon Lansman lobbying Labour to adopt full IHRA with examples' *Jewish News* (8 August 2018) <https://archive.ph/082AW> [Accessed March 2022].

21 Asa Winstanley, 'How Jon Lansman joined Labour's witch hunt' *Electronic Intifada* (7 October 2019) <https://archive.ph/5gNP7> [Accessed April 2022].

22 International Holocaust Remembrance Alliance, 'About the IHRA non-legally binding working definition of antisemitism' *IHRA* (26 May 2016) <https://archive.ph/jso35> [Accessed March 2022].

23 Ali Younes, 'Nakba Day: For Palestinians, not just an historical event' *Al Jazeera* (15 May 2020) <https://archive.ph/Wj3BR> [Accessed April 2022].

24 Chris Knight, 'Nine Holocaust survivors compare Zionist policies to those of the Nazis' *Labour Briefing* (30 July 2019) <https://archive.ph/TPFaa> [Accessed March 2022].

25 Hansard, 'Column 407' *UK Parliament* (15 January 2009) <https://archive.ph/GwgEK> [Accessed March 2022].

26 Board of Deputies of British Jews, 'Statement following Board of Deputies and Jewish Leadership Council meeting with Jeremy Corbyn' *BoD* (25 April 2018) <https://archive.ph/rjaSj> [Accessed April 2022].

27 Chris Williamson, *Twitter* (29 October 2020) <https://twitter.com/DerbyChrisW/status/1321814415503740928> [Accessed April 2022].

28 JC Reporter, '"Jew-baiter" MP says he is being referred for expulsion from Labour' *Jewish Chronicle* (31 July 2019) <https://archive.ph/6hHnI> [Accessed April 2022].

29 Ben Weich, 'Williamson under investigation for "pattern of behaviour"' *Jewish Chronicle* (27 February 2019) <https://archive.ph/XDGdO> [Accessed April 2022].

30 Leo Panitch and Colin Leys, 'Tony Benn at 95' *Tribune* (3 April 2020) <https://archive.ph/rrEFW> [Accessed April 2022].

31 Andy Beckett, 'Unfriendly fire: would a Corbyn government lead to a military revolt?' *Guardian* (25 January 2016) <https://archive.ph/IqXVo> [Accessed April 2022].

32 Susan Ratcliffe (eds), 'Harold Wilson 1916–95' in *Oxford Essential Quotations* (5th edn, OUP 2017).

33 Laura Hughes, Helen Warrell and Jim Pickard, 'Police launch criminal probe into Labour anti-Semitism allegations' *Financial Times* (2 November 2018) <https://archive.ph/vcwme> [Accessed April 2022].

34 Sienna Rodgers, 'Labour student clubs boycott Westminster CLP over Chris Williamson invitation' *LabourList* (21 November 2018) <https://web.archive.org/web/20181124174228/https://labourlist.org/2018/11/labour-student-clubs-boycott-westminster-clp-over-chris-williamson-invitation/> [Accessed March 2022].

35 LSE SU Labour, *Twitter* (21 November 2018) <https://archive.ph/6qbbl> [Accessed April 2022].

36 Charity Commission, 'Board of Deputies Charitable Foundation: Trustees' Report and Consolidated Accounts for the year ended 31 December 2020', p. 5.

37 Jonathan Cook, 'Is Israel's hand behind the attacks on Jeremy Corbyn?' *Middle East Eye* (30 August 2018) <https://archive.ph/lxiWn> [Accessed March 2022].

NOTES

38 Benjamin Netanyahu, *Twitter* (13 August 2018) <https://archive.ph/ISk5D> [Accessed March 2022].

39 Chris Williamson, *Twitter* (21 January 2019) <https://archive.ph/Lvp1h> [Accessed April 2022].

40 Jonathan Goldstein, *Letter* (23 January 2019) <https://web.archive.org/web/20200924123410/https://d3n8a8pro7vhmx.cloudfront.net/jlc/pages/2190/attachments/original/1548260989/Letter_from_JLC_Chair_to_Chris_Williamson_MP_-_23_Jan_2019.pdf?1548260989> [Accessed March 2022].

41 Rachel Riley, *Twitter* (23 January 2019) <https://archive.ph/68lEA> [Accessed April 2022].

42 Board of Deputies of British Jews, *Twitter* (26 February 2019) <https://archive.ph/Be3a4> [Accessed April 2022].

43 Rachel Riley, *Twitter* (27 February 2019) <https://archive.ph/7q4IW> [Accessed April 2022].

44 Jessica Elgot and Heather Stewart, 'Momentum's Jon Lansman confirms run for Labour general secretary' *Guardian* (1 March 2018) <https://archive.ph/dZLRs> [Accessed April 2022].

45 Hansard, 'Military Action Overseas: Parliamentary Approval, Volume 639' *UK Parliament* (16 April 2018) <https://archive.ph/0zEv4> [Accessed April 2022].

46 Jon Pullman, *WitchHunt* (2019) <https://archive.ph/Xu9If> [Accessed April 2022].

47 Paul Waugh, *Twitter* (25 February 2019) <https://archive.ph/xV1jN> [Accessed April 2022].

48 Jessica Elgot, 'Watson says Labour must restore trust in party on antisemitism' *Guardian* (12 September 2018) <https://archive.ph/8FHLw> [Accessed April 2022].

49 Ibid.

50 Companies House, 'Labour Friends of Israel Ltd' *Companies House* <https://archive.ph/dEtLx> [Accessed April 2022].

51 Asa Winstanley, 'Is Labour Friends of Israel an Israeli embassy front?' *Electronic Intifada* (12 January 2017) <https://archive.ph/3B84I> [Accessed April 2022].

52 Neville Teller, 'The Conservative Friends of Israel' *Jerusalem Post* (19 March 2020) <https://archive.ph/VjMq2> [Accessed April 2022].

53 Hansard, 'Antisemitism in Modern Society, Volume 654' *UK Parliament* (20 February 2019) <https://archive.ph/LC6gr> [Accessed April 2022].

54 Ibid.

55 Ibid.

56 Ibid.

57 BBC News, 'Ivan Lewis quits Labour Party as sex harassment row drags on' *BBC News* (21 December 2018) <https://archive.ph/2GHiC> [Accessed April 2022].

58 Hansard, 'Antisemitism in Modern Society' (n 53).

59 Ibid.

60 Nick Robinson, *Twitter* (26 February 2019) <https://archive.ph/VVezK> [Accessed April 2022].

61 Responses to Nick Robinson, *Twitter* (23 February 2019) <https://archive.ph/UzQuH> [Accessed April 2022].

62 Richard Ferrer, 'Nick Robinson tells Holocaust Educational Trust: Jewish MPs are being driven out' *Jewish News* (8 October 2019) <https://archive.ph/8raH4> [Accessed April 2022].

63 Holocaust Educational Trust, 'Nick Robinson Speech HET 2019 Appeal Dinner' *Vimeo* <https://vimeo.com/365713349> [Accessed April 2022].

64 Sienna Rodgers, 'Jennie Formby provides numbers on Labour antisemitism cases' *LabourList* (11 February 2019) <https://archive.ph/XQr5i> [Accessed April 2022].

NOTES

CHAPTER THIRTEEN – BETRAYAL

1 Fréa Lockley, 'Revealed: the truth about antisemitism allegations against expelled Labour MP Chris Williamson' *Canary* (3 May 2020) <https://archive.ph/bWZTt> [Accessed March 2022].

2 Liz Bates, *Twitter* (26 February 2019) <http://web.archive.org/web/20210831100431/https://twitter.com/wizbates/status/1100471552678735873> [Accessed March 2022].

3 Elizabeth Bates, 'Chris Williamson: Labour has been too apologetic about anti-Semitism' *Yorkshire Post* (26 February 2019) <https://archive.ph/sAZje> [Accessed April 2022].

4 Northern Echo, 'Anger among North-East MPs over Chris Williamson's anti-Semitism remarks' *Northern Echo* (27 February 2019) <https://archive.ph/EcefH> [Accessed April 2022].

5 Greg Heffer and Rebecca Taylor, 'Theresa May and Labour deputy Tom Watson call for MP's suspension over antisemitism' *Sky News* (27 February 2019) <https://archive.ph/F9Asf> [Accessed April 2022].

6 Lee Harpin, 'Formby not recognising left antisemitism' *Jewish Chronicle* (4 July 2019) <https://archive.ph/8UTTG> [Accessed April 2022].

7 Henry Zeffman, *Twitter* (27 February 2019) <https://archive.ph/yYVce> [Accessed April 2022].

8 Sienna Rodgers, 'Chris Williamson suspended from the Labour Party' *LabourList* (27th February 2019) <https://archive.ph/ZedI5> [Accessed April 2022].

9 Aaron Bastani and Charlotte England, 'Tim Roache Resigned Amid Allegations of Sexual Assault, Cover up and a 'Casting Couch' Culture at GMB' *Novara Media* (1 May 2020) <https://archive.ph/ftLEx> [Accessed March 2022].

10 Norman Finkelstein, 'Solution for Israel-Palestine Conflict' *Norman Finkelstein* (4 August 2014) <http://web.archive.org/web/20210411003109/http://normanfinkelstein.com/2014/08/04/solution-for-israel-palestine-conflict%E2%80%8F/> [Accessed March 2022].

11 Congressional Research Service, 'U.S. Foreign Aid to Israel - Updated February 18, 2022' (16 November 2020) <https://web.archive.org/web/20220330211209/https://sgp.fas.org/crs/mideast/RL33222.pdf> [Accessed April 2022].

12 Naz Shah, *Twitter* (26 April 2016) <https://archive.ph/VnyeY> [Accessed April 2022].

13 Hansard, 'Points of Order, Volume 608' *UK Parliament* (27 April 2016) <https://archive.ph/YWqqJ> [Accessed April 2022].

14 Aubrey Allegretti, 'Labour MP Chris Williamson suspended over antisemitism row' *Sky News* (27 February 2019) <https://web.archive.org/web/20190227232740/https://news.sky.com/story/labour-mp-chris-williamson-suspended-over-antisemitism-row-11650005> [Accessed April 2022].

15 Ibid.

16 Guido Fawkes, 'Labour MP: Israelis should face "transportation" out of Middle East' *Guido Fawkes* (26 April 2016) <https://archive.ph/i3lx4> [Accessed March 2022].

17 Guido Fawkes, 'About' *Guido Fawkes* <https://archive.ph/mjxjH> [Accessed April 2022].

18 Asa Winstanley, 'UK charity with Mossad links secretly denounced anti-Zionist Jews to government' *Electronic Intifada* (21 December 2011) <https://archive.ph/sb6Op> [Accessed April 2022].

19 Home Affairs Select Committee, 'Antisemitism in the UK Contents: Political discourse and leadership' *UK Parliament* (14 October 2016) <https://archive.ph/28ThA> [Accessed April 2022].

20 Home Office, 'Home Office grants £14 million funding for security at Jewish institutions' *UK Government* (1 April 2020) <https://archive.ph/071As> [Accessed April 2022].

21 CST Blog, 'Jeremy Corbyn and antisemitism: questions to answer' *CST* (8 July 2015) <https://archive.ph/WotB7> [Accessed April 2022].

NOTES

22 CST Blog, 'Report shows why British Jews' fear of Corbyn was not unfounded' *CST* (29 October 2020) <https://archive.ph/xu486> [Accessed April 2022].

23 CST Blog, 'Engine of Hate: the online networks behind the Labour Party's antisemitism crisis' *CST* (4 August 2019) <https://web.archive.org/web/20210421230820/https://cst.org.uk/news/blog/2019/08/04/engine-of-hate-the-online-networks-behind-the-labour-partys-antisemitism-crisis> [Accessed April 2022].

24 Charity Commission, 'MP Fact Sheet: Charities, politics and campaigning' *UK Government* <https://web.archive.org/web/20190726030031/https://assets.publishing.service.gov.uk/government/uploads/system/uploads/attachment_data/file/354727/Charities_politics_and_campaigning_MP_factsheet_6.pdf> [Accessed April 2022].

25 Tania Mason, 'Commission unfairly targets Muslim charities, says think tank' *Civil Society News* (17 November 2014) <https://archive.ph/ksrbQ> [Accessed April 2022].

CHAPTER FOURTEEN – "THE SILENCE OF OUR FRIENDS"

1 Stuart Anderson, '"Burn neoliberalism, not people" – Norwich MP Clive Lewis stirs debate after Grenfell Tower blaze' *Eastern Daily Press* (18 June 2017) <https://archive.ph/usSFy> [Accessed April 2022].

2 Clive Lewis, *Twitter* (16 June 2017) <https://archive.ph/93fLK> [Accessed March 2022].

3 Al Jazeera, 'The Lobby' *YouTube* (12 January 2017) <https://www.youtube.com/watch?v=L3dn-VV3czc> [Accessed April 2022].

4 Ibid.

5 Ibid.

6 Sonia Mota, *Twitter* (17 February 2019) <http://web.archive.org/web/20200928023631/https://twitter.com/SoniaKatiMota/status/1097024445326200832> [Accessed March 2022].

7 BBC Two, 'Diversity in TV | How to Break into the Elite' *Facebook* (30 July 2019) <www.facebook.com/watch/?v=2216647381767726> | Facebook> [Accessed March 2022].

8 Chris Williamson, *Twitter* (2 August 2019) <https://archive.ph/7ALiW> [Accessed April 2022].

9 Clive Lewis MP, *Twitter* (8 August 2019) <https://archive.ph/K5pVF> [Accessed April 2022].

10 Labour Voices, 'Labour Voices: Guy Matthews' *YouTube* (28 May 2019) <www.youtube.com/watch?v=JgrstsdrI7U> [Accessed April 2022].

11 Tony Greenstein, 'Why Anti-Semitism is no longer a form of racism –it's a Marginal Prejudice confined to the fascist fringe' *Tony Greenstein* (11 June 2021) <https://archive.ph/6VMd2> [Accessed April 2022].

12 James Martin, *Twitter* (25 April 2019) <https://archive.ph/wVmDW> [Accessed April 2022].

13 Michael Walker, *Twitter* (19 July 2019) <https://archive.ph/Lvyqg> [Accessed April 2022].

14 Michael Walker, *Twitter* (16 November 2021) <https://archive.ph/54otq> [Accessed March 2022].

15 Michael Walker, *Twitter* (7 April 2022) <https://archive.ph/rvQFT> [Accessed April 2022].

16 Ash Sarkar, *Twitter* (27 February 2019) <https://archive.ph/jvfiy> [Accessed April 2022].

17 Intelligence Squared, 'Jeremy Corbyn is unfit to be prime minister' *Intelligence Squared* (14 September 2018) <www.intelligencesquared.com/events/jeremy-corbyn-is-unfit-to-be-prime-minister/> [Accessed April 2022].

18 Chris Williamson, 'Trump Not Welcome | Chris Williamson MP' *YouTube* (16 July 2018) <www.youtube.com/watch?v=SRLGoVry_C8> [Accessed April 2022].

NOTES

19 Scroll, '"I'm a Communist, you idiot": British TV host Piers Morgan gets a mouthful on live television' *Scroll* (14 July 2018) <https://archive.ph/wh818> [Accessed April 2022].

20 Aaron Bastani, *Twitter* (5 July 2019) <https://archive.ph/dZdaJ> [Accessed April 2022].

21 Richard Seymour, 'Your hot take on Chris Williamson' *Patreon* (28 February 2019) <https://archive.ph/BOa9X> [Accessed April 2022].

22 Ibid.

23 Ibid.

24 Ibid.

25 Billy Bragg, *Twitter* (4 July 2019) <https://archive.ph/bPElF> [Accessed April 2022].

26 Liam Devitt, 'How Britain's Red Wedge tried to bring pop into politics and politics into pop' *Jacobin* (26 June 2021) <https://archive.ph/s99Z3> [Accessed April 2022].

CHAPTER FIFTEEN – A KAFKAESQUE NIGHTMARE

1 Vox Political, 'Was the man who posted lies on Chris Williamson's office really a Tory Councillor?' *Vox Political* (2 March 2019) <https://archive.ph/4gLw2> [Accessed April 2022].

2 'Carl Sargeant not given natural justice, family says' *BBC News* (8 November 2017) <https://archive.ph/ac6Ao> [Accessed April 2022].

1 Michael Crick, *Militant* (first published 1984, Biteback Publishing 2016).

2 Matthew Tempest, 'Tony Benn defends Galloway to party' *Guardian* (22 October 2003) <https://archive.ph/3Zpaf> [Accessed March 2022].

3 Conor Pope, 'Ken Livingstone must be expelled from party, Labour MPs demand' *LabourList* (29 April 2016) <https://archive.ph/2BKrb> [Accessed March 2022].

4 Chris Williamson, 'The Future of Parliament' *YouTube* (5 February 2018) <www.youtube.com/watch?v=nUIi8_p3h74> [Accessed March 2022].

5 Aneurin Bevan, *In Place of Fear* (William Heinemann Ltd 1952), pp. 6–7.

6 Brendan Carlin, 'Jeremy Corbyn is embroiled in fresh anti-Semitism storm after being accused of calling Labour MP suspended over row a "comrade"' *Daily Mail* (17 March 2019) <https://archive.ph/nkuRq> [Accessed April 2022].

7 Lee Harpin, 'Corbyn called "Jew-baiter" MP Williamson 'comrade"' *Jewish Chronicle* (17 March 2019) <https://archive.ph/tAsVA> [Accessed April 2022].

8 Hansard, 'Border Controls, Volume 586' *UK Parliament* (13 October 2014) <https://archive.ph/fCoBP> [Accessed April 2022].

9 Jonathan Walker, 'Labour MP Ian Austin: Make it more difficult for immigrants to claim benefits' *Birmingham Mail* (29 October 2019) <https://archive.ph/S2Gxz> [Accessed April 2022].

10 Ian Austin, 'People are concerned about immigration – Labour must come up with fair answers rather than hiding from it' *LabourList* (18 November 2016) <https://archive.ph/ZBnF5> [Accessed April 2022].

11 Simon Rocker, 'Jon Lansman faces sceptical audience at Limmud' *Jewish Chronicle* (24 December 2018) <https://archive.ph/l6I3m> [Accessed April 2022].

12 Asa Winstanley, 'Jewish Labour Movement was refounded to fight Corbyn' *Electronic Intifada* (7 March 2019) <https://archive.ph/KlFCF> [Accessed March 2022].

13 Ibid.

14 American Jewish Committee, 'Addressing the Rise of Global Anti-Semitism' *YouTube* (3 June 2019) <www.youtube.com/watch?v=nhsxyDdTH8I> [Accessed April 2022].

NOTES

CHAPTER SIXTEEN – RANK COWARDICE

1 Kevin Scofield, 'Keith Vaz says decision to let Chris Williamson back into Labour party should be reconsidered' *Politics Home* (27 June 2019) <https://archive.ph/N76ys> [Accessed April 2022].

2 Ibid.

3 'Suspending Chris Williamson – the fury and the fakery' *Media Lens* (4 July 2019) <https://archive.ph/aDrVJ> [Accessed April 2022].

4 Boris Johnson, *Twitter* (26 June 2019) <https://archive.ph/mDmQe> [Accessed March 2022].

5 Boris Johnson, *Seventy-Two Virgins: A Comedy of Errors* (HarperCollins 2004)

6 '90 Labour MPs and peers condemn Williamson "antisemitism" decision' *Sky News* (28 June 2019) <http://web.archive.org/web/20210617072139/https://news.sky.com/story/scores-of-labour-mps-and-peers-condemn-williamson-decision-11750073> [Accessed April 2022].

7 George Allen, 'Jeremy Corbyn denies Derby MP Chris Williamson is anti-Jewish on visit to Ilkeston' *Derby Telegraph* (31 January 2019) <https://archive.ph/l3JUt> [Accessed April 2022].

8 Ibid.

9 Frances Perraudin, 'Labour MP Jess Phillips will "knife Corbyn in the front" if he damages party' *Guardian* (14 December 2015) <https://archive.ph/qRIZZ> [Accessed March 2022].

10 LBC, 'Corbyn must withdraw the whip from Chris Williamson "as a matter of principle"' *LBC* (28 June 2019) <https://archive.ph/94CML> [Accessed April 2022].

11 Ibid.

12 Kevin Schofield, 'Jewish and non-Jewish Labour staff demand party review Chris Williamson re-admission' *Politics Home* (27 June 2019) <https://archive.ph/k6G2p> [Accessed April 2022].

13 Benjamin Kentish, 'Chris Williamson: 90 Labour MPs and peers demand Corbyn withdraw whip from MP over antisemitism row' *Independent* (27 June 2019) <https://archive.ph/SlnAY> [Accessed April 2022].

14 Gillian Merron and Simon Johnson, 'Chris Williamson's reprieve is a disgraceful step backwards in Labour's half-baked "fight" against antisemitism' *Independent* (27 June 2019) <https://archive.ph/oxo8Q> [Accessed April 2022].

15 Hansard, 'Social Security Bill, Volume 302' *UK Parliament* (10 December 1997) <https://archive.ph/JZ5vq> [Accessed April 2022].

16 Hansard, 'Iraq, Volume 401' *UK Parliament* (18 March 2003) <https://archive.ph/7QOXK> [Accessed April 2022].

17 Justin Cohen, 'Former Foreign Office minister appointed to lead the Board' *Jewish News* (7 May 2014) <https://archive.ph/7pB5L> [Accessed April 2022].

18 Graeme Wilson, 'MP uses taxpayers' cash to rent Lampard's luxury pad' *Sun* (6 April 2016) <https://archive.ph/lzFnu> [Accessed April 2022].

19 David Ottewell and Paul Whitelam, 'How Lincolnshire MPs made hundreds of thousands of pounds selling property that YOUR money helped fund' *Lincolnshire Echo* (15 July 2019) <https://archive.ph/MynRT> [Accessed April 2022].

20 Jon Lansman, *Twitter* (27 June 2019) <https://archive.ph/dnK11> [Accessed April 2022].

21 Editorial, 'Ex-kibbutznik who is Corbyn's left-hand man' *Jewish Chronicle* (28 January 2016) <https://archive.ph/JpY9h> [Accessed March 2022].

22 Lee Harpin, 'Momentum founder to discuss Corbyn in Israel' *Jewish Chronicle* (19 June 2018) <https://archive.ph/8c2zr> [Accessed April 2022].

23 James Wright, 'Momentum founder under fire after claiming left-wing Jews are "not part" of the Jewish community' *Canary* (19 June 2019) <https://archive.ph/WzyzW> [Accessed April 2022].

NOTES

24 Asa Winstanley, '"Ally" Jon Lansman wanted Jeremy Corbyn removed' *Electronic Intifada* (6 September 2019) <https://archive.ph/0KcCI> [Accessed April 2022].

25 Jon Lansman, *Twitter* (9 January 2022) <https://archive.ph/PiR46> [Accessed April 2022].

26 Going Underground, 'Chris Williamson MP blasts antisemitism allegations: I've spent my life fighting racism!' *Odysee* (1 July 2019) <https://odysee.com/@GoingUndergroundRT:0/chris-williamson-mp-blasts-antisemitism:8> [Accessed April 2022].

27 Connor Creaghan, 'Lincoln MP condemns antisemitism after deleting post' *Lincolnite* (27 June 2019) <https://archive.ph/5Ngps> [Accessed April 2022].

28 Karen Lee, *Twitter* (27 June 2019) <https://archive.ph/U23Hw> [Accessed April 2022].

29 Tony Greenstein, 'Open Letter to John McDonnell – Stand up to Tom Watson and Get a Backbone' *Tony Greenstein's Blog* (4 March 2019) <https://archive.ph/yyzQT> [Accessed April 2022].

30 BBC Radio 5 Live, *Twitter* (1 July 2019) <https://twitter.com/bbc5live/status/1145641404296650752>[Accessed April 2022].

31 Ibid.

32 Ibid.

33 Charles Falconer, 'Labour urgently needs an independent process to root out antisemitism' *Guardian* (9 July 2019) <https://archive.ph/Acwhb> [Accessed March 2022].

34 Ibid.

35 Kate Proctor, 'Row over "bullying" of pregnant Labour MP Ellie Reeves rocks party' *Evening Standard* (3 July 2019) <https://archive.ph/r1Ebt> [Accessed March 2022].

36 Steve Walker, '"Hilariously disingenuous" Watson "obnoxious bully" at full NEC meeting. But gets 'pasting' in return' *Skwawkbox* (30 March 2019) <https://archive.ph/BIkl4> [Accessed March 2022].

37 LBC, '"Tom Watson Is A Cynical Old Fixer", Says Former Labour MP Denis MacShane' *LBC* (21 September 2019) <http://web.archive.org/web/20210414204257/https://www.lbc.co.uk/radio/presenters/matt-frei/tom-watson-is-a-cynical-old-fixer-denis-macshane/> [Accessed March 2022].

38 BBC News, 'Harriet Harman: Pregnant Labour MPs should not face deselection' *BBC News* (9 July 2019) <https://archive.ph/9R3gq> [Accessed March 2022].

39 Mattha Busby and Peter Walker, 'MP who criticised Chris Williamson will not face no-confidence vote' *Guardian* (3 July 2019) <https://archive.ph/ALU4Y> [Accessed March 2022].

40 Ibid.

41 Paul Waugh, 'Ellie Reeves: Corbyn Blocks Attempt To Deselect Pregnant Labour MP After "Backlash" *HuffPost* (3 July 2019) <https://archive.ph/7s81X> [Accessed April 2022].

42 Ibid.

43 Darren Loucaides, 'The anti-Semitism crisis tearing the UK Labour Party apart, explained' *Vox* (8 March 2019) <https://archive.ph/DFazP> [Accessed April 2022].

44 Benjamin Kentish, '"The abuse made me physically ill": Luciana Berger reveals toll of fighting antisemitism while Labour MPs refused to stand by her' *Independent* (9 November 2019) <https://archive.ph/zuww3> [Accessed April 2022].

45 LabourList, '"This is your legacy Mr Corbyn": 67 Labour peers' advert on antisemitism' *LabourList* (17 July 2019) <https://archive.ph/uhdtA> [Accessed April 2022].

46 Ibid.

NOTES

CHAPTER SEVENTEEN – FIGHTING BACK

1. Labour Against the Witch-Hunt, 'Model Motions: 'Reinstate Chris Williamson MP!'' *LAW* (28 February 2019) <https://archive.ph/3b8cv> [Accessed April 2022].
2. Sienna Rodgers, 'Exclusive: Labour HQ tells local parties not to accept motions on disciplinary cases' *LabourList* (5 March 2019) <https://archive.ph/pJPRh> [Accessed April 2022].
3. Jon Craig, 'Tony Benn: 'Controversial, But Courteous'' *Sky News* (14 March 2014) <https://archive.ph/dADiu> [Accessed April 2022].
4. Thames TV, 'Tony Benn | Labour Party | Political Struggle |1981' *YouTube* (25 March 2017) (first shown 28 May 1981) <http://web.archive.org/web/20200228004725/https://www.youtube.com/watch?v=t0PQMvH3DYU> [Accessed April 2022], at 0:20.
5. 'Chris Williamson and Francesca Martinez, 'JC4PM General Election Now!' *YouTube* (26 October 2018) <www.youtube.com/watch?v=ELMvDgO_6rs> [Accessed April 2022].
6. Left Legal Fighting Fund, *Twitter* (12 August 2019) <https://twitter.com/Fighting_Fund/status/1160925291910447106> [Accessed April 2022].
7. Noam Chomsky and others, 'Jewish support for Chris Williamson' *Guardian* (8 July 2019) <https://web.archive.org/web/20190708173939/https://www.theguardian.com/news/2019/jul/08/jewish-support-for-chris-williamson> [Accessed April 2022].
8. Home Office, '£770,000 awarded through Building a Stronger Britain Together' *Home Office* (28 June 2019) <http://web.archive.org/web/20210514072047/https://www.gov.uk/government/news/770000-awarded-through-building-a-stronger-britain-together> [Accessed April 2022].
9. Guardian, 'Removed: article' *Guardian* (9 July 2019) <https://archive.ph/bvk0R> [Accessed March 2022].

CHAPTER EIGHTEEN – TOTAL WAR

1. Chris Williamson, 'Democracy Roadshow: The Sequel' *YouTube* (21 Aug 2019) <www.youtube.com/watch?v=7US30mDy6xg> [Accessed April 2022].
2. Arthur Stanley Newens, *In Quest of a Fairer Society: My Life and Politics* (The Memoir Club 2013).
3. Jody Doherty-Cove, 'Chris Williamson event cancelled by venue after MP's intervention' *Argus* (24 July 2019) <https://archive.ph/VeqPh> [Accessed April 2022].
4. Ibid.
5. Guido Fawkes, 'Chris Williamson's Brighton event cancelled a third time' *Guido Fawkes* (8 August 2019) <https://archive.ph/luJzT> [Accessed April 2022].
6. Jewish Telegraph, 'Electric Shock for Williamson' *Facebook* (15 August 2019) <https://archive.ph/hEyoJ> [Accessed April 2022].
7. Ibid.
8. Hannah Mitchell, 'Concerns raised over suspended MP Chris Williamson giving lecture at University of Nottingham' *Nottingham Post* (8 October 2019) <https://archive.ph/pzcCT> [Accessed April 2022].
9. Ibid.
10. University of Nottingham, 'Statement on the invitation to Chris Williamson MP' *University of Nottingham* (4 October 2019) <https://archive.ph/2eCTZ> [Accessed April 2022].
11. Asa Winstanley, 'David Miller was cleared of anti-Semitism, leaked document shows' *Electronic Intifada* (22 October 2021) <https://archive.ph/9N5w3> [Accessed April 2022].
12. Kit Klarenberg, 'Meet Edward Isaacs, the student waging a campus war for Israel' *Electronic Intifada* (16 December 2021) <https://archive.ph/PPxNj> [Accessed April 2022].

NOTES

13 Joshua Lee, *LinkedIn* (archived 18 December 2021) <https://archive.md/hv1ub> [Accessed March 2022].

14 CAMERA, 'A Brief History of CAMERA' *CAMERA* <https://archive.ph/BFuvA> [Accessed April 2022].

15 Rania Khalek, 'Pro-Israel groups vow to "eliminate" BDS' *Electronic Intifada* (7 June 2016) <https://archive.ph/GSNy3> [Accessed April 2022].

16 CAMERA, 'Ha'aretz Allegation of War Crime Unfounded' *CAMERA* <https://archive.ph/7yMY6> [Accessed April 2022].

17 CAMERA on Campus, 'About Us' *CAMERA on Campus* <https://archive.ph/qDqfW> [Accessed April 2022].

18 Joshua Lee (n 13).

19 Masa Israel Journey, 'About the Masa Application' <https://archive.ph/OVmAf> [Accessed April 2022].

20 Masa Israel Journey, 'About us' *Masa Israel Journey* <https://archive.fo/om8hy> [Accessed April 2022].

21 Joshua Lee (n 13).

22 Joanne Greenaway, 'Leadership is not about the ego – it is about the duty' *Jewish News* (17 July 2021) <https://archive.ph/VbkEp> [Accessed April 2022].

23 Ronald Heifetz and Marty Linsky, *Leadership on the Line: Staying Alive Through the Dangers of Change* (Harvard Business Review Press 2002), pp. 11–13, p. 42.

24 Ilan Pappé, 'The 1948 Ethnic Cleansing of Palestine' (2006) 36(1) *Journal of Palestine Studies*, p. 18.

25 Los Angeles Times, 'Colonel Says Rabin Ordered Breaking of Palestinians' Bones' (22 June 1990) *Los Angeles Times* <https://archive.ph/JxOc8> [Accessed April 2022].

26 Joshua Lee (n 13).

27 Masa Israel Journey, 'Our Leadership Approach' *Masa Israel Journey* <https://archive.ph/4zhKE> [Accessed April 2022].

28 Joshua Lee (n 13).

29 JISS, 'JISS Experts' *JISS* <https://archive.ph/6EBL2> [Accessed April 2022].

30 Joshua Lee (n 13).

CHAPTER NINETEEN – THE FIX

1 Benjamin Kentish, 'Labour facing fresh Chris Williamson row as suspended MP set to speak at 'multiple' events at party conference' *Independent* (5 August 2019) <https://archive.ph/fC7to> [Accessed April 2022].

2 Ibid.

3 Mohamed Elmaazi, 'Waterstones shuts down book launch exposing the antisemitism witch hunt against the left' *Canary* (24 September 2019) <https://archive.ph/OakuL> [Accessed April 2022].

4 Greg Philo, Mike Berry, Justin Schlosberg, Antony Lerman and David Miller, *Bad News for Labour: Antisemitism, the Party and Public Belief* (Pluto Press 2019)

5 Zach Dorfman, Sean D Naylor and Michael Isikoff, 'Kidnapping, assassination and a London shoot-out: Inside the CIA's secret war plans against WikiLeaks' *Yahoo News* (26 September 2021) <https://archive.ph/JM66e> [Accessed March 2022].

6 Tom Porter, 'The CIA pitched Trump officials plans to assassinate Julian Assange while he was hiding in a London embassy in 2017, report says' *Yahoo News* (27 September 2021) <https://archive.ph/moUgq> [Accessed April 2022].

7 Sonam Sheth, 'The CIA's massive 'Vault 7' leak resulted from 'woefully lax' security protocols within the agency's own network, an internal report found' *Business Insider* (16 June 2020) <https://archive.ph/M9iXY> [Accessed April 2022.].

8 Ewen MacAskill, Sam Thielman and Philip Oltermann, 'WikiLeaks publishes "biggest ever leak of secret CIA documents"' *Guardian* (7 March 2017) <https://archive.ph/J4YA4> [Accessed March 2022].

NOTES

CHAPTER TWENTY – JUDGMENT DAY

1 Media Show, 'Investigating Michael Jackson' *BBC Radio 4* (6 March 2019) <http://web.archive.org/web/20220410021314/https://www.bbc.co.uk/sounds/play/m0002zcz> [Accessed April 2022], at 18:00.
2 Ibid, at 17:20.
3 *Williamson MP v Formby* [2019] EWHC 2639 (QB).
4 Linda Tsang, 'Lawyer of the week: Rachel Crasnow, who defended the Labour Party against Chris Williamson MP' *Times* (17 October 2019) <https://archive.ph/honDM> [Accessed March 2022].
5 Chris Williamson, *Twitter* (10 October 2019) <https://archive.ph/vp3Mb> [Accessed April 2022].

CHAPTER TWENTY-ONE – TURKEYS VOTING FOR CHRISTMAS

1 Sienna Rodgers, *Twitter* (6 November 2019) <https://archive.ph/HuM2w> [Accessed April 2022].
2 Heather Stewart, 'Tom Watson urges Labour members to sign remain declaration' *Guardian* (4 July 2019) <https://archive.ph/m3TRR> [Accessed April 2022].
3 Peter Walker, 'Tom Watson peerage rejected by Lords vetting commission' *Guardian* (1 June 2020) <https://archive.ph/oxLKx> [Accessed April 2022].

CHAPTER TWENTY-TWO – INDEPENDENCE

1 Morning Star, 'Former Aslef president calls on Labour not to field a candidate against Chris Williamson' *Morning Star* (13 November 2019) <https://archive.ph/idbiX> [Accessed April 2022].
2 Morning Star, 'Britain's capitalist class will do all it can to stop Corbyn becoming PM, Communist Party warns' *Morning Star* (14 November 2019) <https://archive.ph/a69Mk>[Accessed April 2022].
3 Heather Stewart, 'Jeremy Corbyn makes Unite's Andrew Murray a part-time consultant' *Guardian* (26 February 2018) <https://archive.ph/g2Di2> [Accessed April 2022].
4 Michael Ashcroft, 'Was it really 'Brexit wot lost it' for Labour?' *Lord Ashcroft Polls* (17 December 2019) <https://archive.ph/91etO> [Accessed March 2022].
5 Rajeev Syal, 'McDonnell: I won't stay neutral in second Brexit referendum' *Guardian* (24 November 2019) <https://archive.ph/WEnqf> [Accessed April 2022].
6 William James and Michael Holden, 'Corbyn – I would stay neutral in a second Brexit referendum' *Reuters* (22 November 2019) <https://archive.ph/1RGtI> [Accessed April 2022].
7 Rachael Revesz, 'Jeremy Paxman grills Jeremy Corbyn on difference between Labour manifesto and personal views and it backfires' *Independent* (30 May 2017) <https://archive.ph/hWK2s> [Accessed April 2022].
8 Ronan Burtenshaw, 'Jeremy Corbyn: 'We Didn't Go Far Enough'' *Tribune* (11 October 2020) <https://archive.ph/MLE9Q> [Accessed March 2022].

CHAPTER TWENTY-THREE – ROAD TO PERDITION

1 Index on Censorship, 'Index on Censorship announces Ruth Smeeth as new chief executive' *Index on Censorship* (15 June 2020) <https://archive.ph/KswNS> [Accessed April 2022].
2 Index on Censorship, '50 Years of Index' *Index on Censorship* <https://archive.ph/gaZOq> [Accessed March 2022].
3 Edelman, 'Edelman UK appoints Luciana Berger, Managing Director, Advocacy and Public Affairs' *Edelman* (1 July 2020) <https://archive.ph/gZpuT> [Accessed April 2022].

NOTES

4 Anna Gross, 'Chuka Umunna joins Edelman as head of ESG' *Financial Times* (7 July 2020) <https://archive.ph/Cp826> [Accessed March 2022].

5 Jim Armitage, 'Former political high-flier Chuka Umunna jumps from Edelman environment role to banking giant JPMorgan' *Evening Standard* (10 February 2021) <https://archive.ph/1EdoQ> [Accessed April 2022].

6 David Kogan, *Protest and Power: The Battle for the Labour Party* (Bloomsbury Publishing 2019), p. 52.

7 Tom Blackburn, 'Starmer's War on Grassroots Politics' *Tribune* (8 February 2021) <https://archive.ph/gpolf> [Accessed March 2022].

8 Labour Party, 'Labour Party Rule Book 2020' *Labour Party* <https://web.archive.org/web/20220129193704/https://labour.org.uk/wp-content/uploads/2020/04/rulebook-2020.pdf> [Accessed April 2022]

9 Support David Miller, 'FAQs' *Support Miller* <https://archive.ph/Q2Kne> [Accessed March 2022].

10 Ibid.

11 Nicola Woolcock, 'Gavin Williamson threatens funding cuts over universities' antisemitism failures' *Times* (9 October 2020) <https://archive.ph/5yLmo> [Accessed April 2022].

12 Bill Bowring, John Hendy, Anthony Hooper, Michael Mansfield, Stephen Sedley, Hugh Tomlinson, Frances Webber and Geoffrey Bindman, 'Antisemitism definition is undermining free speech' *Guardian* (7 January 2021) <https://archive.ph/pHwEA> [Accessed March 2022].

13 Higher Education (Freedom of Speech) HC Bill 012 2021–22.

14 'Bristol University: Politicians urge action over professor's comments' *BBC News* (8 March 2021) <https://archive.ph/bWlH9> [Accessed April 2022].

15 Lee Harpin, 'MPs and peers accuse Miller of "inciting hate"' *Jewish Chronicle* (4 March 2012) <https://archive.ph/H8nf1> [Accessed April 2022].

16 Eleanor Busby, 'Universities may face cuts if they reject definition of antisemitism, says education minister' *Independent* (9 October 2020) <https://archive.ph/iCXYw> [Accessed March 2022].

17 Support David Miller, 'Israel Gravy Train' <https://archive.ph/KYzBT> *Support Miller* [Accessed March 2022].

18 Asa Winstanley, 'Professor David Miller fired after Israel lobby smear campaign' *Electronic Intifada* (1 October 2021) <https://archive.ph/chHQ0> [Accessed April 2022].

19 University of Bristol, 'Statement on Professor David Miller' *University of Bristol* (1 October 2021) <https://archive.ph/ILabg> [Accessed April 2022].

20 Ibid.

21 Spinwatch, 'About Spinwatch' *Spinwatch* <https://archive.ph/W4ZtP> [Accessed April 2022].

22 Ibid.

23 Powerbase, 'Main Page' *Powerbase* <https://archive.ph/DfDTC> [Accessed April 2022].

24 Hansard, 'Public Bill Committees' *UK Parliament* (13 September 2001) <https://archive.ph/ieWL3> [Accessed April 2022].

25 Guido Fawkes, 'Diane Abbott launched report by Jewish-obsessed conspiracist who was suspended over anti-Semitism' *Guido Fawkes* (28 March 2019) <https://archive.ph/f5FTA> [Accessed March 2022].

CHAPTER TWENTY-FOUR - THE "ANTISEMITISM" AGENDA

1 Democracy Now!, 'Israel's First Lady of Human Rights: A Conversation with Shulamit Aloni' *Democracy Now!* (14 August 2002) <http://web.archive.org/web/20220117161843/www.democracynow.org/2002/8/14/israels_first_lady_of_human_rights> [Accessed March 2022].

NOTES

2 Owen Jones, *This Land: The Story of a Movement* (Allen Lane 2020).

3 Ibid, p. 251.

4 Ibid, p. 214.

5 Ibid, p. 250.

6 Ed McNally, 'Jeremy Corbyn Was Successful When He Stuck to His Socialist Principles' *Jacobin* (7 October 2020) <https://archive.ph/FcORE> [Accessed March 2022].

7 Jonathan Judaken, 'Introduction – AHR Roundtable: Rethinking Anti-Semitism' (2018) 123(4) *The American Historical Review*, p. 1125.

8 Owen Jones (n 2), p. 212.

9 Ofer Aderet, 'Renowned Jewish Historian: Stop Using the Term "Antisemitism"' *Haaretz* (29 September 2020) <https://archive.ph/XEPlo> [Accessed March 2022].

10 Shlomo Sand, 'Antisemitism? Better Call It Judeophobia' *Haaretz* (24 November 2020) <https://archive.ph/9zlfW> [Accessed March 2022].

11 Jonathan Judaken (n 7), p.1132.

12 Abba Eban, 'Our place in the human scheme' (1973) 40(6) *Congress Bi-Weekly*, pp. 5–9.

13 Jonathan Judaken (n 7), p. 1125.

14 Ibid, p. 1126.

15 Ibid, p. 1129.

16 Ibid, p. 1126.

17 Ibid.

18 Ibid, p. 1127.

19 Ibid, p. 1136.

20 Daniel Schroeter, '"Islamic Anti-Semitism" in Historical Discourse – AHR Roundtable: Rethinking Anti-Semitism' (2018) 123 (4) *The American Historical Review*, p. 1180.

21 Owen Jones (n 2), p. 215.

22 Ibid, p. 212.

23 Jonathan Judaken (n 7), p. 1131.

24 Owen Jones (n 2), p. 218.

25 Ibid, p. 217.

26 Naeim Giladi, *Ben Gurion's Scandals: How the Hagannah and The Mossad Eliminated Jews* (2nd edn, Debdelion Books 2003), p. 163.

27 Sabrina Toppa, 'Europe's Jews Should Move to Israel, Says Israel's Prime Minister' *Time* (16 February 2015) <https://archive.ph/4aR9B> [Accessed March 2022].

28 Owen Jones (n 2), pp. 219–20.

29 Nora Scholtes, 'Bulwark against Asia': Zionist Exclusivism and Palestinian Responses' (PhD Thesis) (University of Kent 2015) <http://web.archive.org/web/20210615152439/https://core.ac.uk/download/pdf/30707675.pdf> [Accessed March 2022], p. 2.

30 Ibid, p. 3.

31 Theodor Herzl, *The Jews' State* (first published 1896, tr Henk Overberg, Rowman and Littlefield Publishers 1997), pp. 91–2.

32 Nur Masalha, *The Politics of Denial: Israel and the Palestinian Refugee Problem* (Pluto Press 2003), p. 15.

33 Ibid, p. 19.

34 David Cronin, 'How Britain wanted a Jewish Ulster in Palestine' *Electronic Intifada* (28 May 2021) <https://archive.ph/yPauu> [Accessed March 2022].

NOTES

35 Benny Morris, *Righteous Victims: A History of the Zionist-Arab Conflict, 1881-1998* (Vintage Books 2001), p. 138.
36 Nur Masalha, *Expulsion of the Palestinians: The Concept of "Transfer" in Zionist Political Thought, 1882-1948* (Institute for Palestine Studies 1992), p. 107.
37 Stanley Porter, Michael Hayes and David Tombs (eds), *Faith in the Millennium* (Sheffield Academic Press 2001), p. 79.
38 Nur Masalha, *The Politics of Denial* (n 32), p. 26.
39 Owen Jones (n 2), p. 219.
40 Oliver Eagleton, 'Vicious, Horrible People' (2021) 127 *New Left Review*, p. 140.
41 Ibid, p. 145.
42 Owen Jones (n 2), p. 218.
43 Norman Rose, 'A *Senseless, Squalid War': Voices from Palestine – 1890s to 1948* (Pimlico 2010), p. 71
44 Owen Jones (n 2), p. 218.
45 Ibid.
46 Decolonize Palestine, 'Redwashing' *Decolonize Palestine* <https://archive.ph/De1dN> [Accessed March 2022].
47 Owen Jones (n 2), p. 255.
48 Dan Hodges, 'Labour's first Jewish leader is losing the Jewish vote' *Daily Telegraph* (30 October 2014) <https://archive.ph/CvLNE> [Accessed March 2022].
49 Owen Jones (n 2), p. 221.
50 Robert Philpot, 'How Ed Miliband lost the Jewish vote' *Spectator* (18 April 2015) <https://archive.ph/mrSWH> [Accessed April 2022].
51 Mark Regev, 'Antisemitism on the left and Jeremy Corbyn' *Guardian* (5 April 2018) <https://archive.ph/rq0uz> [Accessed March 2022].
52 Jonathan Cook, 'Is Israel's hand behind the attacks on Jeremy Corbyn?' *Middle East Eye* (30 August 2018) <https://archive.ph/lxiWn> [Accessed March 2022].
53 Benjamin Netanyahu, *Twitter* (13 August 2018) <https://archive.ph/ISk5D> [Accessed March 2022].
54 Owen Jones (n 2), p. 232.
55 Ibid, p. 236.
56 Ibid, p. 240.
57 Ibid, p. 238.

CHAPTER TWENTY-FIVE – "IF YOU DON'T FIGHT, YOU WILL ALWAYS LOSE"

1 Thomas Sankara, We *Are Heirs of the World's Revolutions: Speeches from the Burkina Faso revolution 1983–87* (2nd edn, Pathfinder Press 2007), p. 70.
2 BBC News, 'UK ghettos claim shocks ministers' *BBC News* (19 September 2005) <https://archive.ph/B7LtM> [Accessed March 2022].
3 Simon Walters, 'Mandelson "tried to persuade Trevor Phillips to quit by promising him a Ministerial post"' *Daily Mail* (2 August 2009) <https://archive.ph/NfNGZ> [Accessed March 2022].
4 Rajeev Syal, 'Equalities body accused of targeting BAME staff for redundancies' *Guardian* (5 March 2017) <https://archive.ph/rIqKt> [Accessed March 2022].
5 Basit Mahmood, 'Ex-equalities commissioners say calling out racism cost their jobs' *Newsweek* (28 July 2020) <https://archive.ph/TW1sG> [Accessed March 2022].
6 Emilio Casalicchio, 'Human Rights Commission chief: Labour must prove it is not racist party after anti-Semitism row' *Politics Home* (26 September 2017) <https://archive.ph/VWkGX> [Accessed March 2022].

NOTES

7 Chris Williamson, 'Response to the EHRC's investigation into 'antisemitism' in the Labour Party' *Left Legal Fighting Fund* (29 October 2020) <https://archive.ph/xXHaC> [Accessed April 2022].

8 Niccolò Machiavelli, *The Prince* (first published 1532, tr Peter Bondanella, OUP 2005), p. 11.

9 Matt Kennard, 'Five questions for new Labour leader Sir Keir Starmer about his UK and US national security establishment links' *Grayzone* (5 July 2020) <https://archive.ph/hhXAT> [Accessed March 2022].

10 Richard Norton-Taylor, 'MI5 officer will not be prosecuted over Binyam Mohamed abuse' *Guardian* (17 November 2010) <https://archive.ph/VDBCB> [Accessed March 2022].

11 Ewen MacAskill and Owen Bowcott, 'UK prosecutors admit destroying key emails in Julian Assange case' *Guardian* (10 November 2017) <https://archive.ph/5LSFB> [Accessed March 2022].

12 Oliver Eagleton, 'Keir Starmer is a Long-Time Servant of the British Security State' *Novara Media* (2 March 2021) <https://archive.is/vsyqJ> [Accessed March 2022].

13 Oliver Eagleton, *The Starmer Project: A Journey to the Right* (Verso 2022), p. 35.

14 David Mills, 'Beware the Trilateral Commission!' *Washington Post* (25 April 1992) <https://archive.is/WWupV> [Accessed November 2022].

15 Michel Crozier, Samuel Huntington and Joji Watanuki, *The Crisis of Democracy: Report on the Governability of Democracies to the Trilateral Commission* (New York University Press 1975), Front Matter.

16 Ibid, p. 113.

17 Ibid, p. 127.

18 Dorset Eye, 'What mystery organisation do Sir Keir Starmer, Henry Kissinger and Jeffrey Epstein... have in common?' *Dorset Eye* (2 February 2020) <https://archive.ph/q2XmO> [Accessed March 2022].

19 Oliver Eagleton, *The Starmer Project* (n 13), p. 56.

20 Ibid, p. 185.

21 Ibid, p. 186.

22 Jennie Formby, *Twitter* (23 August 2021) <https://archive.ph/6NGn4> [Accessed April 2022].

23 Sienna Rodgers, 'Exclusive: Labour HQ tells local parties not to accept motions on disciplinary cases' *LabourList* (5 March 2019) <https://archive.ph/pJPRh> [Accessed April 2022].

24 Jessica Elgot, 'Labour MPs and members ordered not to discuss Corbyn's suspension' *Guardian* (27 November 2020) <https://archive.ph/8B2Oc> [Accessed April 2022].

25 Ben Butcher and Alex Clark, 'All-time lows for Labour in Batley and Spen despite overall win' *Daily Telegraph* (2 July 2021) <https://archive.ph/dCPKf> [Accessed March 2022].

26 Paul Mason, 'Labour's victory in Batley and Spen shows the party is learning how to fight back' *New Statesman* (2 July 2021) <https://archive.ph/yOT3q> [Accessed March 2022].

27 Peter Oborne, 'Starmer's Labour has found a culprit for losing the Red Wall: Muslim voters' *Middle East Eye* (25 June 2021) <https://archive.ph/4qqoa> [Accessed March 2022].

28 David Wilcock, Dave Rudge and Claire Ellicott, 'Labour accused of 'dog-whistle racism' by one of its OWN MPs over 'anti-Hindu' leaflet amid deepening dirty tricks row in Batley & Spen by-election campaign – as furious row breaks out between George Galloway supporters and local councillors' *Daily Mail* (29 June 2019) <https://archive.ph/YE2bLl> [Accessed March 2022].

29 *Neslen and others v Evans* [2021] EWHC 1909 (QB).

NOTES

30 Ammar Kazmi, 'Labour on Trial: The Slow Death of Blairism' *Medium* (8 July 2021) <https://archive.is/9gg8i> [Accessed March 2022].

31 Keir Starmer, 'Keir Starmer's statement in response to EHRC's report into antisemitism' *Labour Party* (29 October 2020) <https://archive.ph/4FkPW> [Accessed March 2022].

32 Aaron Bastani, 'Why is Labour Broke?' *Novara Media* (27 January 2022) <https://archive.ph/RSWpc> [Accessed March 2022].

33 Esther Webber and Eleni Courea, 'UK Labour asks staff to take pay cut amid cash crunch' *Politico* (14 January 2022) <https://archive.is/Q3g7K> [Accessed March 2022].

CHAPTER TWENTY-SIX – MAKING THE REVOLUTION

1 Harrison James, 'Keir Starmer refuses to outline all donors funding his Labour leadership bid' *Metro* (4 March 2020) <https://archive.is/0MrkB> [Accessed March 2022].

2 John McEvoy, 'Keir Starmer received £50,000 donation from pro-Israel lobbyist in leadership bid' *Canary* (17 April 2020) <https://archive.ph/D8RP7> [Accessed March 2022].

3 Lee Harpin, 'Starmer tells JLM hustings he would not call himself a Zionist' *Jewish Chronicle* (14 February 2020) <https://archive.is/XteiK> [Accessed March 2022].

4 Board of Deputies of British Jews, 'The Board of Deputies launches its Ten Pledges for Labour leadership and deputy leadership candidates' *BoD* (13 January 2020) <https://archive.ph/IHISj> [Accessed March 2022].

5 Asa Winstanley, 'UK Labour Party hires former Israeli spy' *Electronic Intifada* (19 January 2021) <https://archive.is/WMOuX> [Accessed March 2022].

6 Lee Harpin, 'Keir Starmer: "Anti-Zionist antisemitism is antithesis of Labour tradition"' *Jewish News* (16 November 2021) <https://archive.ph/bwIVa> [Accessed March 2022].

7 Alex MacDonald, 'Labour leader Keir Starmer slammed for 'colonial' speech on Israel and BDS' *Middle East Eye* (17 November 2021) <https://archive.is/shDac> [Accessed March 2022].

8 Decolonize Palestine, 'Myth: Israel made the desert bloom' *Decolonize Palestine* <https://archive.ph/P64hH> [Accessed March 2022].

9 UK Parliament, 'Engagements – Volume 707: debated on Wednesday 19 January 2022' *Hansard* (19 January 2022) <https://archive.ph/yFhUf> [Accessed March 2022].

10 UK Parliament, 'The Register of Members' Financial Interests: Wakeford, Christian (Bury South)' *UK Parliament* (21 December 2020) <https://archive.ph/efgym> [Accessed March 2022].

11 Josh Kaplan, 'Tory MP and co-chair of the Parliamentary group on British Jews defects to Labour' *Jewish Chronicle* (19 January 2022) <https://archive.ph/Hp10G> [Accessed March 2022].

12 Jake Wallis Simons, 'Israel is not an apartheid state, says Keir Starmer as he apologises for the Corbyn years' *Jewish Chronicle* (7 April 2022) <https://archive.ph/vePlx> [Accessed April 2022].

13 Ibid.

14 Keir Starmer, 'Under my leadership, Labour's commitment to NATO is unshakable' *Guardian* (10 February 2022) <https://archive.ph/mxPbp> [Accessed March 2022].

15 Stop the War Coalition, 'List of Signatories: Stop the War Statement on the Crisis Over Ukraine' *Stop the War Coalition* (18 February 2022) <https://archive.ph/Pljda> [Accessed March 2022].

16 Peter Walker, 'Labour MPs drop backing for statement criticising NATO after Starmer warning' (24 February 2022) *Guardian* <https://archive.ph/uJg7s> [Accessed March 2022].

17 Jessica Elgot, 'Corbyn will not regain Labour whip while endorsing Stop the War, suggests Starmer' *Guardian* (11 April 2022) <https://archive.ph/zYbhR> [Accessed April 2022]

NOTES

18 Paul Waugh, 'Keir Starmer Expels Far-Left Corbyn Supporters from Labour' *HuffPost* (20 July 2021) <https://archive.ph/DhsC2> [Accessed March 2022].

19 Ibid.

20 Ibid.

21 Sienna Rodgers, 'Labour NEC bans three more groups "not compatible" with party rules or values' *LabourList* (29 March 2022) <https://archive.ph/MVKzU> [Accessed March 2022].

22 Steve Walker, 'Starmer abolishes fairness and natural justice from Labour's expulsion rules. In as many words' *Skwawkbox* (6 April 2022) <https://archive.ph/Hl77Y> [Accessed April 2022].

23 Ken Loach, *Twitter* (14 August 2021) <https://archive.ph/zr5kc> [Accessed March 2022].

24 Tom D. Rogers, 'The Labour Party is on the verge of bankruptcy' *Evolve Politics* (10 January 2022) <https://archive.ph/RxUrg> [Accessed March 2022].

25 George Parker and Jim Pickard, 'Labour Party is now 'pro-business', vows Rachel Reeves' *Financial Times* (19 January 2022) <https://archive.ph/O4tVa> [Accessed March 2022].

26 Labour Party, 'Labour Party Annual Report 2020' *Labour Party* <https://web.archive.org/web/20210616191332/https://labour.org.uk/wp-content/uploads/2020/11/AnnualReport2020.pdf> [Accessed March 2022], p. 65.

27 Ammar Kazmi, 'The British Establishment's Forever War Against Jeremy Corbyn' *Jacobin* (12 December 2020) <https://archive.is/KHdJU> [Accessed March 2022].

28 John McDonnell, *Twitter* (17 July 2021) <https://archive.ph/cUchl> [Accessed March 2022].

29 Jeremy Corbyn, *Twitter* (20 July 2021) <https://archive.ph/tTvwN> [Accessed March 2022].

30 Vladimir Lenin, 'Lenin's Speech on Affiliation to the British Labour Party: The Second Congress of the Communist International – July 19-August 7, 1920' *Marxist* <www.marxist.net/openturn/historic/script.htm?lenin.htm> [Accessed August 2021].

31 Sam Shead, 'Westminster politicians hold directorships in firms with annual revenues of £220 billion and only 40% of them are declared' *Business Insider* (26 May 2016) <https://archive.ph/vYPyb> [Accessed March 2022].

32 Susan Ratcliffe (eds), 'Political Parties' in *Oxford Essential Quotations* (4th edn, OUP 2016) <https://archive.ph/D04Ll> [Accessed March 2022].

33 Mike Wayne, 'Roadmaps After Corbyn' 131 *New Left Review* (September-October 2021) <https://archive.ph/CYJyG> [Accessed March 2022].

34 Vladimir Lenin, 'What Is to Be Done?' in Henry M Christman (eds) *Essential Works of Lenin* (first published 1901-02, Dover Publications 1987), p. 95.

35 Ibid, p. 105.

36 Martin Luther King Jr, *Letter from Birmingham Jail* (first published 1964, Penguin Books 2018), pp. 15–16.

37 Ernesto Guevara, *Obras Escogidas* (Resma 2004), p. 199.

38 Aneurin Bevan, *In Place of Fear* (William Heinemann Ltd 1952), p. 21.

APPENDIX

1 Kevin Rawlinson, 'Jewish event at Labour conference abandoned after bomb scare' *Guardian* (25 September 2018) <https://archive.ph/osaAo> [Accessed April 2022].

2 Al Jazeera, 'The Lobby P3: An Anti-Semitic Trope' *YouTube* (12 January 2017) <www.youtube.com/watch?v=L3dn-VV3czc> [Accessed April 2022].

3 Asa Winstanley 'Jeremy Corbyn must stop pandering to Labour's Israel lobby' *Electronic Intifada* (28 March 2018) <https://archive.ph/8b8U1> [Accessed April 2022].

NOTES

4 Gideon Rachman, 'Why the new nationalists love Israel' *Financial Times* (1 April 2019) <https://archive.ph/bWJoJ> [Accessed April 2022].

5 Steve Walker, 'Ryan loses no-confidence vote' *Skwawkbox* (6 September 2018) <https://archive.ph/9GFaz> [Accessed April 2022].

6 Joan Ryan, *Twitter* (6 September 2015) <https://archive.ph/igFug> [Accessed April 2022].

7 Steve Walker, 'Enfield/Caliskan scandal grows – ALL black councillors were deselected' *Skwawkbox* (11 June 2018) <https://archive.ph/yIxrd> [Accessed April 2022].

8 Al Jazeera, 'The Lobby P3' (n 2).

9 Asa Winstanley, 'How the Israel lobby fakes anti-Semitism' *Electronic Intifada* (14 January 2017) <https://archive.ph/IxHpr> [Accessed April 2022].

10 Al Jazeera, 'The Lobby P2: The Training Session' *YouTube* (12 January 2017) <http://web.archive.org/web/20220201114452/https://www.youtube.com/watch?v=Vuk1EhkEctE> [Accessed December 2021].

11 Jerusalem Post, 'UK's Corbyn calls for investigation into Israeli meddling after embassy row' *Jerusalem Post* (16 January 2017) <https://archive.ph/3cb4X> [Accessed April 2022].

12 Alex MacDonald, 'Israel embassy plot: Labour pushes for inquiry into Shai Masot scandal' *Middle East Eye* (12 January 2017) <https://archive.ph/zHFvI> [Accessed April 2022].

13 Asa Winstanley, 'Israel lobby funders back breakaway British MPs' *Electronic Intifada* (27 February 2019) <https://archive.ph/cqbxT> [Accessed April 2022].

14 Jewish News, 'Joan Ryan tells AIPAC: Labour "seeks to demonise and delegitimise Israel"' *Jewish News* (25 March 2019) <https://archive.ph/sxweu> [Accessed April 2022].

15 Ed Poole, *Twitter* (14 April 2019) <https://archive.ph/d1cWd> [Accessed April 2022].

16 Adam McGibbon, *Twitter* (15 April 2019) <https://archive.ph/no92s> [Accessed April 2022].

17 Alastair Thompson, *Twitter* (21 December 2018) <https://archive.ph/JBMln> [Accessed April 2022].

18 Asa Winstanley, 'Fake Labour accounts fueling "anti-Semitism crisis"' *Electronic Intifada* (17 January 2019) <https://archive.ph/Bfedd> [Accessed April 2022].

19 Lee Harpin, 'Schism grows between groups over how to respond to hate' *Jewish Chronicle* (26 October 2018) <https://archive.ph/QZ8c2> [Accessed April 2022].

20 Iggy Ostanin deleted the reference in his Twitter biography to his former employer, Bellingcat, but an archived version is still available [see: https://archive.ph/ca7OK]. It appears that Ostanin was the 'source' of several media stories targeting Jeremy Corbyn as a 'threat to national security' and intimating that Corbyn is an 'antisemite'.

21 Zoe Drewett, 'Labour MP turns on Jeremy Corbyn calling him a "f***ing anti-Semite and a racist"' *Metro* (18 July 2018) <https://archive.ph/Lonip> [Accessed April 2022].

22 Gavin Cordon, 'Jeremy Corbyn blasts Margaret Hodge for "breach of trust" in anti-Semitism row' *Daily Mirror* (6 March 2019) <https://archive.ph/OdDf8> [Accessed April 2022].

23 Tim Shipman, Sean Rayment, Richard Kerbaj and James Lyons, 'Corbyn hit by mutiny on airstrikes' *Times* (20 September 2015) <https://archive.ph/4885l> [Accessed April 2022].

24 Francis Elliott, 'Former head of MI6 Sir Richard Dearlove 'troubled' by Corbyn' *Sunday Times* (7 October 2018) <https://archive.ph/ANvUK> [Accessed April 2022].

25 Tim Shipman and Richard Kerbaj, 'MI5 head Andrew Parker summons Jeremy Corbyn for "facts of life" talk on terror' *Sunday Times* (2 September 2018) <https://archive.ph/U3hZU> [Accessed April 2022].

NOTES

26 Henry Zeffman, 'Brexit-weary voters long for political strongman' *Times* (8 April 2019) <https://archive.ph/FQzHu> [Accessed March 2022].

27 Bart Cammaerts, Brooks DeCillia, João Magalhães and César Jimenez-Martínez, 'Journalistic Representations of Jeremy Corbyn in the British Press: From Watchdog to Attackdog' (August 2016) <http://web.archive.org/web/20220215111142/https://www.lse.ac.uk/media-and-communications/assets/documents/research/projects/corbyn/Cobyn-Report.pdf> [Accessed March 2022].

28 Justin Schlosberg, 'Should he stay or should he go?' *Media Reform Coalition* (28 July 2016) <http://web.archive.org/web/20220210134617/https://www.mediareform.org.uk/wp-content/uploads/2016/07/Corbynresearch.pdf> [Accessed March 2022].

29 YouGov, 'Survey Results' *YouGov* (29 August 2016) <https://web.archive.org/web/20210531054132/https://d25d2506sfb94s.cloudfront.net/cumulus_uploads/document/pvxdr2lh73/InternalResults_160830_LabourSelectorate.pdf> [Accessed March 2022].

30 Jewish Socialists' Group, 'Statement on "Labour's problem with antisemitism"' *Jewish Socialists' Group* (28 April 2016) <https://archive.ph/XicPn> [Accessed March 2022].

31 Des Freedman and others, 'Stop Jeremy Corbyn's trial by media over antisemitism' *Guardian* (2 April 2018) <https://archive.ph/ynHlU> [Accessed March 2022].

32 Chuka Umunna, 'Clause IV tells us to live in "solidarity, tolerance and respect" but Labour has failed on anti-Semitism' *LabourList* (16 October 2016) <https://archive.ph/BcXjD> [Accessed March 2022].

33 Chuka Umunna, 'Labour can't talk with credibility about racism until we tackle the antisemitism in our ranks' *Independent* (23 April 2018) <https://archive.ph/eovBk> [Accessed March 2022].

34 LabourList, 'Siobhain McDonagh links anti-capitalism to antisemitism in Labour' *LabourList* (4 March 2019) <https://archive.ph/ATQYB> [Accessed March 2022].

35 I'm a JSA Claimant, 'Margaret Hodge: Anti-zionism is antisemitism' *Channel 4 News* (7 March 2019) <http://web.archive.org/web/20220310022103/https://www.youtube.com/watch?v=5fpaBaoN_jw> [Accessed March 2022].

36 Joe Millis, 'Chris Williamson accused of 'whitewashing prejudices' by signing Holocaust book' *Jewish News* (23 January 2019) <https://archive.ph/onUQh> [Accessed March 2022].

37 Shami Chakrabarti, 'The Shami Chakrabarti Inquiry' *Labour Party* (30 June 2016) <https://web.archive.org/web/20211228191005/https://labour.org.uk/wp-content/uploads/2017/10/Chakrabarti-Inquiry-Report-30June16.pdf> [Accessed March 2022].

38 Tony Greenstein and others, 'Jeremy Corbyn and antisemitism claims' *Guardian* (20 August 2015) <https://archive.ph/ggXjf> [Accessed March 2022].

39 Jewish Chronicle, 'Luciana Berger targeted by antisemites after jailing of abusive internet troll' *Jewish Chronicle* (25 November 2016) <https://archive.ph/OjYjZ> [Accessed March 2022].

40 Samuel Osborne, 'Neo-Nazi given two-year sentence for 'vile antisemitic abuse' of Labour MP Luciana Berger' *Independent* (8 December 2016) <https://archive.ph/Nhjji> [Accessed March 2022].

41 Tom White, 'Jail for internet troll who told Luciana Berger she would "get it like Jo Cox"' *Liverpool Echo* (10 February 2017) <https://archive.ph/MeEiB> [Accessed March 2022].

42 Lee Harpin, 'Teen boasted he wanted to kill Jewish MP' *Jewish Chronicle* (19 July 2018) <https://archive.ph/mBjTf> [Accessed March 2022].

NAME INDEX

Abbott, Diane 4, 114-116, 238, 260, 261, 270, 302, 347
Adonis, Andrew 10, 28
Akehurst, Luke 84
Alexander, Douglas 10, 37
Allen, Charles 8
Allen, Dave 237
Allen, Graham 22
Allende, Salvador 159
Aloni, Shulamit 272
Álvarez, Laura 254
Amsbury, Maggie viii
Andrew, Stuart 73
Ashcroft, Michael 102
Ashworth, Jonathan 15, 16, 37
Asner, Ed 214
Assange, Julian 237-240, 291, 292
Atzmon, Gilad 140, 141, 204, 319, 320, 335
Augustine, Cathy 222
Austin, Ian 12, 78, 103-106, 186, 324
Azam, Mo 49

Baddiel, David 212
Bailey, Luke 360
Balls, Ed 6, 7, 28, 33, 38
Banwait, Ranjit 49-51
Barnett, Emma 202, 203, 269
Baron, John 22
Bash, Graham 178
Bassett, Lewis 92
Bastani, Aaron 172, 173
Bates, Liz 151, 241, 242
Beckett, Andy 369
Beckett, Leo 211
Beckett, Margaret 45, 92, 211, 253
Beckett, Steve 250, 256-258
Beeley, Vanessa 322, 323

Begin, Menachem 90, 130, 311
Bell, Steve 216
Bell, Torsten 37
Bellos, Linda 51
Ben-Gurion, David 228, 280, 281, 283
Benn, Hilary 9, 12, 13, 16-18, 20
Benn, Tony 46, 71, 72, 136, 174, 181, 182, 196, 211, 264, 282
Bercow, John 157
Berger, Luciana 20, 34, 85, 147, 148, 208, 264, 334
Berrisford, Nicole 50
Bevan, Nye 184, 185, 282, 308
Biggs, John 297
Blackman-Woods, Roberta 13
Blair, Tony 4, 5, 9, 10, 35, 42, 62, 66, 71, 72, 149, 181, 182, 203, 206, 264, 265, 293, 302
Blanchard, Olivier 5
Blanchflower, Danny 6, 7
Bloch, Ben 226
Blomfield, Paul 13
Blunkett, David 28
Bonehill-Paine, Joshua 334
Bookbinder, David 51
Bragg, Billy 174-176, 186, 212
Bromley, Pam 289
Brown, Gordon 6, 11, 16, 26, 37, 62, 66, 80, 89, 90, 103, 181, 264, 265
Brown, Lyn 20, 124
Burgon, Richard 58, 92, 95, 114-116, 163, 201, 202, 238, 302
Burnham, Andy 20, 67, 261
Butcher, (Mr Justice) Christopher 298
Byrne, Liam 11, 12, 13

Cable, Vince 26
Callaghan, Jim 14, 66, 67

NAME INDEX

Cameron, David 11, 14, 29, 44, 103
Campbell, Alan 19,
Campbell, Ronnie 22, 238
Chakrabarti, Shami 78, 82-84, 112, 114-116, 213, 331, 332
Chalmers, Alex 77
Chapman, Jenny 37, 114
Chávez, Hugo 100, 101, 107
Chilson, Cyril 135, 84
Cholewka, Stefan 223
Chomsky, Noam 212, 214
Churchill, Winston 101
Cleverly, James 153
Clwyd, Ann 238
Coffey, Ann 58
Cohen, Justin 369, 374
Cohen, Nick 107, 108
Collier, David 266
Collins, Ray 72-74
Connarty, Michael 33
Connolly, James 230
Cooper, John 40
Cooper, Yvette 38, 261
Corbyn, Jeremy v, ix, x, 3, 4, 10, 18, 22-24, 29-31, 34, 37, 38, 42-71, 74-86, 88, 89, 91-100, 102, 104-108, 110-113, 115-123, 125-132, 134-137, 139, 140, 142-149, 151-155, 158-160, 162, 163, 165-167, 170-173, 175, 177, 181-183, 185, 187-189, 191-197, 199, 201-204, 206-211, 213, 224, 230, 234, 237-240, 242, 246, 247, 249-254, 256, 258-266, 271-273, 283-287, 289, 290, 292-295, 299, 302-305, 307-311, 313, 317, 321-323, 325, 326-328, 333, 338, 341, 343, 346, 348, 349, 352
Corbyn, Seb 197
Cortes, Manuel 108, 109
Coulson, Jack 334
Cousins, Maggie 84
Cox, Jo 145, 220

Coyle, Neil 126
Crasnow, Rachel 233, 243, 245
Creagh, Mary 27, 261
Creaghan, Connor 375
Creasy, Stella 170
Crick, Michael 107
Crosby, Lynton 59
Cryer, John 27, 144
Curtice, John 94

Daly, Clare 238
Dar, Yasmine 253
Darling, Alistair 37
Davies, Alan 222-224
Davies, Harry 356
Davies, Peter 92
De Piero, Gloria 37
De Zayas, Alfred 100
Dean, Elaine 210, 211
Dearlove, Richard 325
Dent Coad, Emma 113, 114
Dick, Cressida 138, 140
Draper, Ronnie 222
Drew, Corrie 140
Drewett, Zoe 385
Dromey, Jack 9, 13, 60
Dugher, Michael 37, 80-82, 283
Duncan Smith, Iain 12, 13
Duncan, Alan 100, 101
Dunn, John 62, 221
Durkan, Mark 22

Eagle, Angela 12, 57
Eagleton, Oliver 281, 282, 292, 293
Efford, Clive 154
Eldret, Lisa 50
Ellman, Louise 85, 147, 182-184
Elmi, Huda 189
Engel, David 247

NAME INDEX

Engels, Friedrich 305
Epstein, Jeffrey 293
Evangelou, Christine 64
Evans, David 294, 297
Evans, Jonathan 292

Falconer, Charles 203-206
Falk, Richard 214
Ferrari, Nick 115, 116
Ferrer, Richard 241, 242
Field, Frank 10
Finkelstein, Norman 80, 155, 212, 214, 341, 342
Fisher, Andrew 285
Flint, Caroline 8-10, 17
Flintoff, Crispin 236, 237
Folley, Ben 111, 196
Foot, Michael 282
Ford, Peter 238, 322
Fordham, Hannah 64
Formby, Jennie 88, 131, 142-144, 146, 149, 153, 154, 158, 172, 178-182, 190, 192, 193, 198, 209, 210, 212, 215, 231, 232, 242, 246, 249, 250, 252, 256, 260, 294, 327
Friedman, Milton 305

Gaddafi, Mu'ammar al- 21
Galloway, George 181, 253, 256, 257, 295, 296
García Hernández, Carlos 361
Gardiner, Barry 22, 111
Gardiner, Thomas 231
Gardner, Mark 161
Garnham, Rachel 153
Garratt, Lee viii, 211
Godsiff, Roger 22
Goldstein, Jonathan 141
Goldstone, David 64
Goodman, Amy 272
Graf, Arnie 30, 31

Granger, Chris 64
Green, Elleanne 234
Greenshields, Bill 258
Greenstein, Tony 135, 161, 169, 178, 201, 255, 348, 351
Greenwood, Lilian 194
Guevara, Ernesto 'Che' 159, 307
Gwynne, Andrew 118-120

Hadfield, Greg 216-220, 235, 236, 347
Halligan, Alex 49
Hardie, Keir 224, 290
Harman, Harriet 15, 46, 47, 153, 206, 207, 249, 287
Harris, Tom 29-31
Hattersley, Roy 124, 125
Hayek, Friedrich 305
Healey, Denis 5, 66, 67, 72
Healey, John 120, 151
Heath, Ted 62, 122
Heffer, Eric 282
Heffer, Greg 371
Heifetz, Ronald 227
Helm, Garron 334
Helm, Toby 365, 359
Henderson, Ann 253
Herzl, Theodor 279, 280, 283
Heseltine, Michael 71
Hess, John 225, 228
Hilling, Julie 37
Hilsenrath, Rebecca 288
Hodge, Margaret 58, 85, 98, 105, 147, 180, 183, 184, 324, 329, 342
Hodges, Dan 381
Hodson, Ian 222
Hoffman, Jonathan 132, 133, 311, 312
Holder, Eric 291
Hoon, Geoff 80
Hopkins, Kelvin 238

NAME INDEX

Howarth, George 189
Hulton, William 223
Hunt, Henry 222, 223
Hunt, Tristram 28
Hussain, Fareed 1

Icke, David 276, 337
Isaacs, Edward 226

Jackson, Amy 86, 119, 130, 146, 151-153, 155, 253
Jansson, Asa 347
Jenkins, Roy 122
Johnson, Alan 5, 6, 57
Johnson, Boris 55, 106, 191, 231, 235, 245, 248, 249, 288, 295
Johnson, Diana 27, 198
Johnson, Steve 258
Jónasson, Ögmundur 238
Jones, Helen 13
Jones, Owen 154, 167, 174, 212, 272-274, 276-279, 281-285
Jowell, Tessa 10
Joyce, Eric 73

Kaufman, Gerald 133
Kazmi, Ammar viii, 92, 94, 127, 215, 220, 230, 232, 242, 244
Kelly, Aaron 230
Kelly, Phil 230
Kelton, Stephanie 69
Kendall, Liz 44, 45, 261
Kennard, Matt 290
Kennedy, Jim 48, 49, 186
Kenny, Paul 10, 54, 55, 73
Khan, Sadiq 155
King Jr, Martin Luther 155, 177, 307
Kinnock, Neil 62, 71, 94, 122, 126, 149, 181, 182, 265

Kissinger, Henry 82, 292
Knight, Ted 51
Kosky, Daniel 225
Koussa, Moussa 22
Kyle, Peter 217, 218

Lansman, Jon 49, 108, 133, 142, 143, 154, 186, 195, 196, 253
Lavery, Ian 33, 80, 105, 152, 200, 261, 302, 324
Laxton, Bob 2, 3, 45
Lee, Jennie 282
Lee, Joshua 226-228
Lee, Karen 108, 200, 201
Leir, Edward 64
Lenszner, Damon 132, 133, 311
Leslie, Chris 46, 69, 85
Levane, Leah 214
Levy, Michael 109, 110, 284
Lewis, Brandon 16
Lewis, Clive 85, 164-170, 260, 331
Lewis, Ivan 148
Lipman, Maureen 283
Livermore, Spencer 37
Livingstone, Ken 9, 44, 51, 79-81, 96, 97, 104, 135, 153, 236, 255, 289
Loach, Ken 212, 221, 303
Long-Bailey, Rebecca 221
Lowkey 212
Lucas, Caroline 22
Luxemburg, Rosa 159

MacDonald, Ramsay 76, 100
Machiavelli, Niccolò 243, 252, 290
Machover, Moshé 332
Mack, Eitay 139
MacShane, Denis 96, 206
Maduro, Nicolás 99, 101, 166
Maguire, Kevin 60, 152, 315
Major, John 28

NAME INDEX

Mallet, Paul viii, 158, 244, 250
Mandela, Nelson 83, 330
Mandelson, Peter 10, 26, 35, 36, 76, 287
Mann, John 46, 79, 85, 96, 97, 158, 187
Manson, Jenny 214
Margolyes, Miriam 212
Martin, James 171
Martinez, Francesca 212
Martins Helen 75
Marx, Karl 101, 305
Mason, Paul 382
Mason, Rowena 94, 355, 362, 364
Mason-Power, Alice 38
Masot, Shai 317
Massey, Becky 235
May, Brian 41
May, Theresa 92, 106, 152, 153, 179, 347
McCarthy, Joe 110
McCluskey, Len 127-129, 149
McColgan, Aileen 233
McDonagh, Elisa 187
McDonagh, Siobhain 329
McDonald, Andy 59
McDonald, Tosh 58, 123, 215, 221, 231, 258
McDonnell, John 4, 13, 22, 40, 47, 48, 53, 58, 64, 67-71, 107, 109, 110, 120, 124, 146, 154, 156, 160, 196-198, 201, 239, 260, 261, 302, 304
McFadden, Pat 54
McGlone, Liz 189, 212
McInnes, Liz 99
McKinnell, Catherine 152
McMahon, Jim 49
McNeill, Lara 253
McNicol, Iain 64, 252, 253
Meacher, Michael 5, 10, 32, 33, 46, 48, 49
Melvin, Melanie 347, 348
Melzer, Nils 239
Merron, Gillian 194

Middleton, Dave viii
Mikardo, Ian 282
Miliband, David 4
Miliband, Ed v, ix, 3-11, 14-18, 20, 23, 25-36, 42, 46, 47, 57, 61, 62, 67, 72-74, 81, 82, 99, 113, 116, 153, 263-265, 283, 284
Miliband, Ralph 76
Miller, David 226, 267-270
Miller, Phil 366
Miller, Sabrina 226
Mills, Tom 325
Milne, Seumas 119, 152, 246, 247, 251, 253
Mirwitch, Miriam 207
Mitchell, Bill 68-70, 235, 236
Mitchell, Hannah 376
Modi, Narendra 295
Mohamed, Binyam 291
Moore-Bick, Martin 113-116
Morgan Britton, Luke 361
Morgan, Nicky 28
Morgan, Piers 68, 172
Morris, Benny (X)
Morris, Grahame 63, 81, 137, 200, 238
Morris, Nigel 355
Morris, Simon 284
Morrison, Toni ix
Mosley, Oswald 165, 315
Muhandis, Abu Mahdi al- 24
Murphy, Karie 18, 73, 88, 142, 143, 152, 158, 161, 180, 181, 251, 252, 284
Murphy, Richard 69
Murray, Andrew 259
Murray, Ian 253
Murray, Marilyn ii
Mussolini, Benito 108
Nandy, Lisa 17, 18, 47, 60
Nelsen, Diana 298
Nelson, Scott 339-341
Netanyahu, Benjamin 140, 217, 278, 284

NAME INDEX

Newens, Arthur Stan 216
Newmark, Jeremy 95, 96, 108, 165, 187
Nimmo, John 334
Nzolameso, Titina 114, 115

O'Brien, James 212
Oberman, Tracy-Ann 212
Oldknow, Emilie 63
Onasanya, Fiona 110
Osborne, George 5-7
Osborne, Samuel 366, 386

Pappé, Ilan 212
Parker, Andrew 325
Pepperall, (Mr Justice) Edward 233, 234, 242-245
Perkins, Toby 37, 43, 44, 46
Phillips, Jess 85, 102, 174, 193
Phillips, Melanie 183
Phillips, Morgan 305
Phillips, Trevor 287
Pickles, Eric 3, 50, 119
Pidcock, Laura 159, 202, 338
Pienaar, John 83
Potter, Jamie 189, 212, 233, 245
Powell, Lucy 37, 123
Poynton, Gregor 73
Prentis, Dave 50
Prescott, David 98, 99, 106, 116
Prescott, John 98, 35

Qureshi, Yasmin 22

Rabin, Yitzhak 90, 228
Rachman, Gideon 312
Rahman, Lutfur 297
Rajan, Amol 167, 241, 242
Rattansi, Afshin 197
Rayner, Angela 58

Rayner, Tom 158
Raynsford, Nick 9
Rees-Mogg, Jacob 102
Reeves, Ellie 206, 207
Reeves, Rachel 7, 303
Regev, Mark 284
Reynolds, Jonathan 27, 70
Riley, Rachel 141, 142, 212
Riordan, Linda 22
Ritchie, Margaret 22
Roache, Tim 55, 155
Roberts, Dave 21, 256, 258
Robinson, Nick 148, 149
Rockefeller, David 292
Rodgers, Sienna 70
Roe, Tony 232
Rosenberg, David 87
Rotheram, Steve 33
Rowley, Danielle 200
Royall, Janet 78
Rubin, Michael 147
Russell, Sarah viii, 43, 92, 210
Russell-Moyle, Lloyd 124, 137, 199, 202, 203, 269, 270
Ryan, Joan 98, 175, 315-318

Sainsbury, David 10
Sanders, Bernie 69, 93, 96
Sands, Bobby 230
Sankara, Thomas 286
Sarkar, Ash 172
Sayle, Alexei 212, 224
Schneider, James 121
Schofield, Kevin 83
Seabeck, Alison 9
Secker, Glyn 146, 332
Seeger, Pete 175
Segalov, Michael 154
Serjeant, Carl 179

NAME INDEX

Seymour, Richard 173, 174
Shabi, Rachel 154, 167
Shah, Naz 124, 155, 156, 160, 161, 178
Sharkey, Greg 238
Sharon, Ariel 226, 227
Shawcross, William 162
Sheerman, Barry 125
Shires, James viii, 39, 50, 92, 157, 158
Short, Ted 63
Sistani, Sayyid Ali al- 24
Skinner, Dennis 4, 22, 58, 199
Slaughter, Andy 32
Smeeth, Ruth 82, 83, 85-87, 89, 95, 144, 145, 170, 180, 213, 234, 263
Smith, Angela 125, 163, 164
Smith, Iain Duncan 12, 13
Smith, Jacqui 10
Smith, John 62, 68
Smith, Laura 116, 250
Smith, Owen 59-63, 80, 256
Snell, Gareth 85, 86, 263
Soames, Nicholas 101
Soleimani, Hajj Qassem 24
Starmer, Keir 45, 102, 114, 172, 194, 265, 289, 290, 292, 293, 295, 299, 301, 303
Steele, Paul 75
Stern, Kenneth 133
Stern-Weiner, Jamie 362, 363
Streeting, Wes 85, 86, 118, 234
Sturgeon, Nicola 58
Sugar, Alan 68

Tami, Mark 19
Taylor, Martin 8
Tebbit, Norman 130
Thatcher, Margaret 1, 14-16, 55, 66, 67, 122
Thornberry, Emily 99, 221, 317, 323, 328
Tinley, Tony 54, 142, 256, 259
Tipping, Paddy 157

Tobin, Sam 233
Turley, Anna 123, 263
Turner, Karl 59-61, 231

Umunna, Chuka 26, 34, 125, 126, 261, 264, 328, 329

Varoufakis, Yanis 212
Vaz, Keith 85, 164, 189, 190, 242, 243, 331
Vine, Jeremy 204, 205

Wadsworth, Marc 79, 82-89, 112, 135, 158, 164, 234, 255, 330, 331
Walker, Jackie 81, 108-112, 135, 142, 144-146, 161, 178, 203, 205, 219, 236, 242, 255, 310, 311, 338, 339, 345
Walker, Jonathan 373
Walker, Michael 171-173
Walker, Peter 364
Wallace, Mick 238
Wallis Simons, Jake 301
Walsh, Séanna 230, 231
Waters, Roger 212
Watson, Ian 360
Watson, Tom 18, 73, 146, 153, 180, 192, 193, 198, 199, 206, 213, 216, 253, 254
Waugh, Paul 118, 145
Wayne, Mike 305
Wayne, Naomi 333
Webbe, Claudia 253
Weizmann, Chaim 280
Werkmann, Tina 210, 211
Western, Anne 43
Whelan, Mick 253
Wilcox, Dave 43
Wilkinson, Jyoti 92
Williams, Darren 253
Williamson, Chris iii, v, 60, 101, 108, 124-126, 135, 139, 141, 142, 145, 146, 148, 151,

393

NAME INDEX

158, 164, 165, 171, 172, 180, 181, 186, 192, 193, 199, 204, 212-214, 219, 221-223, 225, 231, 234, 237, 241, 242, 244, 245, 250, 258, 261, 351-354

Williamson, Fionnbharr 39

Williamson, Gavin 266-268

Williamson, Simone 39

Willmott, Ross 15

Willsman, Pete 203

Wilson, Harold 66, 137, 211

Wimborne-Idrissi, Naomi 87, 137, 146

Winstanley, Asa 140, 236

Winterton, Rosie 19, 20, 37

Wolf, Martin 70, 71

Wolfson, Rhea 154

Wood, Mike 22

Woodcock, John 52, 54, 55

Wrack, Matt 14

Wright, James 374

Wright, Matthew 167

X, Malcolm 174

Zapata, Emiliano 214

Zyl, van der Marie 321